D1739491

TEXꞱXET

Studies in Comparative Literature 56

Series Editors
C.C. Barfoot and Theo D'haen

Investigating Identities

Questions of Identity in Contemporary International Crime Fiction

Edited by

Marieke Krajenbrink
and Kate M. Quinn

Amsterdam - New York, NY
2009

Cover design: Pier Post

The paper on which this book is printed meets the requirements of
'ISO 9706: 1994, Information and documentation - Paper for
documents - Requirements for permanence'.

ISBN: 978-90-420-2529-5
© Editions Rodopi B.V., Amsterdam - New York, NY 2009
Printed in The Netherlands

Printed by Printforce, the Netherlands

In memoriam

Henk Krajenbrink
1923-2004

Helen Mackin Quinn
1938-2006

Contents

Acknowledgements

We gratefully acknowledge the support of our respective institutions, in particular the Millennium Fund and Grant in Aid of Publications of the National University of Ireland, Galway, as well as the University of Limerick's Seed Funding, and the Department of Languages and Cultural Studies at UL.

We are grateful to those who helped in the technical preparation of the final manuscript of this work: John Armstrong, Sabine Besenfelder, Maíread Conneely and Joachim Lerchenmueller.

We also thank all those who provided assistance with translation, especially Tina Browne and Fiona Fincannon. Further thanks go to the many colleagues and friends who also helped in so many ways: Mel Boland, Nuria Borrull, Sharon Campbell-Shaw, Martin Chappell, Jean E. Conacher, Joachim Fischer, Gisela Holfter, Dominique LeMeur, Patricia Lynch, Anna Pairaló, Cinta Ramblado-Minero, Serge Rivière, Teresa Rogers-Jenner and Birgit Ryschka.

Special thanks are due to the *Textxet* series editors, Theo D'haen for being so supportive of this project from the outset, and Cedric Barfoot for his invaluable assistance throughout the preparation of this volume. We also wish to thank the following people at Rodopi: Fred van der Zee, Suzanne Roberts, Esther Roth, and particularly Marieke Schilling for her unfailing helpfulness and patience.

We also wish to express our gratitude to Jean-Philippe Imbert for his enthusiastic participation in the early stages of this project.

Finally, and on a more personal note, we would like to warmly thank our families, and especially Wim van Schie to whom we dedicate this book.

Introduction: Investigating Identities

MARIEKE KRAJENBRINK and KATE M. QUINN

This volume presents twenty critical essays based on literatures from a range of different language areas and different national and cultural contexts. The collection aims to explore the ways in which the crime genre, which has proved popular all over the world, has been used in recent decades to articulate and investigate notions of identity.

Questions of identity have traditionally been central to crime and detective fiction. The term "whodunnit" points to the importance of unmasking the criminal and identifying the wrongdoer. However, over time, questions of identity raised within the genre have become more complex. The quest to discover the identity of the person responsible for a particular crime has come, in many cases, to serve as a pretext for, or to provide a framework for a wider interrogation of society or of what constitutes criminality. The adaptability of the genre is such that it can be used to affirm and also to undermine all concepts of identity, be these at the level of nation, ethnicity, culture, or at the level of gender and genre. Indeed, the genre has increasingly been used as a vehicle for a philosophical enquiry into the epistemological dimensions of looking for clues, and for an interrogation of the possibility of a restoration of order. Even the very idea of a stable self-identity had been subjected to scrutiny.

Much attention has been devoted to research on specific aspects of the crime genre in recent years, for instance on the various schools such as classic, hard-boiled or police procedural, and on specific area studies such as French, Latin American and European production, or on feminist and postcolonial detective fiction. However, there have been relatively few projects that aim to take a broader look at points of common interest that exist within the genre at an international level. Yet, such a comparative approach can shed light on processes of adaptation and appropriation of the genre to specific national, regional or local contexts, and can also uncover similarities between the works of authors from very different areas. From a variety of perspectives, the contributors to this collection address a whole range of issues pertaining to identity, and a brief examination of their contributions will illustrate the ways in which they mutually inform and complement each other.

The first essay in the collection is Eva Erdmann's "Nationality International: Detective Fiction in the Late Twentieth Century". Erdmann takes a comparative approach as she provides a wide-ranging overview of current trends within the crime genre and focuses on its international proliferation in recent decades. She investigates the connection between the global presence of the genre and the increasing importance given to specifically local and regional settings. Indeed, the investigation of the setting has replaced that of the crime in many of the works to which she refers. As Erdmann shows, this development often reinforces stereotypes about exotic places and identities, but it can also be used to question preconceived ideas and associations connected with the locale and its inhabitants.

Following on from Erdmann, we have three contributions on detective fiction from Spain that raise questions about national and cultural identity. While all three are from within the geographical boundaries of Spain, they are very different in their focus and approach. Stewart King in "Articulating and Disarticulating Culture and Identity in Vázquez Montalbán's *Serie Carvalho*" looks at the work of one of the most famous modern European crime writers, whose series of detective novels provided a chronicle of post-Franco Barcelona, reflecting on the changes and conflicts in contemporary Spanish and Catalan society. King examines the way in which the author challenges problematic conventional notions of both Spanish and Catalan identities, more specifically with regard to the formation and celebration of national and regional identities in post-Franco Spain. The complexity and contradictions of cultural identities are foregrounded and traditional discourses on nationalism are exposed to new interpretations.

The next essay also deals with Catalonia, but Anne M. White and Shelley Godsland's "Popular Genre and the Politics of the Periphery: Catalan Crime Fiction by Women" focuses on issues of marginalization on the grounds of gender and language. They discuss the relationship between minority language writing and popular genre in terms of transcultural re-inscription, a process of hybridization in which conventions from different cultures are borrowed and confronted, thus creating new aesthetic forms. White and Godsland trace the particular history of these dynamics in women detective writers in Catalonia and, on a wider contemporary plane, suggest a connection with strategies of glocalization: resisting homogenization by critically rewriting the rules of an imported genre. They also consider the reshaping of what has traditionally been a male-dominated genre.

Anne L. Walsh in "Questions of Identity: An Exploration of Spanish Detective Fiction" addresses the question of what is specifically Spanish about detective fiction produced in that country. She gives a highly informative overview of the development of the genre there (in which we also find reference to the body of Catalan crime fiction discussed by King, and White and Godsland). She looks at how early Spanish detective fiction was adapted from foreign models and then traces how the genre came to prominence in the Eighties and Nineties. Walsh then focuses on Arturo Pérez-Reverte's *El club Dumas* as an example of a dominant contemporary trend in the national arena towards ironic use of the detective formula, and the production of postmodernist metafiction. She rounds off her essay by comparing the book with Roman Polanski's cinematic adaptation, *The Ninth Gate*.

With the next two contributions, we move from Spain to France. Sjef Houppermans' "Abyss of the Senses: *Les Rivières pourpres* by Jean-Christophe Grangé" gives a detailed study of this recent novel which has also received cinematic treatment. Like Walsh, he opens with a history of the development of the genre in the national context, which serves to situate Grangé's novel within the body of French detective fiction production. Houppermans' analysis of the novel throws up many different questions on identity related to race, ethnicity and gender. Against the backdrop of a multicultural France, a young *Beur* detective investigates a murder at a remote university campus. The investigation uncovers a case of eugenic manipulation and concealment and eradication of identity, in a story of bloody vengeance and horrific violence that links the mythical with the modern.

Issues of race, ethnicity and nationality surface again in Agnès Maillot's "Fractured Identities: Jean-Claude Izzo's *Total Khéops*". In an essay with a strong sociological focus, Maillot analyses the present socio-political factors influencing the debate on national identity in

France. More specifically, she examines these issues against the backdrop of the importance of the Marseilles setting for Jean-Claude Izzo's novels. Marseilles is presented as a place with a rich cultural diversity, having historically been a city of immigrants, of whom North African *Beurs* are but some of the most recent. Maillot looks at how Izzo confronts the problem of social and racial exclusion by positing the option of a *Marseillais* identity which he considers more relevant than those based on a narrow definition of Frenchness.

The next contribution, Arlene A. Teraoka's "Detecting Ethnicity: Jakob Arjouni and the Case of the Missing German Detective Novel", also examines the relation of race and ethnicity to national identity, but this time in the context of the Germany of the Eighties and Nineties. Teraoka opens by considering why the hard-boiled form was so long neglected in Germany and examines the reasons for the enormous popularity enjoyed by police detective series on national television. She then goes on to examine the emergence of the long-awaited hard-boiled in the novels of Jakob Arjouni which, through the deployment of an ethnic Turk as detective, bring into focus German discourses on race and nationhood and stereotypical attitudes concerning foreignness and criminality. Teraoka also looks at how the identity of the author can become an issue of interest to critics, and how the use of a pseudonym can itself become a comment on ideas about identity.

Race and ethnicity are also a central concern in John Scaggs' "Double Identity: Hard-Boiled Detective Fiction and the Divided 'I'", which looks at the works of Raymond Chandler, Walter Mosley and Tony Hillerman, examining the way in which each addresses the difference between the private and the public self within the figure of the detective. Scaggs finds their respective detectives to be deeply divided figures and, particularly in Mosley and Hillerman, this is often related to language, race and ethnicity. Detectives find themselves having to act within multiple cultural spaces and having to adopt disguises and switch linguistic codes in order to do so. In the novels of these writers identity is often a performance, tailored to fit the expectations of others, that permits them to blend into a particular context.

Similar issues are raised by Theo D'haen in his essay "Plum's the Girl! Janet Evanovich and the Empowerment of Ms Common America". D'haen begins with an examination of genre tradition within the USA, especially the development of the hard-boiled against the socio-political background of the New Deal. He goes on to look at the significance of the contribution of minority groups to the genre, most notably that of black writers. Like Scaggs, he considers the position in society occupied by marginalized groups and the strategies they adopt to negotiate linguistic and cultural boundaries, and he adds another category to this group – that of women. He examines feminist appropriations of the form and then situates Evanovich's work within the context of trends in women's detective fiction since the Eighties, identifying in it an innovative crossover between the private eye novel and the serial romance.

Interestingly, we find an examination of a similar combination of love story and detective narrative in Willem G. Weststeijn's essay "Russian Women Detective Writers". Here Weststeijn analyses the recent proliferation and popularity of the love-detective novel in post-perestroika Russia. He also highlights the difference between these novels and the kinds of state-sponsored detective fiction produced before 1990. Looking at a number of present-day woman authors, Weststeijn argues that they have chosen to add a romantic element to their crime novels in order to make these more appealing to a readership looking for an escape from the harsh realities of contemporary Russia. Conversely, he argues that the elements of crime and violence present in these novels add the dimension of suffering that has so rich a tradition in Russian literature and that he sees as central in the formation of the Russian self-image.

Hans Ester's "Perspectives on the Detective Novel in Afrikaans" examines a similar phenomenon of hybridization, in this case the combination of the detective novel and the specifically South African genre of the farm novel that was long used as a vehicle for proclaiming Afrikaans identity. He opens with a discussion of the changing status of Afrikaans language and literature within South Africa, and briefly comments on recent developments in the crime genre, before moving on to a detailed analysis of works that play with the conventions of both the detective and the farm novel. Ester charts how Etienne Leroux in the Sixties used this new form in a critical way, and how Etienne van Heerden has more recently positioned it within South African postmodernism. Ester shows how van Heerden's novels foreground philosophical and epistemological issues, and also engage in a critical re-examination of history.

We remain in Africa, although moving to another postcolonial context, with Beate Burtscher-Bechter's "Wanted: National Algerian Identity". This essay traces the development of a francophone Algerian crime novel since Independence from France in 1962. She charts how the genre has moved from proclaiming and affirming official state ideology in the Seventies to criticizing the state and exploring alternative views of Algerian identity in the Nineties. Burtscher-Bechter provides a socio-historical background for this transition from state-sponsored spy novels to critical *roman noir*, ending with a discussion of Yasmina Khadra's use of this genre as an instrument for socio-political criticism. In the case of Khadra, as with Jakob Arjouni, the identity of the author and the use of a pseudonym is again the subject of comment.

Literature and politics is also the focus of Marisol Morales Ladrón's essay "'Troubling' Thrillers: Politics and Popular Fiction in Northern Ireland". Here Morales Ladrón discusses this sub-genre and the ways in which the "Troubles" Thriller has emerged as a specific local variant of this form. She points to the existence of two kinds of such works – those that reinforce the idea of fixed identities based on nationality, religion or politics, and those that question these and their attendant ideologies. She analyses three novels that offer a more complex meditation on the sectarian conflicts of Northern Ireland and looks at the way in which they challenge essentialist positions, and binary oppositions with regard to identity.

Sabine Vanacker's "Double Dutch: Image and Identity in Dutch and Flemish Crime Fiction" examines how authors write themselves into a larger international tradition by adapting the genre to a specific context, and analyses how imagotypical suggestions of a national, regional or communal identity feature in the crime genre in the Netherlands and in Flanders. She looks at how language influences identity formation, and points to how the different histories of these neighbouring countries have impacted on the kind of detective fiction produced in each, and the mutual images they hold of each other. She closes with a discussion of the elaborate play with stereotypes and clichés in the work of Janwillem van de Wetering, and looks at how he appeals to very different local and international readerships in America and the Netherlands.

Christopher Jones also reveals an interest in stereotypes in his essay on "Cultural Identity in German Swiss Detective Fiction", especially clichés about Switzerland as a rich and isolated country. He analyses how Swiss crimes are differentiated from those perpetrated by outsiders. In common with Vanacker, he looks at the way in which history is interrogated in German Swiss detective novels, where he identifies an emphasis on moral failures in the recent past of the nation, particularly with regard to opportunistic collaboration with the Nazis. Jones argues that stereotypical representations in this body of crime fiction are most often deployed against the Swiss themselves and used to criticize aspects of contemporary society.

We remain with German-language detective fiction in Marieke Krajenbrink's "Unresolved Identities in Roth and Rabinovici: Re-working the Crime Genre in Austrian Literature". Krajenbrink offers a brief history of Austria and examines the problematic nature of its national identity formation. She goes on to look at the way Gerhard Roth and Doron Rabinovici both work within and against genre tradition to examine issues related to identity – family, ethnic, minority, collective, political and historical. Central to the work of both is a strong criticism of attempts to impose an historical amnesia with regard to Austria's Nazi past. Krajenbrink analyses how these authors use detective elements in a very creative and innovative way that undermines any notions of simple resolutions and reassuring restorations of narrative and ethical order, and that reject reductive notions of identity.

Costantino C. M. Maeder's "Crime Novels in Italy" gives a broad panorama of the development of the genre in Italy and situates this within the context of the wider intellectual and philosophical trends that have influenced national literary production – particularly the influence of Leopardi and Pirandello. He looks at the old guard of Sciascia, Eco and Tabucchi, and at the younger generation of authors like Lucarelli and Camilleri, finding a constant in the playful irony that characterizes all of their production and that he considers so important to the genre in Italy. He argues that a profound scepticism informs the modernist approach found in Sciascia, while the new *gialli* of the Nineties display a playful acceptance of the chaos that has followed the loss of the idea of grand narratives.

Chaos and indeterminacy reappear as central concerns in Philip Swanson's essay, "The Detective and the Disappeared: Memory, Forgetting and other Confusions in Juan José Saer". Swanson begins by bringing the reader up to date with recent theoretical debate about the role and position of the genre in Latin America. Then he situates the work of Argentine writer, Saer, in the wider context of post-colonial and postmodern writing. His analysis of *La pesquisa* considers the relevance of a political reading connected to the policy of disappearance widely used under the military dictatorship, but Swanson argues in favour of a more plural interpretation of this complex and challenging text that displays a concern with metaphysical and psychological dimensions of identity and reality.

We move to Chile with the next contribution from Kate M. Quinn who examines "Cases of Identity Concealed and Revealed in Chilean Detective Fiction". Quinn begins by briefly examining the emergence of a politically-inflected type of detective fiction in late-Eighties and early-Nineties Chile. She then looks at the way in which identity is explored in recent novels by Roberto Ampuero and Marcela Serrano with plots that centre around the reconstruction of an absent person's identity. In Ampuero's case this involves a critical reassessment of radical political activism, while Serrano's focus is on the desire for personal and artistic freedom on the part of a female author. Quinn examines the way in which the respective investigations illustrate the fragmentary and elusive nature of identity, arguing that, particularly in the case of Serrano, this militates against conventional closure.

A refusal of conventional closure and resolution marks the final essay in the collection, Brian Duffy's "From a Good Firm Knot to a Mess of Loose Ends: Identity and Solution in Martin Amis' *Night Train*". Duffy shows how Amis, in this novel, presents a radical reversal of the most basic elements and expectations of the crime novel and of its readers. Even at the level of plot we have no murder but rather a suicide, and the investigation reveals that there is no ready explanation for this act. Amis' concern with the enigma and incoherence of suicide has led him to produce a work that questions the intelligibility of the world. Far removed from conventional detective narrative and facile solutions, Duffy argues that *Night Train* is designed to force the reader to experience the uncertainty of existence and to confront the elusive nature of identity.

As this brief summary indicates, a number of the contributions collected in this book focus on very specific themes or areas, while others set out to map more general tendencies and developments within the contemporary international crime genre. Taken together, the twenty essays complement and mutually enrich each other in often unexpected ways. This book provides a further contribution to the growing field of crime fiction studies and also is of relevance to the ongoing debate on questions of identity. It is clear that there is great scope for further work in this area.

NATIONALITY INTERNATIONAL: DETECTIVE FICTION IN THE LATE TWENTIETH CENTURY

EVA ERDMANN

At the beginning of the twenty-first century, crime fiction is a top-ranking literary genre, and has become part of mainstream culture. The crime novel's position of pre-eminence derives from its broad fan base and its readership, with publishing houses devoting whole series and large print runs to the genre.[1] Evidence of the prevalence of a popular obsession with crime stories is also to be found in the sophisticated typological variety of crime fiction, present in literature and in film. Readers who favour novels with female detectives are not necessarily enamoured of ethno-detective novels, while hard-boiled thrillers differ significantly from fantasy detective fiction. Among the television shows starring detectives, every variety of the genre is represented. In recent decades we have also seen crime fiction gain in popularity in the spheres of literary experiment[2] and literary theory.[3]

---

[1] Examples include DuMont's and Rowohlt's crime series on the German book market, the *gialli* in Italy and Gallimard's *folio policier* in France.

[2] Recent novels whose narrative model is based on that of the detective story include: Georg Klein, *Barbar Rosa: Eine Detektivgeschichte* (Berlin: Alexander Fest, 2001); Thomas Hettche, *Der Fall Arbogast* (Cologne: DuMont, 2001); Haruki Murakami, *A Wild Sheep Chase* (Tokyo: Kodansha International, 1989 – originally published as *Hitsuji wo meguru Bohken*, 1982); and Paul Auster, *Leviathan* (New York: Faber and Faber, 1992).

[3] The frequently repeated schema of the thriller plot seduces the reader into abstract reflections on trails of suspicion, victims or suspicion itself. For a theoretical basis, see Tzvetan Todorov, "Typologie du roman policier", in *Poétique de la prose*, Paris: Seuil, 1971; Hans Sanders, "Die Welt ist, was der Fall ist: Poetologische Randnotizen zum Kriminalroman", *Romanistische Zeitschrift für Literaturgeschichte/Cahiers d'Histoire des Littératures Romanes*, XVII/3-4 (1993), 387-403.

The pursuit of criminals and the solving of crime have developed into a cultural code, even a cultural ritual.

Since the Seventies, there has been a real boom in crime fiction, with many new authors adopting the genre. The dominant form is the series detective novel where each book is complete in itself, but the same protagonist or protagonists appear in succeeding books. The interest resides equally in the solution of different cases and in the representation of the detective's daily life. Professional and personal successes or crises are given equal attention in this new crime fiction. Surprisingly, the crime novel of the last decades is distinguished by the fact that the main focus is not on the crime itself, but on the setting, the place where the detective and the victims live and to which they are bound by ties of attachment. The surroundings where the investigations take place are portrayed with increasing inventiveness, to the extent that the crime itself appears to be at best merely a successful stunt. It almost seems as if the inventories of criminal motives and case histories have been exhausted, so that crime fiction's primary distinguishing characteristic has become the *locus criminalis*.

While serialization becomes more common, the cultural surroundings become more and more original. Social, cultural, historical and political conditions become the object of exhaustive inquiries. We find, for example, descriptions of daily life in the kibbutz,[4] British class snobbery in its everyday garb,[5] images of women being updated,[6] and analyses of the era of Franco's dictatorship in Spain.[7]

---

[4]   See Batya Gur, *Murder on a Kibbutz: A Communal Case*, New York: Harper Collins, 1995.

[5]   The unbalanced detective duo of Elizabeth George's novels, Thomas Lynley and Barbara Havers, ensure continuing conflicts (both comic and serious) between the upper class and a weak middle class. See, for example, *A Great Deliverance*, 1988; *Missing Joseph*, 1993; *Payment in Blood*, 1989; *Well-schooled in Murder*, 1990; *A Suitable Vengeance*, 1991; *For the Sake of Elena*, 1992; *Playing for the Ashes*, 1994, among others (all London: Bantam).

[6]   Three very different examples of female detective stories with their different images of women illustrate the current diversity: the lecturer in literature, Kate Franzler, in the crime novels of Amanda Cross; the middle-aged commissioner in Doris Gercke's novels; the unmarried private detective in Valerie Wilson Wesley's books.

[7]   For a more detailed discussion of this, see Stewart King's essay on Manuel Vázquez Montalbán in this collection.

Detective fiction written in the last decades is more suitable for comparative study than almost any other material, for the *tertium comparationis,* the fixed course of events in the genre, remains the same – first murder, then suspicion, sometimes a false trail, and in the end, resolution. It is the wide variety of new scenes of the crime that ensures that contrasts exist between the various novels. In recent decades, detective fiction has described so many customs and mores from different parts of the world that it is impossible to get an overview. The treatments of them are so detailed that many detective novels can also be considered milieu studies and social novels. Until now, the majority of analyses of current crime fiction, both in literature and film, have taken a monographic approach or followed a logic of genre or national philology. They have only seldom gone beyond the limits of such a focus.[8]

Global crime

In literature, the spread of crime has taken on topographic proportions that reflect the globalization processes of the late twentieth century. In crime novels at the beginning of the twenty-first century, investigations take place all over the world and anyone who went to the trouble of totting up the sum of fictional scenes of the crime would be undertaking a project of international cartography. On the map of the world there are hardly any areas uncharted by crime fiction, hardly any places that have not yet become the setting for a detective novel.

Criminal investigations have been pursued in Newark by Tamara Hayle (Valerie Wilson Wesley) and in the *Bahnhofsviertel,* the red

---

[8] For a comparative examination that goes beyond national and linguistic boundaries, see Ulrike Leonhardt, *Mord ist ihr Beruf: Eine Geschichte des Kriminalromans,* Munich: C. H. Beck, 1990; Jochen Schmidt, *Gangster, Opfer, Detektive: Eine Typengeschichte des Kriminalromans,* Frankfurt am Main: Ullstein, 1987; and Joan Ramon Resina, *El cadáver en la cocina: La novela criminal en la cultura del desencanto,* Barcelona: Anthropos, 1997. On the issue of genre, see Ulrich Schulz-Buschhaus, *Formen und Ideologien des Kriminalromans: Ein gattungsgeschichtlicher Essay,* Frankfurt am Main: Athenaion, 1975. For film and cinematic history of the genre, see Georg Seeßlen, *Detektive: Mord im Kino,* Marburg: Schüren, 1998 and *Zur Geschichte des Kriminalfilms: Arbeitsheft zur Schulfernsehsendung "Der Fall Derrick",* Berlin: Wissenschaftlicher Verlag, 1987.

light district in Frankfurt by Kemal Kayankaya (Jakob Arjouni),[9] in
Berlin by Karin Lietze (Pieke Biermann), in Marseilles by Fabio
Montale (Jean-Claude Izzo),[10] in the Belleville quarter of Paris by
Malaussène (Daniel Pennac), in London by Helen West and Geoffrey
Bailey (Frances Fyfield) as well as Chief Inspector Reginald Wexford
(Ruth Rendell), in Zaïre (Achille F. Ngoye), in Moscow (Alexandra
Marinina),[11] in Japan (Sujata Massey), in Helsinki (Jouko Raivio), in
the North of England (Val McDermid), in Edinburgh (Ian Rankin), in
Greece (Petros Markaris), in China (Wang Shuo), in Canada, Cuba,
Mexico, Australia, and in Algeria.[12] In recent decades, detective
stories in film and literature have been set in many different locations.
European detective fiction production no longer takes second place to
American, even though the USA still leaves its traces conceptually and
intertextually in individual works.[13]

Crime plots have been located on every continent and in every
country, even in the remotest of places. Until the middle of the twentieth century, the classic works of European detective fiction, the cases
investigated by Commissioner Maigret and those of Nestor Burma,
were directly associated with French metropolitan flair and the Quai
d'Orfèvres was known even to those who had never been to Paris.
Now, formerly privileged settings for crime such as Paris have given
way to the omnipresence of crime and the cities must vie for attention
with the provinces. This merely reflects the fact that from the earliest
times, village gossip and family histories have been an inexhaustible
source of inspiration for storytellers.

In the early twentieth century, the French and the English crime
series were already well established, and the plot of a detective novel

---

[9]   Jakob Arjouni and his work are discussed in detail in Arlene Teraoka's essay in
      this collection.
[10] For a more detailed discussion of Jean-Claude Izzo, see Agnès Maillot's essay in
      this collection.
[11] For further details on both Marinina and contemporary Russian crime narrative,
      see Willem G. Weststeijn's essay in this collection.
[12] On the Algerian crime novel, see Beate Burtscher-Bechter, *Algerien – ein Land
      sucht seine Mörder: Die Entwicklung des frankophonen algerischen Kriminal-
      romans (1970-1998)*, Frankfurt am Main: IKO, 1999, and see also her essay in this
      collection.
[13] See Anne Mullen and Emer O'Beirne, *Crime Scenes: Detective Narratives in
      European Culture since 1945*, Amsterdam: Rodopi, 2000.

was expected to exhibit a certain national flair. The new crime series, as milieu studies and novels of customs and mores, have specialized in international background and location studies, becoming the exponents and chroniclers for the settings of their plots. In Robert van Gulik's series about Judge Dee, published from 1949 to 1968, we find an early example of the geographically determined crime series that came into being after 1945 – it created the Chinese detective novel.[14] The Judge Dee detective stories are set in China in the Middle Ages and are derived from the reports of a seventh-century regional judge. The narrative themes, plots and criminal types draw on the rich, culturally specific Chinese context and Chinese history. Today's reader is introduced to the world of Taoism, swords, princesses, temples and monasteries. In this connection, it is significant that van Gulik, a Dutchman, tells his story from the perspective of an outsider, for the narrative thereby enters into the domain of travel writing. In other, subsequent series, the seemingly necessary alien perspective continues to be a mechanism that endows the new crime novel with a touristic character. Even the publishers' marketing blurb for successful crime novels today draws on the nomadic biographies of authors who travel throughout the world, authors like Henning Mankell, the Swede living in Mozambique, and Giorgio Scerbanenco and Donna Leon, the Russian and American living in Italy.

Gradually, topographic references are becoming ever more exhaustive, profuse and detailed. The range of investigators and detectives operating at a national level is being expanded and completed. Batya Gur's Michael Ochajon and Vázquez Montalbán's Pepe Carvalho have already achieved autonomy as literary figures and, like Miss Marple and Sherlock Holmes, represent the different national habits and quirks of Catalonia and Israel, their respective countries of origin. In crime novels and series, the heinousness of crime is increasingly being replaced by the search for more colourful settings and, by

---

[14] See, for instance, Robert van Gulik, *Oudejaarsavond in Lan-fang* (*New Year's Eve in Lan-Fang*), 1958; *Het Chinese lakscherm* (*The Lacquer Screen*), 1962; *Zes zaken voor rechter Tie* (*Judge Dee at Work*), 1961 (all The Hague: Van Hoeve). See also Hartmut Walravens, "Richter Di bei der Arbeit: Zu Robert von Guliks chinesischen Kriminalromanen", in *Orient extremus. Zeitschrift für Sprache, Kunst und Kultur der Länder des fernen Ostens*, XXXVI/2 (1993), 223-34.

means of a specific local connection, the crime novel takes on the function of a new type of *Heimatroman*.[15]

Among the works with the more exotic settings are the detective stories of the journalist Tony Hillerman which derive from the author's interest in the conditions, the histories and the rites of the Navajo on their reservations. In these ethno-thrillers, the thrill of discovery supplements the thrill associated with the detective story itself; it is paratextually supported by maps of Anasazi Country or regions in Colorado. The plots of the entire series are based on the Navajo people's cultural conflict with the United States government, which even extends to judicial concepts. In solving their cases, the detective duo of Lieutenant Leaphorn and Jim Chee always have to take both cultures into account. In Hillerman's *A Thief of Time*, they become involved in a search for a vanished anthropologist while at the same time pursuing grave robbers and researching the anthropology of Navajo law.[16]

The new crime novel is also distinguished by a sort of outward internationality that can be discerned in the reception of thrillers. Some authors such as Donna Leon, Henning Mankell and Elizabeth George have an international audience and their books have been translated into many languages. The internationality of crime in fiction is accompanied by the real international popularity of the crime novel, which makes its readers into a community of conspirators.[17] While the internationality of crime fiction is due in part to book marketing and publishing house strategies, it is also due to the narrative strategies

---

[15]   *Heimatroman* can be translated as "homeland novel", although the concept *Heimat* is traditionally much more emotionally and ideologically loaded. It stands for everything that the home locality involves – such as types of buildings, traditional costumes, customs and values, local dialects – with an emphasis on rural rather than urban life. It can also be understood in the sense that it is used by the ethnologist Clifford Geertz, as the primordial tie to an ethnic group (Clifford Geertz, *The Interpretation of Culture: Selected Essays*, New York: Basic Books, 1973).

[16]   Tony Hillerman, *A Thief of Time*, New York: Harper Collins, 1988. For further discussion of Hillerman's work, see the essay by John Scaggs in this volume.

[17]   The supporters also present themselves on the internet in reader and fan pages. See, for example, a detective story forum and a crime database at the following site, http://www.krimi-forum.de. See, also, a fan page for Henning Mankell at http://www.buecher4um.de/AutorHM.htm, and a page by Valerie Wilson Wesley at http://www.tamarahayle.com.

used in the portrayal of local settings. It is precisely the characteristic element of the surroundings at the scene of the crime that contributes significantly to the success of these novels.

The paradox of the series

Deep within our crime fiction world as it comes alive in books and in film, there is a paradox that is hardly noticed any more. The unusual occurrence of murder has become the norm. The extensive production of crime series and the frequency with which they come into being have made capital crime into an everyday event. We have an un-interrupted daily supply of corpses, crime motives and convicted crim-inals, from the regular Monday detective thriller through the new Mankell to *Tatort*, the show that has been a mainstay of the weekend broadcasting programme for West German television for the last twenty years.[18]

When there are murders waiting for us around every corner, the predetermined course of events in the plot becomes ever more stereo-typical, the variations in crime motives, murder weapons and mur-derers' profiles ever more transparent. Audiences too can use a matrix to see how things are going to work out:

Motive: passion, jealousy, fanaticism, humiliation, self-defence, greed, vanity, anti-Semitism.

Murderer: psychopath, abandoned woman, head of the investi-gating agency, abused child, female rival, sect, drug lord, outcast.

Investigator: amateur with moral obligation (lawyer, barrister, journalist, priest), the duo, female private detective, commissioner, pathologist, competing investigative agencies (FBI against the local police).

Victim: mistaken identity, chance victim, deliberately murdered victim, prominent victim, vanished victim, victim of mass murder, feigned victim.

Scene of the crime: public spaces (park, crowd, lift) and private spaces (shower, bed, TV lounger).

---

[18] See the illustrated book by Holger Wacker, *Tatort: Krimis, Köpfe, Kommissare*, Berlin: Henschel, 1998, which offers a topographic overview of the German *Tatort* series.

Weapon: dagger, edge of table, poison, fist, cement mixer, fall
out of a window, machine gun.[19]

The enigmatic riddles of the detective stories of yore, which kept
their secrets until the final pages, have given way to crossword
puzzles in which the same combinations of letters always repeat themselves. The investigation works with stereotypical sentence patterns:
"Did the deceased have enemies?", "Where were you between one and
three in the morning?", "Put the gun down, you're only going to make
things worse for yourself." Serial production of detective fiction turns
murder into a banality. Current headlines quickly turn up in crime
stories: white-collar crime, computer crime, racism and xenophobia,
smuggler criminality and white slaving are quickly processed.[20] While
real massacres, like those in sects' houses or in schools such as
Littleton in 1998 or in Erfurt in the eastern part of Germany in April
2002, prove the impossibility of controlling crime – bank raids and
kidnappings in kindergartens turn into live media events. The boom in
crime fiction can be understood as a reaction to the hysteria of crime
in real life: the relief of tension supplied by the resolution of criminal
intrigues in literature and in film stands in reverse proportion to the
media's presentation of spectacular crimes and their uncontrollability.

The macrocosm of the scene of the crime: culture and society

Even in fiction, film and the modern fairy tale, a daily murder ritual
becomes boring in the long run if there are no other elements of suspense. These are created when the foreseeable riddle of the whodunnit
is replaced by mysterious surroundings that the investigative troops

---

[19] I thank Nicole Weiß, Sylvere Mbondobari Ebamangoye, Christoph Schulz and the
      summer 1998 Seminar on Detective Fiction at the Department of General and
      Comparative Literature at the University of Bayreuth for many references and for
      collaborating on a project to create a comprehensive schema of crime fiction
      topoi. The work on this essay is also linked to the *Crime and Nation* project,
      carried out with Immacolata Amodeo.
[20] See, for example, the film *Sperling und der brennende Arm* (Germany 1997/98,
      director Dominik Graf, script Rolf Basedow), an Albanian thriller set in Hamburg
      that deals with the Mafia methods of Albanian exiles in Germany, which was
      awarded the best television movie prize by the Deutsche Akademie der Darstel-
      lenden Künste in 1999.

explore; knowledge of the local environment becomes the fundamental competence necessary to investigative work: "Only a native
could successfully follow another person through the narrow streets of
the city; only a native would know the sudden stops, the hidden turns,
the dead ends."[21] If Auguste Dupin began his analyses from the arm-
chair and arranged his hypotheses in a logical chain of statements,
today's social thriller definitely takes place at the scene of the crime.
The reading of crime novels becomes an ethnographic reading; the
scene of the crime becomes the *locus genius* of the cultural tragedy.

At first glance, in the context of the continuing topicality of migrations, multiculturalism and postcolonialism, which have challenged
uni-dimensional cultural and national identities, this narrative strategy
is surprising. However, it is precisely in societies that produce theoretically highly complex discourses on multiculturalism, and in societies that regard multiculturalism as part of their political self-
understanding and their national identity, like the USA and Israel, that
interest in the status of nationality is returning.[22] In Europe, where the
historical formation of nineteenth-century nation building is itself
becoming history, there is growing affirmation, even a sort of re-
animation of the culture of nationality.[23] In the second half of the
twentieth century, gradually at first, and then increasingly, as the
boom in crime fiction took off, the pursuit of the criminal was displaced by the search for cultural identity. The genre of crime fiction
has thus thematically returned to the tradition of the search for identity
of classical antiquity, as typified by the crime of *Oedipus Rex*, where
the murder of the king sets in motion a process of questioning and
revelation of identity.

Now that capital crime cases and their guaranteed solution have
become normality in books and films in the twentieth century, it is the
fictional world of victims, suspects, detectives and commissioners that

---

[21]   Donna Leon, *Acqua Alta*, London: Pan, 1997, 241.
[22]   See David A. Hollinger, *Post-Ethnic America: Beyond Multiculturalism*, New
       York: Basic Books, 1995; and Pheng Cheah and Bruce Robbins, *Cosmopolitics:
       Thinking and Feeling beyond the Nation*, Minnesota: University of Minnesota
       Press, 1998.
[23]   On the hypocrisy of the multicultural discourses of postmodernism and on the
       connection between multicultural and nationalist discourses, see Slavoj Žižek,
       *Liebe Deinen Nächsten, nein danke! Die Sackgasse des Sozialen in der Post-
       moderne*, Berlin: Volk und Welt, 1999, 5-21.

is to generate new suspense. The criminological search for the trail of evidence is transposed to epistemologies of cultural anthropology, ethnographic and national characteristics, and the structure of the genre is governed by the spectrum of cultural identities. The new crime novels are characterized by their variously staked out territorial contexts that encompass ethnic groups, nations, regions, provinces or cities, but only by degrees. The distinguishing feature that they share remains the representation of the territory and its cultural conditions.[24]

In today's crime novels, milieu studies ranging across the world no longer seek to create an experience of alterity exclusively in the un-canny nature of the crime which would be resolved in a happy ending that provides a return to normality and justice, instead they seek such an experience in local cultures alien to the reader. The effect of the *étrange*, the strange and uncanny, as evoked in the double murder in Edgar Allan Poe's *The Murders in the Rue Morgue*, has been gradually shifting since the middle of the nineteenth century to the point where it has now been replaced by the effect of the *étranger*, the unfamiliar and alien.[25] In the development of the genre, crime is taking a back seat to the representation of alterity, which implies an almost embarrassed hiding of the experience of identity.

Now the search for experiences of alterity and identity is by no means culturally specific, but universal. From a perspective of post-modernism – the standpoints and practices of which were the subject of debate at the same time as the boom in crime fiction was taking off, and which accompanied it theoretically – (Western) identities were at the top of the agenda because of the perceived loss of collective and social structures, the loss of biographic certainties and the fragmen-tation of life stories. While literary theory and cultural criticism in the late twentieth century questioned the basic features of identity, that is, gender and nationality, as historical constructs, crime fiction sought to

---

[24] Karl Heinz Kohl points out that there are no hierarchies among these elements. Even in the twentieth century, ethnicity is not an alternative to nationalism. Kohl identifies "ethnic group" as a technical term and an ideological construction (see Karl Heinz Kohl, "Ethnizität und Tra dition aus ethnologischer Sicht", in *Identi-täten: Erinnerung, Geschichte, Identität 3*, eds Aleida Assmann and Heidrun Friese, Frankfurt am Main: Suhrkamp, 1998, 282).

[25] The orangutan and the strange voices that the witnesses cannot identify are both the components of the *étrange-étranger* contained in *The Murders in the Rue Morgue* (1841).

affirm a sense of national and gender identity all the more intensively. While theory deconstructed identities, crime fiction restored them to wholeness; indeed, it succeeded in giving parity to satisfying both the need for identity and the need for alterity. With its narrative detail in which the outlines of the criminal cases are lost in the minute documentation of everyday life in a foreign country, crime fiction retains that postmodern indecisiveness in which attempts are made to deal with ambivalent identities.[26] Sociology and cultural criticism diverge in the assessment of this ambivalence of defining what is one's own and wanting something alien as well. The fans of crime fiction differ in this question too, what some readers experience as familiar and beloved is unutterably boring for others. One crime author says:

> Of course I have often wondered why Kurt Wallander is so popular. I dare say that it's due to the content of the books. They deal with things that concern many people, but I believe it also has to do with the fact that Wallander himself is continually changing, like you and me. The literary credibility lies in the fact that one describes a person's inconsistency. I personally detest the sort of book where I know all about a figure after a few pages and after that, no more changes occur. By contrast, Kurt Wallander is quite different in the seventh book to what he was in the first one. That makes him believable, since to that extent, he is similar to us.[27]

A reviewer says:

> There can be no doubt about it, people read Mankell because they want to be bored, because they feel at home with his very bureaucratic language, which strings together trivialities without rhyme or reason, and when pretending to go into something deeper, only repeats itself shamelessly. People like Wallander because he is like them.[28]

---

[26] See Etienne Balibar and Immanuel Wallerstein, *Race, Nation, Class: Ambiguous Identities*, London: Verso, 1991.

[27] Henning Mankell, "Ein Fuß im Schnee und einer im Sand", available at the following site: http://www.schwedenkrimi.de/mankell_vortrag.htm.

[28] Gerd Friedrich Marenke, "Die Ödnis der schonischen Ebene", 2003, available at the following site: http://www.kaliber38.de/features/marenke/mankell.htm.

Nationality as folklore

How can one make a place that is narrowly circumscribed interesting
for a wide, potentially international audience? This is achieved by
having recourse to cultural stereotypes and clichés that are affirma-
tively used, ironically used or problematized. The clichés that are best
known worldwide are national stereotypes, with which crime fiction
most often plays. National characteristics are embroidered upon for
the representation of fictional figures; thus, the distinguishing feature
of Scottish or Greek crime fiction is not that it is written by a Scot or a
Greek, but that it attempts to convey a Scottish or a Greek atmosphere.

The most popular example of internationally read crime novels is
the Commissioner Brunetti series by the American Donna Leon; the
volumes are numerically subtitled.[29] His investigations are set in
Venice which, because of its island setting and because it has for
centuries been favoured by newly-weds, is seen as the most Utopian
of cities in European cultural history. Brunetti's cases take place
against the backdrop of an *italianità* in which the Mafia, the opera, the
palazzi, art and patrician history reappear in the narrower context of a
venezianità in which the canals, the bridges, the carnival and even the
tourists (the readers) come into play.[30] There is method in the author's
recourse to national stereotypes, which is not confined to the *italianità*
of the Italian protagonists but also extends to many minor characters
of foreign extraction. If they come from Germany, like the conductor
Hellmut Wellauer in Brunetti's first case, *Death at la Fenice*, the solution lies in the dark Nazi past; files requested from Germany show
German thoroughness, while one never understands the languages of
the Romanians and Bulgarians, etc.

In much the same way as travel guides give foreigners basic linguistic help, Leon's insertion of Italian sentence and word fragments

---

[29] Donna Leon, *Death at la Fenice*, London: Chapmans, 1992; *Death in a Strange
Country*, London: Chapmans, 1993; *A Venetian Reckoning*, London: Macmillan,
1995; *Acqua Alta*, London: Pan, 1997; *A Noble Radiance*, London: Heinemann,
1998; *Wilful Behaviour*, London: Heinemann, 2002.

[30] Donna Leon has forbidden the translation of her work into Italian and thereby has
specified her target readership as those who do not know Italy. It is primarily for
the Americans and Europeans outside Italy that these crime novels have been
written and for whom the rudimentary cultural anthropology and Italian local
colour have been introduced.

and her explanation of these is part and parcel of the repeated thematization of national idiosyncrasies. It is sometimes useful and sometimes very specific. Examples from *Acqua Alta* are:

> Obviously, Signora Petrelli had been at work on the hospital staff, see-
> ing that the little envelopes, *bustarelle*, were delivered into the proper
> hands. (39)

> "*Pantegane*", he explained, giving the Venetian name for rat, a word
> which, though it named them clearly rat still managed to make them,
> in the naming, somehow charming and domestic. (61)

> The first one turned to the barman and said, "*Due* vanilla and choco-
> latto, please." (77)

> His hand was underneath his jacket, pulling at his revolver, when they
> heard Flavia shout, "*Porco vacca*", and then both of them heard the
> unmistakable sound of champagne splashing from the neck of a bottle
> on to the floor. (144)

> "*Ricca sfondata*", she explained. Bottomless riches. (155)

> I did some business with him when he first opened his shop here,
> years ago, and he's *un vero figlio di puttana*. (173)

> "*Buon giorno?*" he called ... (198)

The novels of Leon do not supply the only examples of national
stereotyping, but they certainly provide the clearest. These stereotypes
often help to solve the cases. Reading the Venetian cases, an
obviously problematic interculturality becomes evident, which, in
spite of a myriad of national differences (Britons, Chinese, Sicilians,
Romanians, Neapolitans and Americans are all represented), is nevertheless accepted. If the characteristic classifications prove correct,
then the investigation proceeds, but ambiguous cultural classifications
confuse the Commissioner: "The French, Brunetti knew, had con-
quered Naples centuries ago, but the usual genetic souvenir of their
long occupation was the red hair sometimes seen in the city, not these

clear, Nordic eyes."[31] The national distinctions eventually even dis-
appear behind the sole dividing line between "foreign" and "local"[32]
that strikes one as stubbornly traditional and which would be
anachronistic in the twentieth century, if it did not derive, as it probably does, from the American author's tourist view of Europe. One
might think, however, that even in Europe, the humorous description
of southern Italians as "immigrants in their own country",[33] and the
emphasis on Venetians by birth as the legitimate residents of Venice
belong to the national conflicts of the past.

However, this naïve repetition of national characteristics becomes
interesting once more in the context of the globalization, not least of
book markets, that relieves the individual nation states of their political and economic decision-making power and renders the nation state
with its distinctive features a collection of individual and local quirks.
In the global village, nationality may be cultivated as folklore. The
thematization of national characteristics in crime fiction becomes
more interesting too when well-known stereotypes are observed from
a new perspective and well-known clichés updated. For example, the
Spanish-Catalan gourmet Carvalho ironically comments on and parodies national stereotypes in the course of his investigations. The
Carvalho novels also show that the alien perspective, if it is not carefully adjusted, cannot produce the defamiliarization of cultural stereotypes when they give superficial treatment to well-known topoi such
as the Mafia. Certainly, Vázquez Montalbán too has recourse to
clichés relating to Spanish society's formation of national identity for
example, the history of the Communist party or Catalan national pride,
but he does so in order to examine them critically on a cultural and
ideological level. Spain's coming to terms with its past becomes a
running gag in his book-burning motif.

The interest in the discourse of nationalism, which can be seen as a
desire to come to terms with nationality and identity crises, is an intercultural one. Such interculturality may serve to relativize and counterbalance the "Unterscheidung von Nationen" (distinguishing of nations

---

[31]   Leon, *Acqua Alta*, 199.
[32]   *Ibid.*, 132.
[33]   *Ibid.*, 261.

from each other).[34] Although individual works of crime fiction have recourse to specific cultures (in Israel to the conflict in Palestine, in post-Franco Spain to coming to terms with the era of the dictatorship, in Australia to the funeral rites of the Aborigines), the interculturality that the works of this genre have in common lies in relativizing the significance of the national. The interculturality of current crime fiction is based on the need of the inhabitants of a global village for similarly global, ethnographic and anthropological general knowledge.

Throughout the world, the genre of crime fiction has assumed the task of describing local cultures and, in addition to the constant restoration of justice, does the work of cultural representation. This comprises the imagological representation of national stereotypes and critical reflection of and upon different milieus and socio-political ideologies, as well as the portrayal of the historical conflicts of individual societies and states.

Within contemporary crime narrative, as the dual narrative strands of crime and investigation come together in the resolution, the reader is offered yet another strand, that of cultural investigation, the inclusion of which constitutes an important shift within the genre. In certain novels the resolution of the murder can be seen to coincide with a restoration of cultural order, whereas in other cases these very orders are questioned.

Although in this regard there is great diversity in current crime writing, there is no contradiction in crime novels with markedly national plot settings being internationally successful. Given the natural desire for the acquisition of general knowledge on the part of the reader, it is logical that a genre dedicating itself increasingly to the fictional description of local cultural knowledge should prove exciting to a wide readership. In the last thirty years crime fiction has gained worldwide currency in two different ways. It has encompassed the globe in terms of its reception, and in terms of its content it has, on an equally global scale, been concerned with the narrative investigation of murder cases in all corners of the earth. At the beginning of the twenty-first century it reflects within a globalized world those local

---

[34] Niklas Luhmann, *Die Gesellschaft der Gesellschaft*, Frankfurt am Main: Suhrkamp, 1998.

milieus and topoi which are now generating fresh excitement and interest.[35]

---

[35]   This essay has been translated by Fiona Fincannon.

ARTICULATING AND DISARTICULATING CULTURE AND IDENTITY IN VÁZQUEZ MONTALBÁN'S *SERIE CARVALHO*

STEWART KING

> La literatura y el cine nos ayudan a imaginar y a suponer nuestra vida y nuestra memoria.[1]

Well-known for his sense of irony, love of food and literary pyromania, Pepe Carvalho is perhaps Spain's most famous fictional detective. This eponymous anti-hero is the protagonist of eighteen novels, six collections of short stories and a recipe book in a series that covered approximately thirty-three years of contemporary Spanish history before Vázquez Montalbán's death in 2004. This series forms what the author describes as his "novelas-crónica".[2] In fact, as the publisher's blurb to *Los mares del Sur* testifies,[3] one of the selling points of the series is the commentary it provides on the changes that Spain has been undergoing since the transition from a dictatorship to a modern democratic state: "Desde la alta sociedad al inframundo de los suburbios, la novela traza un intenso cuadro de personajes y ambientes

---

[1] Manuel Vázquez Montalbán, *El laberinto griego*, Barcelona: Planeta, 1991, 23: "Literature and cinema help us to imagine our lives and memories." Unless stated otherwise all translations are my own.

[2] Manuel Vázquez Montalbán, *Historias de política ficción*, Barcelona: Planeta, 1989, 5.

[3] According to Patricia Hart, *The Spanish Sleuth: The Detective in Spanish Fiction*, London: Associated University Press, 1987 (cited in Luis F. Costa, 1987, "La nueva novela negra española: el caso de Pepe Carvalho", *Hispanic Science-Fiction/Fantasy and the Thriller*, special issue of *Monographic Review/Revista monográfica*, III/1-2 [1987], 305), the publisher's blurbs are written by Vázquez Montalbán himself.

que refleja los conflictos personales y colectivos de la España actual."[4]
These changes and conflicts are what I wish to highlight by framing
the Carvalho series within the problematic formation and celebration
of national and regional cultural identities in post-Franco Spain, especially as they pertain to Catalonia.

According to Benedict Anderson, the reader's identification between the fictional and real worlds is critical in creating a sense of
national consciousness. In his analysis of *El periquillo sarniento*, a
nineteenth-century Mexican novel by José Joaquín Fernández de
Lizardi, he writes that:

> We see the "national imagination" at work in the movement of a soli-
> tary hero through a sociological landscape of a fixity that fuses the
> world inside the novel with the world outside. This picaresque *tour
> d'horison* – hospitals, prisons, remote villages, monasteries, Indians,
> Negroes – is nonetheless not a *tour du monde*. The horizon is clearly
> bounded: it is that of colonial Mexico.[5]

For Anderson, the importance of realist fiction, newspapers and now
television and radio in the creation of a national consciousness – of
what he calls an imagined community – rests in their ability to describe a social space through the constant repetition of images and
ideas with which the citizens of a nation or the members of a cultural
group identify.

Like the fictional world represented in *El periquillo sarniento*, the
Carvalho series provides the reader with a readily recognizable sociocultural landscape which comprises the many different layers of Spanish society:

> No era su oficio [el de Carvalho] salvar vidas o destruirlas, sino obser-
> varlas en un fragmento determinado de su recorrido, sin preocuparse
> por el origen, ni por el final. Había visto fragmentos de vida de

---

4   Manuel Vázquez Montalbán, *Los mares del Sur*, Barcelona: Planeta, 1979: "From
     high society to the underdeveloped world of the suburbs, the novel charts a vivid
     portrait of characters and situations which reflect the personal and collective con-
     flicts of contemporary Spain."
5   Benedict Anderson, *Imagined Communities: Reflections on the Origin and Spread
     of Nationalism*, London: Verso, 1991, 30.

Andrés, de su familia, de la Sociedad Deportiva Albacete Balompié, de un ciego de Águilas, de dos monjas peatonales de Jaravía.[6]

In an interview which appeared in one of the earliest studies of Spanish detective fiction, Vázquez Montalbán highlights the realist elements of the series and the possibilities that it offers:

> Creo que el ciclo Carvalho tiene unas reglas poéticas propias. Tiene un punto de vista que te permite hacer una crónica de lo real, un tiempo literario que corresponde con el tiempo histórico, y tiene un lenguaje que traduce la sensibilidad de carácter urbano. El lenguaje, por lo tanto, refleja la realidad urbana.[7]

In his daily work, Carvalho encounters families from all social classes, politicians, businessmen and women, immigrants, bootblacks, prostitutes, footballers, even real-life famous people, such as King Juan Carlos and Juan Antonio Samaranch, and, despite being based primarily in Barcelona, he travels to other parts of Spain and internationally when the need arises. Given that the internal time of the series parallels that of historical time, the reader is confronted over the thirty-three years of the series with a Carvalho, who like the reader, grows older. During this time, we are witness to his topsy-turvy relationship with his often neglected girlfriend, the prostitute Charo; his friendships with a wide variety of people who appear regularly, like Biscuter, his secretary cum chef, Enric Fuster, his Valencian neighbour and fellow gourmand, and the bootblack, Bromuro. Other characters that appear sporadically, such as Teresa Marsé (*Los mares del Sur, Tatuaje, Los pájaros de Bangkok*), Carmela in Madrid (*Asesinato en el Comité Central, El premio*), and Yésica (*Los mares*

---

[6]   Manuel Vázquez Montalbán, *La rosa de Alejandría*, Barcelona: Planeta, 1991, 229: "It was not his job to save lives or destroy them, but to observe them in a specific fragment of their journey, without worrying about their origin or their end. He had seen fragments of Andrés' life, of his family's, of the Albacete Football Club, of a blind man from Águilas, of two strolling nuns from Jaravía."

[7]   Vázquez Montalbán quoted in Hart, *The Spanish Sleuth*, 95: "I believe the Carvalho cycle has its own poetic rules. It has a point of view which allows you to make a chronicle of the real, a literary time which corresponds to historical time, and it has a language which translates the sensibility of the urban character. Its language, then, reflects the urban reality."

del Sur, El hombre de mi vida[8]) create a sense of continuity throughout the series. Alongside the lives of these characters, the reader is presented with references to recent events, such as the victory of the Spanish Socialist Workers' Party in 1982 in *Los pájaros de Bangkok,* the Barcelona Olympic Games in *Sabotaje olímpico,*[9] and the disappearance of the ex-director of the Civil Guard in *Roldán, ni vivo ni muerto.*[10] The series also charts the social and cultural transformations affecting Spain on a micro scale, such as changing streetscapes caused by immigration from North Africa and land speculation in which whole suburbs, and the memories and histories which they contain, are being destroyed in the modernization of Barcelona.

The relationship between literature and national consciousness is not a new idea. Herder and other Romantics had linked the two in the late eighteenth and early nineteenth centuries. However, instead of seeing one's cultural identity as existing outside of representation, as the Romantics had argued, Homi Bhabha, following on from Anderson, presents an alternative view in which he argues that cultural identities exist through representation. For Bhabha, nations, "as a system of cultural signification", are themselves narrations through which they come into being.[11] In this sense, the role of narrative in creating a national identity resides in its ability to represent an image not only for and of ourselves but for others as well. As such, national and cultural identities are not something simply found in narratives. According to Stuart Hall they are not unchanging, shaped once and for all at the beginning of time; rather they take shape in the very act of representation.[12]

Like Hall, Vázquez Montalbán is wary of essentialist notions of identity. In fact, he sees identity as being shaped by popular, especially Hollywood, representations of behaviour: "No hay ser humano que no recurra a un modelo interpretativo dominante, sobre todo

---

[8]   Manuel Vázquez Montalbán, *Asesinato en el Comité Central* (1981), *Los pájaros de Bangkok* (1983), *Tatuaje* (1989), *El premio* (1996), *El hombre de mi vida* (2000), all Bareclona: Planeta.

[9]   Manuel Vázquez Montalbán, *Sabotaje olímpico*, Barcelona: Planeta, 1993.

[10]   Manuel Vázquez Montalbán, *Roldán, no vivo ni muerto*, Barcelona: Planeta, 1994.

[11]   Introduction to *Nation and Narration*, ed. Homi K. Bhabha, London: Routledge, 1990, 1.

[12]   See Stuart Hall, "Cultural Identity and Cinematic Representation", *Framework*, 36 (1989), 71 and 80.

cuando le toca vivir situaciones anormales que hasta entonces sólo ha visto en el teatro, en el cine, en la televisión o quizá leído en las novelas."[13] Carvalho himself is not immune to this and adopts roles from popular culture. For example, in an act of self-parody, he questions:

> ¿A quién debo imitar? ¿A Bogart interpretando a Chandler? ¿A Alan Ladd en los personajes de Hammet? ¿Paul Newman en Harper? ¿Gene Hackman? En la soledad de su coche … Carvalho asumía los tics de cada cual.[14]

Later in the same book, he is accused of acting like a Hollywood detective.[15]

Carvalho is a contradictory figure. He once was a militant in the Spanish Communist Party and later worked for the CIA, claiming he killed Kennedy, before returning to Spain to become a private detective. Like the classic detective of American hard-boiled fiction, he is a relatively solitary figure, a loner, who constantly challenges traditional modes of identification. A Galician born in Barcelona and a Catalan who doesn't speak the language, his loyalty is not to any country or region but to the landscape of his childhood, Barcelona's *barrio chino*, where he works and feels most comfortable, even nostalgic at times.

The representation of Catalonia and Catalans in the Carvalho series has been criticized by Joan Ramon Resina for being essentially centralist and anti-Catalan. For Resina, the repeated criminality and the cruel parody of the characteristics and values of the Catalan bourgeoisie serve to attribute negative qualities to Catalan identity, which reinforce centralist attitudes towards Catalonia.[16] While there is some truth to Resina's argument, I would argue that the representation and

---

[13] Vázquez Montalbán, *Los pájaros de Bangkok*, 23: "There isn't a human being who does not resort to a dominant interpretative model, especially when they are in unusual situations which, until then, they had only seen in the theatre, in the cinema, on television or perhaps read in novels."

[14] Manuel Vázquez Montalbán, *La soledad del manager*, Barcelona: Planeta, 1977, 95: "Who should I imitate? Bogart playing Chandler? Alan Ladd as one of Hammett's characters? Paul Newman as Harper? Gene Hackman? In the solitude of his car, Carvalho took on the tics of each of them."

[15] *Ibid.*, 141.

[16] Joan Ramon Resina, "La figura del criminal en las novelas policiacas de Manuel Vázquez Montalbán", *Indiana Journal of Hispanic Literatures*, II/2 (1994), 231 and 237.

articulation of Catalanness and Spanishness is more complex than Resina would suggest. In fact, I would posit that due to the often rigid borders that separate Spanish and Catalan cultures, the Carvalho series, like works by other Spanish-language writers from Catalonia, sits on the margins of both Spanish and Catalan literatures and cultures, not belonging completely to either, whilst questioning the internal coherence of both literatures and cultures. Yet, the series shares with both literatures the articulation and disarticulation of conventional notions of Spanish and Catalan national identity and culture. The purpose of this essay is to explore the ways in which Vázquez Montalbán's Carvalho series disrupts homogeneous Spanish notions of culture and identity through the articulation of a Catalan point of view, before focusing on how his work challenges these same categories in a Catalan context.

In order to understand Vázquez Montalbán's critique of the traditional nationalist discourse of Spanishness, it is first necessary to understand the cultural politics carried out by the Franco regime (1939-1975). During the almost forty years of his dictatorship, Franco tried to create a culturally and politically homogeneous society. To this end, the regime sought to eradicate anything or anyone that did not conform to its vision of Spain. This included political parties, trade unions, freemasons, atheists and regional cultures and languages.[17] In fact, claims for greater autonomy or independence by the Catalans and Basques were, according to Franco,[18] a major reason for the military uprising in 1936 and, consequently, after the war, the regime set about protecting what it understood as the national unity. The regime did this by creating a discourse of Spanishness based on Castilian language and culture. Franco himself stated that Spain had "una sola len-

---

[17] See Mike Richards, "'Terror and Progress': Industrialisation, Modernity and the Making of Francoism", in *Spanish Cultural Studies: An Introduction. The Struggle for Modernity*, eds Helen Graham and Jo Labanyi, Oxford: Oxford University Press, 1995, 176.

[18] Francisco Franco Bahamonde, *Colección de proclamas y arengas del General don Francisco Franco por José Emilio Díez*, Seville: Carmona, 1937, 114.

gua, el castellano, y una sola personalidad, la española".[19] This proved disastrous for Catalonia, the Basque Country and Galicia. In Catalonia, for example, speaking and writing Catalan was banned. Catalan books were destroyed; the Catalan flag, traditional music and dances were also prohibited for being separatist, as were personal and topographic names.

The first detective book of the series, *Tatuaje*,[20] was written almost at the end of the regime and the series is often marked by Francoist cultural politics. Although Vázquez Montalbán is not considered a Catalan author because he does not write in Catalan, he has stated that he uses, whenever possible, his "lengua literaria y profesional en defensa de las reivindicaciones de la cultura catalana e incluso de la realidad nacional catalana, pero sin dar el paso de ponerme a escribir ahora en catalán".[21] This defence of Catalan culture leads him to question traditional concepts of Spanish culture and identity. For example, in *La rosa de Alejandría*, Vázquez Montalbán highlights the effect of forty years of Francoism in Catalonia. In a conversation between the Catalan Narcís and Carvalho, the former asks Carvalho:

> – ¿Sabe usted quién era Carner?
> – Me suena.
> – Ha sido uno de los más grandes poetas de este siglo. Más grande que Elliot (sic), que Saint John Perse, que Maiakovski … pero … era catalán y eso se paga.
> – ¿Qué precio tiene el ser catalán?

---

[19] *Palabras del Caudillo: 19 abril 1937-31 diciembre 1938*, Barcelona: Fe, 1939, 226 "… a single language, Castilian, and a single personality, the Spanish one" (quoted in Norman L. Jones, "The Catalan Question Since the Civil War", in *Spain in Crisis: The Evolution and Decline of the Franco Regime*, ed. Paul Preston, New York: Barnes and Noble, 1976, 236).

[20] Although Pepe Carvalho makes his first appearance in *Yo maté a Kennedy*, Barcelona: Planeta, 1972, the first book in the series, this avant-garde novel does not truly form part of the series. *Tatuaje*, written in 1974, is considered the first novel.

[21] Vázquez Montalbán quoted in Antonio Beneyto, *Censura y política en los escritores españoles*, Barcelona: Euros, 1975, 218: "… literary and professional language in defence of Catalan culture and the Catalan national reality, but without taking the step to sit down and write in Catalan."

> – El de casi no ser. Ni siquiera consta que lo eres en el carnet de iden-
> tidad. Y no digamos ya en el pasaporte.[22]

In Narcís' words, to be Catalan is effectively not to exist. Subsumed under the blanket term Spanish as represented by the identity card and passport, it means being marginalized by a nation-state which associates being Spanish with the dominant culture.

In contrast with the attempted silencing of Catalan culture, Vázquez Montalbán constantly disarticulates the myth of Spanish cultural homogeneity based on Castilian language and culture. Given that the regime tried to eradicate Catalan, Basque and Galician, Vázquez Montalbán inscribes cultural difference in his writings by the use of Catalan words, expressions, and syntactical structures. This code switching between the two languages occurs not only in dialogues where one would normally expect these to appear in order to achieve greater realism, or simply as local colour, but also as part of the narrator's voice. Catalan words, names, etc, in Castilian-language texts, such as appear in the Carvalho series, go beyond local colour, functioning instead as metonyms of cultural difference, where the part stands for the whole. *Los pájaros de Bangkok* is illustrative of this metonymic function. In a scene between Carvalho and a client, the businessman Daurella, the latter explains:

> – Me están robando. Nos están robando.
> Habían sido las primeras palabras de Daurella, sentado ante la mesa de despacho de Carvalho. Su mujer, la señora Mercè, había hecho personalmente un balance durante meses y meses, fin de semana tras fin de semana, en la torrecita que tenían los viejos en Vallirana. Había un inmenso hueco de seis millones de pesetas.
> – Mi mujer sabe lo que se dice. No es una vieja chocha. *Hi toca. Hi toca* [1].

---

[22] Vázquez Montalbán, *La rosa de Alejandría*, 44: "– Do you know who Carner was?
– Sounds familiar.
– He was one of this century's greatest poets. Greater than Elliot (sic), than Saint John Perse, than Maiakovski … but … he was Catalan and that has a price.
– What is the price of being Catalan?
– That of almost not being. It's not even recorded on your identity card. And let's not start on your passport."

Insistía el señor Daurella en catalán.
– Fue una de las primeras mujeres tenedoras de libros que salieron de la academia Cots. Antes de la guerra, ya lo creo. Es que mi suegro era un hombre de ideas y quiso que la Mercè estudiara como un hombre. Mi suegro era de Estat Català, muy de la *ceba* [2], mucho. [23]

This passage contains many of the diverse techniques which Vázquez Montalbán and other Castilian-language writers from Catalonia use to inscribe cultural difference, that is, Catalanness, in their texts. The first technique involves the use of personal names. Daurella uses his family's Catalan names, such as Mercè, instead of the Castilian Mercedes. A little further on in the narrative, proper names are linked to specific cultures. Daurella, when talking about his children, says "el marido de la Esperança, el Pau, o mejor dicho, Pablo como dicen ustedes en castellano"[24] and so doing, marks Castilian-speakers as different, Other, despite using that very language.

Another linguistic technique used by Vázquez Montalbán is that of referring the reader to an external body of knowledge necessary for understanding the text. This is the case of the two footnotes which accompany the text in the above passage. In the first footnote, the author simply offers a translation of the Catalan expression "*hi toca*": "Sabe lo que se hace."[25] The second footnote provides the meaning of the popular Catalan expression to describe an extreme form of Cata-lanism "muy de la *ceba*" because it cannot be translated literally:

---

[23] Vázquez Montalbán, *Los pájaros de Bangkok*, 20:
"–They're robbing me. They're robbing us.
These were the first words Daurella had said as he sat before the desk in Carvalho's office. His wife, Mercè, had personally done the bookkeeping for months and months, weekend after weekend, in the house which the old couple had in Vallirana. There was an immense hole of some six million pesetas.
– My wife knows what she's talking about. She's not a doting old woman. She knows what she's doing. She knows what she's doing [1].
Insisted Mr Daurella in Catalan.
– She was one of the first women bookkeepers who graduated from the Cots Academy. Before the war, indeed. My father-in-law was a man of ideas and he wanted Mercè to study just like a man. My father-in-law was a member of Estat Català, a very serious Catalan nationalist [2]."
[24] *Ibid.*, 21: "Esperança's husband, Pau. Or Pablo as you say in Castilian."
[25] "She knows what she is doing."

"Muy catalanista (muy de la cebolla)."[26] These footnotes serve to articulate cultural difference as readers unfamiliar with Catalan culture need to refer to them for extra-textual cultural information. The need for such information highlights the gap between the culture of the text and that of the reader, showing them to be separate cultures, at least for the non-Catalan-speaking reader.

A third strategy which Vázquez Montalbán uses to emphasize a different cultural reality to that of the rest of Spain is the use of words and expressions typical amongst Castilian-speakers from Catalonia, what he describes as peripheral Castilian.[27] The same passage quoted above contains several different examples of this. For example, the narrator speaks of "la torrecita que tenían los viejos en Vallirana",[28] "la torre", here meaning a "house", is a linguistic phenomenon particular to Catalonia. Another example of this occurs in Vázquez Montalbán's *Asesinato en el Comité Central* where the narrator states that "Carvalho cerró la radio y se puso a ordenar los papeles".[29] The use of the verb *cerrar* comes from the Catalan verb *tancar*, meaning, in this context, to turn off the radio. Unlike the previous examples where Catalan words and expressions found their way into footnotes, in these last examples, the author does not believe it is necessary to explain the specific meaning of *cerrar* and *torre*, supposing that, although a non-Catalan-speaker may find these words a little strange, they should encounter little trouble in grasping their meaning.

Traditionally, the difference between the standard language of the narrator and the regional language of the characters has been used to emphasize the exotic nature of the latter, classifying it as non-standard, inferior and abnormal.[30] Yet, the use of this peripheral, or non-standard, Castilian by a traditional third person narrator, as occurs

---

[26] "Very Catalanist (very much an onion)."

[27] See Manuel Vázquez Montalbán and Jaume Fuster, *Diàlegs a Barcelona*, Barcelona: Ajuntament de Barcelona/Laia, 1985, 137.

[28] "The little house the old couple had in Vallirana."

[29] Vázquez Montalbán, *Asesinato en el Comité Central*, 25: "Carvalho turned off the radio and set about organising the papers."

[30] This is also a characteristic of imperialist attitudes to language. According to Bill Ashcroft, Gareth Griffiths and Helen Tiffin, *The Empire Writes Back: Theory and Practice in Post-Colonial Literatures*, London: Routledge, 1989, 7-8 and 38-77, imperialist discourse establishes a standard form of the metropolitan language which marginalizes all variants as impure, hence, non-standard.

in *Los pájaros de Bangkok*, shows that local colour is not the reason behind its appearance in the text but rather the articulation of difference.

The juxtaposition of two or more languages is fundamental in constructing cultural identity within a multicultural context, such as the Catalan one. Sneja Gunew, in a study of multicultural literature, suggests that foreign words act as signs of untranslatability. Drawing on New Zealand examples, she states that a foreign language – in this case Maori – within a predominantly anglophone context functions as something which "threatens meaning and subject formation, including the idea of a coherent national identity".[31] We can see this clearly by contrasting another detective novel, *Barcelona connection* by Andreu Martín, with the above examples. Martín began his literary career in 1979 exclusively in Castilian before adopting the unusual practice of incorporating both Catalan and Castilian simultaneously in the writing process.[32] In the Castilian version of *Barcelona connection*, the Catalan cultural references, including personal and topographic names, as well as regional dialects are almost totally eliminated. The suppression of Catalan references is so thorough that even when, in the Catalan version, the protagonist reflects on the need to invent a Catalan word for the Mafia, in the Castilian version, this becomes a Castilian word.[33] By changing the linguistic context of the narrative, Martín effectively erases the Catalan cultural references from the sociocultural landscape he describes.[34] In contrast to Martín's *Barcelona connection*, if we examine the above example by Vázquez Montalbán, we can see how

---

[31] Sneja Gunew, "Feminism and the Politics of Irreducible Differences: Multiculturalism/Ethnicity/Race", in *Feminism and the Politics of Difference*, eds Sneja Gunew and Anna Yeatman, St Leonards, NSW: Allen and Unwin, 1993, 15. By foreign language I mean a language different to the principal language of the text. I do not wish to suggest that Maori is a foreign language in New Zealand literature.

[32] According to Ute Heinemann, *Novel·la entre dues llengües: El dilema català o castellà*, Kassel: Reichenberger, 1996, 81, Martín writes a first draft in Catalan before writing a second draft in Castilian. He then rewrites the first draft in Catalan taking into account the changes made in the second (Castilian) draft. Both works are published simultaneously.

[33] Andreu Martín, *Barcelona connection*, Barcelona: Ediciones B, 1987, 140.

[34] Heinemann, *Novel·la entre dues llengües*, 85.

the presence of Catalan in his works serves to disrupt the idea of Spanishness constructed on notions of Castilian linguistic purity.

Vázquez Montalbán's critique of Spanish nationalism does not inhibit him from simultaneously criticizing these very same categories in a Catalan cultural context. Just as he questions the Castiliancentric discourse by way of the articulation of alternative cultural voices, Vázquez Montalbán challenges fixed notions of Catalanness and cultural homogeneity based on language. In *El hombre de mi vida*, Carvalho and Quimet, a Catalan businessman and one of Charo's regular clients whose offer of work allows her to give up the game, discuss exactly what Catalonia is:

> – ¿Qué piensa usted de Cataluña?
> – ¿A quién se refiere?
> – A Cataluña.
> – No acabo de entender la pregunta. ¿Quién es Cataluña? Una entidad geográfica, administrativa, emblemática, simbólica.
> – Nacional. Cataluña es una nación.
> – No lo pongo en duda. Un sujeto colectivo, vamos, colectivo y virtual.[35]

Simply by offering possible definitions, Carvalho questions the very meaning of Catalonia as it can be several things to different people at the same time: a geographic, administrative, emblematic or symbolic space. His idea of Catalonia as a virtual collective, reminiscent of Anderson's imagined community updated for the new millennium, highlights the assertion that cultural identities are abstract.

In direct opposition to the conventional discourses in which the national is constructed on the belief that cultures and identities are different and that there are rigid borders that separate them,[36] Vázquez

---

[35] Vázquez Montalbán, *El hombre de mi vida*, 22:
     "– What do you think about Catalonia?
     – To whom are you referring?
     – To Catalonia.
     – I don't get the question. Who is Catalonia? A geographic, administrative, emblematic, symbolic ... entity.'
     – National. Catalonia is a nation.
     – I don't doubt that. A collective subject, well, collective and virtual."
[36] See Anne Brewster, *Literary Formations: Post-Colonialism, Nationalism, Globalism*, Melbourne: Melbourne University Press, 1995, 13.

Montalbán, in his Prologue to Carlota Solé's study on immigration in Catalonia, argues that Catalan and Spanish cultures should not be considered impermeable. Instead, he proposes that one should listen to "la gente que habla *como un catalán*", despite speaking in Castilian. Similarly, it is important to "distinguirla de la que no habla como un catalán aunque hable en catalán".[37] For Vázquez Montalbán, being attentive to new ways of conceiving Catalan identity demands that we go beyond stereotypes, and that the question of cultural identity be examined in all its complexity. This attempt to go beyond the stereotypes can be seen in *La soledad del manager*, published seven years before the ideas expressed in Solé's work. In this novel, Oriol Alemany, a Catalan "de pura cepa" (traditional Catalan) and close friend of Lluís Companys, the President of Catalonia during the Second Republic, questions Carvalho about his identity:

– Ahora dicen que vamos hacia la democracia. ¿De la mano de quién? Pues de los mismos charnegos que hicieron el caldo gordo al franquismo .... ¿Es usted catalán?

– No lo sé. Yo más bien diría que soy charnego.
–En Catalunya los verdaderos charnegos son algunos catalanes. Como Samaranch, Porta y otros *botiflers* que han hecho el caldo gordo al franquismo. Ésos son los charnegos de primera.[38]

In twisting the meaning of the word *charnego* – a Spanish-speaking immigrant in Catalonia – Alemany does not change its pejorative

---

[37] Manuel Vázquez Montalbán, "Para una nueva conciencia nacional catalana", in *Los inmigrantes en la sociedad y cultura catalanas*, ed. Carlota Solé, Barcelona: Península, 1982, 12: "... people who speak *like a Catalan*"; "... distinguish them from those who do not speak like a Catalan despite speaking in Catalan."

[38] Vázquez Montalbán, *La soledad del manager*, 102:
"– Now they say that we're heading for democracy. And who's taking us there? The same traitors [charnegos] who had it good under Franco .... Are you a Catalan?
– I don't know. I'd say I'm probably one of those 'traitors'.
– In Catalonia, the real foreigners [charnegos] are actually Catalans – people like Samaranch, Porta, and other moneybags who lined their pockets under Franco. They're your real foreigners [charnegos]."
(Vázquez Montalbán, *The Angst-Ridden Executive*, trans. Ed Emery, London: Serpent's Tail, 1990, 139. Modifications mine.)

meaning but rather extends the range of meanings to include anyone who is believed to have acted against Catalonia, in this case, Juan Antonio Samaranch, who before becoming the president of the International Olympic Committee was minister of sport during the Franco regime.

Although Vázquez Montalbán has no illusions about working-class life, as represented by Ana Briongos' family in *Los mares del Sur*, he does not represent working-class immigrants – the "charnegos" – as a threat to community in Catalonia.[39] In fact, Carvalho encounters immigrant families, such as the Abellán family, which are "en plena evolución de lo español a lo catalán", especially in the case of Andrés who "piensa como un catalán, habla muy bien el catalán y poco a poco va cortando las raíces que le ligan al mundo de su madre".[40]

In contrast to the growing working-class immigrant association with Catalonia, Vázquez Montalbán reserves his strongest criticism, as can be seen in the statements by Señor Alemany above, for the Catalan bourgeoisie. At its most obvious, Vázquez Montalbán demonstrates this in his critique of the Catalan haute bourgeoisie which deliberately tries to dissociate itself from Catalonia. For example, in *La soledad del manager*, Gausachs speaks "un castellano forzado para evitar las relajadas vocales catalanas, falsamente acastizado para estar a la altura de gentes importantes de Madrid".[41] Similarly, in *Los mares del Sur*, the Marqués de Munt's speech is characterized as "la de un actor radiofónico catalán que trata continuamente de desimular su acento".[42] In a cultural situation in which national identity is determined by language, the use of a Castilian with all traces of its Catalan origins deliberately removed can be interpreted as a denial of Catalan culture.

Vázquez Montalbán's strongest critique of the Catalan bourgeoisie occurs in *El delantero centro fue asesinado al atardecer*, whose sub-

---

[39] Vázquez Montalbán, *Los mares del Sur*, 254.
[40] Vázquez Montalbán, *La rosa de Alejandría*, 44-45: "... in the process of evolving from Spanish to Catalan"; "... thinks like a Catalan, speaks Catalan very well and who little by little is cutting the ties that bind him to his mother's world."
[41] Vázquez Montalbán, *La soledad del manager*, 66: "... a forced Castilian in order to avoid the relaxed Catalan vowels, falsely purified [acastizado] to be on the same level as important people from Madrid."
[42] Vázquez Montalbán, *Los mares del Sur*, 47: "... that of a Catalan radio actor who tries continuously to hide his accent."

ject is big business, land speculation and an unnamed Barcelona Football Club. In this work, he seeks to expose the "palabras [y símbolos] que [cada época] necesita para enmascararse".[43] To this end, he criticizes a disproportionate focus on outward signs of cultural identification in Catalonia. For example, at the beginning of the book, in an interview with Jack Mortimer, the English centre-forward recently contracted to the club, a group of journalists are interested primarily in whether he will make the effort to learn Catalan and whether he will give his as yet unborn children Catalan names (17). Similarly, later in the narrative, the president of the club, Basté de Linyola, describes the club as "más que un club ... el ejército simbólico y desarmado de Cataluña".[44] In this sense, "Barça" is representative of the wider Catalan community and functions as a channel for Catalan nationalism. At the same time, de Linyola is clandestinely involved in attempting to close down a local football club which has great community support in order to be able to buy the land and sell it at a profit before the Barcelona Olympics. Although de Linyola's public utterances of Catalanness are at odds with his private acts, he is able to achieve his aims without scrutiny because the public and the journalists appear obsessed with outward expressions of support for Catalonia.

Critics, such as José F. Colmeiro, have emphasized Carvalho's marginal, in-betweenness, and the fact that he never assumes a fixed cultural identity.[45] When asked by James Wonderful, an ex-CIA colleague, whether he is Galician, Carvalho responds that he is a "mestizo".[46] Nor does he identify as Catalan. When asked if he is Catalan in *El premio* he responds with a political slogan designed to make immigrants feel Catalan: "vivo y trabajo en Cataluña."[47] For Carvalho, coming from a Galician family living in Barcelona, national identities are too abstract:

---

[43] Manuel Vázquez Montalbán, *El delantero centro fue asesinado al atardecer*, Barcelona: Planeta, 1988, 105: "... words [and symbols] that [each era] needs in order to mask itself."

[44] *Ibid.*, 101: "... more than a club ... the symbolic and unarmed army of Catalonia."

[45] José F. Colmeiro, *Crónica del desencanto: la narrativa de Manuel Vázquez Montalbán*, Coral Gables, FL: North South Center Press/University of Miami, 1986, 182.

[46] Vázquez Montalbán, *Asesinato en el Comité Central*, 104.

[47] Vázquez Montalbán, *El premio*, 229: "I live and work in Catalonia."

"Lo que tengo muy claro es que yo no soy una nación. Bastante me cuesta ser un individuo y no confío en los pueblos. Los individuos pueden tener compasión, los pueblos no. Ser una nación me complicaría demasiado la vida."[48]

Rather than being anti-Catalanist, as Resina claims,[49] it is from Carvalho's position on the margins of traditional modes of identification that Vázquez Montalbán is simultaneously able to articulate and disarticulate current discourse on cultural identities in Spain in an attempt to wrest this discourse from traditional nationalisms and to expose it to new interpretations.

---

[48] Vázquez Montalbán, *El hombre de mi vida*, 22: "What is clear to me is that I am not a nation. I find it difficult enough to be an individual and I have no trust in a people. Individuals can have compassion, a people cannot. Being a nation would complicate my life too much."
[49] See Joan Ramon Resina, *El cadáver en la cocina: la novela criminal en la cultura del desencanto*, Barcelona: Anthropos, 1997, 135.

POPULAR GENRE AND THE POLITICS OF THE PERIPHERY: CATALAN CRIME FICTION BY WOMEN

ANNE M. WHITE AND SHELLEY GODSLAND

Language and identity: the case of Catalonia

In the Introduction to her history of Spanish women's writing, Catherine Davies makes a crucial point that merits repetition here:

> Literature in Spain is written in at least four languages, each with its own national, cultural and literary traditions. This should never be forgotten. In Spain, gender politics are inflected by nationalism as well as by class.[1]

The four languages to which she refers are Spanish (castellano), Basque (euskera), Galician (galego) and Catalan. Our contribution to this collection will be concerned mainly with crime fiction written by women who have chosen to express themselves in the latter of these languages and it will examine a number of issues relating to the complex links that can exist between language, nation, gender and genre, illustrating these with analyses of a number of relevant works.

We will begin, however, by highlighting some of the general issues relating to the importance of the politics of language and nation in the specific case of Catalan and Catalonia. As Kathryn Woolard notes, although Catalan is spoken by a number of communities both within Spain and beyond its borders,[2] this language plays a particular role in Catalonia, where "it has served [in the twentieth century] as a prime

---

[1] Catherine Davies, *Spanish Women's Writing 1849-1996*, London: Athlone Press, 1998, 8-9.

[2] Catalan is spoken not only in Catalonia but also in Valencia, the Balearic Islands, Rousillon in France, Alguer in Sardinia and is the official language of Andorra. Some estimates put the number of Catalan speakers as high as ten million.

symbolic reserve of Catalan nationalism".[3] This role has its origins in the nineteenth century when the cultural movement known as the *Renaixença* or Renaissance created renewed interest in all aspects of Catalan identity. This, coupled with increasing frustration at the perceived inadequacies of Spain's highly centralized political system based in Madrid, helped to fuel nationalist sentiments.

Catalan thus became a "highly successful and visible badge of ... identity", functioning as a means of creating the kind of imagined community central to Benedict Anderson's (1983) definition of the nation. It helped to construct Catalonia as the peripheral Other, and has meant that this autonomous region has frequently been perceived by successive centralist regimes as "a very acute thorn in the flesh of Spanish nation-building".[4] Given its importance as a political symbol, it is hardly surprising that during the dictatorship of Primo de Rivera (1923-1930) and that of Franco (1939-1975), spoken and written expression in Catalan and its teaching were subject to varying degrees of control and surveillance, by legislation and other means.[5] Even in the last decade of the twentieth century, there was little evidence that this language's potency as a political symbol was on the wane. When King Juan Carlos I chose to make the opening remarks of his speech in Catalan at the 1992 Barcelona Olympics, it generated massive media coverage and heated debate about the future of Spain's identity as a nation. Shortly after, further changes to language policies in Catalonia were perceived by many inhabitants of other regions as a worrying development and there was talk of discrimination against Castilian speakers in a region which has always attracted large numbers of migrant workers from other areas of Spain. One Madrid-based right-wing daily, *ABC*, even went so far as to run a story with what many considered a shocking headline: "Igual que Franco pero al revés: per-

---

[3]   Kathryn Woolard, *Double Talk: Bilingualism and the Politics of Ethnicity in Catalonia*, Stanford: Stanford University Press, 1989, 1.

[4]   Clare Mar-Molinero, *The Politics of Language in the Spanish-Speaking World*, London: Routledge, 2000, 47.

[5]   For more information on the current linguistic situation, see Clare Mar-Molinero's "The Politics of Language: Spain's Minority Languages", in *Spanish Cultural Studies*, eds Helen Graham and Jo Labanyi, Oxford: Oxford University Press, 1995, 336-42.

secución del castellano en Cataluña",[6] evidence of the intense feelings which could still be stirred up by this language. In 1998, the central role long attributed to language in defining Catalan identity was clearly acknowledged in the Preamble to the new law on linguistic policy in Catalonia:

> La llengua catalana és un element fonamental de la formació i la personalitat nacional de Catalunya, un instrument bàsic de comunicació, d'integració i de cohesió social dels ciutadans i ciutadanes .... A més ha estat el testimoni de fidelitat del poble català envers la seva terra y la seva cultura específica.[7]

The sentiments expressed in the law ratified by the Catalan Parliament thus echoed what cultural theorist Iain Chambers had observed in another context, namely that: "Language is not primarily a means of communication; it is, above all, a means of cultural construction in which our very selves and sense are constituted."[8]

Transcultural re-inscription

The importance of the role that language can play in the construction of a writer's sense of cultural identity was clearly voiced by Manuel de Pedrolo, one of the region's most respected writers and promoters of crime fiction written in Catalan, who commented in an interview: "I do not belong to any history of Spanish literature – detective or not, since today Spanish and Castilian are the same thing, ... a writer belongs to the dominion of the language in which he writes, in my case Catalan."[9]

---

[6]   *ABC*, 12 September 1993: "Just like Franco but the other way round: the persecution of Castilian in Catalonia" (unless otherwise stated, all translations are our own).

[7]   Law of Linguistic Policy 1, 7 January 1998, cited in Clare Mar-Molinero, *The Politics of Language in the Spanish-Speaking World*, 166: "The Catalan language is a fundamental element of the formation and the national character of Catalonia, a basic instrument of communication, integration and social cohesion for its citizens, male and female .... Furthermore it has been the evidence of the loyalty of the Catalan people towards their land and their particular culture."

[8]   Iain Chambers, *Migrancy, Culture, Identity*, London: Routledge, 1994, 22.

[9]   Patricia Hart, *The Spanish Sleuth: The Detective in Spanish Fiction*, London: Associated University Press, 1987, 238.

For the purposes of our discussion here, however, one of the most interesting features of de Pedrolo's statement is that it suggests something of the complexity of the relationship that exists between texts written in a minority language and a popular genre like detective fiction. For although de Pedrolo's choice of Catalan as a medium of expression situates his work within a very specific sociolinguistic and cultural tradition, his choice of genre places his work within a much broader transnational and transcultural frame. What de Pedrolo fails to acknowledge in his decision to distance his own work from the Spanish tradition of crime writing is the crucial fact that both are products of a kind of textual interaction, which might be labelled transcultural re-inscription. The term was originally coined by Marsha Kinder in the context of her study of the nature of the relationship between Spanish and Hollywood cinema, in which she examines how film directors in Spain have imported conventions borrowed from other cinematic cultures and creatively reworked these for their own aesthetic and political purposes. However, her definition of transcultural re-inscription as "the ideological re-inscription of conventions that are borrowed from other cultures and set in conflict with each other, a process of hybridization that is capable of carving out a new aesthetic language"[10] suggests that this idea might also be fruitfully explored in relation to work by women who choose to write crime fiction in Catalan.

It should be said firstly that the transcultural re-inscription of crime fiction by female writers using Catalan is not a recent literary development but has a history which can be traced back at least to the Thirties with the publication of Mercè Rodoreda's *Crim* (1936),[11] a parody of the ratiocinative school of crime writing much favoured by English authors like Conan Doyle or Christie. Rodoreda, who was later to receive international recognition for her novels such as *La plaça del Diamant*,[12] renounced the novel some years after publication and never allowed it to be included in collections of her work. One can only speculate on the reasons for this, but perhaps this early engagement with a popular genre later proved an embarrassment for a writer

---

[10]   Marsha Kinder, *Blood Cinema: The Reconstruction of National Identity in Spain*, Berkeley: University of California Press, 1993, 11.
[11]   Mercè Rodoreda, *Crim*, Barcelona: Edicions de la Rosa dels Vents, 1936.
[12]   Mercè Rodoreda, *La plaça del Diamant*, Barcelona: Club Editor, 1962.

who was to become one of the iconic figures of modern Catalan literature. It is perhaps a sign of a shift in the contemporary cultural climate
of Catalonia that in more recent times many well-respected Catalan
writers, both male and female, have engaged with the crime genre and
won critical acclaim for their efforts.

Ironically, in the Fifties, the genre that Rodoreda apparently despised was to play a crucial role in attempts to revive the fortunes of
Catalan as a literary medium, when Maria Aurèlia Capmany and other
like-minded writers (including Manuel de Pedrolo) made concerted
efforts to produce a popular novel which would encourage the general
public to read in Catalan.[13] Part of their strategy involved the publication of Catalan translations of French *Série Noire* works and American hard-boiled classics, to provide readers either with an alternative
to the existing Spanish translations or with completely new material.
In addition, however, Capmany wrote several crime novels directly
inspired by these models, the first of which was ironically entitled
Traduït de l'americà (1959), thus clearly signalling the source of its
influences.[14] Indeed the novel often does read as though it has been
translated – another form of transcultural re-inscription – in terms of
the plot, characters and setting which initially appear to have little of
relevance to the political situation in which Catalonia found itself
under Franco's regime. However, it was not difficult for Catalans,
whom censorship had trained to read between the lines, to decipher
Capmany's reasons for setting the main action of the novel in Albania.
As the critic Guillem-Jordi Graells has commented, "el que hi ha de
voluntat paral·lelística Albània-Catalunya, dos països petits i riberencs
de la Mediterrània, desconeguts i en una situació política precària, és
prou evident".[15] Capmany clearly knew that for readers in Catalonia,

---

[13]   For more details, see Ramon Espelt's *Ficció criminal a Barcelona 1950-1963*,
       Barcelona: Laertes, 1998.
[14]   When the novel was reissued in 1980 (Barcelona: Laia) she changed the title to
       Vés-te'n, ianqui! o, si voleu traduït de l'americà (*Yankie go home! or, if you wish,
       translated from the American*).
[15]   Cited in Espelt *Ficció criminal a Barcelona 1950-1963*, 87: "The fact that there is
       an intention to draw a parallel between Albania and Catalonia, two small countries
       on the shores of the Mediterranean, unknown and in a precarious political
       situation, is quite obvious." For more on the ability of Spanish audiences to read
       between the lines under Francoism, see Barry Jordan and Rikki Morgan-

her descriptions of everyday conditions for Albanians living under a totalitarian regime would have proved strangely familiar.

Under the strict censorship laws of Franco's regime, then, the transcultural re-inscription of various imported forms often proved to be a useful means of discussing subjects which were taboo in that particular political context. However, contemporary female writers using Catalan as their medium of expression continue to engage creatively and critically with imported crime genres, but this process can now perhaps be seen as a response to a more widespread cultural shift in which, as Featherstone and Lash suggest, "the global begins to replace the nation-state as the decisive framework for social life".[16] Transcultural re-inscription can become a means of resisting this move towards homogenization by inflecting the global with a local accent, a strategy which has come to be known as *glocalization*.

Undoubtedly the best example of this particular kind of resistance by rewriting is to be found in the work of Majorcan born author, Maria-Antònia Oliver.[17] Oliver draws heavily upon the conventions used in the type of detective novel established by North American feminist authors in the mould of Sara Paretsky and her V. I. Warshawski series. Like Paretsky's protagonist, Oliver's own Private Investigator, Lònia Guiu, is feisty, fiercely independent, quick-witted and capable of defending herself when physical force is needed. However, unlike Warshawski who operates for the most part within the clearly delimited urban territory of Chicago, Guiu's own wanderlust and the cases that she takes on often give the series a sense of displacement that is rarely found in the genre. Scales of geographical space are often made to seem unimportant: dividing lines between home and away, between the local and global become blurred, neatly illustrated by the fact that in *Antípodes* (1988),[18] the second book in the series, as Guiu sees it, when travelling from Majorca to Australia,

Tamosunas, *Contemporary Spanish Cinema*, Manchester: Manchester University Press, 1998, 19.

[16] Mike Featherstone and Scott Lash, "Globalization, Modernity and the Spatialization of Social Theory: An Introduction", in *Global Modernities*, eds Mike Featherstone, Scott Lash and Roland Robertson, London: Sage, 1995, 1-2.

[17] Strictly speaking, as a native of Majorca, Oliver is not a Catalan, but since she has lived and worked in Catalonia for many years and is considered to form part of Catalan literary circles, we have included her work in this analysis.

[18] Maria-Antònia Oliver, *Antípodes*, Barcelona: La Magrana, 1988.

she is merely leaving one island for another. The crimes with which she deals are also best described as glocalized: they are carried out via global networks, making use of the free flow of capital and goods or exploiting such phenomena as tourism or economic migration but crucially, they are also shown to impact most acutely at the local level. Ultimately all the victims of these globally oriented crimes that Guiu comes into contact with originate from or have close links to Majorca. This intermeshing of the global and local is further marked by Oliver in the text through the language which she uses, since on many occasions the communication between the globetrotting Guiu and the victims she is assisting is conducted in *mallorquí*, a dialectal variant of Catalan, and a proud assertion of a distinctive local identity. Significantly, all of Oliver's works in the Lònia Guiu series have been translated by American scholars, suggesting that perhaps the transcultural flow is no longer unidirectional.

Rewriting the rules of the genre

It is important to note that some feminist critics have argued that all female writers who choose to work with the crime novel are involved to a greater or lesser extent in a form of cultural re-inscription when they engage with a genre which in Sally Munt's words "can foreground masculine and misogynistic structures".[19] Kathleen Gregory Klein has taken the argument further and claimed that the future vitality of the genre itself will only be assured by the efforts of feminist authors who are able to "rethink it, reformulate it, re-vision it".[20] Certainly during the Nineties, the publishing industry in Spain began to realize that female crime novelists, whether writing in Spanish or in Catalan, had begun to reshape the contours of the genre and their work began to receive increased promotion and almost constant coverage in cultural supplements and popular literature magazines such as *Qué Leer*.

This led to an intriguing blurring of the lines between what had formerly been viewed as the marginal and the mainstream. Thus, at the

---

[19]   Sally Munt, *Murder by the Book? Feminism and the Crime Novel*, London: Routledge, 1994, 10.

[20]   Kathleen Gregory Klein, *The Woman Detective: Gender and Genre*, Chicago: University of Illinois Press, 1988, 227.

start of the Nineties, Blanca Álvarez explored new territory in the genre with her lesbian protagonist, Baby, and her portrayal of the dark and violent world of drug addition in *La soledad del monstruo*.[21] Midway through the decade, Alicia Giménez-Bartlett produced the first police procedural by a Spanish author to feature a female police inspector, *Ritos de muerte*[22] with Petra Delicado. The series has achieved best-seller status, whilst a television series based on the books ran for several months during 1999-2000. New writer Matilde Asensi used her first novel in the genre, *El salón de ámbar*,[23] to comment critically on Europe's painful past and also became the first Spanish writer to focus on the criminal possibilities offered by cyberspace in the present.

Various female writers have used their novels to extend the thematic and stylistic diversity of the genre by thought-provoking treatment of subject matter that had previously been excluded, such as sexual harassment and exploitation in the work place (for example Assumpta Margenat's *Escapa't d'Andorra*).[24] Others, like Maria-Antònia Oliver, provided a feminist point of view on themes that had previously been dealt with in a sensationalist or voyeuristic fashion such as sex crimes, and so far her protagonist Lònia Guiu has investigated issues such as rape-revenge killing, prostitution and paedophile rings. Moreover, Oliver clearly signalled her intention to re-inscribe male-oriented literary conventions by calling her first book *Estudi en lila*,[25] an allusion to one of the key works of the male crime-writing canon, Conan Doyle's *A Study in Scarlet* (1888).

Crime fiction and Catalan identity

More recently, there have been further attempts by Catalan women writers to push the limits of the genre. Thus the Catalan journalist, Anna Grau took the crime novel in yet another direction when she succeeded in combining murder and political parody in *El dia que va*

[21]   Blanca Álvarez, *La soledad del monstruo*, Madrid: Grupo Libro 88, 1992.
[22]   Alicia Giménez-Bartlett, *Ritos de muerte*, Barcelona: Grijalbo, 1996.
[23]   Matilde Asensi, *El salón de ámbar*, Barcelona: Plaza y Janés, 1999.
[24]   Assumpta Margenat, *Escapa't d'Andorra*, Barcelona: La Magrana, 1989.
[25]   Maria-Antònia Oliver, *Estudi en lila*, Barcelona: La Magrana, 1985.

morir el president,[26] a highly entertaining spoof on the crime thriller which follows the misadventures of the novel's anti-hero, an inept young male journalist who is catapulted to fame when he becomes the sole witness of the murder of the Prime Minister of the *Generalitat* (the autonomous Catalan government). A wild goose chase ensues as the journalist is pursued across Barcelona by various representatives of the Spanish and Catalan forces of Law and Order, together with members of a radical Catalan separatist group and assorted indi-viduals.[27] Grau draws humorously grotesque caricatures of both Cata-lan and Spanish identities, including, for example, Glòria, the Catalan undercover agent who sports a flamenco dress, dances *sevillanas*, and affects an Andalusian accent in an attempt to convince the novel's protagonist of her Spanishness. The treatment of the politics of nationalism is equally parodic. The radical Catalan separatist group, the *Almogàvers*, have taken their name from the Catalan soldiers of the Middle Ages but spend their time smoking dope and eating dough-nuts. Clearly Grau's novel is primarily intended to entertain. However, on another level, like all of the other works cited above, it can also be said to raise a number of serious concerns pertaining to identity.

The theme of identity has, of course, traditionally been of central importance in detective fiction, with the narrative typically revolving around the attempts made by the professional investigator or amateur sleuth to determine whodunnit. More generally, crime-related fiction makes constant use of identity-related themes and motifs such as double agents, going undercover, assuming disguises or changing appearance. Sally Munt has argued that one of the key aspects of crime novels as a genre, what she calls the "driving mystery" of this multifarious literary form, is "a search for identity – not just the mur-derer's, but by extension the reader's too".[28] This may well account not only for the enduring popularity of this literary form but may also

---

[26] Anna Grau, *El dia que va morir el president*, Barcelona: Editorial Empúries, 1999.

[27] Although political thrillers were much in vogue generally as a crime sub-genre in the Nineties, Grau probably had a more specific source of inspiration in Francesc Bellmunt's *El complot dels anells* (*The Conspiracy of the Rings*, 1988), a contro-versial film which explored the possibility of the threat of terrorism by an extreme nationalist group at the 1992 Barcelona Olympics. A novelization of the film written by Assumpció Maresma Matas was published in 1989.

[28] Munt, *Murder by the Book?*, 207.

go some way to explaining the current interest in crime-related fiction in Spain and Catalonia, both amongst producers and consumers of the genre. For perhaps this popular genre provides the ideal vehicle for safely exploring the dynamics of identity politics within a pluri-lingual and multicultural society.

This would seem to be particularly true in the case of the final work to be discussed here, Isabel Olesti's extraordinary *El marit invisible*,[29] which is the author's first novel with a crime-related theme. As with Grau's novel, violent death functions as a major device within the narrative, but here the emphasis is on what caused the crime to be committed, not on the consequences that it brings. Whilst trying to reconstruct in his own mind how his mother was murdered, the male narrator sets in motion a train of reminiscences about her past and also that of his grandmother and of his sister. As the blurb on the book jacket suggests "es pot llegir com una novel·la de misteri però també com un gran fresc de tota una època",[30] and the narration of the personal stories of these three very different women effectively provides the author with a means of recounting the history of Catalonia. This technique of presenting history through the family saga has been used many times before, particularly in other popular genres in Catalonia such as soap operas.[31] However, the version of history Olesti presents in her novel is an unusual one since it challenges any notion of Catalan identity as a pure unchanging essence.

The cultural theorist Stuart Hall has argued that:

> We need to situate the debates about identity within all those historic-
> ally specific developments and practices which have disturbed the
> relatively "settled" character of many populations and cultures, above
> all in relation to the processes of globalization ... and the processes of
> forced and "free" migration which have become a global phenomenon
> of the so-called "post-colonial" world.

---

[29] Isabel Olesti, *El marit invisible*, Barcelona: Columna Edicions, 1999.
[30] *Ibid.*: "It can be read as a mystery novel but also as a vast fresco of a whole era."
[31] See Hugh O'Donnell, "Recounting the Nation: The Domestic Catalan *Tele-novela*", in *Cultura Popular*, eds Shelley Godsland and Anne M. White, Bern: Peter Lang, 2001, 243-62.

He later sums up his notion about what identity is by stating that it should be about "not the so-called return to roots but a coming-to-terms with our 'routes'".[32]

It is exactly this position Olesti assumes in her novel, since the personal stories that are narrated there show the positive benefits of the movement of individuals out of and into Catalonia. At the same time, they also emphasize the negative effects of remaining anchored to particular places or of becoming overly attached to tradition. Thus the narrator's grandmother, a confirmed Republican, flees Catalonia to Tangiers in order to avoid Nationalist reprisals for having assisted Republican soldiers during the Civil War. Whilst there, she has a daughter with Mohamed, a dealer in contraband, who later follows her back to Barcelona. The narrator himself repeats her journey many years later, but this time it is a voyage of self-discovery freely-chosen rather than an imposed flight into exile. His mother, however, is represented as being obsessively attached to the family flat, content to live out her life in its narrow, claustrophobic confines filled with mosquitoes, further evidence of the stagnating atmosphere she inhabits. Even when her own mother's decaying body fills the apartment with the stench of death, she remains oblivious to the smell. Ultimately the narrator discovers that this refusal to consider change has led to her being murdered by her own daughter, who has been driven to despair and madness by her mother's attempts to prevent her living an independent life away from the family home.

On one level, then, Olesti's novel can be read as a narration about the meanings of nation, offering two contrasting visions of Catalan identity: one that is outward-looking and vital, an evolving concept, another that is inward-looking and static, with a tendency towards fossilization and ultimately, even self-destruction. On another level, it could be read as the latest attempt by a female author writing in Catalan to push the limits of the crime genre, beginning with the style that is a truly innovative mix. In places, it is reminiscent of the type of Magical Realism that emerged from Latin America in the Sixties, as Olesti constructs a curious world of strange coincidences and marvel-

---

[32] Stuart Hall, "Introduction: Who Needs Identity?", in *Questions of Cultural Identity*, eds Stuart Hall and Paul du Gay, London: Sage, 1996, 4.

lous happenings, recounting whimsical tales of women who levitate at will and of a flat inhabited by the whistling spirits of the dead.

Elsewhere, though, the tone is much darker, with graphic descriptions of a back-street abortion and a body ravaged by cancer. Olesti also challenges one of the key conventions of the crime genre. For although the central mystery at the core of novel is finally solved, there is no neat resolution since the narrator makes it plain he has no intention of telling the police what he knows, leaving the guilty party unpunished. In addition, the myriad smaller mysteries that litter the pages of the novel remain unsolved. Thus, the true identity of the narrator's grandfather cannot be established; the purpose of the bizarre phone call that sends the narrator's family on a wild goose chase to claim a non-existent competition prize remains unclear, and the reason why an unknown neighbour commits suicide is never explained. These and many more enigmatic episodes are left as tantalizing loose threads in a murder mystery that resists the closure that the genre normally demands.

Moreover, Olesti uses her novel to comment critically on the brand of masculinity conventionally featured in the hard-boiled crime genre. Thus the implicit metaphorical link between gun and phallus that has become a cliché of the form is made shockingly explicit and literal in a scene witnessed by the young narrator in which his mother's lover, a police inspector, uses his pistol to penetrate her. Generally, in this text, the kinds of male characters who would traditionally be at the centre of the action in the crime genre are sidelined and more marginal masculinities are featured: it is revealed, for instance, that the narrator is homosexual. Crucially, too, although the novel's title seems to suggest that a male character will constitute the central interest of the story, this is another of Olesti's ironic touches. For the narrator explains that his mother's Invisible Husband, the ideal man that she falls in love with and remains faithful to until her dying day, is none other than the film star Tyrone Power playing the role of Zorro. The supposed key male protagonist is nothing more than an illusion, a mere trick of the light.

A quotation from Homi Bhabha's Introduction to the collection of essays, *Nation and Narration*, will provide a fitting and thought-provoking conclusion to this examination of Catalan crime fiction written by women, in which we have considered some of the complexities of the relationship that can exist between language, national identity, gender and genre. Writing at the start of the Nineties about what he saw to be the key developments in narrative, Bhabha commented that: "the margins of the nation displace the centre; the peoples of the periphery return to rewrite the history and fiction of the metropolis."[33] Although he was referring on that occasion to literature written in English, his words would also seem eminently suitable as a means of describing the cultural changes that have taken place in Spain with the coming of democracy, a process in which previously marginalized forms, such as crime fiction, have played a key role in allowing those peripheral peoples who were once silenced to voice their concerns and literally write the wrongs suffered during the years of Franco's dictatorship.

---

[33]   Homi K. Bhabha, *Nation and Narration*, London: Routledge, 1990, 7.

QUESTIONS OF IDENTITY: AN EXPLORATION OF SPANISH DETECTIVE FICTION

ANNE L. WALSH

The origins of Spanish detective fiction are well documented and the consensus is indisputable: Spain imported detective fiction from England, France and the United States and, for quite some time, added very little that was home-grown. What this present analysis intends to address is how what began as an imported subgenre of little literary merit gradually achieved its present noteworthy status. Following a brief look at the background to the specific factors that contributed to what came to be known as the literary boom of the Eighties and Nineties, a particular case will be examined: *El club Dumas* by Arturo Pérez-Reverte.[1]

Published in 1993, *El club Dumas* contains many elements that are easily identifiable as coming from the detective formula: a protagonist who must solve a mystery, a *femme fatale*, murders, criminals, corrupt police, and so on. Yet, the use of the formula will be shown to go beyond the recreation of a cliché. Rather, contemporary Spanish detective fiction, as represented by this particular example, uses the formula ironically, drawing attention to that formula and effectively blurring the boundaries between what is identifiably fiction and what is an examination of that fiction; in short, it has entered the area of postmodern metafiction. A comparison between Pérez-Reverte's *El club Dumas* and Roman Polanski's film adaptation, *The Ninth Gate*, will serve as a conclusion by highlighting what elements may be considered specifically Spanish in Spain's own brand of detective fiction.

Prior to the outbreak of the Spanish Civil War in 1936, writers of detective fiction in Spain had followed the lead of foreign writers such

---

[1]   Arturo Pérez-Reverte, *El club Dumas: La novena puerta*, Madrid: Alfaguara, 1999.

as Edgar Allan Poe and Arthur Conan Doyle. Following that war, detective fiction was subjected to the same strict censorship criteria under the Franco regime as the rest of Spain's literary output: to ensure publication, criticism of the regime was to be avoided, sexual tensions diluted, religious and moral messages expounded. Again, translations of foreign texts played a significant role in the spread of the detective fiction formula, though emphasis was on the *novela-problema* rather than on the *novela policiaca negra*. In other words, novels of the Agatha Christie type were encouraged, where a problem was solved without any deep criticism of social norms, and where, after the initial crime, excessive violence or sexual activity was absent.[2] Any Spanish writer who adopted this particular genre in the Forties usually used foreign settings and English-sounding pseudo-nyms.[3] In this way, they could not be accused of undermining the regime and its values. Notwithstanding the difficulties, by the Fifties several writers had made progress, in particular Mario Lacruz and Francisco García Pavón, the latter's *Plinio* series spanning the Sixties. Their works offered a view of the detective that was apt for the Spanish environment: human, fallible, disillusioned, inhabiting a far from just world.

The scene was thus set for what has been called the boom in Spanish detective fiction, though some would dispute both the term and the event.[4] Nonetheless, the Seventies and Eighties saw a huge increase in the publication of homegrown detective novels. Writers such as Manuel Vázquez Montalbán and Eduardo Mendoza, to name but two, discovered that the formula suited their own ends. The consequence was that, for the first time, Spain could claim to have its own brand of detective novel, with characteristics that were particularly appropriate in the Spanish context. José F. Colmeiro points to certain elements identifiable in the early works of Vázquez Montalbán and Mendoza

---

[2]   José F. Colmeiro, *La novela policiaca española: teoría e historia crítica*, Barcelona: Anthropos, 1994, 130-31.

[3]   Patricia Hart, *The Spanish Sleuth: The Detective in Spanish Fiction*, London: Associated University Presses, 1987, 25.

[4]   When interviewed in 1983 by Patricia Hart, Juan Madrid was emphatic: "Yo no creo que haya ningún 'boom' de novela policiaca en España, que eso es un error" (Hart, *The Spanish Sleuth*, 168: "I do not believe there is any 'boom' in the detective novel in Spain, that is a mistake"). Unless otherwise indicated, all translations into English are my own.

that were to provide the seeds for future Spanish detective fiction. These may be paraphrased as: a playful element; an interest in the pleasure of the processes of reading and writing; the presence of intrigue and humour as part of a pattern of complicity between author and reader; themes of crime and marginality used as social criticism; intertextuality; an ironic use of the past; a blurring of boundaries between genres as well as between high and popular literature.[5] Add to these elements "a jaundiced view of contemporary politics" and a need for "the illusion that there is an explanation and that there is justice",[6] and a theory may be formulated as to why detective fiction became so popular in post-Franco Spain: it was ideally suited to express the social, political and literary concerns of postmodern Spanish writers and their readers.

As the Seventies came to an end, detective fiction was a secure presence in Spanish literary output. 1979 saw the publication of three notable novels: Eduardo Mendoza's *El misterio de la cripta embrujada*,[7] Jorge Martínez Reverte's *Demasiado para Gálvez*,[8] and Manuel Vázquez Montalbán's *Los mares del Sur*.[9] It is no coincidence that all three of these writers are Catalan. Their geographical location could explain their less than positive view of contemporary Spanish society. Political corruption, intrigue and disillusionment form the backdrop against which the detective (whether the alleged madman of Mendoza's creation or Julio Gálvez or Pepe Carvalho) solves a case.

Our first introduction to Vázquez Montalbán's Pepe Carvalho in *Los mares del Sur* provides a good definition of the role of the fictional detective in the late Seventies and early Eighties:

---

[5]   Colmeiro, *La novela policiaca española: teoría e historia crítica*, 195.

[6]   Paul Preston, "Materialism and *Serie Negra*", in *Leeds Papers on Thrillers in the Transition: "Novela Negra" and Political Change in Spain*, ed. Rob Rix, Leeds: Trinity and All Saints College, 1992, 14-15.

[7]   Eduardo Mendoza, *El misterio de la cripta embrujada*, Barcelona: Seix Barral, 1979.

[8]   Jorge Martínez Reverte, *Demasiado para Gálvez*, Madrid: Debate, 1979.

[9]   Manuel Vázquez Montálban, *Los mares del Sur*, Barcelona: Planeta, 1979.

"Los detectives privados somos los termómetros de la moral estable-
cida, Biscuter. Yo te digo que esta sociedad está podrida. No cree en
nada."[10]

Throughout the novel, Carvalho is depicted as the classic hard-boiled
detective, with a soft centre. He smokes and drinks too much, struggles to pay the bills and is cautious to the point of coldness when it
comes to sentimental attachments. Yet, he adopts a puppy at the
beginning of the story and, though he struggles to remain detached,
that struggle inevitably fails. Bleda, the puppy, is cruelly killed as a
consequence of Carvalho solving the main crime. *Los mares del Sur*
ends with a poignant burial scene, during which Carvalho contains his
tears as he lays his dog to rest: "Recubrió la tierra con la gravilla que
había separado, tiró la pala, se sentó sobre la baranda del muro y se
aferró con las manos a los bordes de ladrillo para que el pecho no se le
rompiera por los sollozos."[11] For this Spanish detective, then, there is
no sense of achievement or of a job well done once the crime has been
solved. Instead, there is heartache, loneliness and a realization that
nothing can turn the tide of crime.

When the type of detective fiction being produced in Spain in the
late Seventies is examined, it becomes very clear that its writers were
acutely aware of following a known formula. That formula owed
much to the earlier imported model: there was a detective with a crime
to solve, a victim, clues to follow and an injustice to challenge. However, now, that injustice was given a particularly Spanish resonance
with the temporal setting: the transition years when Spain moved from
being ruled by dictatorship to becoming a democratic monarchy. Also,
while some writers continued with the basic formula, others chose to
use it ironically, even to parodic levels. As time progressed, those
writers increased the parodic aspects until the appearance, in 1991, of
Eduardo Mendoza's *Sin noticias de Gurb*.[12] The detective is no longer
portrayed even superficially as a Spaniard but has become an extra-

---

[10]   *Ibid.*, 15: "Do you realize, Biscuter – we private eyes are the barometers of estab-
       lished morality. I tell you, this society is rotten. It doesn't believe in anything"
       (*The Southern Seas*, trans. Patrick Camiller, London: Pluto 1986, 7).
[11]   *Ibid.*, 287: "He topped off the grave with a layer of gravel. Then he flung the
       spade away, sat on the wall, and gripped the edge of the brickwork to prevent his
       chest from bursting with sobs" (*The Southern Seas*, 214).
[12]   Eduardo Mendoza, *Sin noticias de Gurb*, Barcelona: Seix Barral, 1991.

terrestrial being, sent to Earth to find a colleague who has disappeared in the metropolis of Barcelona, a message perhaps covertly saying that the fictional detective was always an alien on Spanish soil. However, as has been noted from the list of elements identified by Colmeiro, Spanish detective fiction does not rely on the nationality of the detective as one of its identifying features. Rather, it is certain elements of rhetoric that point to its specific Spanish identity. In general, writers in the Seventies and Eighties used the recognizable formula of an imported detective fiction to highlight homegrown social ailments. The general consensus was a pessimistic one. The opportunity for social improvement offered by the collapse of the Francoist regime had been missed, and, pointedly, Mendoza has his mad protagonist declare: "¡En este país no se puede vivir!"[13] So, the scene was set for the writers of the Nineties who would extend the formula to accommodate other concerns.

Even while using the formula of detective fiction for socially critical ends, writers of the Seventies and Eighties were also pointing to an awareness of the transparency of fiction by breaking conventions and directly addressing their readers in a variety of ways. Mendoza indicates just such an awareness in the opening chapter of *El laberinto de las aceitunas*:

> No pude por menos de preguntarme lo que tal vez algún ávido lector se esté preguntando ya .... Y a ello responderé diciendo que precisamente en Madrid dio comienzo una de las aventuras más peligrosas, enrevesadas y, para quien de este relato sepa extraer provecho, edificantes de mi azarosa vida.[14]

Vázquez Montalbán demonstrates a surprising disregard for books and literature by having his hero (or antihero), Carvalho, heat his apartment by burning the books in his library. We see him burning

---

[13]   Eduardo Mendoza, *El laberinto de las aceitunas*, Barcelona: Seix Barral, 1982, 38: "No one can live in this country."

[14]   *Ibid.*, 7-8: "I couldn't help asking myself what an avid reader must be wondering already ... and I will answer that by saying that it was precisely in Madrid where one of the most dangerous, complicated and, for whoever can get something positive out of this story, the most edifying adventures of my eventful life started."

Forster's *Maurice*: "porque es una chorrada, como todos los libros."[15] Ironically, if we agree with Carvalho, there is not much point in continuing to read. What Vázquez Montalbán achieves in *Los mares del Sur*, in John Macklin's words, is to destroy "the innocence of realism by ensuring that his critique of society is fully integrated with his constant foregrounding of the conventions of the genre".[16]

What had begun, then, in the transition years, and has come to fruition in the last decade, was a view that fiction may be used self-consciously to examine the role of literature and, by association, the role of the reader in approaching a text. Detective fiction is by no means the only genre to be used to encompass such a view; in a similar way, the genres of the historical novel, the gothic novel, the science fiction novel are all being exploited. Of course, it could be argued that the exploitation of formulae is not a phenomenon restricted to Spain. Rather, using past models ironically may be viewed as part of a more general and extensive postmodern trend. However, it is interesting to note that the consequence of such a trend is that previous subgenres, such as detective fiction, which could have been termed marginalized, have now become an integral part of the whole. Furthermore, there is a general trend within that whole towards a phenomenon that José Colmeiro has termed "la interfecundación de géneros" or the cross-fertilization of genres.[17] The lines defining which novels may be termed detective, and which may not, are unclear, leading to the paradox of one of the most famous writers of Spanish detective fiction declaring: "No escribo novelas negras."[18] It seems it is almost incidental to present-day Spanish writers which formula they incorporate; what matters is to highlight a conscious use of formula so as, in turn, to draw attention to the act of writing and, consequently, to the game of literature. The remainder of this analysis will attempt to explore one example of this game, in an attempt to illustrate the extent

---

[15] Manuel Vázquez Montalbán, *Los mares del Sur*, 34: "Because it's garbage, like all books" (*The Southern Seas*, 21).
[16] John Macklin, "Myth, Mimesis and the *Novela Negra*", in *Leeds Papers on Thrillers in the Transition*, 64.
[17] Colmeiro, *La novela policiaca española*, 169.
[18] Manuel Vázquez Montalbán, "No escribo novelas negras", *El Urogallo*, 1987, 9-10, 26-27: "I don't write detective novels." For a more detailed examination of the Carvalho series, see Stewart King's essay in this collection.

to which the boundaries between detective fiction and metaficion have become blurred.

The novel, *El club Dumas* has been chosen for special attention here for several reasons. Its author, Arturo Pérez-Reverte, is not uniquely a writer of detective fiction but he does blend the detective formula with others to form a postmodern pastiche that may be considered representative of the general trend. Indeed, it may be said that the trend comes to some culmination in *El club Dumas*. What readers find is that *El club Dumas* is a postmodern metafiction disguised as a classic detective story. All the expected elements of a detective fiction, already alluded to, are present: a puzzle to solve, a gin-drinking sleuth complete with overcoat to solve it, dead bodies, a beautiful girl, a *femme fatale*, an urban setting, and so on. However, another set of references runs parallel to such clichés. The sleuth in question is a book hunter, a mercenary bibliophile who seeks and finds valuable books for the highest bidder. He, Lucas Corso, finds himself involved in two seemingly linked cases: hired by Varo Borja to search for two copies of *Las nueve puertas*, a book supposedly containing directions on how to summon the devil, and also hired by Flavio La Ponte to verify the authenticity of *Le Vin d'Anjou*, the supposed twenty-second chapter of Alexander Dumas' *The Three Musketeers*. The two searches intertwine to such an extent that it is a shock to discover at the end of the tale that they were not linked in any way except through the character of Lucas Corso, and because of the narrative playfulness of Pérez-Reverte.

The narrative complications begin when Lucas Corso comes to see Boris Balkan, the narrator, with a copy of *Le Vin d'Anjou* under his arm. What follows is a report by Balkan of that meeting, the conversation the two men had, and the impression Corso made on Balkan — in other words, a traditional first-person narrative. However, very quickly, the rules of tradition are broken: the narrator, Balkan, informs us that "antes de ir a verme le echó un vistazo a cuanto sobre mí pudo encontrar".[19] How does Balkan know that? He seems too definite to be simply surmising the other man's conscientiousness, which he may

---

[19] Pérez-Reverte, *El club Dumas*, 20: "Before coming to see me he'd looked at everything about me he could lay his hands on" (*The Dumas Club*, trans. Sonia Soto, London: Harvill, 1996, 6)

have been able to do if he had known Corso well. Yet, at the time of
the meeting, this seems not to be the case. Several times we are told of
information Balkan will find out later:

> Con el tiempo supe que también era capaz de sonreír como un lobo
> despiadado y flaco, y que podía componer uno u otro gesto según lo
> exigieran las circunstancias; pero eso fue mucho más tarde;[20]

> Después, cuando lo conocí mejor, llegué a preguntarme si la admira-
> ción era sincera;[21]

> Más tarde supe que vivía solo.[22]

So, at the time Corso presented himself at Balkan's house, the two
men were not very well acquainted. Later, they seem to have become
closer, but nothing in the story explains how. In fact, the events narrated later provide enough information to lead to an understanding that
Corso would prefer never to meet Balkan again.

In itself, of course, the questionable omniscience of the first-person
narrator means very little. It is only as the plot unfolds that it may be
seen as just one of a series of narrative games being played. In the first
place, the opening line is not really the opening line but comes after an
untitled, italicized Preface that sets the scene of the crime (11-13): a
body hanging from the ceiling light, hands tied, a broken vase on the
floor, a book open at a certain page, police searching for fingerprints,
police photographer taking flash photographs. Is it murder or suicide?
The scene is set for the detective to take over. What happens is that
Boris Balkan introduces himself, leading us to consider that he will
explain the significance of the opening scene. He does not. Nor does
he even refer to a crime, at least, not until the final lines of his introduction when we are told:

---

[20]   *Ibid.*, 16: "In time I found out he could also smile like a cruel, hungry wolf, and
that he would choose a smile to suit the circumstances. But that was much later"
(*The Dumas Club*, 4).

[21]   *Ibid.*, 28: "Later, when I came to know him better, I wondered whether his admiration was sincere" (*The Dumas Club*, 11).

[22]   *Ibid.*, 29: "I found out later that he lived alone" (*The Dumas Club*, 12).

> Enrique Taillefer llevaba muerto una semana. Lo habían encontrado ahorcado en el salón de su casa: el cordón del batín de seda en torno al cuello y los pies girando en el vacío, sobre un libro abierto y un jarrón de porcelana hecho pedazos.[23]

Thus, after an unsettling delay, the scene is set in true detective-fiction style. We have a body, a crime scene and a mystery to solve: who killed Enrique Taillefer and why? The reader settles back to enjoy the challenge, but the irony is that the murder is proven to be a suicide and the why has very little to do with the main thrust of the story. As we read, we experience a very unsettling feeling, much as if a carpet had been pulled from under us.

Very quickly a second complication occurs with a change in narrative. Though Boris Balkan acts initially as first-person narrator, he soon steps back from the centre and he changes from a narrator-character with a subjective point of view to a third-person narrator who adopts Lucas Corso's viewpoint. His explanation is credible:

> Algún tiempo después, cuando todo hubo terminado, Corso accedió a contarme el resto de la historia. Puedo así reconstruir ahora con razonable fidelidad ciertos hechos que no presencié: el encadenamiento de circunstancias que condujeron al fatal desenlace y la resolución del enigma en torno a El club Dumas.[24]

More is happening at narrative level here than meets the eye. By providing us with a rational explanation for a change of narrative, Balkan (or more correctly Pérez-Reverte) is drawing attention to that narrative as a device. By handing over the narrative to Corso, he becomes, in his own words, the "Doctor Watson" of the story (31). Curiously, what story he means is ambiguous. The italicized title, *El club Dumas*, may refer either to Corso's discovery of a club of that name or, more

---

[23] *Ibid.*, 30: "Enrique Taillefer had been dead a week. He had been found hanged in his house, the cord of his silk robe around his neck and his feet dangling in empty space, over an open book and a porcelain vase smashed into pieces" (*The Dumas Club*, 13).

[24] *Ibid.*, 31: "Some time later, when it was all over, Corso agreed to tell me the rest of the story. So I can now give a fairly accurate picture of a chain of events that I didn't witness, leading to the fatal dénouement and the solution to the mystery surrounding the Dumas Club" (*The Dumas Club*, 13).

interestingly, it could refer to the book itself, a metafictional self-reference.

Had Balkan remained in the background for the rest of the novel, little else could be said. However, he interrupts the third-person narrative on two more occasions, in the fifth and fifteenth chapters. Chapter V opens with: "Es aquí donde entro en escena por segunda vez, pues fue entonces cuando Corso recurrió a mí de nuevo."[25] A few pages later, he steps back again: "De nuevo tengo que pasar a segundo plano, como narrador casi omnisciente de las andanzas de Lucas Corso."[26] It is difficult to explain the reasons for such a narrative interruption, unless it is simply to draw attention to itself.

If Boris Balkan is Dr Watson in this story, then, we might ask, is Lucas Corso the Spanish Sherlock Holmes? That is what seems to be implied; Corso is constantly referred to as a hunter, perhaps recalling Holmes' traditional garb, but, curiously, what he hunts are books:

> Corso era un mercenario de la bibliofilia; un cazador de libros por cuenta ajena;[27]

> El cazador de libros pasó más páginas;[28]

> El cazador junto a la pieza, había dicho Nikon en voz baja.[29]

Our detective, then, sets out to track down, not a murder suspect, but a book. He visits Boris Balkan in an effort to verify authorship of *Le Vin d'Anjou* and from Spain travels to Sintra, Paris, Meung, and, finally, back to Spain again, all the time carrying Varo Borja's copy of *Las nueve puertas*, for he must also track down the other two existing copies of that book. So, two stories become entangled, and because of that entanglement, the reader is not presented with all the clues neces-

---

[25] *Ibid.*, 127: "This is the point at which I enter the stage for the second time. Corso came to me again" (*The Dumas Club*, 82).

[26] *Ibid.*, 142: "I must now once more move into the background, as the near-omniscient narrator of Lucas Corso's adventures" (*The Dumas Club*, 92).

[27] *Ibid.*, 15: "Corso was a mercenary of the book world, hunting down books for other people" (*The Dumas Club*, 3).

[28] *Ibid.*, 79: "The bookhunter turned more pages" (*The Dumas Club*, 45).

[29] *Ibid.*, 342: "The hunter with his prey, Nikon had whispered" (*The Dumas Club*, 228).

sary for the solution of the enigma: *El club Dumas* is not an example of a fair play novel as defined by Ian Michael.[30]

It seems paradoxical that a novel that starts with a narrator declaring his identity should be hinged on narrative confusion. "Me llamo Boris Balkan", the first-person narrator declares in the very first line of *El club Dumas*.[31] He continues by giving details of his own life: he translated *La cartuja de Parma*; he is an expert on the nineteenth-century novel; he organizes summer schools on contemporary writers. However, we quickly discover that all that information has little, if anything, to do with the story. Moreover, the details tell us little about who Boris Balkan really is; they merely tell us what he does, or more correctly, what he says he does. And so, the rules of the game are laid down: we are given information but not all that information is pertinent. Some has to do with *Le Vin d'Anjou*, some has to do with *Las nueve puertas* and some has to do with very little at all. The real twist is that we find it difficult, if not impossible, to separate the various strands.

Yet, it is not our fault if we fall into the various traps set for us, for they are very cleverly laid: we foolishly believe that a suicide that looks like a suicide is a murder for – "hay homicidios que se disfrazan de suicidios",[32] and vice versa. Likewise, we believe that the people Corso meets are modern-day reincarnations of the characters in *The Three Musketeers*. Thus, in our eyes, Boris Balkan takes on characteristics of Richelieu, Replinger resembles Porthos (443), Liana Taillefer becomes Milady de Winter, Enrique Taillefer is Athos (437), Flavio La Ponte is Aramis (414) and even Corso himself fills the role of D'Artagnan admirably (413-14). Due to Lucas Corso's convictions, it becomes impossible to believe that those characters interested in *Le Vin d'Anjou* (Boris Balkan, Replinger, Liana and Flavio) have nothing to do with the search for the copies of *Las nueve puertas*. It is as if we are trapped in quicksand, a feeling that culminates when Corso is brought to meet face to face with the character supposedly responsible

---

[30] Ian Michael, "From Scarlet Study to Novela Negra: The Detective Story in Spanish", in *Leeds Papers on Thrillers in the Transition*, 17-47.

[31] Pérez-Reverte, *El club Dumas*: "My name is Boris Balkan" (*The Dumas Club*, 3).

[32] *Ibid.*, 12 and 15 "Sometimes homicide disguises itself as suicide" (*The Dumas Club*, 2 and 3).

for all the previous machinations, the "respuesta del enigma" (428), the answer to the puzzle.

Everything points to a diabolical, gothic conclusion with such details as a medieval castle, a raging storm and the dead of night. Several immediate narrative clues to the identity of this character add to the tension: the streets are deserted – "no se veía un alma"; the electric discharges are like "truenos del Diablo"; Corso would have followed his escort to "las mismas puertas del infierno".[33] Everything points to the meeting being a supernatural one between Corso and the Devil himself. However, Chapter XV opens with a most striking narrative trick, and we are abruptly brought back to consider the game of literature. The narrative perspective changes from third to first, consequently requiring a shift in viewpoint, and causing a subsequent change in theme. The mystery no longer concerns who is behind the problems encountered by our fictional hero; rather it centres on the identity of who is behind the narrative. Consider the opening paragraph of the penultimate chapter, entitled "Corso and Richelieu", quoted at length to give an accurate impression:

> Ha llegado el momento de situar nuestro punto de vista narrativo. Fiel al viejo principio de que en los relatos de misterio el lector debe poseer la misma información que el protagonista, he procurado ceñirme a los hechos desde la óptica de Lucas Corso, excepto en dos ocasiones: los capítulos primero y quinto de esta historia, donde no tuve otro remedio que plantear mi propia aparición. En ambos casos, como ahora me dispongo a hacer por tercera y última vez, recurrí a la primera persona del pretérito imperfecto por razones de coherencia; resulta absurdo citarme a mí mismo como él, truco publicitario que, si bien aportó rentas de imagen a Cayo Julio César en su campaña de las Galias, en mi caso habría sido calificado, y con razón, de pedantería injustificable. También hay otra causa, quizá relativamente perversa: contar la historia a la manera de un doctor Sheppard frente a Poirot se me antojaba, más que ingenioso – ahora esas cosas las hace todo el mundo –, un truco divertido. Y a fin de cuentas, la gente escribe por diversión, para vivir más, para quererse a sí misma o para que la quieran otros. Yo incluyo algunos de tales propósitos. Citando al viejo Eugenio Sue, los malvados de una sola pieza, si me permiten la

---

[33] *Ibid.*, 428: "Not a soul to be seen"; "thunder from hell"; "the very gates of Hell" (*The Dumas Club*, 278).

expresión, son fenómenos muy raros. Suponiendo – tal vez sea mucho suponer – que yo sea de verdad un malvado.[34]

This passage represents a carefully crafted interruption to what has appeared thus far to be the main plot. Yet, to dismiss it as simply an interruption would be to miss the whole point of *El club Dumas*. This opening paragraph may even be considered a *mise en abyme*: a microcosm of all that *El club Dumas* has to offer its readers. First, the playfulness of the tone highlights the metafictional concerns behind it. We have been led to expect a meeting with the devil, disguised as Richelieu. Nothing in the paragraph contradicts that; indeed we may be reading the devil's own words. Yet, if that is the case, then the devil is a writer, the writer behind the story we have been reading. The "I" of the text overlaps between author, his narrator and, in our manipulated minds, Satan himself. Therefore, this introductory paragraph serves to bring us back to the central focus of *El club Dumas*: a concern with narrative games. This focus is further defined and refined when Balkan, the first-person narrator, congratulates Corso on his success, saying: "Ha sido capaz de seguir el juego hasta el final."[35] It is not too much to consider that Corso is not the only one being congratulated, since the reader too shares in the accolades. Yet, any feeling of self-

---

[34] *Ibid.*, 429: "The time has come to identify the viewpoint of the narrator. Faithful to the tradition that the reader of mystery novels must have the same information as the protagonist, I have tried to present the facts only from Lucas Corso's perspective, except on two occasions: chapters one and five of this story, when I had no choice but to appear myself. In both these cases, and as now for the third and final time, I used the first person for the sake of coherence. It would have been absurd to refer to myself as 'he', a publicity stunt that may have yielded dividends for Julius Caesar in his campaign in Gaul but would, in my case, have been judged, entirely reasonably, as unpardonable pedantry. There is another, fairly perverse reason: telling the story as if I were Dr Sheppard addressing Poirot struck me as, if not ingenious (everybody does that sort of thing now), then an amusing device. After all, people write for amusement, or excitement, or out of self-love, or to have others love them. I write for some of the same reasons. To quote Eugène Sue, villains who are all of a piece, if you'll permit me the expression, are very rare phenomena. Assuming – and it may be too much to assume – that I really am a villain" (*The Dumas Club*, 282).

[35] *Ibid.*, 430: "You've managed to play the game right to the end" (*The Dumas Club*, 283).

congratulation is dissipated when we discover that, yes, we played the game until the end but came to all the wrong conclusions.

That *El club Dumas* is a book about the role of the reader is further emphasized in the ensuing conversation between Balkan and Corso. The chapter is replete with intertextual references: the opening lines of famous novels; the literary licence taken by Alexandre Dumas with the character of Richelieu; fictional characters who live outside their texts. The tension steadily builds as we wait for the final piece of the puzzle, which we surely will be given when the clock strikes midnight. Instead, we are deceived again: no Devil is revealed; the suicide was a suicide; the Musketeer characters were just members of an elite club, not given to crime or satanic rites. The gathering of the suspects, yet another recognizable element of detective fiction, yields no criminal, no crime and certainly no cleverness on the part of the detective. For, we are told: "la novela policíaca debe usted buscarla en otra parte."[36] We have been fooled all along; we thought we were reading a detective novel; all the ingredients were there. Now, almost at the very end, we see that those ingredients were an illusion. Even the mystery of the characters in the story, the Taillefers, Achille Replinger, Balkan, was no mystery. Had we taken the title of the book to heart, the Dumas club was staring us in the face all along. So, what are we left with?: "Al cazador de libros tan sólo le quedaba su vieja bolsa de lona con el último ejemplar de *Las nueve puertas* dentro. Y la chica."[37] There is still doubt about the girl, Irene Adler. Is she or is she not a supernatural being, a demon or an angel? Corso leans toward the former: "Todo te lo daré, si postrándote, me adoras ... ¿No vas a ofrecerme algo de eso?"[38] She seems to confirm her diabolical origins:

> Peleé cien días y cien noches sin cuartel ni esperanza ... ése es mi único orgullo, Corso: haber luchado hasta el final. Retrocedí sin volver la espalda, entre otros que también caían de lo alto, ronca de gritar mi coraje, el miedo y la fatiga ... Por fin me vi, después de la batalla,

---

[36] *Ibid.*, 458: "... you'll have to look for the crime novel elsewhere" (*The Dumas Club*, 301).

[37] *Ibid.*, 460: "All that remained was his old canvas bag containing the remaining copy of The Nine Doors. And the girl" (*The Dumas Club*, 302).

[38] *Ibid.*, 463: "'I'll give you everything, if you prostrate yourself and adore me...' Isn't that the kind of offer you're going to make me?" (*The Dumas Club*, 304-305).

caminando por un páramo desolado; tan sola como fría es la eternidad
... Todavía, a veces, encuentro una señal del combate, o un antiguo
compañero que cruza por mi lado sin atreverse a levantar los ojos.[39]

So the final chapter of *El club Dumas* is really about *Las nueve
puertas*, a book that supposedly holds the secret of how to summon
Satan himself. Yet, that book too is not what it seems. Three copies
are needed to solve the riddle, but as the final engraving in each was a
forgery, we will never know if Satan could really have been
summoned. Like *El club Dumas*, *Las nueve puertas* is incomplete: its
readers, too, embodied in the character of Varo Borja, have been led
astray.

What, then, may be concluded from a reading of *El club Dumas*? Two
stories run intertwined; both have to do with identity. The first, that
linked with *Le Vin d'Anjou*, leads our detective, Lucas Corso, to discover the existence of the Dumas Club, and so the identity of its
membership. The second, linked with *Las nueve puertas*, has a supernatural twist to it. We expect to discover the identity of the devil himself and are thwarted. Yet, still we conclude that that there may be
more to the world than visible reality. The fact that the two stories
only separate in the last two chapters causes us to experience deception first hand. What seems a detective story, (the *Dumas Club* story)
in the traditional sense of the term, turns out to have no crime
attached. What crimes do occur, the murders of Victor Fargas and the
Baroness Ungern, were committed by Varo Borja, who was "la clave
que ordenaba todos los hechos inexplicables del otro hilo argumental;
la faceta diabólica del problema."[40] Such is the resolution offered in
the final chapter.

---

[39] *Ibid.*, 468: "I fought for a hundred days and a hundred nights without hope or
refuge ... that's the only thing I'm proud of – having fought to the end. I retreated
but didn't turn my back, surrounded by others also falling from on high. I was
hoarse from shouting out my fury, my fear and exhaustion ... After the battle I
walked across a desolate plateau, as lonely as eternity is cold ... I still sometimes
come across a trace of the battle, or an old comrade who passes by without daring
to look up" (*The Dumas Club*, 308).

[40] *Ibid.*, 474: "... the key to all the inexplicable events of that other, diabolic, strand
of the plot" (*The Dumas Club*, 311).

However, the sensation on concluding that chapter is not one of satisfied curiosity, a vicarious thrill at having solved a difficult puzzle, or, indeed, a surprise that the fictional detective has outwitted us. Instead, we are left at odds. We have, in truth, been outwitted, but not by Lucas Corso. The clever mind in this story is its author, Arturo Pérez-Reverte, for, as the closing line of *El club Dumas* reads:

> Reía entre dientes, como un lobo cruel, cuando inclinó la cabeza para encender el último cigarrillo. Los libros gastan ese tipo de bromas, se dijo. Y cada cual tiene el diablo que merece.[41]

What has happened is that Pérez-Reverte has taken the elements of a genre that is very familiar, and he has used those elements against us.

Why? I would suggest that he has done so to draw attention to the arts of writing and reading; to challenge readers to seek out the truth, a truth that has to do with the role of literature in reality and with the consequent interpretation of that reality. Lucas Corso has acted as our guide throughout the pages of the tale, but he has been a faulty guide. He has seen patterns where none existed; he has seen guilt where there was innocence; and, finally, he has expected payment and received nothing for his efforts.

What if we consider that Corso is the fictional representation of the reader? We, too, have expected to find patterns – crime fiction is replete with them – and have been led astray. We assumed that Liana and company were the criminals and we were wrong; and we, too, expected final payment in the form of a satisfactory resolution, and, instead, we are rewarded by the uncomfortable feeling that the author is laughing, like a cruel wolf, at our naïvety. So, we are faced with questions of identity. We happily followed the story from Corso's perspective, only to discover too late that that perspective was influenced by Boris Balkan. We thought we could play the role of detective, as all readers of detective fiction do. We followed Corso as he discovered each piece of puzzle and only discovered when he did that there were two unconnected jigsaws and not one. We acted in good faith,

---

[41]   *Ibid.*, 493: "He was laughing under his breath, like a cruel wolf, as he leant over to light his last cigarette. Books play that kind of trick, he thought. And everyone gets the Devil he deserves" (*The Dumas Club*, 323).

becoming, to a certain extent, Lucas Corso, the hunter of books, the book detective.

The comparison is underlined time and again within the pages of *El club Dumas*: readers of books are detectives. To take one example, having congratulated Corso on reaching the *Chateau de Meung-sur-Loire*, and thus, the end of the game, Balkan continues:

> Sí, juego. Tensión, incertidumbre, destreza, habilidad ... Acción libre, según reglas obligatorias, que tiene su fin en sí misma y va acompaña-da de un sentimiento de tensión y de la alegría de actuar de otro modo que en la vida corriente .... Los niños son jugadores y lectores per-fectos: todo lo hacen con la mayor seriedad. En el fondo, el juego es la única actividad universalmente seria; ahí no vale el escepticismo, ¿no cree? ... Por muy incrédulo y descreído que uno sea, si se quiere par-ticipar no hay más opción que atenerse a las reglas. Sólo quien respeta esas reglas, o al menos las conoce y utiliza, puede vencer ... Ocurre lo mismo al leer un libro: hay que asumir la trama y los personajes para disfrutar la historia.[42]

The metaphor is crystal clear and so too are the reasons behind Pérez-Reverte's choice of a detective story on which to hinge *El club Dumas*: to read is to detect; the detective genre becomes a meta-fictional one. As has been seen earlier, Pérez-Reverte was not the first to use detective fiction to examine the relationship between writer-text-reader. He is following a trend that began when Spanish writers first used the detective genre self-consciously. It was initially second-ary to the desire to use the genre for socially critical ends. Now, it has developed into full-blown metafiction, using fiction to explore the effects of fiction with specific emphasis on communication between real author and reader.

---

[42] *Ibid.*, 430-31: "Yes, game. Tension, uncertainty, a high level of skill ... The possi-bility of acting freely, but according to obligatory rules, as an end in itself. To-gether with a sense of tension and pleasure at the difference from ordinary life .... Children are the perfect players and readers: they do everything with the utmost seriousness. In essence, games are the only universally serious activity. They leave no room for scepticism, wouldn't you agree? However incredulous or doubting one might be, if one wants to play one has no choice but to follow the rules. Only the person who respects the rules, or at least knows and applies them, can win ... Reading a book is the same: one has to accept the plot and the char-acters to enjoy the story" (*The Dumas Club*, 283).

To highlight what is particularly Spanish about Spanish detective fiction, finally I will look at what happens if a story, originally grounded
in Hispanic culture, is transposed to both a new medium and a new environment. The release of Roman Polanski's interpretation of *El club
Dumas* (*The Ninth Gate*, 2000) offers food for thought. While, in general terms, the storyline is very similar in both versions, several
significant changes have been made in Polanski's film: Lucas Corso
becomes Dean Corso, played by the recognizably American actor,
Johnny Depp, and the opening scenes placing him in New York rather
than Madrid. Therefore, he loses any connection with Spain and, when
travelling in Europe, he remains the outsider.

This screen Corso tracks down the Dumas Club, as he does in the
book. However, he is not confronted by his own stupidity when he
finds the Musketeer characters gathered at the *Chateau de Meung*, for
indeed they are in league with Satan. The two stories, which were confused erroneously by the textual Corso, are visibly and conclusively
linked on screen. The effect of such a link is to show the detective in a
much more positive light. He has succeeded in his task and is not the
questioning, lost, disturbed, confused representative of postmodern
humanity that his written counterpart embodies. Finally, the scenes
depicting the isolated house, (set in Madrid suburbia in the text),
where Boris Balkan (Varo Borja in the text) attempts to summon up
Satan, burning as Corso and the Girl have passionate sex, leave very
little room for doubt as to the Girl's diabolic connections.

In summary, the film provides the viewer with entertainment, a
story that is intriguing, and that has a right to be called a thriller. However, what it cannot be called is a Spanish thriller. Removing the
Spanish identity of the detective is partly responsible for the loss, but
as seen earlier, identity is not exclusively bound to that. Nor is the loss
merely one of language. (After all, the English translation of *El club
Dumas* arguably retains its Spanishness.) The particular Spanish flavour to be gained by a Spanish protagonist in a Spanish setting is, to a
certain extent, a superficiality. What is more to be regretted is that
viewers of *The Ninth Gate* are not challenged to the same extent as
readers of the original. The feelings of confusion, mistrust and intrigue
are largely absent. The worldview presented goes against the disjointed, unconnected world of *El club Dumas*. Instead, a recognizable
formula is maintained, the mystery is solved, loose ends are tied up
and supernatural elements are relied on to provide the twist in the tale.

Even the presence of such otherworldly elements cannot dent the impression that the world is a logical, coherent place and not the chaotic, disjointed environment presented in *El club Dumas*. In short, what is missing is an ironic, wry view of life, a sense of playfulness, of communication or even of collaboration between author and reader, the very elements that are vital in the Spanish game of literature.

ABYSS OF THE SENSES: *LES RIVIÈRES POURPRES* BY JEAN-CHRISTOPHE GRANGÉ

SJEF HOUPPERMANS

Tables, verres, bouteilles, ustensiles de ménage, tabourets dépaillés, tout était renversé, jeté pêle-mêle, brisé, haché menu.

Près de la cheminée, en travers, deux hommes étaient étendus à terre, sur le dos, les bras en croix, immobiles. Un troisième gisait au milieu de la pièce.

A droite, dans le fond, sur les premières marches de l'escalier conduisant à l'étage supérieur, une femme était accroupie. Elle avait relevé son tablier sur sa tête, et poussait des gémissements inarticulés. En face, dans le cadre d'une porte de communication grande ouverte, un homme se tenait debout, raide et blême, ayant devant lui, comme un rempart, une lourde table de chêne.

Il était d'un certain âge, de taille moyenne, et portait toute sa barbe.

Son costume, qui était celui des déchargeurs de bateaux du quai de la Gare, était en lambeaux et souillé de boue, de vin et de sang.

Celui-là certainement était le meurtrier.

L'expression de son visage était atroce. La folie furieuse flamboyait dans ses yeux, et un ricanement convulsif contractait ses traits. Il avait au cou et à la joue deux blessures qui saignaient abondamment.[1]

---

[1] Emile Gaboriau, *Monsieur Lecoq*, Paris: Liana Levi, 1992:
"Tables, glasses, bottles, household utensils, stools – all had been overturned, thrown about, smashed and chopped into little pieces. Near the fireplace, two men lay cross-wise on the floor. They were on their backs and motionless, with their arms crossed in front of them. A third man was stretched out in the middle of the room. At the back of the room on the right, a woman crouched at the bottom of a stairway leading to the floor above. She had thrown her apron over her head, and was groaning unintelligibly. Just opposite, in a large open doorway which led to an adjoining room, a man stood, rigid and pale. A heavy oak table stood in front of him, almost like a rampart. He was middle-aged, of average height and wore a full beard. His clothes were those of a dockworker, torn to shreds and soiled with mud, wine and blood. This was most certainly the murderer. He had a terrible expression on his face. A mad fury blazed in his eyes, and a convulsive sneer

This passage is to be found in the first chapter of *Monsieur Lecoq*, written by Emile Gaboriau and dating from 1868. This immensely successful book, first serialized in Moïse Millaud's *Le Petit Journal*, is considered to be the first example of the detective novel in France. Gaboriau was a journalist in search of the new and the modern who had moved up to Paris from Saujon in the region of Charente Maritime. There is no doubt that his literary triumph can be attributed to one masterly device: the powerful combination of the story of a brilliant and impatient young detective, Lecoq (in which Gaboriau's own aspirations are reflected), with that of a melodramatic and long-running family saga. A precarious balance is struck between horror and intellect, sending delightful shivers down the reader's spine. Edgar Allan Poe, the founding father of the genre, had understood this device very well when he set his brutal massacre in a middle-class residence against the refined sophistication of his hero, Dupin. As Carlo Ginsburg has observed, the detective is markedly modern in his examination of the evidence, and only he, through his patience and tenacity, can quell the murderous surge. The author's craftsmanship is felt here, as it is reflected in the sagacity of the detective, a technique exemplified in the opening chapters of *Monsieur Lecoq*, where black footprints on white snow melt away only to reappear as vital evidence some five-hundred pages later:

> Lecoq, à genoux, étudiait les empreintes avec l'attention d'un chiro-mancier s'efforçant de lire l'avenir dans la main d'un riche client .... Il conclut .... Ce terrain vague, couvert de neige, est comme une im-mense page blanche où les gens que nous cherchons ont écrit, non seulement leurs mouvements et leur démarches, mais encore leurs secrètes pensées, les espérances et les angoisses qui les agitaient.[2]

The uncertain ground is in fact the area that extends as far as the gates of Paris, from the Tolbiac side in particular, near the Rue du Château-

---

distorted his features. On his neck and cheek two wounds bled profusely." (Unless otherwise stated, all translations are by Tina Browne).

[2] *Ibid.*, 32: "On his knees, Lecoq studied the footprints with the same attention that a fortune-teller would apply when trying to read the future in the hand of a rich client .... He concluded .... This uncertain ground, covered in snow, is like an enormous blank page upon which those whom we seek have recorded not only their movements, but also their intimate thoughts, their hopes and fears."

des-Rentiers, where one of Léo Malet's most successful mysteries, *Brouillard au Pont de Tolbiac*, is also set. In this place, violence usurps all desire for order, and excessive violence is shown as a fundamental reality within the family.

The history of the detective novel in France is marked by a series of variations of this pattern, where violence and intellect are intertwined and where one or other of the main characters is prosperous and highly respected. That is not to say that Gaboriau's legacy was immediately assured. The literary novel tended towards Naturalism or alternatively veered off towards Symbolism, whereas the popular novel was full of mystery and emotion. Verne's work, somewhere between the two types, was made up of tales of travel and adventure. It was not until the turn of the century that two great authors definitively established the bounds of the French detective novel. The first author, Gaston Leroux, favours the combination of the journalistic profession with a passion for investigation, and the energetic movement of his literary creation, Rouletabille, is appealing to the reader. In his two masterpieces, *Le Mystère de la chambre jaune* and *Le Parfum de la dame en noir*, the impulsive reporter is transformed into a modern-day hero, who takes on the dark forces of crime and violence, even risking his own life if necessary. In the face of persistent and systematic research, the hermetically sealed room, fascinating because of the corpse, horrifying because of the signs of violence within, must yield up its secret. With regard to *Le Parfum de la dame en noir*, however, it is as though the fiction is being overtaken by its own past: the young reporter gets caught up in his own family saga, and only a miraculous intervention will save him.

It has been said of Gaboriau "qu'il lança dans le monde le roman policier sans le comprendre";[3] as for Maurice Leblanc, he stated: "Je prends la plume, et Arsène Lupin s'impose à moi."[4] Arsène Lupin is a fundamentally ambiguous figure. This ambiguity was to characterize a number of his successors: while the gentleman burglar commits his crime with great panache, he has no qualms about crossing the line and resorting to brute force with relish. One of the consequences of this is that Leblanc can on occasion directly pit Arsène Lupin against

---

[3]   Jacques Dubois, *Le Roman policier*, Paris: Nathan, 1992, 46: "without realising it, he had launched the detective novel on the world."
[4]   *Ibid.*: "I put pen to paper, and Arsène Lupin takes over."

Sherlock Holmes. Without doubt it is the author's reactionary side that leads him to commend the aristocratic freedom enjoyed by Lupin over the bourgeois sense of duty that characterizes Conan Doyle's hero. Corruption through violence is at the very heart of the *polar*, however.

The second large wave of detective literature in France started in the Nineteen Thirties, but did not reach its peak until after the war. Two great names emerged simultaneously: Georges Simenon who created his superintendent Jules Maigret, and Léo Malet whose character Nestor Burma was to captivate generations of readers. Jacques Dubois has cleverly explained how, through a formula of psychological understanding, Maigret's character allowed the creation of the great myth of social consensus beyond class barriers. Violence is structured according to the pattern of social evils. Malet, on the other hand, belongs more to the American hard-boiled school – Hammett and Chandler are his teachers. His creation Burma is the private eye who uses efficient methods, yet is also regularly the victim. Violence can only just be mastered, supposing one is lucky. While the plot and appeal of the characters reminds us of the American novel, the setting has a very local colour (acknowledging Eugène Sue, *Les Nouveaux mystères de Paris* would become the title of a series of investigations set in turn in each of the twenty *arrondissements* of Paris). In addition, Nestor's use of irony gives a typically French flavour to the Yankee cynicism.

While humour serves as an antidote in Malet's works, it takes centre stage in the drawn-out series *San Antonio* by Frédéric Dard. He brings us incredible adventures, wild fantasies, gargantuan images of Bérurier and other loud-mouthed and gluttonous characters. For better or worse, however, the work is above all an enormous celebration of language. The excesses of the narrative and the style both lighten and darken a world of basic frantic movement. The couple Boileau and Narcejac specialize rather more in that other American device: subtle suspense. Their work *Sueurs froides* would become the basis of Hitchcock's masterpiece *Vertigo*. In it a veil of sophistication disguises brute force, yet the Minotaur of unbridled desires lurks at the heart of the maze of deception.

From the Seventies onwards, two main strands of the French detective novel emerge. The first adheres to the basic whodunnit tradition, but tries to refine certain ingredients or to highlight the historical, social or political elements. Fred Vargas, René Reouven and

Daniel Pennac are on a par with P. D. James, Patricia Highsmith and Paul Auster. Above all, Didier Daeninckx creates an essentially French variety of this narrative type: his mysteries reflect the re-examining of France's blacker history, an exercise the country was forced to undertake in order to become reconciled with her past. *Meurtres pour mémoire* is a good example of this, where violence is shown as an evil that will continue to poison society unless it is completely and irrevocably eradicated.[5]

The story revolves around the massacre of French-based Algerians in Paris, following a large protest meeting in 1962. The massacre was expressly ordered by the Ministry of Internal Affairs where the person in charge was none other than Maurice Papon (whose trial in Bordeaux at the end of the Nineties revealed a most unsavoury past during the Occupation). A young man has to die when he opens an investigation into the disappearance of his father who, due to a combination of circumstances, was implicated in the violence of 1962. This investigation can only succeed through the perseverance of a particularly motivated police officer. The anamnesis made possible by the novel allows the hastily buried scandals of the past to be uncovered, allows the concealed violence to be unearthed, so as to give it its rightful place, not to justify it, but to try and understand it.

Nevertheless, one suspects the case can never be fully closed: you cannot dig without getting your hands dirty. The bitterness of the investigator is indicative of this, set in a cynical world where there is a constant threat of recurring violence (instigated by the *Front National*, for example, which prefers to rewrite French history in order to justify its own nostalgic aims). As much as stirring up the quagmires of the past, Daeninckx is also intent on describing the depths of present-day social despair, as it manifests itself through crime (see, for example, his short story collection *Zapping*[6]).

The second important strand of detective literature after 1970 is that of the modern *roman noir*, in which the investigative work of the detective no longer plays the main role. Instead, acts of violence and the struggle between the conflicting forces of crime and repression take centre stage. Jean-Patrick Manchette was the most important

---

[5]   Didier Daeninckx, *Meurtres pour mémoire*, Paris: Gallimard, 1984.
[6]   Didier Daeninckx, *Zapping*, Paris: Gallimard, 1992.

author in this field, with such works as *Nada* and *Que d'os*. While the cynicism of the protagonists provides no catharsis, except in the void that follows total annihilation, and while the excessive violence may leave any human breathless or worse still, it is the mechanics of the story and the construction of the narrative that render this world of absolute evil artificial and consequently aesthetic. The best examples of the deliberate exaggeration of violence are to be found in the work of René Belletto (*La Machine*). By its sophisticated excesses, the detective novel here resembles the fantasy genre and the neo-gothic form.

Nowadays, the *roman policier* is characterized above all by the variety of directions it can take and the enormous scope for differentiation that exists within it. It is necessary to point out that the *polar* is now more popular than ever, as much in its least intellectual form where the plot can be easily followed – something assured by a series such as *Fleuve noir* for example, the kind of book read in the metro – as in novels where all the possibilities of the genre are exploited, for instance in the celebrated *Série noire*, or which draw on other genres such as science fiction, the historical novel, or indeed in novels which feed into investigative literature (Echenoz, Carrère, Gailly). Parallel to this, it continues to interact as intensely as ever with the cinema, and one can also observe the textual proliferation of *Poulpe* (a detective series in which different authors follow each other through a virtually endless series of variants and quotations). This was in turn supplemented by the *Polarweb* and other websites, where a large body of archival material is already building up, and where the beginnings of some future plot are probably brewing.

It is in this context that *Les Rivières pourpres* by Jean-Christophe Grangé was published in 1998, in the *Spécial Suspense* series, until then largely comprised of works translated from English. Inside the cover of the book, the editor, Albin Michel, made the following comment on the publication:

> Pourquoi un Spécial "Spécial Suspense"? Parce qu'il s'agit tout simplement d'un grand et vrai roman par un nouvel auteur étonnant. Par son imagination, son originalité, son art du récit, Jean-Christophe

GRANGÉ fait pâlir bien des auteurs américains parmi les plus grands.
GRANGÉ, un nom bien français, qui marquera l'univers du thriller.[7]

Even allowing for publicity rhetoric, the need to distance oneself from
any American influence is evident in this area, as in many others.
Without doubt, this particular aspect contributed greatly to the success
of the book in France, where it went on to become a bestseller, and
was also made into a film. Mathieu Kassovitz (the director of *La
Haine*) started filming in 1999, and the film was released in cinemas
in October 2000.[8] This was not the first novel published by Grangé as
Le Vol des cigognes[9] had already attracted media attention to the work
of this former great reporter. In this novel, he combines his liking of
tales of travel to distant lands with a colourful story of international
diamond trafficking. The word play in the title comprising the ideas of
flight and theft, reminiscent of Raymond Queneau, points to the thrilling and playful nature of this work.

If the editor insists on the author's fine French name, it is undoubtedly because English-speaking authors largely feature in the
Spécial Suspense series. This area is clearly dominated by the American formula, itself largely sustained by its close collaboration with its
domestic film industry. It is an area in which the predominance of
action sequences, rapid cutting, efficient use of cinematic cliffhanger
techniques, oblique links between the Mafia and terrorists, as well as
the ever-present urban slums all play an essential role. Grangé has
succeeded in combining the successful ingredients of this type of production (serialization or a comparison with *The Silence of the Lambs*,
for example, would undoubtedly be telling in this respect) with a cer-

---

[7] Jean-Christophe Grangé, *Les Rivières pourpres*, Paris: Michel Albin, 1998: "Why
a special 'Special Suspense'? Quite simply because this is a great and true novel
by a remarkable new author. By his imagination, his originality, and his narrative
style, Jean-Christophe GRANGÉ overshadows even some of the greatest American
authors. GRANGÉ, a very French name, will make his mark in the genre of the
thriller."

[8] The film was a highly successful box-office hit, starring Jean Reno and Vincent
Cassel. However, lovers of the book will miss the subtleties of the narrative style,
since in the film all the emphasis is on the spectacular scenes of violence that
Kassovitz uses.

[9] Jean-Christophe Grangé, *Le Vol des cigognes*, Paris: Michel Albin, 1994. The title
plays on the word *vol*, which can either mean "theft" or "flight".

tain number of elements more typical of the French context. Chief among these is the theme of French authenticity and specificity.

There are few other countries where the resistance to an enforced globalization has aroused as much emotion and has mobilized as many forces as it has in France. The movement has taken on many diverse forms, ranging, generally speaking, from the demand for a return to the France of Old made by the huntsmen of Saint-Josse to the anti-globalization demonstrations of José Bové and his supporters, extending then to Jacques Lang's *l'exception française*. Therefore, it is not by accident that the action in Grangé's novel develops around an important case of genetic manipulation, destined to influence the individuality of society's future leaders.

It is also worth noting that events unfold in an artisanal and mechanical way rather than through the use of high technology or sophisticated methods. Kidnapping is chosen over bio-technological hijacking. This approach is probably due to a particular family story, which is at the very root of the dilemma in question. It is the story of twin girls, of a murdered father, and of a vengeful mother. France is desperately searching for her identity, hidden between the memories of a perennial world and the vehemence of a postmodern society, between the parochialism of her infancy and the nomadism of increasing deracination. This quest is reflected in Grangé's deeply ambivalent story where the invasion of doubles and mirror images reflects the wide-spread crisis of identity. The vista becomes rather unclear, shrouded in a violence which is just barely under control, in much the same way as the unrelenting destiny of a Greek tragedy. In the parting scenes, the torrent waters are the colour of blood, and the young *Beur*[10] inspector, himself despairing, sees in them, not the breaking of dawn but the depths of night.

One of the strengths of *Les Rivières pourpres* is undoubtedly the way in which the book combines several traditional strands of the detective novel. Dubois identifies the following four categories: the mystery novel, the investigative novel, *roman noir*, the suspense novel.[11] In our view, Grangé's success can best be explained by the measured fusion of the main elements of each of these different

---

[10]   A French word used to describe those of North African origin born in France of immigrant parents.

[11]   Jacques Dubois, *Le Roman policier*, 54.

approaches. Violence, once again at the very centre and the periphery of the infernal nerve-centre of the text (that is, it pervades the entire work), benefits from, and justifies, the merging of narrative types.

It is a mystery novel because at the start of the story a corpse is found in Guernon, a fictitious university town situated far away at the foot of a mountain near Grenoble. The corpse is enigmatic, a sort of cryptogram: buried in a high recess of the cliff, it is covered with wounds and signs of torture; the eyes have been gouged out and re-placed by drops of water. The body is that of a young university librarian, Rémy Caillois, and we have to wait until the end of the novel before finding out who killed him, and more particularly, the motive for his murder. In fact, the mystery holds a terrible secret and the murder turns out to be part of a plot for revenge. This immediately establishes a strong link between the mystery element and the investi-gation. The suspense is created by the skillfully elaborated progression of the enquiry, which inevitably leads to the discovery that more bodies are to follow: an assistant at the university hospital will be found in a high mountain crevice, then an ophthalmologist from Annecy and finally a young police officer who had gone too far in his enquiry.

The *roman noir* element is cultivated by diverse means: the cruelty of the mutilations, the horror of revenge rooted in an unspeakable past, the harshness of the police detectives. At this juncture, it must be pointed out that one of the great merits of the story lies in the fact that two investigations progress simultaneously. The other investigation is based on events in an imaginary village Sarzac, in the department of Lot, where a grave has been desecrated and school files have gone missing. The link between the two cases, imperceptible at first, becomes increasingly more complicated as the book progresses and the chapters devoted to the two mysteries alternate.

In the meantime, we become acquainted with the realities of daily life in this peculiar university, where the ideal of creating a certain type of superman, combining a high level of intelligence with a superb physique, is upheld. One senses that the crux of the mystery lies in this desire to interfere with the very origins of life. A variety of characters play their part in this: Sophie Caillois, Rémy's wife who shares his ideal of a superior race; the rector who is overwhelmed by events; the director of a private clinic for blind people and, most especially, the magnificent Fanny Ferreira. In Sarzac, the other investigation uncovers the remains of a child. The mother had wanted to hide this child from persecutors, but it was eventually to be killed in a car accident. Meanwhile, it turns out that the clues left by those who desecrated the grave lead the police to Guernon, a development which brings the two investigations together.

A double discovery finally allows the gaps to be filled: a set of duplicates in the university archives reveals that the birth statistics had been tampered with over a long period of time. Moreover, it transpires that the fingerprints of the child killed in the accident in Sarzac are identical to those of the murderer now prowling Guernon. The solution lends a highly neo-gothic quality to the story: Rémy Caillois' father and the father of the second victim, Philippe Sertys, were at one time the principal players in a sinister exchange of babies at the university clinic. They used to replace the feeble and delicate babies of intellectuals with the babies of virile and sturdy mountain people. This was done to obtain fresh blood for a population whose physical constitution was declining due to its isolation. The intellectuals' infants were strangled before being replaced by the victims of eugenic abduction. By later orchestrating meetings and marriages between the old elite and the new blood (by placing them in a specific way in the library, amongst other things), they succeeded in creating an exceptional generation. The sons obsessively managed their fathers' legacy.

This terrible mystery at a tribal level takes on the form of a family secret in what becomes a spectacular case. It is at this point that the two investigations come together. In Guernon, the wife of a crystal miner, Fabienne Hérault, gives birth to identical twin girls. One of the daughters is swapped over while the other is left to grow up with her real parents by mistake. The secret is in danger of being discovered when the mother, a teacher, is transferred to Guernon. The father is killed by the manipulators, who then set out in pursuit of the mother. She in turn finds refuge in Sarzac and conceals her child's identity, disguising her as a little boy and naming her "Jude Itero". As the threat of discovery is ever-present, she stages a car accident in which the body of a young dead child is mutilated beyond recognition. In fact, it is a body that she had exhumed and fitted with the fingertip of her own daughter. The two young girls go and live in Guernon in perfect harmony and swear that they will one day avenge the death of their father.

Caillois is to become the first victim, followed by Sertys who, in the meantime, had undertaken a trip to Sarzac to revisit the tomb. The ophthalmologist Edmond Chernecé, the third victim, had also taken part in the baby-swapping programme, having guessed the game of the conspirators, and had killed a young police officer who was over-zealous in trying to pre-empt the path of destiny. Through these people, a link is also established between the fantastical dimension of the satanic undertaking, taking place as it does in a highly artificial context, and the real world which is overrun by primitive violence. From Guernon to Grenoble, then in Annecy, horror becomes reality. The term "demons" is used on several occasions to describe the criminals who interfere with the process of reproduction. Their attempt to manipulate the future of humanity is recounted like a primordial myth. In this isolated mountain where the basic elements of rock, alpine floods, mountain air, and unrelenting sun reign supreme, an inescapable tragedy is played out, the terror of which has implications for the world that exists outside its boundaries. In this context, the detective novel takes on a fatalistic quality, which endows it with characteristics similar to the great tragic stories and the founding epics of the nation.

The combination of realism and fantasy is constantly renewed, its *charme* (fascination) lies in the adulteration of both. As has already been pointed out, anything concerning reproductive techniques and genetic manipulation is very topical in France and mobilizes at the same time the profound forces of the imagination. When we consider the two policemen who lead the inquiry, this combination of the archaic and the modern is even more apparent. There is Karim Abdouf, a young *Beur* who was trained in the jungle of Nanterre, a world "peuplé d'êtres surviolents".[12] He is an expert on drugs and urban crime, and has been sent to this backwater by an administration that did not approve of his activities in Nanterre. He injects all the energy of a hunter fighting evil into the affair, identifying more and more with the persecuted child. Faced with having to kill her at the end of their journey, his last thought (indeed the last sentence of the book) is: "Il ne voyait pas quel genre de soleil pouvait éclairer les

---

[12] Grangé, *Les Rivières pourpres*, 64: "peopled by ultra-violent beings" (*Blood-Red Rivers*, trans. Ian Monk, London: Vintage, 2003, 46).

ténèbres qui emprisonnaient son cœur."[13] A multicultural France (symbolized by her national football team that won the World Cup in 1998) serves as the background. It is challenged by a racist mentality that is held in check. However, the threat remains and no perspectives to counter this are presented, a failure symbolized by the irrepressible wave of violence surrounding the football match with which the book opens.

The other twin girl deals mainly with the other policeman, chief superintendent Pierre Niémans, who asserts himself as the boss. In a sense, he is the real protagonist. To some extent, he sees some of his own shadows and the reflection of his inner darkness in the violence he is trying to suppress in Guernon. His entire struggle against crime and disrespect for the law is a continuous effort to appease his inner turmoil, which the barking of killer dogs symbolizes and brings home to him. The tone is set at the beginning of the book by the scene of the football match, which initially appears to be unrelated to what follows.

In this tale of procreation and succession, however, it is the ideological and fictional base of all the fury that is about to be unleashed. At the same time, the reader can identify with the scene. Niémans – presented as a police officer through external focalization, as through a cold camera-eye – is head of the Public Order Service during an international game between an English side and a Spanish one. As the crowds leave the stadium, scuffles break out, and then spread quickly and wildly. Niémans is irresistibly swept along by the wave of violence and loses all control in the pursuit of a hooligan who has just settled his score with an English supporter from an opposing club. The reader is initiated into the violent world of the novel with a description such as:

> Il cogna, cogna, puis s'arrêta soudainement, fixant les traits ensan-
> glantés du hooligan. Des saillies d'os pointaient sous les chairs déchi-
> quetées. Un globe oculaire pendait au bout d'un treillis de fibres.[14]

---

[13]   *Ibid.*, 404: "He wondered how much sunlight would be needed to chase away the shadows that were folding around his heart" (*Blood-Red Rivers*, 328).

[14]   *Ibid.*, 18: "Again and again he hit him, then suddenly stopped and looked down at the hooligan's bloodied features. His bones were sticking up through the shreds of his skin. An eyeball dangled down on a mess of fibres" (*Blood-Red Rivers*, 7-8).

The consequences of these cuts and wounds will impact on the commissioner during his investigation in Guernon: the comatose Englishman dies in the end and his death will represent a death sentence for his executioner.

At the end of the pursuit of Fanny, the other murderous twin, who had in the meantime become his lover, the couple perishes in a bloody and fatal embrace. Niémans, a man whose very name denies the existence of his fears, embodies, on the side of the police, the same *lex talionis*,[15] the essential law of primeval revenge, which explains the actions of the alpine Erinyes: "Il songea à ces accès de violence incontrolables qui aveuglaient sa conscience, déchirant le temps et l'espace, au point de lui faire commettre le pire."[16] Justice is indeed blind in this story of gouged eyes and blinding truth. Niémans is cast in the role of a modern-day Oedipus, fleeing his own internal hell only to find it again. Karim is more like an Orestes who avenges himself on the wrong party.

In his character we also see the deep complexities of the world of violence: "des accès de fureur le transperçaient parfois, stupéfiants et incontrôlables."[17] First, we see how he makes himself sole judge and executioner in a narcotics case where his former friend had died, and again during a raid on some skinheads. This story seems superfluous to the main story, but it heralds the main story by the very cruelty and severity of the altercation. The *fafas* and their *birds*, a type of wild fauna, are pinned to the ground, limp and burnt out by means of their preferred drug, glue used for repairing bicycle punctures. This violence is the hallmark of contemporary society, plunged into its high-tech primitivism. Another example is found in the words of an old man who carried out the autopsy on the little girl killed in the accident on the motorway; he comments on the carnage of the roads: "Comme une espèce de guerre souterraine, tu vois, qui surgirait de temps en

---

[15]   Latin name for the law best described by the maxim "an eye for an eye and a tooth for a tooth".

[16]   *Ibid.*, 21: "He thought about his uncontrollable fits of violence, which blinded his conscience, ripping apart time and space, causing him to commit outrageous acts" (*Blood-Red Rivers*, 11).

[17]   *Ibid.*, 65: "He was occasionally gripped by uncontrollable fits of violent rage" (*Blood-Red Rivers*, 47).

temps, avec une violence de terreur."[18] In the mountain landscape,
Niémans also senses the fatal presence of this violence:

> Il avait l'impression de saisir, à travers ces horizons solitaires, une vé-
> rité profonde de notre planète. Une vérité soudain mise à nu, violente,
> incorruptible, qui résisterait toujours aux volontés de l'homme.[19]

The novel thus presents a clever mix of realism and fantasy, where the
laws of a world ordered by signs give way to an unbridled desire,
fuelled by the imagination. This also indicates a confrontation between the rational consciousness and the subconscious driven by other
motives, which becomes visible through the intermediary of the characters and as events unfold. It is as if a system of associations and
repetitions permeates the text, causing the book to function at the level
of this fundamental opposition. By its nature and since its inception,
the detective novel seeks obsessively to achieve order out of chaos and
to tame primal violence. This is because it is aware that its own forces,
its most fundamental motives are inextricably linked with the world of
primeval rage. This is why its system of reasoning, the construction of
its narrative, its fictional autonomy, a sign of triumph over distortion
and disorganization, take on an enormous importance.

Les Rivières pourpres is a meticulously constructed novel in which
the narrator imposes implacable and rigorous order on the chaos. This
deep-seated ambivalence can be seen in the many reflections and
mirror images. On the one hand, they form a complete explanation,
and embody the inescapability of the course of events. On the other,
they are excessive and cracks begin to appear within them. Gaps are
widened and the hymen of the Other is destroyed. By the end, one can
hardly make sense of the frenzy of doubles and of the disorientation
caused by the multiple retrospections. They leave readers breathless as
they accompany the surviving law-enforcer in his distress. The order
imposed does not promise a new future. The nature of the vengeance
is the most striking aspect of the mirror games. This is because it

---

[18] *Ibid.*, 232: "It's like an underground war, get me? Which breaks out from time to
time in horrific violence" (*Blood-Red Rivers*, 188).
[19] *Ibid.*, 167: "Crossing these lonely horizons, he felt as if he had grasped a hidden
truth about our planet. A violent, incorruptible truth that had abruptly been exposed, which would always resist the will of mankind" (*Blood-Red Rivers*, 133).

fanatically imitates the details of the crime and follows the *lex talionis*, which demands that the criminal be punished in the same way as he sinned. Since their misdeed can be defined as the abduction of the children's identity, their own bodies are rendered unrecognizable. This is achieved most notably by the removal of their eyes and their fingers, the marks of their individuality. The key question arising out of this spectacle is: "Qu'avaient donc fait ces hommes pour être réduits à l'état de reflets, pour que leur chair soit privée de toute marque distinctive?"[20]

Madness and schizophrenia reveal their indomitable nature because they equally affect the guilty victims as well as their persecuting judges and the agents of law and order. We are plunged into an uncanny world characterized by the unending contemplation of double meanings, by perpetual exchange, and by the doubt that they cast over life or death. This world has a strangely familiar quality, where ontological terror is to be found in the deepest shadows. Any attempt to exorcize the primeval horror of the mysterious destruction of life by death, all the Totems and Taboos cannot prevent rage from wreaking havoc in the darkness. The obsessive repetition plunges the protagonists of this tragedy into the abyss, beyond the pleasure principle and far beyond the desire to restore equilibrium in the world. The *rivières pourpres*, rivers of blood, represent both family bloodlines and savage butchery. The story is indeed presented like the unfolding of a classic tragedy, with the story very precisely concentrated into a twenty-four-hour period, and told in a series of tableaus (as indicated by the expression "faille théatrale"),[21] which constitute a long ritual of purification. Only the excessive repetition softens the horror: Thanatos beyond all regulatory principle. The message of the novel is that in today's world, life is just a frantic rush towards death. In the end, everything crumbles, breaks down and is pulverized; a return to primary matter, to ash and bone. Jude's tomb is filled with a large quan-

---

[20] *Ibid.*, 277: "What, then, had these men done to deserve being reduced to mirror-images, to being deprived of their biological signatures?" (*Blood-Red Rivers*, 225).

[21] *Ibid.*, 46: "theatrical rock fault" (*Blood-Red Rivers*, 33). This is where the first victim is found.

tity of rodent skeletons, "luisant de reflets préhistoriques".[22] The desire for vengeance culminates in the idea "qu'il fallait éclater leur corps en plusieurs reflets, comme on casserait une carafe, avec plein d'éclats".[23] In these last pages, the fragmented narrative comes together, the pieces all carefully stuck together in a mosaic. In the centre, however, there is a kind of black hole, where a dull rumbling noise appears to engulf the characters: Fanny riddled with bullets, Pierre butchered with a knife, Judith stabbed in the heart. Karim remains because he is the "sphinx", who in this version does not throw himself into the chasm, but remains frozen at the edge of the abyss and personifies the mystery of blood. The book has been deciphered but the crypt of the pages closes in on these central characters. The reconstructed truth yielded by the investigation and the narration (*homoiosis*) is coupled with *in fine* another truth, *aletheia* revealing the other side of the mirror. In an exemplary fashion, *Les Rivières pourpres* thus succeeds in combining the profile of French society today, torn between its nostalgic recollections and its openness to the world, with a story of desire. The unconscious ramifications of this story present the truth of violence (a novelistic truth as defined by René Girard in his *Mensonge romantique et vérité romanesque*[24]).

This intense planning of the narrative can also be perceived in the fundamental resonance of the text, wherever its powerful music plays. A single piece of music serves as a base of a number of elements, among which are the voices that vibrate, the rhythm of the narrative, the succession of victims, the groaning of the mountains. Fabienne Hérault was a gifted pianist who, at the most painful moments of her own life and her daughter's, played Chopin's Second Piano Sonata in B-flat minor. Judith subsequently uses the piano wire of a B flat tone to strangle her victims. Karim had already suspected this as he had discovered this music score on the mother's piano. On closer examination, we learn that the third movement of this sonata is the famous Funeral March. The beginning and end of the march obsessively

---

[22]   *Ibid.*, 348. In the English translation of the novel, this is rendered as follows: "Those myriads of skeletons, reflecting in the beam of his torch, looked like a mass prehistoric grave" (*Blood-Red Rivers*, 281).

[23]   *Ibid.*, 404: "that we ought to smash their bodies into a set of different reflections, like the shards of a broken mirror" (*Blood-Red Rivers*, 326).

[24]   René Girard, *Mensonge romantique et vérité romanesque*, Paris: Grasset, 1961.

repeat two bass chords, while a softer melody makes up the middle movement. Sadness unfolds in many ways, notably by the cruel presence of death that surrounds the melancholic sadness of the person who survives the tragedy. In this sense, the music may seem programmed (an aspect underscored in the novel, as it follows the movements of the music). Furthermore, it has been said of these pages of the Chopin sonata, that they are "des plus mystérieuses avec des harmonies dures, modernes, souvent dissonantes".[25] The blindness of the text is lost in the mysteries of the music, and the reader tiptoes away.[26]

---

[25] "Most mysterious, and contain hard, modern, and often dissonant harmonies." See Arthur Hedley's *Chopin*, Rotterdam: Ad Donker, 1958, and also *Dictionnaire des oeuvres*, eds Laffont-Bompiani, Paris: Laffont, 1980.

[26] *Le Concile de pierre* is the title of the third novel Jean-Christophe Grangé published in September 2000 (Paris: Michel Albin). Again it is the story of a child martyr, this time originating in far-off Mongolia. The quest for happiness, and even more so the search for truth, seem to come to a head after four-hundred pages of bloody suspense: the resurrection of the sleeping child during the Sonata in B-flat minor, opus 35. In 2002 *L'Empire des loups* was published, where the extreme violence surrounding the trafficking of drugs from Turkey is combined with mental manipulation of the main character. The overdose of horror (with a particularly gothic setting) is measured against the paintings of Francis Bacon, which are set in a *mise en abyme*. The very organized structure of the text once again attempts to counterbalance the fundamental disorder; the imbalance nevertheless runs the risk of deepening ... something from which literature could well suffer.

Fractured Identities: Jean-Claude Izzo's *Total Khéops*

AGNÈS MAILLOT

Jean-Claude Izzo, poet and novelist, former Communist and journalist, late-comer to the detective novel, gave the genre in France a new school, that of the *polar aïoli*, or *Marseillais* detective fiction, in which he cast a distinctive hero, Fabio Montale, and a distinctive heroine, Marseilles. Before finally succumbing to lung cancer, in January 2000, Izzo became mentor to a young generation of Marseilles authors who, following his lead, gained confidence and popularity.[1] According to author François Thomazeau, "entre Pagnol et Izzo il n'y a quasiment rien eu à Marseille. Grâce à lui, des vocations sont nées, il a décomplexé les intellectuels marseillais."[2] Izzo's trilogy was among the best-selling French-based detective novels of the Nineties in France. He wrote *Total Khéops* in five months, chapter by chapter, sending one each week to his son who was at the time doing his military service. The novel was published in 1995 and sold 150,000 copies. The success of this first book encouraged Izzo to write a sequel, *Chourmo*, published a year later, and then, *Soléa*.[3] The success of Izzo's trilogy is partly due to the themes that are tackled in all three books, which include violence, unemployment, racism, corruption and multicultural relations, but also to the hugely successful literary phenomenon that

---

[1] Amongst this new generation of *polar* writers are Philippe Carrese, author of *Trois jours d'engatse* and François Thomazeau, author of *La Faute à Dégun*.

[2] Quoted in Sophie Huet, "Jean-Claude Izzo, un pilier du 'polar marseillais'", *Agence France Presse*, 26 January 2000: "Between Pagnol and Izzo, there was practically nothing in Marseilles. Thanks to him, vocations were born, he has rid the Marseilles intellectuals of their complexes." (Unless stated otherwise, all translations are my own.)

[3] Jean-Claude Izzo: *Total Khéops* (1995), *Chourmo* (1996), *Soléa* (1998), all Paris: Gallimard. *Soléa*, the last of the trilogy, sold an impressive 40,000 copies in the very first week.

the genre of *roman policier*, or detective novel has become in France, both in translated texts and in a new generation of French writers.

The plot on which *Total Khéops* is based is quite conventional. A hero, disenchanted cop Fabio Montale, sets out to uncover the identity of the killer or killers of his two childhood friends, Ugo and Manu, both shot in mysterious circumstances. His quest for the truth leads him down a trail of murders, rapes, betrayals, taking him to the under-world of Marseilles, its derelict suburbs (*banlieues*), its shabby back streets, but also its more picturesque bars, restaurants and alleyways with their provençal atmosphere, light and smells. Montale meets with a mixture of characters: crooked cops, Mafia-type mobsters, good-hearted prostitutes, chatty ageing Marseilles barmen and cordon-bleu gourmets who could have come straight out of a Pagnol novel, and also befriends second-generation *Beurs*.[4] One of the novel's recurrent themes is the loss of identity of the characters, against the backdrop of a city quickly surrendering its idiosyncrasies to a pattern of French identity that is becoming increasingly blurred. This essay will analyse Izzo's treatment of the question of identity in *Total Khéops*, focusing first on the concept of *Marseillais* identity and then analysing how Izzo approaches and ultimately condemns the notions of integration and Frenchness through the depiction of first and second-generation immigrants. In this study, we will establish to what extent the *polar* genre is a suitable vehicle for multicultural fiction.

Marseilles boasts a long tradition of immigration, being a cross-roads of cultures and ethnicities. It is, historically, a city of migration. Founded by a Greek, Phocee, in 600 BC, Marseilles' history starts with an immigrant. Its geographical location makes it the obvious port of arrival of Mediterranean immigration. At present, the city's population of foreign origin is 110,000, out of a total of 800,000 people, although if the number of immigrants who have become naturalized is taken into account, the total figure of foreigners is 56,000, that is 7% of the population. Marseilles is made up of long established communities, from the Italians who arrived in the second half of the nineteenth century to the Armenians who fled the genocide in 1915-16 and joined one of the oldest and biggest communities of the city, 80,000 strong, dating from the eighteenth century. It was not until after the Second

---

[4]   *Beur* is the slang term for second-generation Arabs, derived from the word *Arabe*.

World War, from 1947 onwards, that North Africans started settling in the city, mirroring the patterns of immigration throughout France. The latest addition to Marseilles' multicultural composition is the Comorean community, representing around 40,000 people. Marseilles is thus characterized by fast-evolving demographic trends. According to sociologist Emile Temime:

> Si l'on tient compte d'une population flottante, des brassages internes (déplacement des fonctionnaires, retraités, etc.) de plus en plus importants, on peut estimer, sans trop de risques, qu'un habitant sur trois est arrivé dans la ville dans les vingt-cinq dernières années.[5]

Marseilles' foreign population, proportionally, does not differ much from that of France overall, being roughly within the French general average of 6.3%. But what makes the city different from the rest of the country, in the eyes of Izzo, is its proven capacity until recent years to integrate newcomers, not just because of its history and location, but also because all its inhabitants share a particular identity, the *Marseillais* identity, far more relevant in his eyes than the ill-defined French national identity. It is both rooted in local history and customs, colloquial vernacular, strong cultural traditions, and loose enough to embrace all those who want to engage in and contribute to its dynamics. In his own words, the city is:

> ...faite d'ailleurs, d'exils, et elle se donne sans résistance à ceux qui savent la prendre, l'aimer. Ici, on est chez soi. D'où que l'on vienne. Et personne, jamais, ne vous demandera d'où vous arrivez, exception faite des flics, la nuit.[6]

---

[5] Quoted in Dominique Pons, "Marseille ou le mythe vacillant de l'intégration", *Le Monde diplomatique*, 16-17 July 1997, 6: "Taking into account the floating population, the internal intermingling (civil servants, old-age pensioners) which is more and more frequent, one can quite accurately estimate that one in three inhabitants has arrived in Marseilles in the last 25 years."

[6] Jean-Claude Izzo, "Petit guide irraisonné de Marseille", http://www.diplomatie.go uv.fr/fr/actions-france_830/documentaire_1045/diffusion-non-commerciale_5378/ collections-video_5374/societe_8874/ville_10302/par-jean-claude-izzo_10330/: "Marseilles is made of elsewhere, of exiles, and she offers herself, without resistance, to those who know how to take her, love her. Here, you are at home. No matter where you are from. And nobody, ever, will ask you where you come from, except for the cops, at night."

Jean-Claude Izzo considered himself the epitome of the *Marseillais*:
born in the city in 1945, of an Italian father, a barman, and a Spanish
mother, a dressmaker, he defined himself as half-Spanish, half-Italian
and half the rest of the world. What unites the people of the city, then,
is precisely the fact of being from everywhere and nowhere at the
same time, thus making a collective identity based on multiple origins
sustainable. In this context, the city itself becomes the cement, the
bond between these citizens of the world.

Izzo's Marseilles identity is largely coloured by his own love for
his native city, plainly evident in the numerous and colourful descriptions he gives of the harbour, the sea, the atmosphere and the people.
Thus, Marseilles is generally defined in sentimental, sometimes even
passionate terms, and the identity that is derived from this definition
would probably not sustain any theoretical scrutiny. But it constitutes
an attempt, however subjective and incomplete, at departing from the
uneasy debate that dominated French politics in the last decade of the
twentieth century, centring on the definition and attributions of
Frenchness. Strictly speaking, be it from a political or legalistic point
of view, French nationality is bound by two essential parameters, *ius
solis* and *ius sanguinis* (*droit du sol* and *droit du sang*). Since the
French Revolution, the weight given to each of these two prerequisites
has shifted, depending on the periods. Nevertheless, overall, and particularly in the last years, the birthright and blood ties have proven
quite restrictive when attempting to overcome the fundamental question of identity in a multicultural environment. What the French
Republican ethos has advocated is a common identity, brought about
through adhesion to shared values and institutions. But this has also
implied, to an extent, the willingness of minorities to renounce their
own identities, be they local, ethnic, religious or cultural. The ideal of
Marseillais identity, as advocated by Izzo and his alter ego Fabio
Montale, cuts across soil and birth, and takes on a more general, albeit
vague, understanding of multicultural relations.

This idea is problematic for several reasons. Firstly, as Patrick
Weil, commissioned by the French government in 1997 to draw up a
report on nationality, remarked, "there is no differentiation in the
French social imagination between identity, citizenship and nation-

ality, between local and national citizenship".[7] Furthermore, while there is no doubt that there is a strong cultural and social dynamic particular to Marseilles, it is not clear how this is sufficient to define the individual in his relationship to his environment and to others. In other words, can this *Marseillais* identity take precedence over the broader French one, and exist, so to speak, in isolation, as Montale seems to suggest? Not according to sociologist Michel Péraldi who argues that:

> une identité territoriale ne peut pas se substituer à une identité sociale. Or Marseille n'a pas d'identité sociale. On n'y a pas recomposé le puzzle qui permet d'exister. Tout ça ne fait pas une identité. Etre marseillais, c'est bien, mais superficiel. La plupart des immigrés sont dans un "non monde" social humiliant.[8]

The potential for a *Marseillais* identity superseding all differences is thus denied by the economic and social problems that the city has experienced in recent years and which have contributed to the break-up of the social fabric. In fact, unemployment and poverty statistics in the mid-Nineties, when *Total Khéops* was written, were amongst the highest in France. Furthermore, the total recorded crimes for 1991 was 117.65 per 1,000 inhabitants, a sharp increase compared to ten years earlier, when the rate was 98.42.[9] This has led to increasingly uneasy relationships between different communities, since what they shared, fundamentally, was no longer a cultural or social space but a feeling of being excluded from society.

The fragmentation of post-industrialized societies has led to a dual sense of belonging, a divide between those who are inside and those who are left on the margins, which President Jacques Chirac, in his 1995 electoral campaign, referred to as *la fracture sociale*. This has

---

[7] Patrick Weil, "Nationalities and Citizenships: The Lessons of the French Experience for Germany and Europe", in *Citizenship, Nationality and Migration in Europe*, eds David Cesarani and Mary Fulbrook, London: Routledge, 1996, 81.

[8] Quoted in Pons, "Marseille ou le mythe vacillant de l'intégration", 7: "A territorial identity cannot be substituted with a social identity. But Marseilles has no social identity. The jigsaw that makes it possible to exist has not been recomposed. This is not an identity. It is a good thing to be a *Marseillais*, but it is superficial. Most of the immigrants are in a humiliating social 'non-world.'"

[9] These statistics are available at: http://europa.eu.int/comm/regional_policy/urban2 audit/indicators/crime.htm.

deep implications for the collective identity of the country as a whole, since there is very little space now available for the excluded sections of the population, and more particularly, for non-nationals, to fit into a general consensus. As sociologist Didier Lapeyronnie analysed:

> L'intégration systémique a été remplacée par la juxtaposition de l'univers des classes moyennes, participant aux flux dominants de l'économie, et les mondes exclus, tenus à distances et à l'écart de cette participation .... L'économie a été séparée de la culture. Mais la pierre angulaire de l'intégration socio-nationale était le lien étroit entre l'insertion économique et l'intégration culturelle dans l'ensemble politique national.[10]

What the immigrants share with their fellow poverty-stricken French citizens is no longer the sense of belonging to a social class, the working class, which has tended to vanish as an actor within French politics and as a unifying space. Being *exclu* is, if anything, divisive, and leads to antagonisms within the marginalized world of exclusion. Jean-Claude Izzo was undoubtedly clearly aware of the decline of the dynamics of working-class politics, being himself a former member of the Communist Party that failed to retain its voice among the working classes and was, to an extent, replaced as a spokesperson for the disadvantaged sections of the French population by the *Front National*.

In *Total Khéops*, detective Fabio Montale concludes that the *Marseillais* have increasingly tended to revert to more tribal behaviour and affiliations, thus no longer giving their allegiances to the city, but to a misleading discourse on *préférence nationale*, which claims that French people should be given priority over non-nationals in issues such as housing and employment. According to Montale, this has been fed partly by successive government policies that have, directly or indirectly, encouraged the division in French collective perceptions,

---

[10] Didier Lapeyronnie, *L'Individu et les minorités: La France et la Grande-Bretagne face à leurs immigrés*, Paris: Presses Universitaires de France, 1993, 61: "Systemic integration has been replaced by the juxtaposition of the universe of the middle classes, participating in the dominant flows of the economy, and the excluded worlds, distanced and kept away from this participation .... Economy has become separated from culture. But the founding stone of socio-national integration was the narrow link between economic insertion and cultural integration within the political national whole."

leaving the immigrant population aside. "La France républicaine avait décidé de laver plus blanc que blanc. Immigration zéro. Le nouveau rêve français",[11] says Montale, in a direct reference to the then Interior Minister, Charles Pasqua, whose objective was effectively an end to all immigration. The controversial Interior Minister claimed in 1993 that France used to be a country of immigration, but no longer wished to be so.

This type of discourse came to a large extent as a response to the emergence and growth of extreme-Right ideas on immigration, which gained momentum in the mid-Eighties. These were particularly relevant in the context of Marseilles, where Jean-Marie Le Pen's party obtained some of its best electoral results. In the first round of the 1995 Presidential election, for instance, the *Front National* candidate topped the poll, with 22.32% votes, ahead of the Socialist Jospin and the right-wing candidates Balladur and Chirac. The municipal elections of the same year saw the *Front National* come third with 22% of the vote in the first round, behind the UDF candidate Gaudin and the Socialist Weygand.[12] What Izzo is combating, through his narrator, is the type of discourse that links identity to the fight against immigration, which was precisely the rhetoric used by the extreme-Right candidate at the 2001 municipal election, Bruno Mégret: "Marseille menacée par une immigration et une insécurité galopantes, peu à peu privée de son identité, victime d'une longue crise économique qui a réduit au chômage une grande partie de la population, résume les périls qui pèsent sur notre pays."[13]

For Izzo, the anti-*Front National* crusade was a mission, and he saw his work as part of the fight against the propagation of extreme-Right ideas: "J'estime, par fidélité à mon père immigré, que j'ai un rôle à jouer dans le combat qui se prépare."[14] Thus, his hero, Fabio

---

[11] Izzo, *Total Khéops*, 17: "Republican France had decided to wash whiter than white. Zero immigration. The new French dream."

[12] For further details, visit: http://www.lafranceelectorale.com

[13] "Lettre de candidature de Bruno Mégret", available at http://www.Mégret-marseille.com/actu.html: "Marseilles, threatened by galloping immigration and insecurity, being deprived little by little of its identity, falling victim to a long economic crisis that has reduced to unemployment a large section of the population, sums up the perils that threaten our country."

[14] Quoted in Huet, "Jean-Claude Izzo, un pilier du 'polar marseillais'": "I think, out of loyalty to my immigrant father, that I have a role to play in the struggle ahead."

Montale, takes every opportunity to denounce the narrowness and
dangerous overtones of this emerging French national idea. Throughout the pages of *Total Khéops*, his mixed feelings, made up of a longing for the past and a strong resentment of the present, are clearly visible. In an interview with the literary magazine *Lire* in 1998, Izzo
conveyed this in the following terms: "Je voulais parler à la fois de
mes nostalgies du passé et de la ville d'aujourd'hui, sa confrontation
entre les différentes migrations."[15]

Montale's nostalgia stems from the fact that he sees his native city
merging rapidly into the broad French model. By doing so, Marseilles
is in danger of losing not simply its identity, by becoming just another
French city, but also its capacity to integrate new and recent waves of
immigrants. Emulating the rest of the country is a dangerous path, as
he bitterly explains in *Total Khéops*:

> Marseille était gagnée par la connerie parisienne. Elle se rêvait capi-
> tale. Capitale du Sud. Oubliant que ce qui la rendait capitale, c'est
> qu'elle était un port. Le carrefour de tous les brassages humains.
> Depuis des siècles.[16]

Losing this sense of intermingling, according to Montale, will inevitably lead to social fragmentation, to new antagonisms that might have
been latent in the past but that certainly did not stand in the way of
collectiveness. Marseilles, according to Montale, cannot and should
not be hijacked by those who want to claim it as theirs. It should not
fall prey to the discourse of those who are seeking to give *la France
aux Français*. Montale's rhetoric in reply to this simplistic and re-
ductionist axiom is quite similar, although it takes the opposite view:
"Marseille appartient à ceux qui y vivent."[17]

Total Khéops is peopled with a myriad of characters who are, for
the most part, immigrants, either first or second generation. Because

---

[15] Quoted in Christine Ferniot, "Jean-Claude Izzo", *Lire*, 267 (July-August 1997),
40: "I wanted to speak both of my nostalgia for the past and the city of today, its
confrontation between the different migrations."

[16] Izzo, *Total Khéops*, 98: "Marseilles was gained by Parisian bullshit. She dreamed
of herself as a capital city. The capital of the South. Forgetting that what made it a
capital was that it was a port. The crossroads of the intermingling of all populations. For centuries."

[17] *Ibid.*, 235: "Marseilles belongs to those who live there."

of his profession, and the tasks that he has been assigned by his superiors, Montale is in constant contact with the youths of the *banlieues*, being an intermediary between them and the police institutions, and has as a mission to avert any clashes in these areas. Through these characters, the narrator can contrast past and present, analysing the changing patterns of *Marseillais* society and of France in general. Montale sees patterns in the way the first generation immigrants integrated, or at least settled, in Marseilles. Far from painting a rosy picture of France before the depression of the Seventies, when immigration was stopped, Montale nevertheless longs for the days when it was possible to arrive and feel at home, to retain one's identity while adopting the cultural traits of the city, to look forward to a future. Fundamentally, what united those immigrants was hope, hope for a better future for them and for their children, hope of a better material life. They all came from difficult situations and had great expectations.

The first group of immigrants was constituted mainly of Southern European migrants from neighbouring countries such as Spain and Italy, who arrived in Marseilles before the war. Fabio's childhood friends, Ugo, Manu and Lole, came from similar backgrounds. Ugo's parents had fled Mussolini's Italy, Manu's father had been shot by Francoists. They took the jobs that the French did not want, they were poor, their clothes smelled of damp, they were laughed at in school. But still, they had something going for them. "Immigrés, exilés, tous débarquaient un jour dans l'une de ces ruelles. Les poches vides et le coeur plein d'espoir",[18] remembers Montale. His parents, both Italian, managed to preserve their own culture alongside that of Marseilles. They ate pasta with tomato sauce, sang popular Italian songs, but inevitably wrapped up the night playing *belote*, thereby becoming so *Marseillais* that they even adopted the local dialect and accent: "Fan! Y va falloir lui mettre les sangsues."[19] In those times, it was still possible to feel and be as *Marseillais* as any character in a Pagnol scene, as shown when Montale's father and his friends clearly re-enact the famous *belote* scene of the 1931 movie *Marius*.

---

[18] *Ibid.*, 18: "Immigrants, exiles, they all ended up in one of those narrow lanes. Their pockets empty and their hearts full of hope."
[19] *Ibid.*, 42: "We're going to have to put the leeches on him."

Even the generation of post-war immigrants, that of the Algerian Mouloud, could still feel that they belonged. Mouloud arrived in France after the war, during the *Trente Glorieuses* (1945-1975), or period of economic boom, and like all his contemporaries, he might have believed that this was El Dorado, or at least that there was a place for him in French society. Montale tends to show quite paternalistic attitudes towards Mouloud, whom he talks about in gentle but at times condescending terms, profiling him as the epitome of the naïve and genuine immigrant who was, inevitably, deceived and betrayed by the very dream he had brought with him. Upon arrival in France, "c'était, à lui tout seul, le rêve de l'immigration".[20] At a time when integration, be it social or economic, was achieved through work, and when the immigrants were seen, first and foremost, as workers and only second, as potential citizens, Mouloud was in more than one way an exemplary immigrant worker, toeing the line while retaining his own cultural identity. Mouloud seemed to be able to find a space between his native and his adopted culture, and to instil both sets of values in his three children:

> Il n'obligea jamais ses enfants à se couper des autres, à ne pas fréquenter les Français. Seulement à éviter les mauvaises relations. Garder le respect d'eux-mêmes. Acquérir des manières convenables. Et réussir le plus haut possible. S'intégrer dans la société sans jamais se renier. Ni sa race, ni son passé.[21]

At the same time, he remained cautious, never completely feeling at home. His integration is not as successful, at the height of his career, as that of Montale's parents' generation. Not only does he not adopt the habits of his French colleagues, leading quite a secluded life, but he never loses his original accent, where Montale's parents were able to reproduce some *Marseillais* colloquialisms. When Mouloud calls Montale for help after his daughter Leila's disappearance, he betrays his incapacity to fully grasp the French language: "Siou plait,

---

[20] *Ibid.*, 57: "He was the quintessential dream of immigration."
[21] *Ibid.*: "He never obliged his children to cut themselves from others, to not socialize with French people. Only to avoid bad relationships. To keep their self-respect. To acquire proper manners. And to succeed as much as possible. To integrate within society without denying themselves. Neither their race, nor their past."

faut qu'tu viennes, M'sieur Montale, c'est pour Leila."[22] Mouloud
soon became, mainly because of external factors, a foreigner to both
worlds, acculturated and distanced from his native Algeria. When he
returns there with his wife and children for a holiday, Mouloud experiences dislocation, and the feeling of estrangement from his childhood
and his past. But France ceases to be his place when he loses his job
and becomes unemployable after having been targeted as a leader in a
strike. His successful integration depended on work, and once this
falls apart, he becomes the quintessential tragic figure, whose dream
for himself and his children has been violently dashed, and who has
nothing to look forward to. The loss of his daughter will seal his fate
forever:

> L'Algérie n'était plus son pays. La France venait de le rejeter défini-
> tivement. Maintenant il n'était plus qu'un pauvre Arabe. Sur son sort,
> personne ne viendrait se pencher.[23]

Mouloud's story is tragic, yet he does not seem to be able or willing to fight. This is in contrast to his children's generation, whose
view of France is rather nihilistic but who invent a new identity for
themselves, one quite different from that of their father, from that of
the migrant worker. This *Beur* generation holds no hope for the future,
but at the same time, does not feel resigned to its lot. In contrast to
their parents, they do not have much to look forward to, precisely,
according to Montale, because the dream of their parents has been
shattered before their very eyes. They are part of both worlds, the
French one and the *exclu* one, and yet, of neither.

According to an opinion poll carried out in 1995, when *Total
Khéops* was published, a vast majority of *Beurs* (seven out of ten) felt
closer to the culture of the French population than to that of their
parents, yet only one third of non-*Beur* respondents said they saw
them as French.[24] This demonstrates the difficulty experienced by

---

22   *Ibid.*: "Please, Mister, you have to come, it's for Leila."
23   *Ibid.*, 108: "Algeria was no longer his country. France had just rejected him de-
     finitively. Now, he was only a miserable Arab. No one would take an interest in
     his fate."
24   See Alec G. Hargreaves, *Immigration, "Race" and Ethnicity in Contemporary
     France*, London: Routledge, 1995, 19.

second-generation immigrants to feel part of a given social group, and to fit into an already existing identity. But nationality as defined in France in the Nineties was certainly not open enough to encompass them. As Maurice Roche explains:

> Common culture is often taken to be the basis for collective identity, which in turn is often taken to be the basis (via nationality) for citizenship. This analysis tends to be more weighed towards "heritage" and "the common past" rather than to the "common future" or indeed even than to the "common present".[25]

It is precisely the lack of a dream, of a vision of a common future that characterizes this generation. Montale's view is that whatever they do, they are doomed. The system will eventually get them, no matter how hard they try:

> Des fils d'immigrés, sans boulot, sans avenir, sans espoir. Il leur suffisait d'ouvrir la télé aux infos pour apprendre qu'on avait baisé leur père, et qu'on s'apprêtait à les baiser eux encore mieux.[26]

Consequently, although not all second generation characters follow the same itinerary in *Total Khéops*, they all end up in the same place – nowhere.

Montale sees two possible ways for the young of the *banlieues* to go. Firstly, the way of the second-generation immigrants who, much like their parents, tried to fit in while retaining their cultural legacy. In some ways, they are better equipped, as they have been educated and brought up in the French environment, and are familiar with its codes and values. Mouloud's daughter Leila is a model of successful integration. She has just completed an MA in modern French literature, quite an achievement, considering that, according to Montale, only one out of a thousand children of immigrants succeed in doing that.

---

[25] "Citizenship, Popular Culture and Europe", in *Culture and Citizenship*, ed. Nick Stevenson, London: Sage Publications, 2001, 75.

[26] Izzo, *Total Khéops*, 101: "Sons of immigrants, without jobs, without a future, without hope. All they had to do was turn on the TV to discover that their father had been fucked around with and that they were just about to be fucked around with even more."

The title of her thesis is in itself a statement: "Poésie et devoir d'iden-tité" ("Poetry and Duty of Identity"):

> Pour elle, enfant de l'Orient, la langue française devenait ce lieu où le migrant tirait à lui toutes ses terres et pouvait enfin poser ses valises. La langue de Rimbaud, de Valéry, de Char, aurait se métisser, affir-mait-elle. Le rêve d'une génération de beurs. A Marseille, ça causait déjà un curieux français, mélange de provençal, d'italien, d'espagnol, d'arabe, avec une pointe d'argot et un zeste de verlan. Et les mômes, ils se comprenaient bien avec ça. Dans la rue. A l'école et à la maison, c'était une autre paire de manches.[27]

Leila has found a way to position herself as a modern French citizen (through language and education) without denying her strong cultural heritage. Her story could be the epitome of success, were it not for her tragic ending, raped and murdered by three men who are avenging on her their resentment and their anger, who are symbolically treating her in the same way French society is treating the rest of her community:

> Après l'avoir violée, ils lui avaient sans doute laissé croire qu'elle était libre. Cela avait dû les exciter de la voir courir nue. Une course vers un espoir qui était au bas du chemin. Au début de la route.[28]

But this does not mean that the *Beur* community, or indeed all second-generation immigrants, have not found a place for themselves and for their own cultural expression in France, and more particularly in Marseilles. Just as Mouloud's restricted mastery of the French language epitomized his limited integration into society, the re-appropriation of the French language by the second generation is a

---

[27] *Ibid.*, 63: "For her, child of the Orient, the French language became this place where the migrant pulled to himself all his land and could finally put down his suitcases. The language of Rimbaud, of Valéry, of Char intermingle, she said. The dream of a generation of *Beurs*. In Marseilles, the French spoken was strange, a mixture of Provençal, of Italian, of Spanish, of Arabic, with a touch of slang and a pinch of *verlan*. And the kids could understand each other with that. In the street. At school and at home, it was another story altogether."

[28] *Ibid.*, 103: "After having raped her, they had no doubt made her believe that she was free. It must have excited them to see her run naked. A race towards a hope that lay at the end of the lane. At the start of the road."

sign of their capacity to find their place within a broader French identity:

> For many immigrants from former colonies, French is still perceived, even if only at an unconscious level, as a language of external domination. Traces of such anxieties are sometimes found among their children, despite their formal mastery of French and this perhaps helps to explain a frequent tendency to inflect the language in directions that de-center it. By injecting liberal doses of slang, and expressions imported from other tongues, they re-appropriate the language so as to make it perceptibly their own.[29]

The language used throughout *Total Khéops* is riddled with slang, no matter who speaks. This abundance of familiar and sometimes crude language is one of the main characteristics of the *polar* genre in France nowadays, where it seems that this vernacular makes the novel more real, or at least closer to the people it depicts. In the case of *Total Khéops*, indeed, most of the action takes place either in the *banlieues*, where *verlan* was invented, or in the underworld, where slang originated. It is thus not surprising to see such a profusion of familiar language used. But what Izzo adds to this is a profusion of references to another type of expression pertaining both to popular and youth culture, rap music. Rap is to be heard throughout the novel, mirroring the success of this musical genre in France nowadays.

Marseilles is one of the French capitals of rap, and it has seen the emergence of some of the biggest French bands of that scene, such as IAM, whose first album came out in 1988. An obvious cultural choice, according to Montale, since

> A Marseille, on tchatche. Le rap n'est rien de plus. De la tchatche, tant et plus.[30]

Musical expression, then, becomes the common denominator, one where groups without a voice can appropriate their own cultural particularities and be given a cultural space. There is another language, that transcends all nationalities and all cultures, and that is to be seen

---

[29] Hargreaves, *Immigration, "Race" and Ethnicity in Contemporary France*, 104.
[30] Izzo, *Total Khéops*, 77: "In Marseilles, we talk. That's all rap is. Talking, as much as possible."

within the very context of Marseilles, that is sung by the popular band Massilia Sound System, who first appeared in 1984 and who combine an age-old tradition, that of the *troubadours*, with reggae sounds, sung in Provençal French. Thus, the band have created a cultural expression that is both alien and common to most of their listeners, both rooted in the local tradition and in world music, and that can transcend the numerous cultural and geographical origins of their listeners. Their political overtones, obvious in the fictional political party they founded which became the name of one of their albums, the *Parti indépendantiste internationaliste marseillais*, also points to the combination of local and world identities that Marseilles boasts.

Second generation immigrants are not the only characters in *Total Khéops* who find themselves at a loss when it comes to defining themselves, not only in relation to others, but in relation to themselves. The fear and resentment that have been generated by the anti-immigration hype have resulted in a narrow definition of Frenchness, and a tendency to define oneself not according to the person one is, but rather to what one is not. This is bred by prejudice, fear and ignorance. Even Montale is not immune to this type of gut reaction. When he meets the cop from the Caribbean, the *Antillais*, for the first time he is immediately suspicious of him.

> Ces gars-là, ils se croient plus français qu'un Auvergnat. Les Arabes, c'est pas vraiment leur verre de rhum. Ni les Gitans.[31]

In other words, for a black French national, the only way of feeling accepted within the metropolitan community is to display the same base feelings towards the ethnic communities as the French, on the whole, seem to do. This is a typical stereotype that Izzo, through his narrator, uses to show how limited the sense of identity has become in contemporary France. Ethnicity, or nationality, which seem to be the defining lines for situating oneself in French society, have become the weapon of the weakest elements of society who are no longer sure what group they belong to. Thus, Varouvian, the Armenian shopkeeper, forgets his own past when he explains to Fabio why he verbally abused the young Arabs:

---

[31] *Ibid.*, 123: "Those guys think they are more French than someone from Auvergne. The Arabs are not their glass of rum. Same goes for Gypsies."

"Le centre, on dirait Alger, ou Oran. Z'y êtes allé, là-bas? Moi oui.
Vé, ça te pue pareil maintenant. Avant, tu bousculais un bougnoule
dans la rue, il s'excusait. Maintenant il te dit: 'tu peux pas t'excuser!'.
Sont arrogants, voilà c'qu'y sont! Se croient chez eux, merde."[32]

The irony of the conversation is obvious, Varouvian probably being
himself a second or third generation immigrant. But the key element
of this gut reaction is fear, the fear of being outnumbered, or overwhelmed, as the *Front National* propaganda explains so often. This
perceived threat is used to justify this type of banal racism. Fear is
what defines those who desperately need to find themselves in a society that has forgotten about them as much as about its immigrants.
Second or third generation immigrants are as guilty of this crime as
their fellow French citizens, since they also experience difficulties in
finding their place in society. When he interviews a taxi-driver of
Spanish origin, Sanchez, Fabio looks at a picture of his kids and is
immediately drawn to conclude that:

Dans leurs yeux, fuyants, aucune lueur de révolte. Des aigris de naissance. Ils n'auront de haine que pour les plus pauvres qu'eux. Et tous
ceux qui boufferont leur pain. Arabes, Noirs, Jaunes. Jamais contre les
riches. On savait déjà ce qu'ils seraient. Peu de chose. Dans le meil-
leur des cas, les garçons chauffeurs de taxi, comme papa. Et la fille,
shampouineuse. Ou vendeuse à Prisunic. Des Français moyens. Des
citoyens de la peur.[33]

Montale is a product of his generation who has grown up in ghettos
but has nevertheless succeeded in entering one of the institutions of
the French state, the police force, although he feels gradually alienated

---

[32] *Ibid.*, 60: "The city centre, you'd think it was Algiers, or Oran. You been there? I
have. Yeah, it all stinks the same now. Before, you bumped into a *bougnoule* in
the street, he apologised. Now he says: 'Can't you apologise?' They're arrogant,
that's what they are. Think they're at home. Shit."
[33] *Ibid.*, 154: "In their eyes, shifty, not the faintest glimmer of revolt. Bitter from
birth. They will only feel hatred for those poorer than themselves. And all those
who will eat their bread. Be they Arab, Black, Yellow. Never against the wealthy.
We already knew what they would become. Not much. At best, the boys would
become taxi drivers, like daddy. And the girl, a hairdresser. Or a salesgirl in
Prisunic. Average French people. Citizens of fear."

from the force he represents. As an intermediary between the state and the individual, the police force has clearly failed, in his eyes, to act as a neutral agent and is increasingly taking sides with the oppressors against the oppressed. Fabio even feels that, somehow, he has sold out, not only in relation to his school friends but also to the community and the ideals to which they aspired, being in effect an instrument of the force that coerces people out of their identity.

Obviously, Montale is the epitome of the outsider, the cynic who is aware of the corruption that surrounds him within the police force and the limitations that are being placed upon him. What seemed to interest Izzo, when he created Montale, was not so much the role of the cop as the latitude that the *polar* genre would give him to tackle the issues that were most important to him, such as the poverty and exclusion that are the lot of most of the immigrants who people his novels. This was at the heart of his project, far more than the detective plot itself. In the interview with *Lire* already mentioned, he explained that:

> Si on enlevait les digressions de mes romans, les retours en arrière, on ne trouverait qu'une fragile histoire policière qui, en elle-même, n'est pas très importante. L'essentiel, c'est le reste. Tout ce qui me tient à cœur du monde réel et du monde intime.[34]

Thus *Total Khéops* is far less a story about a cop's journey through a murder trail than a maze of fractured identities and broken destinies, a parabola of what France has become, in the eyes of Izzo, in the last years of the twentieth century: a society incapable of accepting, let alone integrating, its foreigners. A society where the Other has become, by definition, suspect and should therefore, as in any investigation, be treated as such as such – a society where the agenda of social and human relations has been subverted by unemployment and violence.

---

[34] Quoted in Ferniot, "Jean-Claude Izzo", 43: "If you were to take away the digressions of my novels, the flash-backs, you would only find a very fragile detective story which, in itself, is not very important. The essential part is all the rest. All that I hold dear of the real and intimate world."

DETECTING ETHNICITY: JAKOB ARJOUNI AND THE CASE OF THE MISSING GERMAN DETECTIVE NOVEL

ARLENE A. TERAOKA

In 1987 the German publishing world witnessed a minor miracle: the successful debut of a writer of hard-boiled detective fiction. The then twenty-three-year-old Jakob Arjouni and his remarkable protagonist, the Turkish German private eye Kemal Kayankaya, became the instant rave of crime fiction fans: with his lean style, urban realism, and wise-cracking hero, Arjouni was hailed as the long awaited German successor to Hammett and Chandler.

What makes Arjouni's success all the more intriguing is that it emerged where critics predicted it would not appear. The question of legitimacy, in fact, haunts the novel's protagonist, who is required to identify himself before a wide array of Germany's residents. Notably, their disbelief – "Privatdetektiv und Türke. Das soll ich glauben?"[1] – is aimed not only at Kayankaya's occupation but also at his German citizenship. Kayankaya, whose Turkish mother had died in childbirth, was brought as an infant to Germany by his Turkish father. His father worked for three years as a garbage collector before he was knocked-down and killed by a car; the orphan was then adopted by liberal Germans. Laden with stereotypes and, in its end, highly improbable, this brief history, recounted by the protagonist, is meant less to explain Kayankaya's identity – the meaningfulness of the category Turk with

---

[1]   Jakob Arjouni, *Mehr Bier*, Zurich: Diogenes 1991, 13: "A private investigator – and a Turk? I'm supposed to believe that?" (*More Beer*, trans. Anselm Hollo, Harpenden: No Exit Press, 1996, 9). There are three further Kayankaya novels: *Happy birthday, Türke!* (1987), *Ein Mann, ein Mord* (1991) and *Kismit* (2001), all Zurich: Diogenes. The present essay is a shortened version, prepared with Alison Guenther-Pal, of my article of the same title published in *The German Quarterly*, 72 (1999), 265-89. Translations for Arjouni's novels are taken from Hollo; all other translations are by Alison Guenther-Pal.

German citizenship – than to trace the phenomenon of his existence, however anomalous it may seem. As I argue in what follows, Kemal Kayankaya's problem of legitimacy – the utter incomprehensibility to Germans of the Turkish German private investigator as a member of their society – requires a wide field of investigation involving the genre of crime fiction, German discourses of race and nationhood, and deep-seated attitudes concerning foreignness and criminality.

I begin with the issue of detective fiction in Germany. Apparently, the genre is missing; or, more accurately, the German detective fiction that does exist is barely worthy of mention. An investigation of the scholarly literature on the topic uncovers a string of titles that bemoan this state of affairs: "Das Rätsel des deutschen Kriminalromans",[2] "Krimi – made in Germany: Literatursoziologischer Nekrolog",[3] or, my favourite, "Zu viele Stümper am Werk: Das Elend des deutschen Kriminalromans".[4] While some scholars attempt to construct a noble line of descent from Schiller's *Der Verbrecher aus verlorener Ehre* (1786) and Hoffmann's *Das Fräulein von Scuderi* (1820) to Hansjörg Martin's *Einer fehlt beim Kurkonzert* (1966) or Friedhelm Werremeier's *Hände hoch, Herr Trimmel!* (1976),[5] others excoriate contemporary German crime novelists for being sexless and pedantic[6] or in-

---

[2] Volker Ladenthin, "Das Rätsel des deutschen Kriminalromans", in *Deutsche Criminalgeschichten*, ed. Volker Ladenthin, Frankfurt am Main: Insel, 1985, 401-24 ("The Mystery of the German Detective Novel").

[3] Richard Albrecht, "Krimi – made in Germany: Literatursoziologischer Nekrolog auf den progressiven bundesdeutschen Serienkrimi", *Frankfurter Hefte*, 3 (1984), 45-54 ("Detective Novel – Made in Germany: A Socio-literary Necrology").

[4] Rainer Stephan, "Zu viele Stümper am Werk: Das Elend des deutschen Kriminalromans", *Süddeutsche Zeitung*, 29-30 October 1983 ("Too Many Hacks at Work: The Misery of the German Detective Novel"). Jochen Schmidt (*Gangster, Opfer, Detektive: Eine Typengeschichte des Kriminalromans*, Frankfurt am Main: Ullstein, 1989) delivers the widest discussion of German crime novels in the postwar period.

[5] Edgar Marsch, *Die Kriminalerzählung: Theorie, Geschichte, Analyse*, Munich: Winkler, 1983, ("The Criminal from Lost Honour", "Mademoiselle de Scudéri", "Someone's Absent from the Spa Concert", and "Hands up, Mr Trimmel!", respectively).

[6] Gabriele Dietze, "Tough Girls and Multicultural Detectives: The German Mystery Novel in the Eighties", *Clues*, XV/2 (1994), 85-97.

competent in German grammar and the basic details of ballistics and *rigor mortis*.[7]

German critics appear fond of quoting George Bernard Shaw, who purportedly claimed that Germans are incapable of two things: a successful revolution and a good crime novel.[8] The two charges, I believe, are not unrelated. Scholars generally distinguish two traditions within detective fiction.[9] One is the British variety associated most famously with Arthur Conan Doyle and Agatha Christie: the crime occurs in middle- or upper-middle-class English circles; the detective operates with scientific knowledge and superior powers of deductive reasoning to solve the mystery and to restore society to its conventional order. The other, the American hard-boiled tradition established by Hammett and Chandler, grew out of the pulp magazines of the Twenties and Thirties in a time of political corruption and economic depression: with distinctly lower-middle-class roots, the hard-boiled detective used hard language, violence, and street smarts to expose the networks that linked public politics, Mafia, and big business.

The hard-boiled private detective is typically seen as a celebration of Western individualism, of a rugged and incorruptible masculinity, of a private and puritanical moral code of male friendship, justice, honour, and sacrifice; he is part chivalric knight, part Robin Hood, part the Wild West frontier hero who (to quote Grella quoting D. H.

---

[7]   Rainer Stephan, "Zu viele Stümper am Werk"; Rudi Kost, "Masse statt Klasse? Über den neuen und den allerneuesten deutschen Kriminalroman", in *Der neue deutsche Kriminalroman: Beiträge zu Darstellung, Interpretation und Kritik eines populären Genres*, eds Karl Ermert and Wolfgang Gast, Rehburg-Loccum: Evangelische Akademie Loccum, 1985, 127-32; Wilhelm Roth, "Krise und Boom: Der neueste deutsche Kriminalroman", *Die Horen*, XXXVIII/4 (1993), 198-207.

[8]   See Dietze, "Tough Girls and Multicultural Detectives" and Ladenthin, "Das Rätsel des deutschen Kriminalromans".

[9]   For clear statements, see W. H. Auden ("The Guilty Vicarage", in *Detective Fiction: A Collection of Critical Essays*, ed. Robin W. Winks, Woodstock: Foul Play, 1988, 15-24), Peter J. Rabinowitz ("Rats behind the Wainscoting: Politics, Convention, and Chandler's *The Big Sleep*", *Texas Studies in Literature and Language*, 22 [1980], 224-45) and the essays by George Grella ("The Formal Detective Novel" and "The Hard-Boiled Detective Novel", in *Detective Fiction: A Collection of Critical Essays*, ed. Robin W. Winks, 84-102 and 103-20, and "Murder and the Mean Streets: The Hard-Boiled Detective Novel", in *Detective Fiction: Crime and Compromise*, eds Dick Allen and David Chacko, New York: Harcourt, 1974, 411-29).

Lawrence on the heroes of James Fenimore Cooper) "turns his back
on white society ... who lives by death, by killing, but who is pure
white".[10] This creates a powerfully seductive, but, at the same time,
dangerous, popular hero. The hard-boiled private eye champions the
struggle of the individual against a corrupt society; yet his violent
rebellion contains fascistic potential, a sadistic and destructive impulse
that manifests itself in his trademark racist, misogynist, and homophobic attitudes. Thus Grella points to the "perversion of the American detective novel" represented by Mickey Spillane's Mike Ham-
mer, whom he characterizes as a "totalitarian moral policeman" and
"the new superman, a plainclothes Nazi".[11] More recently, this socio-
pathic tendency in hard-boiled fiction has led Ogdon to place the
genre within the context of *Freikorps* literature as analysed by Klaus
Theweleit: the hard-boiled hero is the hard, cold, clean soldier who
battles the threat of degeneration embodied by the foreigner, the
working masses, and the "Red Whore".[12]

If two distinct tendencies, one the individualist rebellion and the
other the pseudo-fascist violence, inhabit the literary figure of the
hard-boiled detective, there are corresponding explanations for his absence in post-war Germany. It is, in fact, respect toward state authority
that defines the one variety of detective that Germans produced with
astounding success: the state-employed police inspectors of German
television. Indeed, the phenomenon of the German police inspector
has been the most enduring, and the largest, triumph of the German
television industry: *Derrick*, which drew an audience of nine million
in Germany (and half a billion internationally), broadcast its last
episode in autumn 1998 after running for more than twenty-three
years. The significance of *Derrick* and its predecessor, *Der Kommissar*, for German audiences can hardly be overestimated: with their
late-middle-aged, authoritative but benevolent paternal heroes, these
series projected a therapeutic image of post-war Germans who were

---

[10]   Grella, "Murder and the Mean Streets", 424.
[11]   *Ibid.*, 425
[12]   Bethany Ogdon, "Hard-boiled Ideology", *Critical Quarterly*, XXXIV/1 (1992),
        71-87.

disciplined, dutiful, and nonviolent.[13] In contrast, the darker, potentially fascistic hard-boiled private detective could not have offered a more undesirable alternative. In fact, the power of the taboo against a hero who would display the racist, sexist, homophobic, and violent impulses of the classic hard-boiled private eye helps to explain the nature of the main German detective fiction that emerged. Written by leftist-liberal intellectuals, informed by sociological theory, and programmatically reformist, the often boring and preachy *Sozio-Krimi* of the Seventies aimed to enlighten audiences about issues such as pollution and organ transplants.[14] Clearly, this was not fruitful ground for the hard-boiled school that pitted an individualist agent of justice and violence against a pervasively corrupt social and political hierarchy. There simply was not, nor could there be, any receptive sympathy for the violent hard-boiled loner in the cultural and ideological climate of post-war Germany.

It was not just genre conventions that legislated against the appearance of Arjouni's novels. Arjouni's Turkish German private eye is himself a figure of illegitimate standing, and this on two counts. Foremost, Turkish German as an identity category makes no sense in Germany, despite its two million permanent Turkish residents. The centuries-long conception of German nationhood anchored in an ethno-cultural identity, rooted in a unitary language, race, and culture, has remained resistant to the demographic changes brought by massive labour immigration since the late Fifties. Indeed, one of the most stubborn legacies of Germany's past has been its definition of citizenship according to the principle of *ius sanguinis*. Based in the Reich Citizenship Law of 1913 and codified in the Nuremberg Laws of 1935 – the principle of blood continued to deny full citizenship rights to second and third

---

[13] Dietze, "Tough Girls and Multicultural Detectives", 86; Harald Martenstein, *Das hat Folgen: Deutschland und seine Fernsehserien*, Leipzig: Reclam, 1996, 63, 67-68.

[14] See Matthias Schmitz and Michael Töteberg, "Mord in der Lüneburger Heide: Über -ky und andere Autoren des neuen deutschen Kriminalromans", *Basis*, 8 (1978), 174-89, 250-52; see also *Der neue deutsche Kriminalroman*, eds Karl Ermert and Wolfgang Gast.

generation Turks born and living in Germany.[15] Germany, as its political leaders have asserted, is not a country of immigration. In addition, Turks face the cultural bias, buttressed by the West's projection of Islam as its new ideological enemy, that they belong to a culture that is fundamentally and categorically different from that of Europe.[16] Even after naturalizations of foreigners increased fourfold from 1985 to 1991 as a result of relaxed requirements,[17] only a fraction of Turks – under three percent – had been granted German citizenship by 1997.[18] This political disenfranchisement, compounded by the absence of anti-discrimination and civil rights legislation, contributed to a sobering material reality: after more than thirty years in Germany, Turks were concentrated at the lowest levels of income, housing, education, vocational training, and employment, with little or no contact with Germans and little evidence of an emergent middle class or intellectual elite.[19] In light of this, Jakob Arjouni's Turk with a German

---

[15]   Rogers Brubaker, *Citizenship and Nationhood in France and Germany*, Cambridge, MA: Harvard University Press, 1992; Nora Räthzel, "Germany: One Race, One Nation?", *Race and Class*, XXXII/3 (1991), 31-48.

[16]   See, for example, remarks to this effect by former Chancellor Helmut Schmidt ("Der Teppich braucht keine neuen Flicken", *Die Zeit*, 27 January 1989, 7) or by Rudolf Augstein, editor of *Der Spiegel* ("Heilmittel 'Doppelbürger'?", *Der Spiegel*, 7 June 1993, 18).

[17]   Thomas Faist, "How to Define a Foreigner? The Symbolic Politics of Immigration in German Partisan Discourse, 1978-1992", *West European Politics*, XVII/2 (1994), 70.

[18]   "Who Should Be German, Then?", *The Economist*, 4 July 1998, 45. Mary Fulbrook ("Germany for the Germans? Citizenship and Nationality in a Divided Nation", in *Citizenship, Nationality, and Migration in Europe*, eds David Cesarani and Mary Fulbrook, London: Routledge, 1996, 88-105) lists the hurdles and deterrents to naturalization. For an overview of German naturalization law, see Detlef Bischoff and Werner Teubner (*Zwischen Einbürgerung und Rückkehr: Ausländerpolitik und Ausländerrecht der Bundesrepublik Deutschland*, Berlin: Hitit, 1992), Stefan Senders ("Laws of Belonging: Legal Dimensions of National Inclusion in Germany", *New German Critique*, 67 [1996], 147-76) and Räthzel ("Germany: One Race, One Nation?"). For more recent developments since this period, see http://www.migration-online.de.

[19]   Eva Kolinsky, "Non-German Minorities in Contemporary German Society" (71-111) and Elçin Kürsat-Ahlers, "The Turkish Minority in German Society" (113-35), both in *Turkish Culture in German Society Today*, eds David Horrocks and Eva Kolinsky, Providence: Berghahn, 1996. Both Ayşe Ş. Çağlar ("German Turks in Berlin: Social Exclusion and Strategies for Social Mobility", *New Community*, XXI/3 [1995], 309-23) and Kevin Robins and David Morley ("Almancı,

passport appeared the embodiment of a socio-political contradiction in terms.

But make the Turkish guestworker a private detective, and the incongruity approaches the absurd.[20] There is, first, a deep-seated Western stereotype of Orientals as irrational, thus as ill suited for the role of detective;[21] Turkish detectives are virtually absent in crime fiction.[22] Furthermore, within the German context, the assumed illegal status of Turkish men, who are often grouped with refugees and asylum-seekers, their projected parasitical position in the German economy, and their imagined un-Christian, brutal ways turn them into symbolic threats to bourgeois German society. The quasi-natural connection between foreignness and criminality has led in fact to the establishment of the term *Ausländerkriminalität* (foreign criminality) in German political and criminological discourse.[23] As an unassimilated, alien,

---

Yabancı", *Cultural Studies*, X/2 [1996], 248-54) insist on a more differentiated presentation of Turkish life in Germany. Zafer Şenocak (*Atlas des tropischen Deutschland*, Berlin: Babel, 1993), however, writes about the absence of developed Turkish German cultural forms and of a self-assured second generation of Turkish immigrants.

[20] John G. Cawelti makes the general observation that "one cannot write a successful adventure story about a social character type that the culture cannot conceive in heroic terms; this is why we have so few adventure stories about plumbers, janitors, or streetsweepers" (*Adventure, Mystery, and Romance: Formula Stories as Art and Popular Culture*, Chicago: University of Chicago Press, 1976, 6).

[21] See Sally R. Munt, *Murder by the Book? Feminism and the Crime Novel*, London: Routledge, 1994, 84.

[22] Kayankaya might be the first Turkish private eye in Western literature. Reeva S. Simon mentions two Turkish heroes in novels by Joan Fleming and Julian Rathbone, but neither is a private detective (*The Middle East in Crime Fiction: Mysteries, Spy Novels, and Thrillers from 1916 to the 1980s*, New York: Lilian Barber, 1989, 84-85).

[23] See Jo Reichertz and Norbert Schröer ("Beschuldigtennationalität und polizeiliche Ermittlungspraxis: Plädoyer für eine qualitative Polizeiforschung", *Kölner Zeitschrift für Soziologie und Soziolpsychologie*, 45 [1993], 755-71); Hans-Jörg Albrecht ("Ethnic Minorities, Crime, and Criminal Justice in Germany", in *Ethnicity, Crime, and Immigration: Comparative and Cross-National Perspectives*, ed. Michael Tonry, Chicago: University of Chicago Press, 1997, 31-99); and Bernhard Villmow ("Ausländerkriminalität", in *Kleines kriminologisches Wörterbuch*, eds Günther Kaiser *et al.*, Heidelberg: C. F. Müller Juristischer Verlag, 1993, 39-48). The continued use of misleading statistical data has led some scholars to argue that the notion of a foreign criminality is a strategy of social control that offers a scapegoat for the economic anxiety of Germans, a legitim-

and criminal presence in German society, foreigners (above all, Turks) would be the last people that a German audience would expect to find as agents of law and justice. Given the prevailing beliefs regarding law and order, state authority, and national identity, the Turkish German private detective hero cannot exist in German political culture: the name Kemal Kayankaya denotes an absence; it is a concept empty of content.

Central to the charge of illegitimacy levelled against Kayankaya is the implied correlative claim that true identity can be recognized. Indeed, it is this claim that makes possible both the notion of German citizenship founded on ethno-cultural origin and the detective novel as a genre. German identity, and thus the claim to citizenship, is based on family genealogy; it is treated as an isolatable fact established on the basis of official records or family artefacts; it is permanent, such that one's Germanness can survive generations of exile in another language or culture. German identity can be proven; ethnicity is capable of detection.

A similar provability of identity, an essentialist ethic, underwrites the profession of private or police investigation. Friedman argues, notably, that the detective emerges as a specialist in identities: able to penetrate disguises; to ferret out crooks; essentially to redress the problem of identity which became, with the development of big cities and the increased mobility and anonymity of immigrants and workers in the nineteenth century, a problem as such for criminal justice.[24] Thomas presents a similar reading that connects the emergence of

---

ation of repressive police practices and conservative political agendas, and a mask for the problem of German racist violence: see Peter-Alexis Albrecht ("Die strafrechtliche Auffälligkeit des 'Ausländers': Kriminologische Verarbeitung und kriminalpolitische Verwendung", *Strafverteidiger*, 6 [1990], 272-79); Jürgen Mansel ("Kriminalisierung als Instrument zur Ausgrenzung und Disziplinierung oder 'Ausländer richten ihre Kinder zum Diebstahl ab'", *Kriminalsoziologische Bibliografie*, 17 [1990], 47-65); Michael Kubink (*Verständnis und Bedeutung von Ausländerkriminalität: Eine Analyse der Konstitution sozialer Probleme*, Pfaffenweiler: Centaurus, 1993); Michael Walter and Michael Kubink ("Ausländerkriminalität – Phänomen oder Phantom der (Kriminal-)Politik?", *Monatsschrift für Kriminologie und Strafrechtsreform*, 76 [1993], 306-17). For one media example, see the feature "Zeitbomben in den Vorstädten", in *Der Spiegel*, 14 April 1997, 78-93.

[24] Lawrence M. Friedman, "True Detective", *Studies in Law, Politics and Society*, 14 (1994), 9-24.

detective fiction to national needs: Sherlock Holmes "should be understood as the literary personification of an elaborate cultural apparatus by which persons were given their true and legitimate identities by someone else";[25] thus the detective became one means by which foreignness was criminalized and the safety of the body politic and England's identity as ruler of an empire were secured.

With Thomas' arguments in particular, the function of the detective novel becomes tied to the project of state consolidation. Within the German context, the endeavour to fix the identity of individuals in a time of massive and seemingly uncontrolled border crossings is similarly implicated in the need to maintain a stable and secure notion of a German nation. In short, the discourses surrounding both the traditional detective novel genre and the concept of citizenship in Germany share at their core the anxiety on the part of citizens to uphold a sense of social and economic stability. This obsession with issues of identity and legitimacy explains a great deal about the critical and popular responses to the appearance of Arjouni's detective.

What struck me from the beginning was the obsessive attention paid to the identity of Kemal Kayankaya and, even more so, to that of his creator. As a whole, German audiences endeavoured to contain both Kayankaya and Arjouni within familiar categories. Arjouni notes, for example, the criticism his novels received from Leftists, who complained that Kayankaya was not a real Turk.[26] This also seems to have been the bone of contention that led Arjouni to dissociate himself from Doris Dörrie's film version of *Happy birthday, Türke!*. Presumably in order to make Kayankaya more authentically Turkish, Dörrie put dark contact lenses on her lead actor, inserted an affair between Kayankaya and a Turkish widow, and replaced Arjouni's depiction of economic pressures and police corruption with an emphasis on the Turks' culture shock. And if Kayankaya had to be made more recognizably – that is, less ambiguously – Turkish for certain German audiences, the identity of his creator had to be pinned down as well.

---

[25] Ronald R. Thomas, "The Fingerprint of the Foreigner: Colonizing the Criminal Body in 1890s Detective Fiction and Criminal Anthropology", *ELH*, 61 (1994), 656.

[26] See John Williams, "Down these Mean Strasse", *The Independent Weekend*, 12 November 1994.

To start with, the creator of a Turkish protagonist had to be Turkish himself, and he had to be a Turk like the one he created: Roth, for one example, explicitly conflates author and protagonist in his treatment of "Kemal/Arjouni".[27] The name Arjouni sounds exotic, Arabic or French perhaps, but not German (although neither is it unambiguously Turkish).[28] Further, Arjouni himself, who has been visible in photographs, public readings, and interviews, looks foreign with his dark curly hair and dark green eyes. Put in the least objectionable terms: neither Arjouni's name nor his appearance would lead audiences to assume that the author is German. Interviews with Arjouni take place in his favourite cafe, which bears the Turkish name "Meyhane".[29] Arjouni speaks about the Germans as though the term did not include him, of their lack of tolerance for people who look different, and of their tendency to judge others on the basis of racial and ethnic background.[30] Finally, critics believe they have found evidence for Arjouni's foreignness in the vicious wit, at times even rage, with which Kayankaya combats the everyday racism of German beer drinkers, bureaucrats, police officers, landlords, and neighbours. As Roth concludes: "So kann nur ein Underdog schreiben, ein Außenseiter, ein Fremder, ein Geschlagener."[31] We can sense in his approving statement some recognition of the Turk's hard life in Germany, an admiring solidarity with the victim who can express his pain in literary form; I am suggesting a manner of reader response here that allows German audiences to ennoble, even celebrate, the hard-boiled Turkish private eye as a victim while recasting Arjouni's biting social criticism

---

27 Wilhelm Roth, "Türke und Detektiv", *Frankfurter Rundschau*, 21 November 1987.
28 "Arjouni", if it is a name of Turkish origin, does not exhibit the expected phenomenon of vowel harmony. Thus while "Arjouni" sounds foreign to German ears, it will not sound Turkish to Turkish ones.
29 See Thomas Schmidt, "Ein Mann, ein Mord!", *Hamburger Abendblatt*, 21 September 1991.
30 Jakob Arjouni, "Besatzer sollen bleiben", Interview with Georg Hoffmann-Ostenhof and Ernst Schmiederer, *Profil*, 14 September 1992; "We Have Great Jobs and Earn Heaps of Money", Interview with Christian Seiler, *The Guardian*, 8 November 1991; "12 Fragen an Jakob Arjouni", *Playboy*, 1 November 1991.
31 Wilhelm Roth, "Türke und Detektiv": "Only an underdog can write like this – an outsider, a stranger, someone who has been beaten."

of contemporary Germany as an indictment of social injustice generally.

This manner of embracing Arjouni's novels, however, hinges on
Arjouni himself – as well as Kayankaya – being a Turk, thereby medi-
ating German audiences' identification with the victim. Therefore,
imagine the outrage of the critics when they discovered that the author
was German and the crime novels were something of a hoax.
Arjouni's real name, reportedly, is Jakob Bothe; he is claimed to be
the offspring of a high-profile liaison in the Sixties between a publisher and a playwright, the product of an elite boarding school education, with nothing in common with his protagonist except his city of
birth.[32] The revelation incited a lively attack: "Das mit dem Türken
war alles Bluff: Vom Balkan, wie er uns jahrelang weismachen wollte,
stammt ... Arjouni nicht!"[33] What is striking about the discourse of
Arjouni's critics is its fixation on the idea of legitimacy, a notion that
Arjouni has apparently betrayed: illegitimate even by birth, the author
has also transgressed the bounds of his true identity (that of a privileged and pedigreed German intellectual) by recreating himself as an
uncouth and back-talking Turk.

The pursuit of Arjouni reflects an ingrained habit to think in terms
of rigid cultural and national identities. This in turn reflects German
political discourse, in which even debates on multiculturalism concern
the optimal manner of regulating the interaction of cultures understood
as separate, stable entities.[34] There is no notion of social identity as
relational, provisional, permeable, and fluid. In this light, any labelling
of Arjouni, the establishment of his identity once and for all, serves to
reduce the provocation of his literary work: if Turkish, he fails to give
us what we expect, namely, a view of life in the minority ghetto. If he
is really German, then he has simply played a joke on us. Yet just as

---

[32] See Thomas Schmidt, "Ein Mann, ein Mord!".

[33] Eva Strasser, "Happy Birthday, Türke!", *Wiener*, 1 December 1991: "All that stuff
about the Turk was a bluff: Arjouni doesn't come from the Balkans, as he had us
believe for years!"

[34] See Sabine von Dirke, "Multikulti: The German Debate on Multiculturalism",
German Studies Review, 17 (1994), 513-36; Arlene A. Teraoka, "Multiculturalism
and the Study of German Literature", in *A User's Guide to German Cultural
Studies*, eds Scott Denham, Irene Kacandes, and Jonathan Petropoulos, Ann
Arbor: University of Michigan Press, 1997, 70-71; Thomas Faist, "How to Define
a Foreigner?", 66-68.

Kayankaya confronts us with the irreducible ambiguity of his identity, so does his creator represent a multiplicity of influences, experiences, and alliances that cannot be reduced to the simple, undifferentiated label of German, Turk, or something in between, namely hoax.[35]

The real problem is not identity *per se* but rather the way in which it is understood. The issue is not Arjouni (or Kemal Kayankaya) being German or Turkish but the very conception of identity according to essential and mutually exclusive categories. Indeed, I would suggest that the obsession with establishing the author's real identity is simultaneously a manifestation of racist thinking and an effort to avoid confronting it. Arjouni tells us quite clearly that his concern is not the identity crisis of Turks but the racism of Germans: "Es gibt keine Ausländerproblematik", Arjouni retorts, "sondern nur eine Nazi-Problematik".[36] His novels, at their core, investigate assumptions that determine the way in which Germans identify themselves and others. In doing so, they do not fix identity so much as confound it.

The Kayankaya novels tell a riveting story. In *Happy birthday, Türke!* the detective is hired by a Turkish widow to find her husband's murderer; Kayankaya discovers that the Turk had been involved in a heroin operation run by high-ranking police. *Mehr Bier* concerns a murdered German chemical industrialist and the environmental activists accused of the crime. Again Kayankaya discovers a scheme of corruption that involves police officials and politicians seeking financial and political gain. *Ein Mann, ein Mord* has Kayankaya searching for a Thai prostitute who disappeared while attempting to buy forged documents that would permit her to remain in Germany; here, too, there is a wider criminal conspiracy, a ring of embezzlers supported

---

[35] Arjouni has claimed that he grew up in a Turkish family and has friends who are Turkish, but that he is not part of the Turkish community; when pressed, he identifies himself, in explicitly non-ethnic terms, as a Frankfurter. It is also difficult to define an ethnic niche for the author by virtue of the imagined Turkishness of his material or his audience: neither does he write about or for a Turkish community, nor does Kayakaya represent a real Turk; as Arjouni insists, the one is diverse, the other, nonexistent (see John Williams, "Down these Mean Strasse").

[36] See Bettina Steiner,"Vom Dienst suspendiert: Jakob Arjouni und sein Detektiv Kayankaya", *Die Presse*, 3 November 1993; Eric Hansen, "Watching the Detectives", *Elan*, 14 June 1991: "There is no foreigner problem, only a Nazi problem."

by police and local business Mafia, all Germans, who are prominent figures in society.

Each novel has at its core a deeply personal relationship that is threatened or destroyed by the systemic crime. In *Happy birthday, Türke!*, it is the story of a Turkish immigrant who is blackmailed into selling drugs and of his hard-working son who struggles to preserve their family. In *Mehr Bier*, it is the story of the tragic love between an industrialist and his father's Polish mistress, who had sought to escape a ruined country by attaching herself to the enemy. In *Ein Mann, ein Mord*, it is the bond between a Thai prostitute and the German artist who kills to save her from her rapist. In every case, Kayankaya displays compassion for the individuals caught in a situation in which they are driven to murder. Ironically, Arjouni gives his readers the criminality that German society projects onto its minority populations. But the crimes of the foreigners – the Turkish worker, the Polish lover, the Thai prostitute – motivated by revenge or desperation, pale in comparison to the crimes perpetrated by those anchored firmly in, and protected by, German institutions.

The most compelling feature of the novels, however, lies in the constant slippage of racial and ethnic identity they display. Above all Kayankaya illustrates the absurdity of determining true origins. He speaks the local dialect and identifies with John McEnroe, champions the underdog yet beats up gays, and rages against German bureaucrats, environmentalists, neo-Nazis and student-movement Leftists alike. Though associated with images of pollution and infection, he is the agent that pursues truth. His complex and heterogeneous choices, attitudes, and actions deny an allegiance to any one identity, any one recognizable type. Moving within a German environment shot through with racial and social stereotypes, Kayankaya embodies, rather, a distinctly foreign notion of identity, one based on impurity and trans-formation.

At one point, for example, Kayankaya takes the place of an illegal immigrant who is to be deported on the next flight to Beirut. His ex-aggerated performance plays on German stereotypes of Muslim men and becomes for that reason totally convincing to the immigration police: Kayankaya babbles on about his twenty-seven wives; he ogles the female immigration officer, makes lewd remarks about the size of his penis, and offers to fuck her in the time remaining before his flight.

What is astounding is that the officials never see through his farce but accept him unquestioningly as an illegal alien.[37]

Another hilarious scene has Kayankaya in a small town asking directions from a German man who is scrubbing the licence plate of his BMW with a toothbrush. The German tries to shoo Kayankaya away in the broken speech imagined to be the language of Germany's foreigners – "Nix brauchen, nix kaufen!".[38] Kayankaya responds, asking whether the friend with the rubber feet and the pipe up its ass has cavities or just bad breath. The German continues to repeat, more loudly each time, his four words of broken German; only after Kayankaya threatens to spit into his tulip beds does he provide the directions that were requested. Kayankaya leaves with thanks and a cheerful word of encouragement:

> Und immer schön Deutsch lernen. Man fühlt sich ja gar nicht mehr wie zu Hause.[39]

The Turkish German reveals himself to be a master of German stereotypes. He effortlessly assumes the posture, language, and attitudes of the foreign male as envisioned by Germans – an uncivilized, disorderly, immoral brute. And with sadistic wit, he also shows that he knows what it takes to be German: in this case, by usurping the role of the German and making him seem the speaker of the guestworker idiom. Kayankaya essentially claims German identity and a German home: what is needed, he shows us, are a certain set of consumerist choices, certain racist attitudes, general ignorance about anything non-German, and, above all, the assumption that people who look different and speak differently threaten the integrity of the German home for its rightful inhabitants. By taking Germans at their word – by adopting, mimicking, and mirroring their attitudes about both themselves and foreigners, Kayankaya proves his own command of Germanness while, at the same time, debunking the notion of Germanness. The

---

[37]   Jakob Arjouni, *Ein Mann, ein Mord*, 125-27 (*One Man, One Murder*, trans. Anselm Hollo, Harpenden: No Exit Press, 1996).

[38]   *Ibid.*, 69: "No need nothing, no buy nothing!" (*One Man, One Murder*, 62)

[39]   *Ibid.*, 69-70: "And keep on studying your German. There are times, these days, when the place feels like a foreign country" (*One Man, One Murder*, 63)

essence of Germanness, it turns out, is a set of stereotypes and be-
haviours. Kayankaya quips:

> Kein Problem für mich. Ich mähe meinen Rasen, lache bei Karneval
> und kann gleichzeitig Bier trinken und Skat spielen. Irgendwo hinter
> München liegt Afrika, da wohnen die Neger. Bei der Sportschau
> möchte ich nicht gestört werden. Mein Couchgarnitur ist pünktlich
> abbezahlt. Und im Grunde meines Herzens bin ich ein tanzender
> Schlesier.[40]

In effect, the deliberate and exaggerated adoption of such notions of
home and national identity works to expose German racism in ironic
fashion. For if Kayankaya, who was brought up by Germans, who
attended a German law school, who speaks Hessian dialect and
Hochdeutsch (standard German) and not Turkish, who moves so
masterfully within German society that he polices it, can still be seen
as not German, then the difference can lie only in his skin colour, his
name, and the assumptions they provoke. Kayankaya is a walking
indictment of policies that claim to support the naturalization of non-
Germans on condition of their cultural assimilation; through him we
see the continued non-acceptance of others on condition of their race.

From the point of view of the Germans in Arjouni's novels, Kayankaya is Turkish, yet his mastery of German customs and attitudes and
his lack of any ties to Turkish language and culture and to a Turkish
family confound this view; at the same time, he cannot, purely on the
basis of his name and appearance, be really German. In a political discourse that conflates culture, race, and national identity, Kayankaya is
a multiple contradiction in terms: he gives the lie both to the accepted
notion of what it is to be German and to the belief in fixed racial categories; by infusing them with irreconcilable elements, he demonstrates their unenforceability.

---

[40] Jakob Arjouni, *Mehr Bier*, 20: "No problem. I mow my lawn, I laugh a lot during
the carnival season, and I manage to drink beer and play skat at the same time.
Somewhere past Munich lies Africa, that's where the Negroes live. I hate inter-
ruptions during sportscasts. My three-piece suite has been paid for. And I'm really
a dancing Silesian at heart" (*More Beer*, 17)

The teeth in Arjouni's work – what makes his detective novels memorable and important, I would argue – are rooted in the genial creation of Kemal Kayankaya, the Turkish German detective hero who is delegitimized by the traditions and conventions of German literature, German crime and law enforcement, and German citizenship law. Throughout Arjouni's novels, Kayankaya faces the constant demand, whether explicitly stated or not, that he prove his legitimacy, his authenticity, his legality, and his competence as a private investigator, as a Turk, and as a German citizen. Yet the question of legitimacy is answered not in its own terms but by the irreducible fact of Kayankaya's existence as a German with the name, physical appearance, and race of a Turk. The significance of Arjouni's novels is that they exist where they should not be; they outsmart the question of essence; they insist not on what one is, but on the fact that one exists – "Ich bin's eben".[41] Thus a young crime writer puts before his audience a figure of honour and merit where previously only the fraud had been projected. In embodying the contradictions within German conceptions of racial and national identity, Kayankaya exposes a fundamental crime: the policing of rigid boundaries separating Turk from German. The cult popularity and the scandal of Jakob Arjouni's crime series lie in Kayankaya's example of a new notion of ethnicity defined by its transgressive, investigatory adventures.

My essay has been concerned broadly with the problem of the hard-boiled detective genre and its connections to German discourses of identity. That the two issues should come together is hardly coincidence. I would end with the suggestion that there is indeed a generic connection between the problem of ethnicity and the project of the private detective. The true mystery of the detective novel genre, Most writes, is the nature of the detective himself: he is a figure without origins, without a past, without family, a figure defined by his freedom from all categories, a figure constantly in motion and never at home.[42] As a liminal figure defined by his pursuit of an impossible ideal (truth, justice), the detective himself can be seen as the embodi-

---

[41]   Jakob Arjouni, *Mehr Bier*, 13: "I just am" (*More Beer*, 9)
[42]   Glenn W. Most, "The Hippocratic Smile: John le Carré and the Traditions of the Detective Novel", in *The Poetics of Murder: Detective Fiction and Literary Theory*, eds Glenn W. Most and William W. Stowe, San Diego: Harcourt, 1983, 342-45.

ment of the contemporary problem of ethnicity. The truth he desires – a satisfactory justice, moral and legal clarity, an irreducible certainty of identity – will prove more often than not to be unattainable; indeed, ambiguity and lack of clarity are what make the hard-boiled detective genre what it is. The very absence of this notion of ambiguity and indefinability in discussions of ethnicity in Germany explains also the absence of the hard-boiled private eye in German culture – the case of the missing detective novel is linked to the case of the missing notion of a fluid ethnicity. Friedman notes that, historically, the figure of the detective as well as the genre of detective fiction were brought about by a "fluid, restless, mobile social system, with endless possibilities for false identity [and] mysterious origins".[43] Conversely, the fact that this mobility was unthinkable in the Germany of the Nineties impaired both an adequate understanding of the dynamics of ethnicity and the adventures of a truly hard-boiled German private eye.

---

[43]   Lawrence M. Friedman, "True Detective".

DOUBLE IDENTITY: HARD-BOILED DETECTIVE FICTION AND THE DIVIDED "I"

JOHN SCAGGS

Raymond Chandler once said that if he ever wrote a non-fiction book, "it would probably turn out to be the autobiography of a split personality".[1] Critics often attribute the division evident in the figure of the private investigator Philip Marlowe to a division in Chandler's own personality, the result (or so this line of argument claims) of his oscillation between American and English culture.[2] Paul Skenazy notes, in the introduction to *Raymond Chandler Speaking*, that Chandler "was a man of two continents, two centuries, and two languages".[3] He was born in Chicago in 1888, his father from Pennsylvania and his mother an Irish immigrant from Waterford. At the age of seven he went with his mother to live in London, where he was educated. He published poems, reviews, and essays in several London literary magazines, but in 1912 he gave up literature and returned to the United States.

Chandler returned to writing in 1932, after twenty years in the world of business. He turned to the tough-guy private eye stories of magazines such as *Black Mask*, and adopted the clipped, colloquial tone of the genre, a tone in stark contrast to the elaborate literary style he had employed in his earlier writings in England. In a letter dated 18 March 1949, Chandler says, "I had to learn American just like a foreign language",[4] and the division implied in such a comment is also

---

[1] Paul Skenazy, "Introduction", in *Raymond Chandler Speaking*, eds Dorothy Gardiner and Kathrine Sorley Walker, Berkeley: University of California Press, 1997, 1.
[2] Ralph Willett, *Hard-Boiled Detective Fiction*, BAAS Pamphlets in American Studies, 23, Staffordshire British Association for American Studies, 1992, 16.
[3] Skenazy, "Introduction", in *Raymond Chandler Speaking*, 1.
[4] *Raymond Chandler Speaking*, 80.

evident in the hard-boiled narrative voice of the P.I. Philip Marlowe that Chandler created.

The conventional first-person narrative of hard-boiled detective fiction, by privileging the voice of the P.I., suggests an element of monological control to the narrative that is often undermined by the merely partial understanding, or local effectiveness, that the P.I. frequently achieves.[5] Furthermore, as Stephen Knight observes, Marlowe's voice is really two voices: an insightful, ironic narrative voice, and a terse, aggressive dialogic voice. According to Knight, "the voice of Marlowe's reverie, both subtle and ironic, is quite different from the voice he uses to other characters". In the guise that he wears in his dealings with others, he is tough and insensitive – the typical hard-boiled detective. However, Knight observes that the divided voice evident in Marlowe's narratives "creates a double man",[6] and this double identity is reflected in other ways in Chandler's novels, and in contemporary American hard-boiled detective fiction in general.

If we view Marlowe's tough talk as a form of protracted disguise, as a form of language as power, which, as Scott R. Christianson observes, asserts his individuality,[7] then the presence of disguised or altered identity as a central motif in hard-boiled detective fiction should come as no surprise. In fact, it rarely surprises Marlowe when he encounters it in the characters, both clients and villains, who populate his narratives. As Liahna Babener notes, "virtually every one of Chandler's seven novels pivots on a case of mistaken, disguised, or altered identity".[8] Examples range from Mildred Haviland in *The Lady in the Lake* (1944), who adopts a new role every time her existing alias comes under threat, to Terry Lennox in *The Long Goodbye* (1953), who adopts a series of fake identities in an attempt to escape from, and eradicate, a tortuous past. However, it is not only the inhabitants of Marlowe's narrative world that cast aside and re-invent

---

[5] Willett, *Hard-Boiled Detective Fiction*, 9.

[6] Stephen Knight, "'A Hard Cheerfulness': An Introduction to Raymond Chandler", in *American Crime Fiction: Studies in the Genre*, ed. Brian Doherty, London: Macmillan, 1998, 81.

[7] Scott R. Christianson, "Tough Talk and Wisecracks: Language as Power in American Detective Fiction", *Journal of Popular Culture*, 23 (1989) 155.

[8] Liahna Babener, "Raymond Chandler's City of Lies", in *Los Angeles in Fiction: A Collection of Essays*, ed. David Fine, Albuquerque: University of New Mexico Press, 1995, 128.

their identities. In Los Angeles, home of Hollywood, where, as Skenazy notes, "you are what you appear to be [and] to act is to become a person",[9] Marlowe himself plays roles. According to Babener, he is "a man of many faces", a man who "plays the tough guy or the pushover, the sharper or the dimwit as circumstances dictate. He invents aliases to broaden his range of action."[10]

In this artificial world of costumes, make-up, and make-believe, Marlowe, as a "double man", plays a dual role. He is an observer, the Private Eye who attempts to see through the facades that the other characters present to him, but he is also the Private "I", the individual self who, in order to solve the crime, hides his true motivation and identity behind a tough-talking mask. This mask, in turn, wears its own masks, like that of Doghouse Reilly in *The Big Sleep* (1939), or the bungling bibliophile alias that Marlowe creates in order to infiltrate a pornographic book-store in the same novel. It is this duality that characterizes not only the private eye Philip Marlowe, but the figure of the private eye in general. Through an examination of the novels of Walter Mosley and Tony Hillerman, it will be established that the hard-boiled detective in contemporary American fiction is always, in one sense or another, a "double agent".

Devil in a Blue Dress (1990), the first novel in Mosley's *Easy Rawlins* cycle, offers a knowing inversion of the opening of Chandler's *Farewell, My Lovely* (1940). In Chandler's novel, Marlowe, the white detective, is in a black neighbourhood, or, more specifically, "one of the mixed blocks over on Central Avenue".[11] He enters a black bar with Moose Molloy, who is searching for his old sweetheart, and Molloy subsequently hires Marlowe to track her down. In Mosley's novel, a white man, Dewitt Albright, enters a black bar in Watts looking for somebody who can track down a white woman, Daphne Monet, known to associate with the musicians of the Watts nightclub scene. The agent of this transgression, and Easy's reaction to it, are described as follows:

---

[9]   Paul Skenazy, "Behind the Territory Ahead", in *Los Angeles in Fiction*, 116.
[10] Babener, "Raymond Chandler's City of Lies", in *Los Angeles in Fiction*, 141.
[11] Raymond Chandler, "Farewell, My Lovely", in *Three Novels*, Harmondsworth: Penguin, 1993, 167.

> I was surprised to see a white man walk into Joppy's bar. It's not just
> that he was white but he wore an off-white linen suit and shirt with a
> Panama straw hat and bone shoes over flashing white silk socks. His
> skin was smooth and pale with just a few freckles. One lick of
> strawberry-blond hair escaped the band of his hat. He stopped in the
> doorway, filling it with his large frame, and surveyed the room with
> pale eyes.[12]

The excessively white (as his name suggests) Albright stops "in the
doorway" of Joppy's bar, highlighting his inability to cross completely
what W. E. B. DuBois in *The Souls of Black Folks* terms "the color
line",[13] a term echoed in *White Butterfly* by Easy Rawlins.[14] What
Albright seeks in Easy is a kind of double agent capable of crossing
that line, someone "able to manage the liminal spaces between black
and white culture",[15] the very spaces that his own excessive whiteness
prohibits him from navigating.

This double agent pattern recurs throughout the Easy Rawlins
novels. In *White Butterfly*, Easy sums up his situation: "Every once in
a while the law sent over one of their few black representatives to ask
me to go into the places where they could never go."[16] These places
are the social spaces of the black community that Easy himself inhabits, the bars, clubs, churches, pool halls, and whorehouses of the
ghetto that he enters in order to act as a representative for those, like
Albright in *Devil in a Blue Dress*, who cannot. Working for Albright,
Easy enters the black world of ghetto jazz clubs to look for Daphne
Monet, a mulatto whose real name is Ruby Hanks, but who successfully passes herself off as white, her double identity fooling even the
double agent Easy. "I looked at her to see the truth", says Easy, "But it
wasn't there. Her nose, her cheeks, her skin color – they were white.
Daphne was a white woman."[17] In *Black Betty*, Easy is hired by Saul
Lynx, another white man, to find a missing black woman, the Black
Betty of the novel's title, because Easy is, as Saul says, "known for

---

[12]   Walter Mosley, *Devil in a Blue Dress*, London: Pan, 1992, 9.
[13]   W. E. B. DuBois, *The Souls of Black Folks*, New York: St Martin's Press, 1997.
[14]   Walter Mosley, *White Butterfly*, London: Serpent's Tail, 1992, 17.
[15]   Gilbert H. Muller, "Double Agent: The Los Angeles Crime Cycle of Walter
       Mosley", in *Los Angeles in Fiction*, 287.
[16]   Mosley, *White Butterfly*, 10.
[17]   Mosley, *Devil in a Blue Dress*, 205.

finding people in the colored part of town".[18] In *White Butterfly*, Easy's services are retained by the Los Angeles Police Department to search for a multiple murderer who is killing black good-time girls.

The focus of the investigation changes, however, when one of the victims breaks the pattern. She is Robin Garnett, a conservative, preppy, University College of Los Angeles coed. Easy's investigations reveal, however, that she has been living a double life as one Cyndi Starr, The White Butterfly, a stripper who lives in the black community of the ghetto. Easy also lives a double life, and Mosley himself, in his essay "The Black Dick", discusses Easy's double nature:

> Now when Easy gets around white people they may be afraid of him, but they never suspect that he has the smarts of some kind of agent trying to glean their secrets. Turn the coin over: when Easy comes into a bar or church in the Watts community everybody thinks they know by his colour that no white man would trust him with a mission. Easy has become invisible by virtue of his skin.[19]

However, as the novels make clear, it is not just the colour of Easy's skin that makes him invisible. On the contrary, Easy is always conscious of racist perspectives, as when, fighting an urge to run in *Devil in a Blue Dress*, he observes that "a patrol car would arrest any sprinting Negro they encountered" (83). In *White Butterfly*, the black policeman Quinten Naylor is, in contrast, too white to do the job that he asks Easy to do. As Easy says, "the black people didn't like him because he talked like a white man and he had a white man's job" (20).

While Easy's invisibility stems from the colour of his skin, his own comments on this invisibility suggest a further element to it. Reflecting on his first experiences of working as a private eye in *Devil in a Blue Dress*, Easy tells himself that "Nobody knew what I was up to and that made me sort of invisible; people thought that they saw me but what they really saw was an illusion of me, something that wasn't real" (135). Here, Easy identifies the duality of identity evident in Marlowe's two voices in the novels of Raymond Chandler, and it is this duality, coupled as it is with his racial invisibility that allows Easy

---

[18]   Walter Mosley, *Black Betty*, London: Serpent's Tail, 1994, 7.
[19]   Walter Mosley, "The Black Dick", in *Critical Fictions: The Politics of Imaginative Writing*, ed. Philomena Mariani, Seattle: Bay Press, 1991, 133.

to function as a double agent in the multicultural world of mid-century Los Angeles.

Like Marlowe, Easy has two voices. In *Devil in a Blue Dress*, he admits that: "I always tried to speak proper English in my life, the kind of English they taught in school, but I found over the years that I could only truly express myself in the natural, 'uneducated' dialect of my upbringing" (17). But Easy is different from Marlowe, in that the voice that Easy employs in his engagement with the external world is rarely stable. As Gilbert Muller observes, Easy shifts "linguistic gears" to suit his environment.[20] In particular, his voice changes in the white environments that his cultural investigations demand that he enter, in order to hide what Mosley terms "the smarts" that white people do not expect of him. Sometimes, however, Mosley's shifting of "linguistic gears" is unintentional, an internalized survival mechanism learned through everyday life in a racist environment.[21] When Easy, in *Devil in a Blue Dress*, goes to call on Albright in a white area of the city "a long drive from Watts" (13), a white porter answers the door and asks Easy who he is looking for. More than simply shifting linguistic gears to compensate for the environment, Easy's voice stalls almost completely:

> "I'm looking for, um … ah …", I stuttered. I forgot the name. I had to squint so that the room wouldn't start spinning. (21)

In the exchange that follows, in which the porter accuses Easy of being a thief, Easy's anger allows him to reassert control over himself, and the voice we hear as it shifts gears from the proper English of his first-person narrative, is more typical of the street voice that he often employs in dialogue, depending on the situation that he is in:

> I was disgusted. "Forget it man", I said. "You just tell him, when you see him, that Mr Rawlins was here. You tell him that the next time he

---

[20]   Muller, "Double Agent", in *Los Angeles in Fiction*, 294.
[21]   Liam Kennedy, "Black *Noir*: Race and Urban Space in Walter Mosley's Detective Fiction", in *Criminal Proceedings: The Contemporary American Crime Novel*, ed. Peter Messent, London: Pluto Press, 1997, 54.

better give me a note because you cain't be lettin' no niggahs comin' in yo' place wit' no notes!"[22]

Easy's voice changes not only in relation to his circumstances, but also in relation to his mood, as an older, and more self-aware Easy observes in *A Little Yellow Dog* (1996). According to Easy, "my language got closer to the street as I got angrier".[23] Easy's linguistic camouflage is often accompanied by his adoption of various aliases. In *A Little Yellow Dog* he presents himself to various different people under various different identities. At one point he is one Arlen Coleman, at another, Brad Koogan, "a name", as he admits, "borrowed from a friend who died at the Battle of the Bulge" (89). In *White Butterfly*, when he calls on the mother of the murder suspect, he calls himself Martin Greer, while earlier in the novel he is one Roger Stockton, an alias complete with a fake Korean War past, an imaginary war wound, and a "smile that would have gotten [him] elected, if [he] was a white man" (162). In each case, the name suggests an identity, as when the man who Easy is questioning in *A Little Yellow Dog* comments that Brad Koogan sounds "like a white man's name" (43), which, of course, it is.

In the same way that the aliases Easy adopts create multiple, albeit short-term, alternative identities, in particular in conjunction with his linguistic camouflage, so too is the name Ezekiel "Easy" Rawlins evidence of a fundamentally divided identity. Mr Ezekiel Rawlins, in *A Red Death* (1991), is an honest workingman, "versed in floor waxes and bleach – not blood".[24] However, as Easy himself wryly observes on occasion, as in *A Little Yellow Dog*, there is a constant struggle between his respectable identity in "the workaday world" (217), and his identity as the street-wise man of action, Easy Rawlins, Easy being his name "before [he] became a respectable workingman" (70). His workaday identity is characterized by a steady income, his family, and his property, in particular the ownership of the house in which he lives. His street identity, on the other hand, is characterized by violence, womanizing, and hard drinking, all of which threaten what he values most in the workaday world.

[22] Mosley, *Devil in a Blue Dress*, 22.
[23] Walter Mosley, *A Little Yellow Dog*, London: Picador, 1997, 8.
[24] Walter Mosley, *A Red Death*, London: Pan, 1993, 1.

Easy therefore goes to great lengths not just to hide, but to suppress his street identity, and to hide his identity as a self-employed property owner that his street identity has given him. He poses as a janitor and handyman on his own properties, as in the opening of *A Red Death*, while his associate Mofass collects the rent for a fictitious "white lady downtown" (14). The fictitious white lady even has a suitably white name: Mrs Davenport. He reprises the role in *White Butterfly* when a consortium of businessmen approach Mofass with the intention of buying what they assume to be his property. Easy often refers to himself in this subservient role in the third person, thereby highlighting this duality of identity, as he does in *A Little Yellow Dog* when, in particular situations, he acts "as if [he] were just a poor peasant afraid of a world that [he] could barely comprehend" (67).

Easy, however, is well aware of the effect that such role-playing has. When he observes, in *Devil in a Blue Dress*, that "what [people] really saw was an illusion of me, something that wasn't real" (135), he is thinking primarily of the advantages that this has for his job as a private investigator. In his private life, however, it has a negative effect. It causes the failure of his marriage in *White Butterfly*, but paradoxically it guarantees his survival, for, as he observes in *A Little Yellow Dog*, "where I came from you kept everything a secret – survival depended on keeping the people around you in the dark" (17). Keeping those around him in the dark, and thereby protecting them by protecting himself, also alienates Easy from them, and this alienation, which springs from his dual identity, is further compounded by his crossing of the colour line. Easy, as Muller observes, is "a double agent attempting to help people in his own community but also serving paradoxically the ends of white representatives who more often than not precipitate evil and destruction",[25] and this paradoxical position compounds not only Easy's alienation, but the alienation that is typical of the private eye/I in contemporary hard-boiled detective fiction.

Easy's attempts to serve his community, the black community of Watts, while simultaneously serving the ends of white representatives whose machinations threaten the stability of that black community, echoes a similar situation in Chandler's novels. As Willett observes,

---

[25]   Muller, "Double Agent", in *Los Angeles in Fiction*, 295.

"Marlowe's appeal is that he satisfies a populist disdain for authority while continuing to work for law and order thereby aligning himself with its agencies".[26] In the novels of Tony Hillerman there is an inversion of the detective's characteristic hostility towards the forces of law and order, and his simultaneous alliance with those forces. Peter Messent identifies a shift from the private-eye novel to the police procedural in contemporary crime fiction,[27] and the figures of Officer Jim Chee and Lieutenant Joe Leaphorn, members of the Navajo Tribal Police Force who feature in Hillerman's novels, would seem to be an example of this changing perspective. Often, Leaphorn and Chee "professionally uphold laws unrelated to, or in conflict with, Navajo sensibility and culture".[28] However, as David Murray observes, the question for Jim Chee "is how to reconcile laws with his instinct and his sense of what is right",[29] and both officers, according to Willett, "bend the law in order to bring about justice".[30] Thus the division evident in Marlowe and Rawlins also surfaces in Hillerman's novels.

Leaphorn, in Willett's view, is "a cross-cultural figure, a participant in the contemporary crime-fighting world of short wave radios and pickup trucks, and the contemporary Amerindian world of poverty, alcoholism and white racism". Unlike Jim Chee, and despite the fact that his grandfather was a singer of curing rituals, Leaphorn's interest in Navajo folklore "is professional and academic",[31] having studied anthropology in university. This university background allows Leaphorn, as Murray observes, "to 'read' both [his] own and other cultures",[32] and his investigations are thus a form of interpretation, the cultures that he moves through becoming, in turn, texts to be interpreted. However, as both observer of, and inhabitant in, these cultural texts, Leaphorn becomes both the analysing subject, and the analysed object. As both the agent of the interpretative act, and the object of the interpretation, he is, literally, a double agent.

---

[26] Willett, *Hard-Boiled Detective Fiction*, 16.
[27] Messent, "Introduction", in *Criminal Proceedings*, 2.
[28] Willett, *Hard-Boiled Detective Fiction*, 48.
[29] David Murray, "Reading the Signs: Detection and Anthropology in the Work of Tony Hillerman", in *Criminal Proceedings*, 142.
[30] Willett, *Hard-Boiled Detective Fiction*, 47.
[31] *Ibid.*, 48-49.
[32] Murray, "Reading the Signs", in *Criminal Proceedings*, 142.

Leaphorn's investigative technique, in its fusion of *Belacani* (white) police procedure and *Dinee* (Navajo) beliefs, further exposes this duality. His approach is a logical one, depending, as outlined in *The Blessing Way* (1970), on "the natural sequence of behaviour; the cause producing the natural effect".[33] However, this logical approach is based on the Navajo Way, as taught to Leaphorn by his grandfather, Hosteen Nashibitti, and described in *Dance Hall of the Dead* (1973):

> Interdependency of nature. Every cause has its effect. Every action its reaction. A reason for everything. In all things a pattern, and in this pattern, the beauty of harmony.[34]

This fusion is further evident in Leaphorn's dealings with the *Dinee* inhabitants of the Navajo Reservation. In *The Blessing Way*, Leaphorn is questioning Sandoval, an older, traditional Navajo about the activities of a Navajo witch, although, as Murray observes, he "personally regards [it] as a destructive and irritating superstition".[35] In this novel, in his questioning, however, Leaphorn follows "the old and patient ways", aware that it is the best way to find the information that he needs, although a negative remark about these witchcraft beliefs immediately causes Sandoval to wonder "if the young man [Leaphorn] believed in witches. The policeman had a white man's haircut".[36] Thus, in the old man's view, Leaphorn is just what Leaphorn has described another character earlier in the novel as being, "another poor soul who didn't quite know how to be a Navajo and couldn't learn to act like a white".[37]

These "poor souls" are often identified by their inability to speak Navajo, the language of their birth, if not of their upbringing. In *The Ghostway* (1984), Leroy Gorman is at least part Navajo, but his inability to speak Navajo points to a cultural division highlighted by the double identity implied by his position in a Witness Protection Pro-

---

[33] Tony Hillerman, *The Blessing Way: The Leaphorn Mysteries*, Harmondsworth: Penguin, 1994, 129.
[34] Tony Hillerman, *Dance Hall of the Dead: The Leaphorn Mysteries*, Harmondsworth: Penguin, 1994, 221-22.
[35] Murray, "Reading the Signs", in *Criminal Proceeding*, 129.
[36] Hillerman, *The Blessing Way*, 60-61.
[37] *Ibid.*, 46.

gramme, living a half-life under the name of Grayson.[38] Similarly, language is an important cultural marker for Leaphorn and Chee, but whereas Leaphorn often uses Navajo to infiltrate *Dinee* culture and disguise his *Belacani* police officer motives, as in the above example in *Dance Hall of the Dead*, Chee is sometimes forced to deny his *Dinee* heritage in his role as a police officer (and in his relationship with the Anglo girl Mary Landon) by refusing to speak Navajo. In *People of Darkness* (1980), Chee is forced to "[stick] to English"[39] when questioning another Navajo because of Mary Landon's presence.

If Joe Leaphorn, in his role as a cross-cultural figure, is a divided figure, then Jim Chee is doubly so. Like Leaphorn, he has studied anthropology, and therefore is capable of reading his own, and other, cultures. However, unlike Leaphorn, Chee's interest in Navajo folklore is more than professional and academic. He is more religious than the sceptical Leaphorn, and is studying to be a *yataalii*, or ceremonial singer. Unlike Leaphorn he finds it difficult to reconcile *Dinee* and *Belacani* culture. When Chee discovers, in *The Ghostway*, that there is a roster of Navajo singers, his reaction to this discovery underlines his difficulty in reconciling his two cultural identities:

> It would be useful to any policeman. And even while he was thinking that, another part of his consciousness was shocked and dismayed. So few names. (256)

In *People of Darkness*, Chee has applied for admission to the Federal Bureau of Investigation, but constantly defers his interview date. His soon-to-be girlfriend, Mary Landon, asks him if he can be, "both a Navajo medicine man and an FBI agent", to which he replies, "'Not really', while he inwardly tells himself, 'You can't be a Navajo away from the People'" (108), thus providing an answer for each culture. In *The Ghostway* we find him, like Marlowe in *Farewell, My Lovely*, and like Dewitt Albright in *Devil in a Blue Dress*, at a liminal point between two cultures. As part of an investigation, Chee must enter a *hogan* (a Navajo dwelling) where somebody has died. However, according to Navajo custom, it is a place of death, and the *chindi*, or

---

[38]   Tony Hillerman, *The Ghostway*, New York: Harper Collins, 1992, 241.
[39]   Tony Hillerman, *People of Darkness*, New York: Harper Collins, 1991, 190.

ghost, associated with that place, must be avoided. Hillerman, as Murray observes,[40] uses the conflict between Chee's duties as a policeman and his beliefs as a Navajo *yataalii* to examine the further reaching divisions of Chee's character:

> At one level of his intellect it seemed a trivial thing .... To the Jim Chee who was an alumnus of the University of New Mexico ... an officer of the Navajo Tribal Police, lover of Mary Landon ... student of anthropology and sociology ... holder of Social Security card 441-28-7272, it was a logical step to take .... How could his logical mind justify not searching it?
>
> But "Jim Chee" was only what his uncle would call his "white man name." His real name, his secret name, his war name, was Long Thinker, given him by Hosteen Frank Sam Nakai, the elder brother of his mother and one of the most respected singers among Four Corners Navajos.[41]

Stepping into the death *hogan* is also, in Chee's mind, "stepping through into the white man's world",[42] the world of social security numbers, of universities, and of law enforcement.

The cultural division suggested by this passage is also indicative of a division of self-identity, a division that is often highlighted in other characters in the novels, such as Gorman/Grayson in *The Ghostway*, or, more emphatically, in the figure of B. J. Vines in *People of Darkness*, where a division between Vines' early life, and his life "after he struck it rich" (237), is evidence of a division much deeper than one based on wealth, and involving a re-invention of his identity that is typical of the novels of Chandler. In this re-invention, the geologist Lebeck fakes his death, and gives his new self a new name: B. J. Vines. Similarly, like Easy Rawlins, Jim Chee has two names, his "white man name", and his *Dinee* name, Long Thinker. For Chee, as he states in *People of Darkness*, this name is "his real and secret identity" (85), the Private "I" that is the product of the distinction between seeing and being seen already identified in relation to Marlowe and Rawlins. However, as Chee is an officer of the Navajo Tribal Police, the private eye, or private investigator aspect of this binary actually

---

[40] Murray, "Reading the Signs", in *Criminal Proceedings*, 135.
[41] Hillerman, *The Ghostway*, 51-52.
[42] *Ibid.*, 64.

becomes a public eye, or public investigator. In this way, the "generic shift" to the police procedural identified by Peter Messent in contemporary crime fiction, which he claims has been prompted by a recognition of the ineffectuality of "the marginal position and limited perspective of the P.I. hero or heroine",[43] actually serves to highlight the division between the private self and the public self, and therefore in turn also highlights the effectiveness of the marginal position and limited perspective of the P.I., either public, or private.

The P.I., as either private investigator or public officer, is a deeply divided figure. His loyalties are divided between the public and the private domain. His voice is similarly divided between these two domains, either through the use of the first-person narrative typical of the genre, or through the cultural division evident in a bilingual or multilingual society. He moves backwards through time in search of a resolution to the events unfolding in the present, and finally he often adopts either cultural or linguistic disguises to move through the multicultural environment in which he must operate. The procedures employed by the P.I. in his or her search to make sense of events, or to restore balance and order, therefore depend paradoxically on the division of the self. This division, however, is not merely cultural, but more fundamentally, it is linguistic. The detective's narrative quest is motivated by the desire to restore a lost unity, such as the harmony of the Navajo way, but ironically it is the presence of the detective in his own narrative that ultimately makes this unity impossible.

---

[43] Messent, "Introduction", in *Criminal Proceedings*, 2.

PLUM'S THE GIRL! JANET EVANOVICH AND THE EMPOWERMENT OF MS COMMON AMERICA

THEO D'HAEN

In this essay, I will discuss Janet Evanovich's Stephanie Plum series – thirteen instalments to date, from *One for the Money* in 1994 to *Lean Mean Thirteen* in 2007,[1] and undoubtedly many more to follow – in the light of some recent theorizing on American crime writing, and particularly on the various forms of empowerment involved.

For a long time, crime writing in general and detective fiction in particular were regarded as merely escapist forms of popular literature, as cheap entertainment for the masses, unworthy of serious consideration, or, worse, as distractions on the road to the cultured appreciation of true or good Literature. In recent years, though, the insight has dawned that, just like its more glamorous high literary counterpart, popular literature too can do what Jane Tompkins has memorably termed "cultural work".[2] Tompkins coined the term primarily with regard to a nineteenth-century American popular genre, sentimental domestic fiction, written by and for women. Specifically, she argued that this kind of writing, rather than the mere drivel it was branded as by contemporary male writers, actually constituted a form of female empowerment. Sean McCann, in *Gumshoe America: Hard-Boiled*

---

[1] Janet Evanovich, *One for the Money*, London: Penguin, 1994 and *Lean Mean Thirteen*, New York, St Martin's Press, 2007. See also *Two for the Dough*, London, Penguin, 1996; *Three to Get Deadly*, London, Penguin, 1997; *Four to Score*, London, Pan, 1999; *High Five*, London: Pan, 2000; *Hot Six*, London: Macmillan, 2000; *Seven Up*, London: Headline, 2002; *Hard Eight*, London: Headline, 2003; *To the Nines*, London: Headline, 2004, *Ten Big Ones*, London: Headline, 2005, *Eleven on Top*, London, Headline, 2006, *Twelve Sharp*, London: Headline, 2007.

[2] Jane Tompkins, *Sensational Designs: The Cultural Work of American Fiction 1790-1860*, Oxford: Oxford University Press, 1985.

Crime Fiction and the Rise and Fall of New Deal Liberalism,[3] makes a
convincing case for classical American hard-boiled crime fiction
doing the same thing for working-class white male Americans between the two World Wars and beyond. For McCann, New Deal
Liberalism posits America, or the United States, as a society where all
men, each in his own right, are equal, and where it is the state's business to make sure that this is so. Realities, however, often being different, it is the hard-boiled detective's task to correct reality where
deficient, so as to make sure that the common American gets a fair
(New) Deal. At the same time, the hard-boiled detective acts as a
representative man of common America. That is why he is a professional, and not, as so often with his British counterpart, a gifted
amateur. In other words, he is a working stiff, not a member of the
leisured class. In fact, more often than not it is precisely the idle rich
that the hard-boiled detective has to contend with – most markedly, of
course, in Raymond Chandler's early novels. Physically, the detective's toughness and his ability to take it, coupled with his rugged good
looks, constitute the working man's idealized rejoinder to the leisured
man's supposed softness. Verbally, the hard-boiled detective's famous
wit deflates all uses of language as an instrument of power, whether it
be that of the arrogant rich who think they own him because they
employ him, of the official representatives of power such as the police
professionals he usually is at odds with and who support the powers
that be, or of the criminals that threaten him with physical violence.
The hard-boiled detective's role as representative New Deal liberal (in
the traditional – that is, economic – sense of the word) individual also
explains why he is a loner, with neither family nor friends. The hard-
boiled detective, in other words, is Mr Common American cast in the
role of urban super-cowboy.

With a term he borrows from the political scientist Robert Dahl, in
A Preface to Democratic Theory (1956), McCann characterizes the
breakdown of New Deal social solidarity under the pressures of
Fifties consumerism as minorities rule. This indicates the change from
a political system where the state supposedly directs things for the
benefit of all, to one whereby the state limits itself to being the arbiter

---

[3]   Sean McCann, *Gumshoe America: Hard-Boiled Crime Fiction and the Rise and
     Fall of New Deal Liberalism*, Durham: Duke University Press, 2000.

between various constituencies vying for the same material pie. At the same time, and because of social and economic, as well as demographic changes, the working common man is displaced from that American centre he had occupied under the New Deal. Minorities rule, then, pits classes, races, and genders against each other. Hard-boiled crime writing follows suit. Chandler's later fictions become increasingly racialized. Jim Thompson casts the ordinary American man as loser. Ross Macdonald has the white common man, in the guise of Lew Archer, get himself an education and an inner life, and thus re-empowers him as a member of the middle class. Mickey Spillane re-empowers that same white common man by having him take the law into his own hands in acts of indiscriminate and violent revenge. At the same time, we see that the hard-boiled genre, and that of crime writing in general, is appropriated by Dahl's minorities for their own attempts at empowerment. Chester Himes, in a series of novels featuring two Harlem police detectives, tries to negotiate between the ideal of a society unified in its legal system and the reality of that same society split along racial lines. In *Plan B*, the final, unfinished, novel in the series, he gives up on this idea and accepts that there is no hope for blacks under a white system of law. Thirty years later Walter Mosley, in a string of novels featuring African American amateur detective Easy Rawlins, arrived at a similar conclusion. From the Nineties on, other racial minorities followed the African American example, and likewise exploited the hard-boiled detective genre to vent their own grievances and hopes, yet – as I have argued elsewhere[4] – without necessarily leading them to the same conclusions as Himes or Mosley. Most important, at least for our present purpose, is that since the early Eighties an ever-increasing number of women has swollen the ranks of American writers working in the hard-boiled crime tradition.

As literary historians have been quick to point out, the repositioning the hard-boiled genre has undergone over the last few decades has also led to changes in the genre's conventions. Stephen F. Soitos, in *The Blues Detective: A Study of African American Detective*

---

[4]   Theo D'haen, "Samurai Sleuths and Dutiful Daughters: The American Way", in *Sleuthing Ethnicity: The Detective in Multiethnic Crime Fiction*, eds Dorothea Fischer-Hornung and Monica Mueller, Madison/Teaneck: Farleigh Dickenson University Press and London: Associated University Presses, 2003, 36-52.

Fiction, claims that what he calls "black detection" distinguishes itself from classic white hard-boiled writing in the following ways. To begin with, black detectives "are aware, and make their readers aware, of their place within the fabric of their black society".[5] Then, true to the double-consciousness pattern that W. E. B. DuBois long ago discerned as typical for an African American culture operating against the backdrop of a wider and more general white American culture, these detectives always engage in role-playing. Third, black detective writing makes elaborate use of what Soitos calls "blackground", the interweaving into the text of "black vernaculars" such as "music/dance, black language, and black cuisine".[6] A fourth element is hoodoo. With the exception of the fourth, highly specialized item, which seems specific only to African American fiction, and arguably not even to all of that, all other items to a greater or lesser degree, and according to the particularities of the group concerned, also apply to minority detective writing other than African American.

As to women's crime writing, Priscilla L. Walton and Manina Jones, in *Detective Agency: Women Rewriting the Hard-Boiled Tradition*,[7] following upon and in many ways summarizing and elaborating upon earlier work by Klein,[8] Munt,[9] and Irons,[10] go a long way to establish a distinct tradition of female crime writing both tributary and alternative to the classic male tradition. Obviously, the dialogue this recently established female tradition conducts with its classic male American counterpart is both elaborate and complex. I will here limit myself to discussing some elements fitting Soitos' three more general accounts – social embedding, role-playing, specific vernaculars – and making for the empowerment of women.

---

[5] Stephen F. Soitos, *The Blues Detective: A Study of African American Detective Fiction*, Amherst: University of Massachusetts Press, 1996, 29.
[6] *Ibid.*, 37.
[7] Priscilla L. Walton and Manina Jones, *Detective Agency: Women Rewriting the Hard-Boiled Tradition*, Berkeley: University of California Press, 1999.
[8] Kathleen Gregory Klein, *The Woman Detective: Gender and Genre*, Urbana: University of Illinois Press, 1988.
[9] Sally R. Munt, *Murder by the Book? Feminism and the Crime Novel*, London: Routledge, 1994.
[10] Glenwood Irons, *Feminism in Women's Detective Fiction*, Toronto: University of Toronto Press, 1995.

For the empowerment of working-class males under the New Deal it was important that the classic hard-boiled detective be a working professional. For female empowerment at the time of the first massive wave of women crime writers, in the Eighties, it is equally important that women detectives then rising to fame are professionals too: Marcia Muller's Sharon McCone, Sue Grafton's Kinsey Millhone, Sara Paretsky's V. I. Warshawski, Linda Barnes' Carlotta Carlyle, Karen Kijewski's Kat Colorado. Like their classic male examples, they are loners in the sense that they do not have any next of kin. Unlike their male forebears, though, they are not social loners. To a certain extent, and *pace* Soitos, all more recent crime writing is more social in setting than the hard-boiled classics, thereby simply reflecting post-Second World War reality, with people becoming ever more enmeshed in an increasingly complex society. Even white male crime writing, as of the Fifties, starts paying more attention to the social embedding of its characters, for instance by converting the hero from a lone private eye into a police detective operating in the appropriate institutional setting.

Eventually, this led to the emergence of a special sub-genre: the police procedural. In this respect it is useful to recall that the novels of Chester Himes, from which Soitos takes most of his examples, likewise feature two black police detectives, not private eyes. Notwithstanding Himes, though, the police procedural has not proved very attractive for minority writers, including women writers. This is understandable if we stop to consider that – at least until recently – minorities were scarce, or in any case underrepresented, and often unwelcome, in real life police forces. In fact, various fictional female private eyes started out as police detectives but found they could not stand the evident gender bias. Kinsey Millhone, for instance, at the beginning of *"B" is for Burglar*[11] details why she quit the police force: macho prejudice and unwelcome sexual attentions. Valerie Wilson Wesley's Tamara Hayle and Grace F. Edwards' Mali Anderson were both handicapped not only by gender but also by race. V. I. Warshawski turned investigator when she became disillusioned with the little she could achieve as a legal aid lawyer. Instead of to the male-tinged camaraderie of the precinct duty room, or even the courthouse, then,

---

[11]   Sue Grafton, *"B" is for Burglar*, New York: Bantam, 1986.

both Kinsey Millhone and V. I. Warshawski turn to support groups of neighbours and friends, composed mostly of women and the occasional much older man – thereby reflecting the everyday social environment of the average housewife rather than that of the working woman. If a younger man does come into the picture, usually as a lover, the relationship between him and the female detective is always tense, and more often than not comes to nothing in the end. Not unusually, the lover in question is a policeman or police detective himself, and fierce battles over the female detective's independence, and over the way she does her job, have become a stock in trade of the genre.

Finally, more often than not, the specific cases these female detectives take on highlight the plight of women. Grafton usually sticks to the level of the personal and of family relations. Paretsky more often than not moves from there to the level of the social, the economic, and the political. With both Grafton and Paretsky, though, there never can be any doubt that, in an endless repetition of what Millhone and Warshawski perceive as their own initial victimization, ultimately it is the patriarchal order of the world that is to blame for the mishaps and tragedies befalling their heroine's clients. In their use of social setting, plot, and character, then, and in the relations between them, these women's private eye novels re-appropriate many elements of the classic male examples in the genre for their own purposes, and turn them against man's world.

Role-playing in women's detective fiction manifests itself in various ways. First, there is the question of names. Female detectives apparently prefer potentially male names: "Kinsey", "Kat", "V. I." occasionally lengthened to "Vic" as short for Victoria. Walton and Jones see this as one way for female women writers to buy into the classic generic conventions while at the same time signalling difference. Then, there is the matter of dress and general appearance. Both Kinsey and Warshawski go out of their way to appear as neutrally professional as possible. With Kinsey this takes the form of not paying any particular attention to such matters as clothes and hairdo, and pointedly telling us so. With Warshawski, on the contrary, it takes the form of dressing the part, rather like Chandler's Marlowe at the begin-

ning of *The Big Sleep*.[12] In all these instances, it is clear that these
female detectives, and their creators, are very much aware of their
playing a role in a script originally written for male detectives in a
male-oriented genre.

As to female vernaculars, Walton and Jones emphasize how in
various instances Kinsey Millhone likens detecting, and particularly
the more tedious aspects of it, to housekeeping. There is also the language of clothes, as when Kinsey – even though she obstinately downplays its importance when it comes to her own person – in *"M" is for
Malice* is perfectly able to judge another woman's sweater as "a
masterpiece of cable stitches, wheat ears, twisted ribs, popcorn
stitches, and picot appliqué".[13] Then there is the language of the body,
not just, as is traditional in crime writing, in terms of violence done to
it – though in both Grafton and Paretsky there is plenty of that too –
but rather as to its most intimate workings, for instance when V. I.
Warshawski details her period. With Paretsky the language of feminism also intervenes, especially in the conversations Warshawski has
with her female friends of the Sixties and Seventies. Finally, there is
the language of food, as when Kinsey discusses recipes with her 80+
landlord, who used to be a baker, or describes the home food she has
at her neighbourhood restaurant. In both cases the food, and the talk
about it, is also a way of forging and fostering social alliances and
relationships. In the last instance, though, these vernaculars, while undoubtedly feminizing the novels in which they appear, at the same
time also serve to demonstrate how the heroines in question transcend
the narrow female concerns invested in them, and thus notwithstanding their femininity can still lay claim to the hallowed territory of the
classic private eye novel.

What is going on, then, in the fiction of Grafton, Paretsky, and
their likes, is a subtle balancing of male generic conventions and
female appropriations of them, via Ms Common America cast as hard-
boiled hero(ine). By the mid-Nineties the female tradition embodied
by these authors apparently had already assumed such firm contours
that newcomer Janet Evanovich could bounce her highly successful

---

[12]   Raymond Chandler, *The Big Sleep*, New York: Random, 1988.
[13]   Sue Grafton, *"M" is for Malice*, New York: Fawcett, 1997, 23.

Stephanie Plum series off of it, and thus seriously question its specific form of empowerment.

Almost blow for blow, and from the very outset, Evanovich posits Stephanie Plum as a send-up of both the male and the female hard-boiled traditions. It is probably not a coincidence that when we first meet Stephanie, in the first novel in the series, *One for the Money*, she is thirty-two years old, exactly the same age Kinsey Millhone gives as hers at the very beginning of *"A" is for Alibi*,[14] the first novel in her series. Both, in the time-honoured tradition of hard-boiled writing, tell their own tale, and do so retrospectively. Both are also professionals, but if Kinsey as a private eye does a tough man's job, Stephanie goes even one step further than her: she is a bounty hunter, though her bounty hunting assignments as a rule very quickly shade over into what can be traditionally termed private eye work. This is where the similarities end, though, because whereas Kinsey made a deliberate choice to become a private eye after having quit the police force, Stephanie in *One for the Money* becomes a bounty hunter almost by accident, after having lost her job as a lingerie buyer for a downmarket clothing store. The contrast here could not be starker, and is immediately indicative of the gap separating Stephanie from the by now traditional female private eye. The beginnings of the two novels in case likewise immediately create a very different atmosphere. Kinsey starts off with:

> My name is Kinsey Millhone. I'm a private investigator, licensed by the state of California. I'm thirty-two years old, twice divorced, no kids. The day before yesterday I killed someone and the fact weighs heavily on my mind.[15]

Stephanie on the other hand, confides to us that:

> There are some men who enter a woman's life and screw it up forever. Joseph Morelli did this to me – not forever; but periodically.[16]

[14] Sue Grafton, *"A" is for Alibi*, New York: Bantam, 1987.
[15] *Ibid.*, 1.
[16] Evanovich, *One for the Money*, 3.

After ten instalments we can ascertain how accurate a description of the entire Stephanie Plum series this initial sentence of *One for the Money* is. Joe Morelli provides the initial motivation for the plot of *One for the Money*, in the sense that he is the first skip Stephanie has to bring in. As a police officer in Trenton, the New Jersey town that both he and Stephanie call home, Joe often also turns out to have an interest in the cases that Stephanie gets involved in. Most importantly, however, Morelli is also the man of Stephanie's life, and each new novel is another episode in their – often stormy – romance. In fact, it is totally appropriate that this aspect should be highlighted even in the first line of that series, because this is precisely one of the innovations Evanovich brings to the genre. Whereas Grafton and Paretsky concentrate on empowering contemporary women by carving out a stake for them in the typically male territory of hard-boiled private eye fiction, Evanovich achieves the same end by having the genre itself shift ground in the direction of the serial romance. Everything in her novels conspires to this end, and specifically those elements that fit Soitos' three general categories of social embedding, role-playing, and specific vernaculars.

It is telling that Kinsey Millhone in *"J" is for Judgement*,[17] the tenth novel in what remains one of the most firmly established and high profile recent female crime writing series, should unexpectedly discover that she still has family left. This reflects the current re-shaping of the crime genre, whereby the personal element, including family ties, is becoming more and more intrusive. In S. J. Rozan's Chinese American Lydia Chin novels, for instance, Lydia's mother is a constant presence, while her brothers put in an occasional appearance. In Valerie Wilson Wesley's Tamara Hayle series, Tamara's teenage son Jamal plays a prominent role, while Grace F. Edwards' Mali Anderson shares a house with her jazz musician father and her orphaned nephew Alvin. In all cases, these family members regularly provide part of a specific novel's plot motivation. Janet Evanovich, however, takes all this much further. Stephanie not only has a mother and father with whom she is in almost daily contact, usually over a very solid dinner, but living with her Hungarian-Italian parents is also Grandma Mazur, who is always in for an adventure – the riskier the

---

[17] Sue Grafton, *"J" is for Judgement*, New York: Fawcett, 1994.

better. Both her mother and grandmother are very much concerned that Stephanie, at thirty-two, is still single.

She used to be married, but divorced her husband, another local boy, when she discovered him one day "bare-assed on [the] dining-room table ... playing hide-the-salami" (as she puts it in *Four to Score*[18]) with a girl that had been Stephanie's rival from high school days. Stephanie's mother and grandmother want to see her fixed up with a good husband again, and to this end they keep inviting to dinner what they deem suitable local candidates – needless to say, Stephanie's idea of a suitable candidate is rather different from theirs. The Plums, and Grandma Mazur in particular, are also very much part of a vibrant local network of female gossip, and anything Stephanie does immediately goes out on the grapevine, often reaching her parents before she can tell them herself.

Indeed, in contrast to Kinsey Millhone or V. I. Warshawski, Stephanie is very much a part of an organic neighbourhood, where people have known one another from childhood, and where families continue to live in the same house for several generations. Moreover, she is also part of an equally organic professional environment. Whereas Kinsey Millhone and V. I. Warshawski work alone, and out of their own house (Kinsey) or out of a shabby office (Warshawski), Stephanie's professional life centres on her cousin Vinnie's bail bond office. Though Vinnie in theory is the boss, he usually hides in his back office, and it is the various women staffing the front office that in effect run his affairs. To a large extent, they do so by gossip and female bonding, thus providing a very effective example of girl power. That Evanovich is not just having some gratuitous fun here with what is often stereotyped as typically female behaviour can be seen from the fact that it is this same female network, both family and office, that often allows Stephanie to beat Joe Morelli to the solution of a case they are both working on – he from the official, she from the private eye side. In this sense, what happens in the public sphere of crime detecting between Stephanie and Morelli parallels the situation in the Plum household, where Stephanie's father is definitely out of it when it comes to knowing what is going on, precisely because he is not plugged in to the unofficial channels of female Trenton. In other

---

[18]   Evanovich, *Four to Score*, 3.

words, Evanovich is here empowering women by very different, but no less effective, means than Grafton or Paretsky do.

Something similar happens when we turn to the role-playing issue. Though Stephanie is occasionally called "Steph", ostensibly bringing her in line with the potentially masculine name bias of traditional female P.I. writing, she much more often goes by her full first name. That first name is obviously a very feminine one; definitely more appropriate to the boudoir – after all, not for nothing was she once a lingerie buyer – than the shooting range. In an ironic twist, it is actually Morelli who calls her "Steph", even though obviously she is all woman to him. Stephanie's last name likewise marks a break with tradition. Names like Millhone and Warshawski sound all business, or are at least neutral except for ethnic pointers. Plum, while it is neutral as to specific ethnic markers, and this regardless of Stephanie's styling herself "the blue-eyed, fair-skinned product of a Hungarian-Italian union",[19] is anything but neutral when it comes to emotional overtones. Read as plain English, and going by the various definitions the *Oxford English Reference Dictionary* provides, the name overtly suggest roundness, ripeness, juiciness, sweetness – plenty of sunshine and good times. It also means "the best of a collection; something especially prized", and in this sense can be used attributively. Hence: a plum girl. That is certainly how most men in the series look upon her.

Kinsey and V. I. not only play at P.I.-ing onomastically, as I argued earlier, they also do so by dressing the part of a private eye, and by taking it like a man when it comes to physical violence. In dress and personal appearance, Stephanie Plum clearly goes against the grain of the female tradition. Her usual (summer) attire is "black spandex sports bra ... matching spandex shorts and a sleeveless oversized Trenton Thunders baseball jersey".[20] This is her idea of dressing the part when Ranger tells her that to lure a young gangster away from the funeral home where his boss is lying in state will take "smooth white skin barely hidden behind a short skirt and tight sweater":[21]

> Fifteen minutes later, I was dressed in four-inch FMPs (short for 'fuck-me-pumps,' because when you walked around in them you

[19] Evanovich, *Two for the Dough*, 9.
[20] Evanovich, *Four to Score*, 1.
[21] *Ibid.*, 39.

looked like whorehouse Wonder Bitch) ... I shimmied into a low-cut
black knit dress that was bought with the intent of losing five pounds,
gunked up my eyes with a lot of black mascara and beefed up my
cleavage by stuffing Nerf balls into my bra.[22]

When it comes to rough play, Stephanie has her own way of handling
this: she calls in the hired help. In her case, the help is called Ricardo
Carlos Manoso, a second generation Cuban-American who goes by
the trade name of "Ranger". The characterization of Ranger at the
same time firmly anchors the Stephanie Plum series in the post-
Second World War hard-boiled tradition and in that of the serial
romance. As to the former, Ranger obviously is a chip off the same
block that also yielded Hawk as sidekick to Robert B. Parker's
Spenser, as well as Pike to Robert Crais' Elvis Cole. Ranger is a crack
bounty hunter, who teaches Stephanie the tricks of the trade, and
comes to her rescue whenever needed – usually after a convenient
phone call from Stephanie. He takes care of most of the shooting and
fisticuffs. At the same time, Ranger is every woman's wet dream. In
fact, Stephanie throughout the series feels more than the occasional
pang of desire for Ranger herself, and he certainly does not seem
averse to a little dallying with her. In the end, though, Stephanie
always sticks with Morelli – her first love and her last love after all.
    Though Stephanie suspects otherwise, she in fact is also Morelli's
one true love. The deftness with which Evanovich plays the love interest between Ranger, Morelli, and Stephanie, and especially the way
she turns Stephanie's agonizing over whom she will allow or invite
into her bed into cliffhangers at the end of the later novels, obviously
fits the serial romance tradition. In fact, though the Stephanie Plum
novels have everything a serious private eye novel needs – plenty of
action, stake-outs, chases, fights, sudden reversals as to suspects, and
plenty of suspense – in the end it is the romance that provides the
frame to the detective story, and not the other way around. This undoubtedly adds to our feeling that what we are witnessing in the
Stephanie Plum novels is role-playing indeed: the romance heroine
playing at private eye.
    In fact, we seem to be supported in this view when Morelli himself,
in *Two for the Dough*, calls Stephanie "the worst bounty hunter in the

---

[22] *Ibid.*, 40.

history of the world".[23] Or when we see that at the beginning of each novel Stephanie is given what seems like an easy assignment, which she invariably bungles. Before we let ourselves be taken in by this, though, it is useful to consider that Stephanie always gets her man in the end, whether it is a skip or Joe himself. In this regard, the first novel in the series sets the pattern for all to follow, as in this first novel it is actually Joe that is Stephanie's first assignment, and in a sense he then is also a sexual and emotional skip on her, having seduced her when they were both in their late teens, and after that having left her to her own designs. In other words, though all conventional odds are against her, she is highly successful in the end, against everyone's expectations and against the better sense of society. Unlike Kinsey and Warshawski, though, Stephanie does not triumph by becoming like a man – in appearance, name, thinking, style of life, etc. – but rather by being very much the plum of femininity: girl power again. Evanovich also stresses girl power in quite a different, and very humorous, way when she makes Lula, an African American 250-pound ex-hooker, and Grandma Mazur, carrying a six-shooter in her pocketbook, stand in for Ranger as back-up for Stephanie.

If the Stephanie Plum novels are full of female vernaculars, relating to food, sewing, hairdressing, and every other female occupation under the sun, the remarkable thing is that Stephanie is so very bad at all of them. Her mother is a superb cook, and though Stephanie usually has misgivings about having to go to her parents' place because as an again unmarried woman they still treat her very much as a daughter, this is certainly not because of the food she gets there, and on which she willingly stuffs herself. On her own, though, she lives on junk food – preferably pizza, especially when Joe Morelli happens to be around. In fact, Joe himself turns out to be a better cook – and housekeeper – than Stephanie when she finally gets to visit him in his own house in *Four to Score*. What is even more remarkable, though, is that none of this seems to affect either Stephanie's figure – though she herself obviously thinks she is gaining weight, and she very occasionally succeeds in pushing herself to run a few laps by way of exercise, most of the men around seem to think her figure perfect – or her sex-appeal.

---

[23]   Evanovich, *Two for the Dough*, 301.

In almost every novel Stephanie goes to the hairdresser's, and this inevitably ends in disaster. In *Three to Get Deadly* she runs out of the hairdresser's because she sees a skip going by. As a result she ends up with orange fizz hair, because her rinse stays on too long. In *Four to Score* she cannot get an appointment with her regular hairdresser, and instead goes to Grandma Mazur's. Predictably, Stephanie comes out with an old lady perm. Just as I have argued earlier, Evanovich makes the point that in order to be a successful bounty hunter / private eye you do not necessarily have to look or talk like the male or even the female stereotype of the genre, here the message seems to be that neither do you have to be a fashion model or a perfect home maker to be successful in love.

All in all, then, Evanovich with her Stephanie Plum series seems to be taking the side not of Ms Superwoman doubling as Mr Superman, looking to right the wrongs of the world, but rather that of everybody's favourite neighbourhood girl – Ms Common America cast as Ms Ideal Common America. This ambition to stay close to everyday American life also speaks from the titles of the successive novels in the series, invariably taken from, or variants upon, well-known American popular cultural icons: a rock song, colloquial expressions, soft drinks. It likewise speaks from the cross with the serial romance – arguably the lowest of popular forms – the private eye novel is here made to undergo. By the same token, and most importantly, Evanovich shifts the very generic ground upon which private eye fiction stands. She thus reaches out to a wholly new audience, potentially empowering a large section of the female reading public hitherto untapped even by traditional female private eye fiction. Commercially, at least, the gamble seems to have paid off, as the Stephanie Plum series indubitably is a tremendous hit.

MURDER AND LOVE: RUSSIAN WOMEN DETECTIVE WRITERS

WILLEM G. WESTSTEIJN

During the carnival in Venice a Russian artist dies from an overdose of drugs. It turns out that he has been employed on a temporary basis by Luigi Giacometti, a well-known producer of masks, who commissioned him to make a number of statues. The lethal dose has been administered through the clothes, which indicates an experienced user or administering by another person. In the latter case it might have been murder. For the sake of convenience the Italian police assume that the artist has killed himself, but the wife of the artist, who comes to Venice to collect the body, has her doubts. After all, just before he left for Italy, her husband had been treated successfully in a drug rehabilitation clinic and had sworn off using drugs. Her doubts are confirmed when, after her return to Russia and after the funeral, she pays a visit to the drug clinic and has an interview with the nurse who had treated her husband. This nurse, Dasya, assures her that it is impossible for the artist to have given himself an injection through his clothes. She herself has fallen in love with the artist during his treatment and he had promised her that, once he returned from Italy, he would leave his wife and live with her.

At first, Dasya does not want to tell this to the artist's wife, but when she decides to do so and calls on her at her house, she finds her dead in her bath with a hairdryer in her hand, presumably electrocuted. Shortly after, Dasya is approached by a certain Igor Vadimovich who is interested in the artist and tells Dasya that he met him in Venice, just before his death. According to him, it is clear that the artist has been murdered. Igor offers his help to find the murderer. He knows that nine statues have recently arrived at a women's club in St Petersburg, sent from Italy in the name of the artist, but evidently not made by him. Dasya has to become a member of the private club in order to find out what exactly is the matter with the statues and ascertain if there are any documents which prove that the club has commissioned them. Igor provides Dasya with an admission ticket for the club, so that she can present herself as a possible new member.

After this rather complex introduction comes the main part of the novel – Dasya's adventures in the women's club. More than two thirds of the novel is devoted to them and much of what is told is only indirectly connected with the murder case. The principal aim of the writer seems to be to confront the reader with the existence of a women's club in contemporary Russia, to show how such a club is organized, how it functions and who its members are. It turns out to be a private club for rich lesbians and Dasya, a poor nurse, whose paltry monthly salary is hardly sufficient for one dinner at the club, is evidently out of place there. That fact that she is admitted at all, and is even offered a free membership is down to the fact that the president of the club, Larisa, falls in love with her and pays everything for her. This enables Dasya to investigate things in the club, but she has to submit to Larisa's amorous attentions. Dasya discovers the statues, which turn out to be rather tasteless plaster figures, and when she inadvertently topples one of them it falls to pieces. The way in which the author confronts the heroine with lesbian love is remarkable. When Dasya spends the night in one of the club guest rooms, much against her liking she has to accept Larisa into her bed. The rape is described rather explicitly – fifteen-years ago Soviet censorship would have categorically deleted the mere mention of a naked breast.

Eventually, the murder is solved. The artist was killed after having completed his assignment to make a number of statues. Instead of these statues, however, plaster figures were sent to Russia in his name and these concealed hidden precious antique statues made by a famous Italian sculptor. A rich Russian art collector was prepared to pay a fortune for them. The women's club acted as an intermediary and thought up a plan to smuggle the statues into Russia.

The novel, *Nezhnoe dykhanie smerti* by Anna Malysheva,[1] summarized above, is typical in many ways of the contemporary Russian detective novel written by women. In the first place, it is striking how much attention is paid, comparatively speaking, to matters that hardly relate to the main line of the plot. Whereas in most detective novels –

---

[1]   Anna Malysheva, *Nezhnoe dykhanie smerti* (*Death's Tender Breath*), Moscow: Centroligraf, 1999.

and this also holds true for the novels of English women detective writers, who have made a considerable contribution to the genre – everything is subservient to the solving of the murder which is usually committed in the first chapter,[2] in the case of the Russian woman detective the solving of the murder and also the murder itself are a matter of secondary importance. Much attention is paid to the main protagonist's personal circumstances. She is usually a young woman in the big city – most often Moscow, although St Petersburg is also a popular setting – who becomes involved in a murder case. Consequently, the appearance of the heroine is confined to one book. When the murder is solved, sometimes with, but sometimes without her assistance, she receives her reward, love or money, but after that her part is played. After all, she is not a professional detective and it would be strange if, in her life as an ordinary woman, she were to be confronted with a murder case more often. But even if the heroine is a detective who appears in many different novels, there is still much digression on secondary matters, especially living conditions in contemporary, post-perestroika Russia. In detective novels written by male authors this is quite different. Often they are set in a political or criminal milieu and sometimes, as in the popular novels by B. Akunin, where the story is set in another age.[3]

What is the origin of this preference by Russian women detective writers for the portrayal of contemporary women's lives? Until recently mass literature or popular literature did not exist in Russia. At the time Gorbachev acceded to power, and until the official abolition of censorship (1990), all the media were under the strict control of the Communist Party. All the publishing companies, papers and journals were owned by the state and nothing could be printed without the consent of *Glavlit*, the censorship authority. Literature had to meet the

---

[2] The plot of a classic detective novel is, in fact, focused on the reconstruction of the story preceding the murder.

[3] B(oris) Akunin is the pseudonym of G. Chkhartishvili, a member of the editorial board of the well-known journal *Inostrannaya literatura* (*Foreign Literature*) and an expert on Japanese culture. He represents an interesting phenomenon in contemporary Russian detective fiction. His novels, whose protagonist is the police detective Erast Fandorin, are set in nineteenth-century Russia and reveal a great deal of knowledge about the Western detective tradition (Conan Doyle, Gaboriau, Chandler, Hammett) as well as Russian literature.

requirements of the official theory of art, Socialist Realism.[4] One of the tenets of Socialist Realism was that art should have an educative value, which implied that it should offer a positive view of Socialist society. Literature that failed to do this was kept away from the Soviet reader. This not only applied to literature that adopted a critical attitude to Soviet society or Soviet history (for instance, Solzhenitsyn's *The Archipelago Gulag*), but also to literature written purely for amusement, such as Western detective novels, novelettes and romances. The popular literature that was permitted, such as the spy novels by Yulian Semyonov or the fervently nationalistic historical novels by Valentin Pikul, always contained a message. This message was that a Russian is stronger, smarter and of higher moral standing than his corrupted rival in the West. The cliché of the good Russian as opposed to the bad Westerner fitted excellently with the leaders' way of thinking.

Gorbachev's perestroika put an end to state control of the media and of literature. As a result the book market became inundated with a flood of literature that had been forbidden during the Soviet regime.[5] Among this new literature were books by famous Russian authors who had emigrated after the revolution (Bunin, Nabokov) and authors who had been expelled from the country by Brezhnev (Solzhenitsyn, Brodsky), and also Western popular fiction. There was an enormous demand for this kind of literature and enterprising publishers hastened to fill the gap in the market. Agatha Christie was extremely popular and her books were devoured by Russian readers. The great success she and other Western writers of popular fiction enjoyed with Russian readers incited the Russians to enter this commercially profitable field themselves. This turned out to be easy, and in the present Russian book market national authors of popular fiction (fantasy, thriller, detective novels) have almost entirely supplanted the foreigners.

---

[4]   This theory was proclaimed for the first time at the first general assembly of the Soviet Writers' Union in 1934 by Stalin's paladin, the writer Maxim Gorky.

[5]   This catching up with the past reached its height in the years 1989-1991. In a period in which paper, and consequently books and journals were comparatively cheap, the circulation of the thick literary journals, in which in Russia, the most recent literature is published, soared. The well-known journal *Novyi mir* (*New World*) had a circulation in those years of more than three million (now nine thousand).

In the genre of the detective novel Russian women writers have gained a dominant position. The uncrowned queen is Alexandra Marinina, a criminologist with a law degree and ex-lieutenant of the Moscow police. Her books are produced in print runs of millions of copies. Many other popular writers of detective novels have a legal background. Tatyana Stepanova was a detective and is working as an officer at the information service of the Moscow police; Marina Serova studied law at Moscow University and worked at the Moscow court of justice. A second group of writers has had a literary or a journalistic education. Anna Malysheva, with whom we began, did a literary course at the well-known Gorky Institute (the writers' academy in Moscow) and so did Polina Dashkova. Tatyana Polyakova studied philology, and Elena Yakovleva journalism.

The great number of women among the authors of detective novels in contemporary Russia can be explained by the fact that the Russian detective genre is, in many cases, a hybrid genre. From the initial discussion of Anna Malysheva's novel *Nezhnoe dykhanie smerti* it is clear that much of what is described in this novel does not have any direct relation with the history of the murder, but rather enters into the daily life and in particular the love life of the heroine. The same can be said of Polina Dashkova's popular novels. In one of these books, *Mesto pod solntsem*,[6] the protagonist is a certain Katya Orlova, a ballet dancer. She is not a great star, it is true, but her performances are made possible by her husband, a casino owner, Mafia boss who is the main sponsor of the theatre in which she is appearing. After one of Katya's opening nights her husband is killed in her presence on their way home.

At the end of the long drawn-out story (more than 450 pages), the murderer is unmasked but before that the reader is confronted with a lot of details unrelated to the murder case. The author enters at length into Katya's past, the way in which she became acquainted with the Mafia boss and, before that, her love affair with a well-known economist. As the story develops, three other young women are introduced: a poor student, a massage prostitute and a film actress who used to be a call girl. Their past is also related – they all went to school together.

---

[6] Polina Dashkova, *Mesto pod solntsem* (*A Place under the Sun*), Moscow: EKSMO Press, 1999.

In a rather complicated manner they are connected with the story of
the murder. The plot is neither very exciting, nor very ingenious. Just
as in Malysheva's books, the main aim seems to be to describe
women's lives in contemporary Russian society. Dashkova spices her
story up with some romance. Unlike Malysheva's novel, her protagonist is not a poor nurse, but rather, from a material viewpoint, an
enviable young woman with a dream profession and a dream life. Not
everybody is like Katya, a ballet dancer with a five-room apartment, a
house in Crete, two cars and a maidservant. Her husband's death does
not turn out badly for her. The inheritance is excellently arranged and
at the end of the novel she is saved from serious trouble by a former
friend who has always been in love with her. Future happiness is
assured.

The novels of writers such as Malysheva and Dashkova, with their
mixture of crime and love intrigue, are a special, but important sub-
genre of the Russian detective novel. They have by now acquired their
own denomination: *lyubovno-detektivnye romany* (Love-Detective
Novels). As such they are taking the place of the pure popular love
story, which hardly exists in contemporary Russian literature. The
western love story or romance (in Russia called "rose novel") has been
extensively translated and evidently meets some need. Just as for the
Western reader, that need is to fantasize about a romantic dream world
in which there is no war, no hunger and no violence, where everything
revolves around a love intrigue with a happy ending. In contrast to the
other popular genres, the rose novel has hardly any Russian prac-
titioners.[7] The reason for this, presumably, is that an original Russian
rose novel would be too unrealistic in Russia's contemporary social
conditions. The Russian reader will be easily carried away by a love
story at an English country estate and will have no problems accepting
the idyllic background associated with it. However, such an idyllic
background cannot be found in present-day Russia. The nobility, with
its palaces and rural estates disappeared a long time ago and the
wealth and luxury of the new Russians is almost always acquired by
means of Mafia-like practices. For most people daily life is hard and

---

[7]   See Olga Vainstein's observations in her article "Rossiiskie damskie romany"
("Russian Ladies' Novels"), in *Novoe literaturnoe obozrenie*, 44 (2000), 441-47.

problematic. A "rose" Russian heroine would be so unrealistic that it would be impossible to identify with her.

The combination of a love story and a detective novel is the ideal means to make the romantic realistic and probable or, at least, more probable. The point of departure in a detective novel is invariably a shocking event, a murder, which generates all kinds of emotional (often someone is murdered who is dear to the principal character) as well as material problems. However, according to the rules of the genre, the detective novel has a happy ending. The murder is solved, thus putting an end to all the problems. Between the murder and its solution much can be told about the difficulties of daily life and the hero or heroine can eventually be rewarded without the story becoming too improbable. In real life the rose is impossible. If you want to offer your reader a satisfying rose picture, you have to add a substantial dose of black.

Apart from Russia's present-day problematic reality there is another important reason why there are hardly any original Russian rose novels. In *Nezhnoe dykhanie smerti* we see that the principal character, Dasya, not only loses a lover, with whom she was on the point of starting the first relationship in her life, but she also has to suffer a traumatic experience – rape. Dasya is described as a sincere, brave and altruistic young girl and the reader easily sympathizes with her. Such harshness towards the heroine would be unthinkable in western popular fiction (in novels like those written by Barbara Cartland, for example). Russian readers have, traditionally, fewer qualms about this. The hard fate of people seems to be more generally accepted. In the nineteenth-century serial novel *Peterburgskie trushchoby* (1866)[8] by the literary hack Vsevolod Krestovsky, one of the principal characters, a charming young woman and mother of two children, is brutally raped by an aristocratic debauchee during the time her husband is unjustly locked away in prison.

The ruthlessness towards the hero or heroine has, in all probability, less to do with the hardness of Russian society than with a masochistic streak in Russians themselves. Suffering and grief are considered natural and necessary experiences. Suffering is even attractive and posi-

---

[8] *Peterburgskie trushchoby* translates as "The Underworld of St Petersburg".

tive, it purifies the soul and raises man above the mere material.[9] It is, perhaps, dangerous to generalize in such a way about the Russian national character, but since Dostoevsky there has been ample reason to do so. The term he served in a Siberian prison camp[10] was a terrible ordeal for Dostoevsky, but at the same time he experienced it as a broadening of the meaning of life and an enrichment of his soul. The purification of the soul through suffering is amply demonstrated in his novels. In *Crime and Punishment*, for instance, Raskolnikov, the student, who robs and murders an old usurer and her sister, is unable to reconcile his deed with his conscience. After a long inner struggle he gives himself up to the police, accepts his punishment and eventually becomes a better man.

Dostoevsky has, of course, not invented the idea that suffering is inevitable and purifies the soul. It was, and is, a commonly held opinion in Russia and Dostoevsky was the first to express it explicitly and generalize it.[11] That Russia and Russians have a difficult fate and are destined to suffer is a recurrent theme in Russian literature[12] and

---

[9]   The Russians realize that they cannot compete economically with the Western countries. They are, however, proud of their soul and are convinced that their spiritual life is richer than that of the materialistic Western people. The Russian soul has been extensively discussed by the philosopher Nikolai Berdyaev (see for example his *Istoki i smysl russkogo kommunizma* [*The Origin and the Significance of Russian Communism*], Paris: YMCA Press, 1955).

[10]   In 1849 Dostoevsky was severely punished for being a member of a secret organization of young socialist radicals, the *Petrashevsky Circle*. All the members of the group were arrested and condemned to death by a military tribunal. A few moments before the execution the Tsar reversed the verdict and granted a reprieve. Dostoevsky was deported to Siberia for ten years: four years prison camp and six years service as an ordinary soldier in a Siberian place of exile.

[11]   One of the first clear statements is in his *Notes from the Underground* (see F. M. Dostoevsky, *Polnoe sobranie sochinenii v tridtsati tomakh*, 5, Leningrad: Nauka, 1973, 99-179), when the underground man declares that "suffering is the sole origin of consciousness" and that "man sometimes terribly passionately loves suffering" (119).

[12]   While working on this essay I read a Natalya Volodina play, *Rossiisky tragifars* (*A Russian Tragicomedy*), *Postskriptum*, 2 (1996) which contains the following dialogue between a Chinese and a Russian:
       "The Russian: 'You know, these days I often wonder: why is Russian history so full of suffering and blood?'

seems to be deep-rooted in the Russian soul. Recent research into urban subculture, in this case focused on stories and diaries of secondary school girls,[13] has shown that most of these stories are about love and almost invariably have a tragic conclusion. In the melodramatic stories murder and suicide are a matter of course and in quite a few stories crimes are publicly confessed in places like courthouses. It is evident that a rose novel does not really fit the schoolgirls' perception of the world, and this is the potential readership of the love-detective novels.

In view of the great value Russians attach to their souls, it is disappointing to notice how important a favourable financial conclusion is to much popular fiction. In *Nezhnoe dykhanie smerti* a dead lover and rape are more or less compensated by the paltry sum (although a lot of money for the heroine) of ten thousand dollars. However, ordeals are considered part of life and, therefore, the money Dasya eventually makes out of her adventures in the women's club seems sufficient compensation for what she has had to endure there. Tatyana Polyakova's *Kak by ne tak*[14] begins altruistically. The heroine is a divorced doctor who does her utmost to save the life of a Mafia boss she found, severely wounded and with a number of bullets in his chest, on her way home from the hospital where she works. When she gets mixed up in a conflict between two rival Mafia gangs and is entrusted with a large sum of money, her only aim becomes to take possession of this money. A good friend she had engaged to help her is even killed for it. The fact that she is not killed herself as well is thanks to her guardian, the cyclopic assistant of the Mafia boss she saved. This

---

The Chinese: 'That is no question at all. Russia is a country of suffering. That is just such an axiom as saying that I am Chinese and you are Russian. Russia is the way it is, it cannot be otherwise. That was the mistake and the root of the downfall of all the liberal governments that wanted to deliver Russia from its suffering. Rubbish. It would be the same as to trying to rescue Russia from itself. For a long time only those with an iron fist – Ivan the Terrible, Peter the Great, Stalin, the Bolsheviks – were able to rule Russia and thus augmented its suffering. The present-day liberals will have to be replaced by the next cruel dictatorship for a considerable time'" (241, my own translation).

[13] See S. Borisov, "Prozaicheskie zhanry devichikh albomov" ("Prose Genres of Girls' Albums"), in *Novoe literaturnoe obozrenie*, 22 (1996), 362-80 and "Devichi rukopisnye lyubovnye rasskazy" ("Girls' Manuscript Love Stories"), in *Russky shkolny folklor*, ed. A. F. Belousov, Moscow: Ladomir / Ast, 1998, 185-268.

[14] Tatyana Polyakova, *Kak by ne tak* (*Not Likely!*), Moscow: EKSMO Press, 1999.

cyclops cuts the throat of many of his rivals in the course of the story and, eventually, has no scruples about killing his own boss in cold blood and making off with his money. Protection and money are an iron combination. The doctor falls for her criminal cyclops and resigns from her job. Together they buy a house in the suburbs to enjoy a quiet, comfortable life. This is a rather bizarre conclusion, in which the heroine, out of self-interest, has strayed far from the ethics of her profession.

The principal character of the love-detective story is invariably a young, independent woman who successfully copes with the problems and difficulties she has to face. This important characteristic of the genre of the love-detective corresponds to the pure detective story written by women. In the latter case, however, the heroine is not just a young woman, but a professional police or private detective who, after a murder case has been solved, can appear again in the next novel. The main character in the action-packed novels by Marina Serova is private detective Zhenya Okhotnikova who has had an excellent education at the school for secret agents, but has lost her job owing to the changing political circumstances and now supports herself as a detective. As part of her education, she has been trained in all kinds of fighting techniques and is afraid of nobody. In one of Serova's novels, *Vpripryzhku za smertyu* she takes a stand against two gorilla-like bodyguards and renders them harmless with her brilliant judo technique. Zhenya's lack of fear reveals itself also in the light-hearted, ironic narrative style – she is both protagonist and narrator of these novels. At the beginning of *Vpripryzhku za smertyu*, Zhenya is nearly killed by a nearby explosion that destroys a Mercedes, killing all of the passengers, and the first thing she thinks of is a funny anecdote, which she relates in detail, with relish. She is not afraid of slang and uses many amusing comparisons. Her old aunt who is addicted to detective stories (an Agatha Christie-like element in Serova's novels) "otkryvaet novy tomik s takim zhe predvkusheniem naslazhdeniya, kak kakoi-nibud' vostochny sultan mog trebovat' sebe ezhednevno ocherednuyu devstvennitsu";[15] the blown-up Mercedes is "kak raz

---

[15] Marina Serova, *Vpripryzhku za smertyu* (*Springing in the Wake of Death*), Moscow: EKSMO Press, 1999), 8-9: "opens a new novel with the same anticipation of pleasure with which some Eastern sultan could each day summon the next virgin."

takaya model', na kotoroi razbilas' printsessa Diana v parizhskom tonnele".[16]

While Zenya Okhotnikova personally disarms her opponents and undertakes dangerous actions to solve murders, Nastya (Anastasia) Kamenskaya, the heroine of Alexandra Marinina's novels, excels by her fine intuition and great analytical power. Nastya is a detective in the Moscow police (as was the author), working at the famous police station at Petrovka Street. She is totally absorbed in her work. In describing her, Marinina has consciously refrained from giving her traditional feminine characteristics. Nastya is not emotional, not very sensitive and not interested in love, sex and beautiful clothes. She is happily married (her husband is an expert in mathematics), but does not like cooking and is a bad housekeeper. Her work means everything to her and gives her great satisfaction, although it is often difficult, hectic and fatiguing. The similarities between Nastya and her male colleagues enhance Nastya's particular qualities. With her exceptional intuition she outstrips all her colleagues, so that murder cases that threaten to come to a standstill through lack of clues can still be solved. Her intuition is particularly useful in cases in which non-rational elements that are scientifically difficult to control, such as telepathy, the possible consequences of traumatic experiences and astrological prophecies, play an important part.

Nastya's helplessness in all matters related to housekeeping does not mean that these matters are absent from Marinina's books. Nastya is the main character of the novels, but in most of them three other women are presented as well. One of these is her friend Tatyana Obraztsova who, like Nastya, is a police detective, but is also a writer of detective stories (a second double of Marinina). She is slightly more inclined to womanly life and in one of the novels she is expecting a baby – something that would be unthinkable in Nastya's case. Nastya's other two young friends are Dasya, her sister-in-law, and Irina, the sister of Tatyana's ex-husband.[17] The four women with their

---

[16]　*Ibid.*, 13: "the same model as the car in which Princess Diana was smashed up in a Parisian tunnel."

[17]　For a comparison of the various female characters in the novels of Marinina, see Hélène Mélat, "Igra Chuzhimi Maskami: Detektivy Aleksandry Marininoi" ("Playing with Other People's Masks: the Detective Novels of Alexandra Marinina"), in *Filologicheskie nauki*, 3 (2000), 93-103.

four different milieus enable Marinina to introduce various psychological portraits and give a varied picture of daily life in present-day Moscow. Furthermore, Nastya's work as a detective brings her into contact with people from all layers of society, again offering an opportunity to describe the various milieus. In *Chuzaya maska*[18] we are given a picture of the world of publishers and see how bestsellers are much more profitable for them than for their authors, we also see the life of politicians and the machinations necessary for being elected, in addition to being shown the goings-on in hospitals and prisons.

A good description of character and milieu, more brainwork than violence and an exciting, ingeniously constructed plot – these are all reasons why Marinina is deservedly at the top of Russian detective literature and is avidly read also by the intelligentsia, including its male readers. Marinina cleverly draws attention to Russian women and shows that they are in no way inferior to men. Thanks to the lack of any feminist bias this is entirely acceptable, all the more because it is true to reality.[19] That Russian women in general do not want to have anything to do with feminism is, I believe, due to the fact that Russian women consciously or unconsciously know that they, and not men, run Russian society. Without women there would be absolute chaos in Russia. Such an awareness of indispensability hardly exists in the West. At the same time, because of the depressing current state of affairs, reality can use a little gloss. With its happy conclusion, conforming to the requirements of the genre, the detective story offers some kind of comfort in the distressing circumstances of everyday life.

---

[18] Alexandra Marinina, *Chuzaya maska* (*Another's Mask*), Moscow: EKSMO Press, 2000.

[19] In Russia feminism has met with relatively little response. This has been attributed to various factors, one of them being the enormous surplus of women after the Second World War and Stalin's terror, which would make women less interested in fighting for their own rights. However, it is worth observing that despite women outnumbering men and nearly all women being employed, even fewer women are found in high places than in the West.

PERSPECTIVES ON THE DETECTIVE NOVEL IN AFRIKAANS

HANS ESTER

After the peaceful revolution in South Africa, beginning with the changeover of power in 1989 (F. W. de Klerk became president after P. W. Botha) and the release of ANC leader Nelson Mandela in 1990, many South Africans were sceptical about the position of the Afrikaans language in the future. In fact, many observers inside and outside South Africa were sure about the inevitable tendency to marginalize Afrikaans in South African society. To a certain extent time has proved them right. In the educational field Afrikaans was forced to clip its wings. Afrikaans as an educational language in the universities today has maintained part of its status, but on a very reduced basis. This reduction also applies to political life and to the administration of justice. The reason for this phenomenon is obvious. A language to bridge the communication gap between South Africans of different descent had to be found. This bridge is English.

However, to a large extent the prophets of the decline of Afrikaans have been proven wrong. This has to do with a surprising awareness of the special quality of being an Afrikaans-speaking South African. Afrikaans has become part of the search of South Africans for something one could describe as a South African identity.[1] Perhaps one could even say that Afrikaans is the reason why South Africa has not become a second Australia or New Zealand. The difference lies in the fact that English does not reign supreme and that Afrikaans is a European alternative with African features.

From the start of the emancipation movement of the language in 1875 in Paarl (former Cape Province), Afrikaans had to fulfil a na-

---

[1] According to the figures of the Census 1996 (the last one, preparations for a new one have already started) Afrikaans is the mother tongue of 14.4 per cent of the population of the Republic of South Africa.

tional task. Literature in Afrikaans was supposed to be a vehicle for nation building, Afrikaans itself being a new language compared with Dutch, a new language that was a symbol of national identity. This idea was consolidated in the years of reconstruction after the second Anglo-Boer war (1899-1902). It would, however, give only a partial image of the development of literature prose, poetry and theatre in Afrikaans, if this literature were presented as a monolith, as an obedient reflection of social aims and moral tasks in favour of a solid Afrikaner society.

To a greater or lesser extent there has always been a margin between social expectations of literature in South Africa and the reality of this literature. Literary critics in South Africa emphasized the fundamental change in the lyrical language, in the identity of the lyrical subject during the 1940s and the fundamental opposition of Afrikaans prose to the political *status quo* by the generation of the *Sestigers* – authors like André Brink, Abraham H. de Vries and Etienne Leroux.

Contemporary production of Afrikaans literature proves that Afrikaans is very much still alive. Without wishing to create an image of competition within the body of South African literature, it seems valid to argue that Afrikaans literature is among the most interesting literature being produced in South Africa today. We are witnesses to an explosion of creativity. Afrikaans literature has turned out to have a surprising vitality.[2]

In terms of crime fiction production, there has been a number of very interesting recent works. Chris Moolman with *Sweepslag* (1996), *Operasie Ché* (1997), *Die asem van Ghaddafi* (1998) and *Komplot* (2000) is an example of how an author can write James Bond-like suspense novels that still maintain an element of historical comment. In all these detective stories the characters' names are recognizable variations on the names of living politicians and other VIPs. Therefore the stories read like inside information about things that have never reached the news. Another popular author is Deon Meyer with his novels *Feniks* and *Orion*. *Orion* (2000) for example, is a story about

---

[2]   This applies to all literary genres. The stress lies on prose. Within Afrikaans prose there is a particular interest in the detective novel, autobiographical writings and fairy tales.

former policeman Zatopek van Heerden's search for a murderer and is also an evocation of the dark side of South African history during the last three decades of the twentieth century.[3]

Within current trends in Afrikaans literature, I wish to focus in this essay on one particularly interesting element – the combination of the farm novel with the genre of the detective novel. I will concentrate on the novels of Etienne Leroux and Etienne van Heerden.

Ideology and the horizons of anticipation: the farm novel

In his book of essays *White Writing* J. M. Coetzee draws attention to a very important phenomenon within the entire body of South African literature – the burden of values that the farm as an ideological space represents in South African fiction. Coetzee discusses in detail the works of Olive Schreiner, especially her *The Story of an African Farm* (1883) and also the novels by the most influential author of farm novels in Afrikaans, C. M. van den Heever (1927-1939). What Coetzee writes in his chapter about van den Heever and about the meaning of the farm novel in general is essential within the context of my essay:

> Not unnaturally, the Afrikaans novel of the 1930s gave extended coverage to the phenomena of strife over inheritance (brother against brother, father against son, widow against children), conflict between farmers and land speculators, the hardening of class boundaries between the landed and the landless, the migration of impoverished rural Afrikaners to the cities, competition between black and white labour on the mines and diggings or on the railways, and the threat to traditional values posed by the city (with its liquor, gambling, prostitution, and foreign ways) and by the penetration of novel forms of gratification into the countryside. Faced with what was more and more clearly an epoch in the history of the Afrikaner, Afrikaans novelists responded in diverse ways: they celebrated the memory of the old rural values or proclaimed their durability or elaborated schemes for

---

[3]   Many critics have remarked on the dominance of female writers in present Afrikaans literature. There certainly is a very strong area of Afrikaans literature that deals with the feminine perspective on life and is written by women. Until now, the genre of the detective novel in Afrikaans is dominated by male authors. It will be very interesting to observe the further development of Afrikaans literature from the gender point of view.

their preservation; they tracked the forces of change to their origins in history (capitalism), society (the Jews), or the cosmic order (God's will, the indifference of the universe); they denounced the rapacity of the new class of speculators; they satirized the pettiness, selfishness, and lack of family feeling of the *verengelste* (anglicized) urban Afrikaner.[4]

What Coetzee says with reference to the Afrikaans novel of the Thirties had an impressive persistence during the entire twentieth century. Even at present, the farm novel in all its varieties is a lively literary genre that offers possibilities for change and adaptation under different social and political conditions. This literary genre is a clear example of the existence of an horizon of anticipation on the side of the Afrikaans reader. It is also an exciting example of the emerging difference between the Afrikaans reader and the reality of Afrikaans literature during the Seventies. This development was not limited to the farm novel, it also took place in other subcategories of the novel such as the detective novel.

An examination of the works of Etienne Leroux will illustrate the change from harmony to disagreement, especially the second part of his *Silberstein Trilogy*, the novel *Een vir Azazel.*[5] In *Een vir Azazel* we find a combination of the farm novel with the detective novel. A murder has been committed, but the search for the offender is very different from what the reader would expect. The horizon of expectations is replaced by a new horizon of grotesque reflections.

Een vir Azazel is set on the estate of Welgevonden, a typical name for an extended South African farm, a name that means and prophesies "well found". Welgevonden tries to create and maintain a social order without disorder; it is a blueprint of social engineering come true. This can already be observed in the first novel of the trilogy, *Sewe dae by die Silbersteins* (1962). Henry van Eeden, a young Afrikaner man with an allegorical name travels to Welgevonden to meet his future bride Salome Silberstein. In the course of seven days Henry is initiated into the world of Welgevonden by taking part in seven

---

[4]   J. M. Coetzee, *White Writing: On the Culture of Letters in South Africa*, New Haven: Yale University Press, 1988, 82-83.

[5]   Etienne Leroux, *Een vir Azazel* (*One for the Devil*), Cape Town: Human and Rousseau, 1964.

different types of ritual. In *Een vir Azazel* their child Adam Kadmon Silberstein has grown up. The novel centres around the murder of a young girl at Welgevonden. The unnatural death of this girl, who later in the novel turns out to be a prostitute, already cracks the order of things at Welgevonden. A detective-sergeant with the name Demosthenes H. de Goede comes to Welgevonden to try and discover the identity of the offender but instead focuses on Adam Kadmon Silberstein. He, the descendant of a Jewish mother and an Afrikaner father, is in fact the real threat to the order of Welgevonden. His body is that of a giant, but his mind is that of a young child. The fury of the mob, which is sparked by the death of the young girl, is aimed at the giant. Kadmon Silberstein is the exception to the rule of perfection. He is a permanent thorn in the aspirations of this microcosm, which represents the microcosm of South Africa.

Finally, Kadmon Silberstein is stoned to death by the angry mob, with the detective throwing the first stone. He is transformed into a scapegoat that has to bear the sins of this world. The detective plays the role of a priest in a mythical ordeal. In fact we are dealing with a pseudo-mythical execution. Although the real offender remains at large, the community can be relieved. We are confronted with a reversal of values and an inversion of expectations. The rules of the detective genre are turned upside down (and inside out) in *Een vir Azazel*. There is no genuine search for the murderer by way of induction and deduction. This fundamental change in the rules of the literary game is reflected by the confusing start of the novel. Reading the first chapter, one readily identifies the body in the water as that of the dead girl. At the end it becomes clear that the novel bites its own tail: the body in the dam is not the girl's body but that of Adam Kadmon Silberstein.

Elsewhere I have tried to make the "grotesque" the keyword for understanding this novel.[6] "Grotesque" comprises the structure of this novel in relation to the reactions of its readers. The readers of these novels would have been part of a traditional structure of communication between author and reader. This pattern of communication is

---

[6] Hans Ester, "Die groteske wêreld van *Een vir Azazel*", *Standpunte*, XXVII/7, 1973, 1-10 and "Die groteske wêreld van *Een vir Azazel*", in *Die oog van die son: Beskouings oor boeke en werk van Etienne Leroux*, ed. Charles Malan, Pretoria: Academica, 1982, 105-16.

confused in order to create space to reflect on the preassumptions of Afrikaans readers who know their tradition. In order to understand the implications of *Een vir Azazel* the reader must reconstruct the historical context in which it is set. In his novels Leroux has demonstrated the possibilities of using the genre of the detective novel and, at the same time, fundamentally changing it.

Toorberg and *Die swye van Mario Salviati*

Etienne van Heerden offers a more recent example of an author working in both the tradition of the detective novel and that of the farm novel. He combines the identifiable tradition of both detective novels and farm novels with the level of thinking laid down by the theory of the meaning of language which is based on the structural inter-dependency of the words used. Surprisingly, the combination of a postmodernist consciousness with the detective novel is almost a universal phenomenon nowadays.[7]

Etienne van Heerden's work is characterized by implicit and explicit reflections on the consequences and limits of postmodernist theories. He studies postmodernist theories from the viewpoint of the situation he finds himself in, that situation being South African society with all its moral dilemmas and obligations. The double-sidedness of his work makes his writing interesting: there is the exploration of a traditional genre and the exploration of the society, the environment of ethical sensitivity.

In his doctoral thesis, *Postmodernisme en Prosa: Vertelstrategieë in vyf verhale van Abraham H. de Vries*, published in 1997,[8] Etienne van Heerden reflects on five short stories written by Abraham H. de Vries. He applies various hypotheses from the theory of postmodernism to these stories and examines the relationship between language and reality, between this text and other texts and between the text and the reader. Van Heerden's conclusions are linked with the restriction

---

[7]   In order to study the background of this phenomenon I will refer to Jack van der Weide's dissertation *Detective en anti-detective: Narratologie, psychoanalyse, postmodernisme*, written in 1996 (published Nijmegen: Vantilt). Van der Weide explains the combination of the requirements of psychoanalysis and the standards of the intellectual debate set by postmodernist thinking.

[8]   Etienne van Heerden, *Postmodernisme en Prosa: Vertelstrategieë in vyf verhale van Abraham H. de Vries*, Cape Town: Human and Rousseau, 1997.

and reservation that other perspectives would have led to other conclusions. His reservation is the consequence of the theoretical introduction that precedes the analyses. He does not accept postmodernism as an established theory with an unassailable status. To him postmodernism is a theory that critically questions its own premises. Van Heerden acknowledges the existence of local varieties of postmodernism and identifies a special South African variant under the umbrella of postmodernism in general. He turns out to be an advocate of a form of postmodernism that criticizes the hierarchies of power not only in society but also within literature itself. This type of postmodernism acquires an ethical dimension because of its questioning of the conventions we use to order the world in systematic patterns.

I do not have the scope in this essay to give a detailed description of van Heerden's entire book, but some of his basic thoughts must be mentioned. One is his assumption of the postmodernist text as being ambivalent. He also calls this text "undecided". This attitude regards the world as being more than text and holds that it is involved in the needs and the physical realities of life. Yet, this idea of approaching literary and other texts cannot deny that a tense relationship exists between word and world. Van Heerden concludes that the reality-making nature of language can coexist very well alongside the ambition to create humanity and responsibility.

In his novel *Toorberg* (literally, "Magic Mountain", published in English as *Ancestral Voices*) van Heerden describes the opposition of facts, rules and decisions with the imponderable motivations to create an image of reality. In *Toorberg* the police magistrate with the symbolic name Van der Ligt (meaning "of the light") pays a long visit to the estate of Toorberg to investigate the strange death of the young boy Noag du Pisani. Fourteen months before Noag, called Druppeltjie du Pisani, fell into a water borehole on the estate (or farm) of Toorberg. The central question is how did Druppeltjie du Pisani come to his bad end? Did the boy die as a result of the fall into the borehole or did somebody shoot the boy through his head when he was immovably stuck in the hole? What is the truth about what has happened? Rumours abound. No other authority than the judiciary can clear up the dark events. Police magistrate Van der Ligt's files are growing and growing but judicial transparency is decreasing proportionally. The enigma in this novel, comparable to Leroux's *Een vir Azazel*, is not the unexplained death but rather reality itself and the incapacity of language to represent its complexity.

The conceptions and notions of reality move to the centre of the literary text. Instead of a satisfactory identification of the murderer of Druppeltjie du Pisani, the construction of the framework of reality becomes the target of searching. The novel illustrates the choices that have been made in order to construct a coherent image of the world. This is central to van Heerden's novel. These choices include the mode of interpreting the past to serve the needs of the present, the dichotomy between culture and nature, and fixation with the mythical space between both sides of the frontier. What the novel *Toorberg* intends to do is to identify the auxiliaries used by human beings to stay in control of the uncertainties of life. Druppeltjie's death does not entirely fade into the background. In fact, the sad end of the little boy embarrasses all the forms of construction. The fate of the boy itself marks the start of the restructuring of human relations and of the efforts undertaken to control life and death, integration and segregation. His life and death lead to the questioning of the social and moral order of Toorberg.

Guilt is one of the most essential notions in van Heerden's work, in his novels and novellas. In many of his novels a crime has been committed and it looks as if the revelation of this crime and the identification of the criminal are the main issues. A very good example of this strategy is the novel *Kikoejoe* (1996) in which the rape of a black girl is the central puzzle. But in *Kikoejoe* as in *Die swye van Mario Salviati* the crime is an excuse to follow a certain trail. One trail manifests itself as a multiplicity of trails. The investigation of the criminal case leads to a confusing analysis of the cobwebs of stories, of narrative knots that succeed each other or ask the reader to pay attention to all simultaneously.

Die swye van Mario Salviati is the story of Ingi Friedländer, a young woman with a university degree in fine arts who is sent to the small village of Tallejare by museum officials in Cape Town. In this village lives the sculptor Jonty Jack Bergh who is in possession of a legendary sculpture, named Visman Steier, which according to Jonty Jack is not man-made but a present from heavenly beings, the angels. Ingi Friedländer is in charge of buying the sculpture and bringing it to Cape Town. The sculpture obviously has a political meaning for her employers and is intended to take a prominent place in the South African parliament. What seems to be a rather simple task reveals itself to be a quest to discover the secrets this inconspicuous village is hiding behind the façade of normality. Ingi Friedländer is increasingly fascinated by the dark backgrounds of the individuals here and of the community as a whole.

Very ingeniously the narrator intertwines various episodes and eras from the past. One of these episodes is the Anglo-Boer war in which a small group of Boer fighters seek to hide the gold treasure of the Transvaal Republic, the "Krüger Pounds". All trace of them disappears in Tallejare. Another era is the Second World War with the arrival of Italian prisoners who are used as labourers on the farms of Tallejare. The most intriguing character next to Jonty Jack Bergh is the Italian deaf-mute Mario Salviati. He assists Groot Karel Bergh, Jonty's father, in constructing a watercourse for the irrigation of the lands on this side of the mountain that dominates this landscape – a construction that was intended to (and finally did) undermine existing ideas about the laws of nature. This transgression of the boundaries of rationality forms an enormous challenge to the willingness of the community of Tallejare to change established ways of thinking. In the course of time a stone has grown along with Mario Salviati's hand. Nothing could be more symbolic of the unity between himself and the world of South Africa. The stone is a symbol and in a certain way a stigma. No word can break his link with this world.

It is this transgression of normality that leads the way to the unveiling of the basic secret of Tallejare, the document in which the location of the Krüger Pounds is described. This part of the past is linked with a terrible crime, the execution of the Boer horsemen who were witnesses to the final destination of the golden treasure. The crime is a common secret. Gradually the reader understands that the description in the Prologue of the novel is the result of the quest at the end of the novel. Groot Karel Bergh disappeared after falling into despair over the supposed failure of the water scheme that he and Mario Salviati had developed. With his horse coach he vanished into a cave. I shall quote part of the Prologue and a small part of one of the last chapters. First the Prologue:

> Die verlede stamp hulle teen die bors. Hulle deins terug, want dit lyk of die swart koets begin beweeg en op hulle afkom. Maar dit is bloot 'n optiese illusie. Die stof is besig om weg te sif en die starendes se pupille vergroot terwyl hulle die donker in tuur.

Die koets is 'n verskynsel; 'n spookkoets wat glinster weens die vuurvlieë wat daaroor swerm en dit bewaak. So lank verwyder van die aandrang van lig en die aanraking van mensehande, het dit bykans splinternuut bewaar gebly. 'n Stalaktiet drup tot teen die koets se dak vas en stalagmiete groei uit die grotbodem om dit van onder te anker. Die aarde steek vingers uit om die onwaarskynlike koets te beskerm.

Op die leiselbankie sit 'n wit geraamte. Hy is nog gekleed, en uit die beendere van ses perde is af te lei dat hulle in die tuig gesterf het. Aan hul skedels roer volstruisvere in die ligte bries.

Ingi Friedländer beur vorentoe om beter te sien. Tussen die vingers van die geraamte se linkerhand sit 'n sigaar, halfpad gerook. Die ander beenhand klem 'n dokument vas. Dit is oud en bros en vergee, en vuurvlieë sit glinsterend op die rande daarvan.

Die derde kaart, dink almal.[9]

And, from the last chapter:

Jonty kom stadig aangestap na die koets, wat in stalaktiete en stalagmiete vasgevang is, asof klipvingers dit dra. Hy steek sy hand uit – en 'n sug gaan op – na die dokument in Karel Skoonveld se hand. Toe hy daaraan raak, verstof dit tot 'n wolkie wat wegdwarrel, en verdwyn. Jonty vryf verbaas sy duim en wysvinger teen mekaar. Daar sit grys poeier aan sy vingertoppe, asof hy aan 'n dooie vuur se as gevat het. Die priester slaan die teken van die kruis, en gaan vorentoe

---

[9]   Etienne van Heerden, *Die swye van Mario Salviati*, Cape Town: Tafelberg-Uitgewers, 2000, 9: "The past goes against the grain with them. They shrink back as it seems that the coach starts moving and bears down upon them. But that is only an optical illusion. Dust is floating down and the pupils of the glancing watchers enlarge while they peer into the dark.
        The coach is an appearance; a ghost-coach that glitters because of the fireflies that swarm around it and watch over it. So long out of the impulse of the light and the touch of human hands, that it has remained almost brand new. A stalactite drips itself into fixation to the roof of the coach and stalagmites grow from the soil of the cave to cramp it from underneath. The earth stretches its fingers to protect the unlikely coach.
        On the front seat there is a white skeleton sitting. He is still dressed and from the bones of six horses one can conclude that they have died in harness. On their skulls ostrich feathers move in the slant of wind.
        Ingi Friedländer leans over to see better. Between the fingers of the skeleton's left hand is a cigar, half smoked. The other hand of bones clasps a document. It is old and frail and yellowed and fireflies sit glancing on its edges.
        The third map, everybody thinks." (Translations my own.)

om Jonty, wat nou aan die bewe is, te help. Maar dit ontgaan Ingi nie dat die gebaar wat Jonty maak, die duim wat vryf teen die wysvinger, die universele teken is vir, ironies, aardse rykdom: geld.[10]

History is reduced to a skeleton. The essential documents and clues are pulverized. There is no access except by way of telling the story from the questions that arise today.

Nobody in this novel has the role of the observer. Everyone is observer and is observed him or herself simultaneously. There is no impartial position from which the world can be appropriately represented. Coming to Tallejare means that one has to give up the position of outsider. Involvement is the only acceptable and possible response. For Ingi Friedländer this means she has to delve into the lines of communication and understanding that lie beneath the surface of ritualized social habits. For her the erotic implications of the accepted manners in Tallejare lead to questions and restlessness. Under the surface a far-reaching sexual aggression is perceptible. The novel describes her hesitating initiation into the closed world of Tallejare. A terrible crime has been committed in the past, almost a hundred years ago. This crime led to distorted social relations and a situation in which almost everyone is the hostage of the other. This might be described as a general sense of imprisonment in the minds of the people of Tallejare. Of course, Ingi Friedländer does not forget that her instruction was to buy the sculpture and, in reality, to steal it from where it belongs. Gradually Ingi becomes part of this confusing world in which the laws of normality are shaken up, or rather replaced by a different balance of rationality and irrationality, of physical existence and spiritual presence. The quest ends and begins with the discovery of vitality. Mario Salviati dies and Ingi lives:

---

[10]   *Ibid.*, 401: "Jonty steps up slowly to the coach. Which is caught in stalactites and stalagmites, as if tone fingers carry it. He stretches his hand – a sigh was heard – to the document in Karel Skoonveld's hand. As soon as he touches it, it pulverises to a cloud of dust that whirls away and disappears. Astonished, Jonty rubs his thumb and forefinger. There is a grey powder on his fingertips, as if he has touched a dead fire. The priest makes the sign of the cross and steps forward to help Jonty who is trembling all over. But Ingi does not fail to see that the gesture that Jonty makes, rubbing his thumb against his forefinger, is the universal sign for, ironically, earthly wealth: money."

Sy neem die handklip van Mario Salviati uit haar jeans se sak, en
sonder om behoorlik daarna te kyk, gooi sy dit so ver sy kan die vlakte
in, tussen ander klippe en lae bossies.
 Dan klim sy weer in haar geel Peugeot, en toe sy oor 'n effense
hoogte kom, sien sy 'n trop springbokke pronkend hul balletspronge
uitvoer. "Mario Salviati," fluister sy aan die trop, terwyl hulle heerlik
uitgelate, rats van sintuig en lewensvreugde, oor die klippe spaander.[11]

The special quality of *Die swye van Mario Salviati* lies in the ways in
which it links the playing with genre conventions and readers' expectations to an exploration of the complexity of human consciousness.
This combination of various traditions within Afrikaans literature with
a questioning of the foundations of human knowledge is a good example of the distinct features of present postcolonial literature in Afrikaans.

---

[11]   *Ibid.*, 403: "She takes the hand-stone of Mario Salviati from the pocket of her
jeans, and without looking properly at it, she throws it as far as she can into the
field, between other stones and low bushes.
 Then she climbs into her yellow Peugeot again. And when she passes a little
hill, she sees a flock of springbok performing its ballet gambols. 'Mario Salviati,'
she whispers towards the flock, while they frolic wonderfully across the rocks,
overflowing with joy, full of life and agile senses."

WANTED: NATIONAL ALGERIAN IDENTITY

BEATE BURTSCHER-BECHTER

The question of an Algerian identity has repeatedly been addressed by both intellectuals and government officials since the release of Algeria into independence in 1962. Therefore, it comes as no surprise that the search for a national identity is also reflected in the development of the francophone Algerian crime novel.[1] Its relatively short history began in 1970 with the spy novels by Youcef Khader. But it was not until two decades later, in the early Nineties, that the genre attained its first high point in the *romans noirs* of Yasmina Khadra. The twenty-three Algerian crime novels published between 1970 and 1998[2] are closely related to the political, social and historical events of the times they were written and clearly show the development of an Algeria in search of itself.[3]

---

[1] When we subsequently speak of the Algerian crime novel the comments refer exclusively to Algerian crime novels written in French.

[2] As with the novels of Yasmina Khadra and their publication in France the Algerian crime novel caught up with the international development of the genre, the end of our period of investigation is set at 1998, the year in which *L'Automne des chimères* (Paris: Éditions Baleine) appeared as the last volume of the series of *romans noirs* by Khadra. For further details concerning the development of the francophone Algerian crime novel, see Beate Burtscher-Bechter, *Algerien – ein Land sucht seine Mörder: Die Entwicklung des frankophonen algerischen Kriminalromans (1970-1998)*, Frankfurt am Main: IKO, 1999.

[3] The text corpus was collected according to the directives of the renowned literary scholar and bibliographer Jean Déjeux (*La Littérature maghrébine d'expression française*, Paris: Presses Universitaires de France, 1992, 88-90) and was merely complemented by the novel *Fredy la rafale* by Mohamed Benayat (Algiers: ENAL, 1991) and the recent publications by Yasmina Khadra. The crime novel *Causse Toujours* published in the series *Le Poulpe* by the Algerian author Moloud Akkouche has not been included as it contains no reference to Algeria. The same applies to the crime novel *Avis déchéance*, published by Akkouche in 1998 in Gallimard's *Série Noire*. The book *De bonnes nouvelles d'Algérie* by the Algerian

By comparing and contrasting the spy novels written by Youcef Khader and the *romans noirs* penned by Yasmina Khadra the search for an Algerian identity, as well as its gradual assertion, can be observed. Whilst the novels of the early Seventies can clearly be identified with the political world view of the Algerian government at that time – they therefore adopt and justify its prejudices unthinkingly and proclaim a national identity as defined by the leaders of the state – the crime novels by Yasmina Khadra, written in the Nineties, stand in stark opposition to the dominant regime and its policies. Twenty years after the publication of the first spy novels, the justification of the regime and the confirmation of the existing systems have been replaced by harsh criticism of the existing system of government and the prevailing social conditions, as well as an authentic view of Algerian reality and a critical analysis of the events of war. At the same time the rooting of these novels in Algerian everyday experience contributes substantially to the affirmation of an *algerianité* that has nothing in common with the idealized national identity of the Seventies.

Algeria after Independence

The euphoria and the expectations of the Algerian population were high, when, after more than 130 years of French rule, Algeria attained its independence in 1962. For more than eight years the Algerians had fought their way to freedom in a bloody war of liberation. Now they placed all their hopes on the FLN (*Front de Libération Nationale*) that had taken over the leadership of the state after the war. One year after the end of the war of liberation the young independent state received its constitution under its first president, Ahmed Ben Bella. Algeria founded a democratic people's republic; Islam became the state religion and Arabic the official language. Leading the young nation into independence, the Algerian rulers voted for the path to socialism. Now they looked towards the Arab World. Yet the fact that Algeria also belonged to the African World was clearly emphasized and expressed in the support for those African peoples still under colonial rule. Thus the *Charte d'Alger* of the year 1964, which can be seen as a

---

author Chawki Amari published in April 1998 in France has been excluded on the basis of formal criteria – this is a collection of twelve *nouvelles noires*.

political and ideological manifesto of the years of Ben Bella, proclaims the common battle of the Arabian and African World against imperialism and neocolonialism and propagates a Muslim and national socialism.[4]

In the years following independence the Algerian population was mainly concerned with trying to cope with the massive changes resulting from long-awaited freedom. Soon after the French colonial powers had left the country, massive convergence upon the cities set in among the rural population. The destitute farmers hoped for work and accommodation left behind by the *pieds noirs*, as the French who lived in Algeria during French rule were called. For most Algerians moving into towns thus also meant a move into unemployment as urbanization was accompanied by a massive population explosion in the Algeria of the Sixties.[5]

The rise of urban society and modern industrial towns in the nineteenth century is generally seen as one of the most significant preconditions for the development of the crime novel in Europe.[6] Thus it is also in Algeria that the gathering pace of urbanization and forced industrialization must be seen as providing the foundations for the birth of the Algerian crime novel. The fact that the plots of the first Algerian novels are not set in Algerian towns, which would provide suitable settings, might seem surprising but can be explained by the fact that the first Algerian crime novels were not the result of an unrestrained development of the genre, but served the purposes of an official state ideology. According to this ideology, crimes could not happen in Algeria and particularly not in Algiers. The location of the novels, and thus crime as such, was placed outside Algeria. Algeria and its townships thus remained untarnished places to which the hero could return after the accomplishment of his mission. Even if the spy novels that form the starting point of the genre in Algeria are not set within the national boundaries, both urbanization and industrialization

---

[4] See Werner Pieck, *Algerien: Die wiedergewonnene Würde*, Hildesheim: G. Olms, 1987, 62-63.

[5] See Benjamin Stora, *Histoire de l'Algérie depuis l'indépendance*, Paris: La Découverte, 1994, 24-25.

[6] See Pierre Boileau and Thomas Narcejac, *Le Roman policier*, Paris: Presses Universitaires de France, 1992, 14-15; and Francis Lacassin, *Mythologie du roman policier*, Paris: Christian Bourgois, 1993, 23-28.

and the decisive changes that accompanied this, at least implicitly constitute an important precondition for the development of the genre, and in particular created the climate in which the crime novel could establish itself on a long-term footing in Algeria.[7]

Agent SM 15 – an Algerian James Bond

With *Délivrez la Fidayia!*[8] – the first of a total of six spy novels by Youcef Khader that were published by the national publishing house SNED[9] – the most renowned Algerian secret agent Mourad Saber, also known as SM 15,[10] entered Algerian literature in 1970. The handsome elite soldier, who works for the counter espionage section of the Algerian secret service, is not merely very good-looking but also possesses substantial technical and linguistic skills, and has mastered not only a great variety of weaponry but also a range of martial arts. That this character is modelled on James Bond is clear.[11] But there are also

---

[7]   During this period of time, in which the leading Algerian members of society were keen to lead and form the young state both politically and ideologically, the Algerian state publishing house SNED (*Société Nationale d'Édition et de Diffusion*) was founded in 1967. It also published the first Algerian spy novels. Thus the publishers were controlled by the state and the authors who wanted to publish their works with a state publisher had to reckon with censorship and bans on publication which amongst other things led to a large proportion of francophone Algerian authors publishing their works abroad. Apart from this, the bureaucratic requirements were enormous and the formal quality of the books very bad. Manuscripts would therefore spend years in drawers without the author ever being informed about what happened to his works. See Stora, *Histoire de l'Algérie depuis l'indépendance*, 59; and Rédha Belhadjoudja, *Traitement de la notion de suspense dans le roman policier algérien, ou la naissance du polar en Algérie*, Diss: Université d'Alger, 1993, 231.

[8]   Youcef Khader, *Délivrez la Fidayia!*, Algiers: SNED, 1970.

[9]   The publication of *Délivrez la Fidayia!* in 1970 was followed by *Halte au plan 'Terreur'* and *La Vengeance passe par Ghaza* in that same year. 1972 saw the publication of *Les Bourreaux meurent aussi* and *Quand les 'Panthères' attaquent* (all Algiers: SNED).

[10]   The letters S and M not only stand for the names of the agent Mourad Saber but also for the unit he works for, the *Sécurité Militaire algérienne*.

[11]   See Zineb Ali Benali and Bouba Tabti, 1984, "Le Roman d'espionnage algérien: Mourad Saber ould James Bond", in *Balades dans la culture en Algérie en 1979*, Algiers: OPU, 1984, 147-75; Aaron Segal, "The Spy as Hero: Algeria's Answer to James Bond", in *New Middle East* 41, (1972), 21-24; and Rédha Belhadjoudja, "L'Homo-Saber: Portrait d'un héros", *Horizons*, 9 November 1987.

substantial differences between the Muslim agent and his western model. In contrast to James Bond, SM 15 exhibits those stereotypical properties of character generally attributed to Muslims: he is presented as completely celibate, drinking no alcohol and abhorring smoking. In this respect SM 15 does not merely differ substantially from his European and American counterparts, these conspicuous character traits also distinguish him from his opponents, particularly the Zionists, who are presented as being driven by animal instincts and obsessed with sex.[12] Agent SM 15 is stylized to an absurd level by his de facto invincibility and invulnerability, his strict moral principles, his asceticism and his strange attitude towards the other sex. An identification of the reader with the Algerian *überhero* is unlikely and yet the adventures Mourad Saber has to survive in the course of the six-part novel series are clearly marked by the proclamation of Algerian national identity.

The patriotic defence of one's own country is generally the explicit aim of the spy novel, and at the same time the triggering element of the plot. The thematic focus of this subspecies of crime novel concentrates on political structures and powers that remain hidden from the reader. In order to distinguish one's own nation and its agents from those of the opponents, the defamation of the political opponent or of the enemy provides an underlying theme for this genre.[13] If we take into account the genre-specific characteristics and aims of the spy novel, it becomes obvious that it was neither easy for the Algerian ruling powers, nor for the Algerian readership at the end of the Sixties to be confronted with an exclusively European choice of spy novels. The racism directed towards the Arab population in the European and American novels as well as the depiction of enemies in no way corresponded to the political expectations of the Algerian leaders.[14] In view

---

[12] See Jochen Schmidt, *Gangster, Opfer, Detektive: Eine Typengeschichte des Kriminalromans*, Frankfurt am Main: Ullstein, 1989, 433-34, who notes that it was customary to present the hero as celibate in the Nazi films of the Thirties, yet to attribute substantial sexual passions to their opponents.

[13] See Peter Nusser, *Der Kriminalroman*, Stuttgart: J. B. Metzler, 1992, 119-26.

[14] See Marc Riglet, "Le Roman d'espionnage algérien", *Maghreb*, 52 (1972), 45: "Il était sans doute insupportable à l'Algérie de voir figurer dans ses kiosques des romans français d'espionnage, qui, sous couvert d'aventures, exposaient des thèmes les plus opposés aux choix algériens de politique étrangère et distillaient un racisme anti-arabe sans fard. Car dans l'ordre des 'méchants', l'Arabe tient une

of these circumstances, intensified by the fact that spy novels generally met with great interest, it is understandable that the Algerian government was keen to encourage the production and publication of an autonomous Algerian spy or rather crime novel, in order to contribute to national identity.[15]

In order to fulfil this aim, Youcef Khader[16] focuses on two types of enemy that are supposed to confirm the political orientation of the new nation. On the one hand, there are the Zionists, Israel and its political allies, in particular the United States of America, depicted as declared enemies of Algeria and the Arab World, and thus membership of the Arab World and solidarity with the Palestinians are emphasized. On the other hand, imperialism, in particular Zionist imperialism, recurs as a stereotypical foe in all the novels and serves the purpose of celebrating the victorious struggle for independence and the solidarity of the Algerian nation towards its still oppressed brother nations.

As an ally of the Arab World, SM 15 fights against Sin-Beth, the Israeli secret service, and Zionism in all the novels. The stereotypical and generalizing descriptions of the conflict between Arabs and Zionists show the Arab nation (in the singular) as an innocent and hapless victim of Zionist aggression. The bone of contention is the foundation of the Zionist and imperialist state of Israel, which as an artificial con-

---

place non négligeable à côté de l'Allemand sadique, du froid robot soviétique ou de l'inquiétant et bien sûr rusé Asiatique." ("It was without doubt unacceptable to Algeria and Algerians to see themselves represented in French spy novels which under the pretext of describing adventures treated themes directly opposed to the aims of Algerian foreign policy and would exhibit a blatant form of anti-Arab racism. For among the evil-doers the Arab retained a position close to that of the sadistic German, the cold Russian robot and the sinister and sly Asian.")

[15] In order to speed up this process the importation of foreign crime novels was increasingly restricted after the publication of *Délivrez la Fidayia!* until they disappeared completely from the Algerian book market. See Belhadjoudja, *Traitement de la notion de suspense dans le roman policier algérien*, 70.

[16] Behind the name Youcef Khader we will find a French author of Catalan descent who acted as ghostwriter for various authors and finally published his memoirs of the Spanish Civil War under various pseudonyms (Jean Lafay, Tim Oger, Roger Vlim, Gil Darcy, G. J. Arnaud and others) with various publishers. Under the pseudonym Youcef Khader he wrote Arabian anti-Zionist spy novels, published by the Algerian publishing house SNED. See Belhadjoudja, *Traitement de la notion de suspense*, 43-44.

struct is deprived of all claim to legitimacy.[17] The struggle of the Algerian agent against Zionists and imperialists and the associated violence is justified by the inimical attitude of the opponent, his destructive hatred and his unpredictable acts of sadism, to which SM 15 responds with equal cruelty. But as his cruel methods serve the aims of the Arab nation, and contribute to the liberation of oppressed peoples, they appear to be fully justified in the representations found in these novels.

Racist elements, stereotypical descriptions and a very biased point of view characterize the series of novels by Youcef Khader, which are obviously driven by one ulterior motive: the proclamation of a national identity devised for Algeria by the politicians in power in order to provide some point of reference to a population in desperate search of its roots after a hundred and thirty years of colonial rule. The same aim is pursued in the idealization of the Algerian War of Independence that also recurs in Youcef Khader's work and becomes a mythical component in Algerian political identity.[18]

"A response and a substitute" – it is under this title that Marc Riglet pointedly characterizes the goals to be attained by the first Algerian spy novels and their protagonists. They represented an answer to the European and American novels, their heroes and their racist, anti-Arab image, and at the same time, they filled the vacuum that had hitherto been represented by the Algerian spy novel.[19] In view of the ideological orientation, which among other things aimed at strengthening national self-esteem, Youcef Khader's novels can also be seen as an answer to the question posed by the Algerian people as to their national identity. The fact that this answer is not a realistic one, but at best an ersatz identity, can be derived from the stereotypes and clichéd presentations.

---

[17] This is illustrated by the fact that in the novels Israel is always used in quotation marks.

[18] This myth lasts into the Eighties and is an essential element in the legitimization of the national party FLN and is literally cultivated by those in power. See Stora, *Histoire de l'Algérie depuis l'indépendance*, 73-75.

[19] Riglet, "Le Roman d'espionnage algérien", 45.

A further development of the genre in fast motion

Up to the end of the Eighties the politics of the ruling FLN, the increase in population and a persistent economic crisis was characteristic of the political, economic and social developments in Algeria. For many years the agricultural sector was neglected in favour of the industrialization of the country and the state provided only very limited means for building accommodation, cultural and social institutions and the development of a suitable transport infrastructure. The need for increasingly large food imports and shrinking income from oil exports as the only national source of income caused foreign debt to explode and plunged the country into a state of continuing crisis.

This was a hasty sketch of the external conditions in which the genre of crime novels was able to gain a foothold in Algeria. Soon after the publication of the novels by Youcef Khader, two spy novels by Abdelaziz Lamrani (*D. contre-attaque* and *Piège à Tel Aviv*[20]) appeared on the market, two works that – like Khader's – place the defence of one's own country as well as the defamation of political opponents at the centre of interest. The protagonist of the series, Emir 17, is not presented in such an infallible and clichéd fashion as the Muslim SM 15, but these novels substantiate the political ideals of the Algerian state with the stereotypes typical of the genre.

Only ten years after the rise of the Algerian crime novel the first half of the Eighties formally led to a transition from the spy novel to the *roman noir* and thus a relocation of events to Algeria. Gradually, the idealized secret agents of the spy novels were replaced by down to earth police officers and detectives, and the sociological dimension of the plots became increasingly important. Thematically the persistent economic crisis of the Eighties can be found in the novels by Larbi Abahri (*Banderilles et muleta*[21]) and Zehira Houfani Berfas (*Le Portrait du disparu* and *Les Pirates du désert*[22]). Industrial crime is discovered as a topic and the protagonists are confronted with the need to protect the Algerian market from external influences and subversive

---

[20] Abdelaziz Lamrani, *D. contre-attaque* (1973) and *Piège à Tel Aviv* (1980), both Algiers: SNED.

[21] Larbi Abahri, *Banderilles et muleta*, Algiers: SNED, 1981.

[22] Zehira Houfani Berfas, *Le Portrait du disparu* and *Les Pirates du desert*, Algiers: ENAL, 1986.

elements within Algerian society. Despite the transition from the spy novel to the *roman noir* these novels remain caught up in clichéd and stereotyped representations, and are still dominated by a polarization of good and bad, friend and foe. Crime represents an exceptional situation and can be overcome at the end of the novel – the Algerian economic system and thus the national esteem of the country have been saved.

In view of the tense economic situation in Algeria, white collar crime remained a dominant theme and was reflected in Djamel Dib's *romans noirs* in the second half of the Eighties (*La Résurrection d'Antar, La Saga des djinns* and *L'Archipel du Stalag*[23]). At the same time the novels by Salim Aïssa (*Mimouna* and *Adel s'emmêle*[24]) are marked by a deeper psychological characterization of victims and thus introduce a new aspect into the development of the Algerian crime novel. During this period the clear distinction between good and evil slowly fades and the authors' view of the characters and their criminal machinations becomes more differentiated. Even the investigator is presented in a new light. Djamel Dib in particular manages to equip his hero, Inspector Antar, with more than the well-known clichéd characteristics, but provides him with individual traits and incorporates him into everyday Algerian life, which is no longer just seen as a backdrop but as a real space with all its specific cultural, social, economic and political problems. In contrast to the novels by Youcef Khader, national identity in the *romans noirs* of Djamel Dib is conveyed through the reader identifying with a hero who is aware of the problems of his home country but initially only comments on the events with humorous remarks. Despite the innovations mentioned, Djamel Dib's novels remain conventional particularly in their endings. At the end of the plot the investigators are able to capture the criminals and restore a healthy and sound world. The dream of a peaceful and free Algeria is upheld.

Before the Algerian novel achieves its first peak in the novels of Yasmina Khadra, at the end of the Eighties and the beginning of the Nineties, we observe a qualitative breakdown in the development of

---

[23]   Djamel Dib, *La Résurrection d'Antar* (1986), *La Saga des djinns* (1986), and *L'Archipel du Stalag* (1989), all Algiers: ENAL.

[24]   Salim Aïssa, *Mimouna*, Algiers: Laphomic, 1987; *Adel s'emmêle*, Algiers: ENAL, 1988.

the genre with the novels of Rabah Zeghouda (*Double Djo pour une muette*[25]) and Mohamed Benayat (*Fredy la Rafale*) in Algeria. Neither the topic nor the characterization of the protagonists endow the novels with significance, but the titles should be mentioned for the sake of completeness.

1988 – The year of transition

After thirty years of exclusive rule by the FLN the country was in a state of economic, political and social disarray. In October 1988 the pent-up aggression of the populace resulted in a spontaneous uprising, which spread like wildfire from Algiers to all other towns in the country and plunged Algeria into chaos such as had been unknown since the War of Independence. Algerians went out on the streets to protest against corruption and economic mismanagement, demanded political and economic reforms and clamoured for freedom and democracy. In view of the consequences resulting from the uprisings, the year 1988 is generally seen as a turning point in the history of the young nation state as the events of that October introduced a new epoch in Algerian politics, which Bernhard Cubertafond so fittingly described as a step towards democracy and a period of uncertainty.[26] A liberalization of the party system and the legalization of the FIS (*Front Islamique du Salut*) resulted from the process of democratization. The decisive victory of this opposition party in the 1990 municipal elections and the large number of votes gained in the first round of the parliamentary elections in 1991 expressed the degree of dissatisfaction of large parts of the population with the FLN and its corrupt bureaucrats. Consequently the Algerian Head of State, Chadli Bendjedid, was forced to abdicate by the army in the early months of 1992. The second election round was annulled, a state of emergency was proclaimed and the FIS, the party that had clearly won the election, declared illegal.

In the summer months of 1992, a series of terrorist attacks shook the country, which resulted in bloody competition between the militant supporters of the FIS and the army and finally ended in civil war. Under General Liamine Zéroual, who had led the country since 1994,

---

[25]   Rabah Zeghouda, *Double Djo pour une muette* Algiers: ENAL, 1988.
[26]   Bernhard Cubertafond, *L'Algérie contemporaine*, Paris: Presses Universitaires de France, 1995, 7-13.

the bloody feuds between fundamentalists and the military achieved depressing dimensions in the Nineties. Assassination attempts on specific targets and terrorist attacks dominated everyday life in Algeria, accompanied by a flourishing black market, constantly increasing unemployment among the younger population, unchecked population explosion and an acute dearth of accommodation. To this are to be added the machinations of influential politicians and of the Algerian financial Mafia, as well as the persistent fear of massacres, abductions and terrorist attacks that had gripped the Algerian population. These events provide the background for the plots of *Morituri*, *Double blanc* and *L'Automne des chimères*,[27] a crime trilogy by Yasmina Khadra, located in the midst of the bloody Algerian conflict.

Commissaire Llob – Idealistic Inspector and patrotic Writer

At the centre of the five crime novels by Yasmina Khadra stands the seemingly rough, but essentially sensitive protagonist of the series, Commissaire Llob.[28] Both as a police officer in the Algerian capital and as an author he stands for justice and enlightenment. The inspector's first two adventures *Le Dingue au bistouri*[29] and *La Foire des enfoirés*[30] appeared in Algeria in 1990 and 1993, as written by the protagonist, Commissaire Llob. *Le Dingue au bistouri* in particular was enthusiastically acclaimed by the critics and the style of the *roman noir*, a successful mixture of humorous, sarcastic, poetic and emotional descriptions, and the anchoring of the work in Algerian everyday life and concrete allusions to non-literary reality were particularly praised. *Le Dingue au bistouri* and *La Foire des enfoirés* were followed by three further novels about Commissaire Llob: *Morituri*, *Double blanc* and *L'Automne des chimères* were published under the pseudonym Yasmina Khadra in 1997 and 1998, and they appeared in France in view of the tense situation in Algeria.

---

[27] Yasmina Khadra, *Morituri* (1997), *Double blanc* (1997) *L'Automne des chimères* (1998), all Paris: Éditions Baleine.

[28] In Arabic the name Llob means "hard core, pure heart".

[29] Yasmina Khadra, *Le Dingue au bistouri*, Paris: Flammarion, 1999. (Reprint of Commissaire Llob, *Le Dingue au bistouri*, Algiers: Laphomic, 1990).

[30] Yasmina Khadra, (as Commissaire Llob), *La Foire des enfoirés*, Algiers: Laphomic, 1993.

Apart from the speculations concerning the real identity of Yasmina Khadra (only in September 1999 did the author admit that a man was hidden behind the female pseudonym;[31] in January 2001, the former officer in the Algerian army threw off the mask and disclosed his real name, Mohamed Moulessehoul),[32] interest was particularly roused by the setting of Algerian reality marked by bomb attacks and assassinations. It is through this thematic orientation that this novel trilogy is clearly distinguishable from the first two volumes of the series. The crisis that shook Algeria in the Nineties is constantly present in the trilogy and the fear of terrorist attacks weighs on the investigating officers and their families. The humorous comments of the inspector running through the first two novels are replaced by bitter comments and critical accusations against those responsible for this calamitous situation.

Following the secret agents and special agents dominating Algerian literature into the Nineties, the figure of Commissaire Llob provides an endpoint to a development that can be compared to the appearance of Maigret in France and can be described as the "civilization of the detective".[33] Just like Maigret, Commissaire Llob is employed in a civil profession – he is a police employee in Algiers, is married and has four children. Apart from that, Llob no longer appears as timeless hero, untouched by the effects of time and age, but ages in the course of the five novels, and the more than fifty-year-old inspector of *Le Dingue au bistouri* awaits his sixtieth birthday in *L'Automne des chimères*. As a police officer, husband and father of a family Brahim Llob is integrated into Algerian society and forms part of the reality of his country. He struggles with everyday problems like the average Algerian citizen, is rooted in the traditions of his home country and in all novels displays his knowledge of the history and culture of his homeland. The rootedness of the protagonist in his country is reflected in the lyrical and sensitive descriptions of the Algerian capital and is also expressed in the inspector's worried comments on the developments in

---

[31] Yasmina Khadra in an interview with Jean-Luc Douin, "Yasmina Khadra lève une part de son mystère", *Le Monde*, 10 September 1999.

[32] Yasmina Khadra in an interview with Jean-Luc Douin, "Yasmina Khadra se démasque", *Le Monde*, 12 January 2001.

[33] Ulrich Schulz-Buschhaus, *Formen und Ideologien des Kriminalromans: Ein gattungsgeschichtlicher Essay*, Frankfurt am Main: Athenaion, 1975, 157.

Algeria and his critical analysis of the crisis in his home country. It is obvious that Commissaire Llob loves his country. His intense criticism of those who have plunged Algeria into civil war is to be seen as an expression of his worries and as proof of his patriotism. In stark contrast to SM 15, the upright average citizen Llob turns into a figure of identification for the reader and bearer of national identity, which has nothing to do with government plans or idealizing visions of the powers that be. The Algerian identity represented by Llob is that of a self-confident and critical citizen, who has a realistic view of the problems his country is confronted with, and gives everything – even his life – to bring the crisis to an end.

Both sociologist and sympathizer,[34] Commissaire Llob analyses the events in his home country and throws a critical eye on the events in the Algerian capital. The impression of Algeria created by Yasmina Khadra through the perspective of his protagonist reflects the complex situation that in the middle of the Nineties led to a crisis, and can be seen as a reflection of prejudiced black and white pictures that see the Islamic fundamentalists as those solely responsible for the civil war. In his trilogy the author shows that the political and social conditions of the past decades are to be held responsible for the Algerian crisis and that the manipulators behind the bloody events were at least partly to be found in government circles, that many Algerians executed the cruel plans themselves for various reasons. Yasmina Khadra makes it unmistakably clear that the perpetrators can be found in all walks of life and he not only points at the cruelties of the conflict but also castigates those profiteers who managed to change sides at the right point in time and who now have parties in well-guarded villas and share money and power amongst themselves, whilst in other quarters of the Algerian capital evils drive the population out into the streets and turn them into criminals. Thus the author exemplifies one aspect of the crisis in Algeria that not only emphasizes its complexity but also its hopelessness.

By combining the solving of a crime in the *roman noir* with the discovery of specific socio-historical aspects the genre attains a critical potential which Yasmina Khadra draws upon in his trilogy. But it

---

[34] Abderrahmane Lounès, "Le polar et la manière", *El-Moudjahid*, 30 July 1991. Lounès uses the play upon words "sociologue" and "soucieux-logue".

is not only for this reason that the author chose the *roman noir* to reflect the bloody events in Algeria. In contrast to the traditional whodunnit à la Agatha Christie this "literature of a time of crisis", as Jean-
François Vilar described the *roman noir*,[35] does not provide definitive
solutions and the hero of the novel only manages to catch the criminal
in a decreasing number of cases, thus reasserting the old order and the
feeling of security associated with it. The investigations are now only
partially successful and this in a limited way, but even in these cases
both blame and justice are relative and the investigators are always left
with a feeling of bitterness and doubt. If we take these characteristics
of the genre into account it becomes obvious that in contrast to the spy
novels the *roman noir* is not suited to the proclamation of an idealized
national identity. The relativization of justice, the differentiated
presentation of characters and events and the restricted scope of solutions leave the readers in a state of disconcertedness and they therefore
depend all the more on the investigator who has committed himself to
the discovery of truth and the perpetration of justice.[36]

This aim is achieved both by Commissaire Llob in his role as crime
inspector and author. In *Morituri, Double blanc* and *L'Automne des
chimères* the first person narrator Llob is presented as a successful
author who publishes his novels under the pseudonym Yasmina
Khadra. In *L'Automne des chimères* Llob is suspended from police
duty due to the publication of *Morituri*. This self-reflective game provides the real author with the possibility of influencing the reception
of his novels and to comment on or emphasize the explosive aspects
of this novel trilogy by critical commentary. The double role as inspector and author lends the reflections on the future of the country
and its inhabitants more weight, as it was always the intellectuals and,
in particular, the writers who put the question of an Algerian identity
at the centre of their works. Both as an inspector and author Llob is
presented as a man of the people and incorporates the self-esteem and
honesty required for the Algerian people to find their way out of the
present crisis. Yasmina Khadra's novels show quite clearly that we
cannot expect solutions from those in government. Hope is rather

---

[35]   Jean-François Vilar, "Noir c'est noir", in *Meurtres exquis: Histoire sociale du
       roman policier*, ed. Ernest Mandel, Montreuil: La Brèche, 1987, 9.
[36]   Jean Pons, "Le Roman noir, littérature réelle", *Les Temps Modernes*, 595 (1997),
       9.

placed in the Algerian people and all those men and women who do not fall silent and who continue to fight for justice and freedom of speech despite all the risks. This hope is personified by the incorruptible and honest figure of Commissaire Llob, whose idealism in view of the events in his home country appears like a relic of a time long gone, in agreement with the statement made by the author Tahar Djaout, who was murdered in broad daylight: "Si tu parles, tu meurs. Si tu te tais, tu meurs. Alors, parle et meurs",[37] which is taken up by Yasmina Khadra in *Morituri*. Here the intrepid police inspector and writer ignores the lethal danger he is exposed to day after day. He goes his way unperturbed, and obeys his conscience and devotes his work as an inspector and author to constructing an Algerian nation in which the inhabitants can finally, after years of hardship, live together in peace and contentment. In *L'Automne des chimères* Commissaire Llob pays for his courage and commitment with his life. "Ils ne lui ont laissé aucune chance",[38] that is the depressing closing sentence of the novel dashing any hopes that might have remained. The honesty and incorruptibility embodied by Commissaire Llob persist even after the death of the hero. Only if there continue to be courageous, unflinching and critical voices, drawing our attention to the evils and nurturing the faith in the future of the country, will the Algerian nation have a chance of finding its way out of a crisis lasting thirty years after the proclamation of independence.[39]

At the end of the Nineties Algeria is still in search of itself. This fact goes unquestioned and the continuing dispute between the military forces and fundamentalists provides ample evidence of this fact. But in contrast to the Seventies, when the Algerian government literally created a national identity and tried to force this upon the population,

---

[37] "If you speak out, you will die. If you keep silent, you will die. Therefore speak out and die."

[38] Khadra, *L'Automne des chimères*, 176: "They did not leave him a ghost of a chance."

[39] In March 2004 Yasmina Khadra published another volume of the Commissaire Llob series: *La Part du mort* (Paris: Julliard) is set in Algiers at the end of the Eighties. However, investigations lead the protagonist back to the historical context of the end of the War of Independence in Algeria, where entire families of *harkis* – Algerians who supported the French colonizers during that war – were killed in August 1962.

the national awareness of the Algerian population can no longer be doubted after the October risings of 1988. In contrast to SM 15, who as an imported fictional character was fitted with Muslim attributes and provided a puppet for the Algerian government, Commissaire Llob represents a typical Algerian average citizen who is deeply rooted in his home country and whose *algerianité* cannot be doubted at any time. National identity as such is not explicitly topicalized in Yasmina Khadra's novels but lived and thus conveyed in a far more convincing fashion. At the centre of these works we find the question of how Algerians, in view of the persisting crisis, are to act to secure the future of their country. The path followed by the idealistic inspector and patriotic writer Brahim Llob in the five novels by Yasmina Khadra can be seen as a possible answer to this question: "Dans une Algérie qui se cherchait désespéremment, parmi les angles morts et les feux de la rampe, alors que chacun s'enrageait à se frayer une place au soleil, Brahim marchait droit."[40]

---

[40] Khadra, *L'Automne des chimères*, 167: "In an Algeria in desperate search of itself, somewhere in between a dead end and sudden exposure, whilst everyone was trying to secure her/himself a place in the sun, Brahim walked straight ahead."

"TROUBLING" THRILLERS: POLITICS AND POPULAR FICTION IN NORTHERN IRELAND LITERATURE

MARISOL MORALES LADRÓN

> Yet, in a sense, it is hardly surprising that the climate of Northern Ireland should be a thriller writer's dream. It provides the perfect setting for a thriller and all the necessary ingredients are available in abundance. Northern Ireland is, after all, a place of "dangerous passion".[1]

Since the beginnings of the Northern Irish Troubles in the late Sixties,[2] interest in exploring the social and political concerns of a region affected by sectarian violence and religious bigotry has produced a significant body of literature within which the popular genre of the thriller has become one of the most suitable forms of expression. Action, suspense and psychological thrillers have in this context acquired a rich political dimension that intersects inevitably with questions of identity, producing what has been called the "Troubles" thriller. The development of this mode has diverged into two cat-

---

[1]   Laura Pelaschiar, *Writing the North: The Contemporary Novel in Northern Ireland*, Trieste: Edizioni Parnaso, 1998, 19.

[2]   Different dates have been given to refer to the origin of the Troubles. In August 1966 there were celebrations of the fiftieth anniversary of the Easter Rising of 1916, which caused some disturbances between Protestants and Catholics. Also in 1968 the Royal Ulster Constabulary intervened violently in a demonstration in favour of civil rights. However, 1969 was the year when British troops became involved in the civil strife. See Andrew Graham-Yooll, "Belfast, 20-23 October 1993", *The Antioch Review*, LII/2 (1994), 289 and Richard Deutsch, "'Within Two Shadows': The Troubles in Northern Ireland", in *The Irish Novel in Our Time*, eds Patrick Rafroidi and Maurice Harmon, Lille: Publications de l'Université de Lille III, 1975-76, 131 for the euphemism associated with the current meaning of the term "Troubles".

egories: the "Troubles-trash", an extremely popular form that, according to Eve Patten, has become one of the most profitable industries in Northern Ireland since the beginning of the conflict,[3] and a more literary form, which draws on serious political matters to reflect upon social and religious disputes that cut across national and cultural identities. Both kinds, however, have been strongly criticized for offering a stagnant and reductive version of the dynamics of the Troubles, one that bases its premises on clear-cut boundaries between opposing poles with regard to nationality, religion or politics. The objective of this essay is to analyse the ways in which these identity issues are echoed in the literary production of Benedict Kiely, Brian Moore and Colin Bateman.

Firstly, however, I would like to briefly address issues regarding the term "thriller" itself. Despite the fact that not all critics would consider the thriller as an independent fictional category and would often include it under umbrella terms such as "crime", "detective", "mystery", "suspense" or even "horror" fictions,[4] differences among these modes abound.[5] Although it is not my intention to explore conceptual considerations in depth, nonetheless for the purpose of a volume

---

[3]   Eve Patten, "Fiction in Conflict: Northern Ireland's Prodigal Novelists", in *Peripheral Visions: Images of Nationhood in Contemporary British Fiction*, ed. Ian A. Bell, Cardiff: University of Wales Press, 1995, 128-29.

[4]   David Glover, "The Stuff that Dreams are Made of: Masculinity, Femininity and the Thriller", in *Reading Popular Fiction: Gender, Genre and Narrative Pleasure*, ed. Derek Longhurst, London: Unwin Hyman, 1989, 73; *The Twentieth Century: A Guide to Literature from 1900 to the Present Day*, ed. Linda R. Williams, London: Bloomsbury, 1992, 144 and 195.

[5]   Chandler, in his famous essay "The Simple Act of Murder", deals with detective and mystery fiction in general (see Raymond Chandler, "The Simple Art of Murder", in *Pearls Are a Nuisance*, London: Penguin, 1980, 181-99). Todorov establishes a clearer distinction between the thriller (the *Série Noire*), the whodunnit and a third category that has developed between these two forms, which is the suspense novel (see Tzvetan Todorov, "The Typology of Detective Fiction", in *Modern Criticism and Theory: A Reader*, ed. David Lodge, London: Longman, 1988, 161-63). Fowler adds that the British term "detective story" and the American "mystery" are not the same at all: "the latter merges easily into the thriller of Hammett, Chandler, or Macdonald, whereas the former remains sharply distinct. Neither the thrillers of Fleming nor the entertainments of Greene could possibly be taken for detective stories" (Alastair Fowler, *Kinds of Literature: An Introduction to the Theory of Genres and Modes*, Cambridge, MA: Harvard University Press, 1982, 133).

mainly concerned with detective fiction, it would be helpful to distinguish here some of the basic traits that characterize each mode.

Crime novels in general share particular features that could be summarized thus: the construction of complex plots; the repetition of fixed patterns that are familiar to the reader; the use of type characters; the inclusion of elements of mystery, so that reading becomes a process of discovery; and the exploration of the conflict between good and evil, integrity and corruption, etc. More particularly, traditional detective fiction has been defined as "a literature of social and psychological adjustment" whose main objective is to "provide reassurance: mysteries are dissipated, crimes cleared up, evil is punished, order restored, and endings satisfy. The experience of reading is one of recuperation, confirming us in the moral universe we know".[6] As a result, the process of detection undertaken by the investigator and the final defeat of crime have traditionally imbued the mode with a conservative ideology.

Though to a certain extent similar, the thriller is organized around specific milieus, characters and situations, rather than around a method of presentation, "in other words, its constitutive character is in its themes ... it is around these few constants that the thriller is constituted: violence, generally sordid crime, [and] the amorality of the characters".[7] In contrast to the ideology underpinning detective novels with their resolution of the crime and protection of society, the thriller mirrors anarchy, horror and destruction. According to Palmer:

> the thriller is based upon the description of deviant acts – murder, rape, burglary, espionage .... The manner in which the description of deviant acts contributes to a consensual view of the world can only be understood on the basis of an analysis of the ideology proposed by the thriller.[8]

It should not come as a surprise then that a mode that has been defined as "the resolution of a mystery in circumstances of physical danger

---

[6] Glover, "The Stuff that Dreams are Made of", in *Reading Popular Fiction*, 67-68.
[7] Todorov, "The Typology of Detective Fiction", in *Modern Criticism and Theory*, ed. David Lodge, 162.
[8] Jerry Palmer, "Thrillers: the Deviant Behind the Consensus", in *The Study of Popular Fiction: A Source Book*, ed. Bob Ashley, London: Printer Publishers, 1989, 187.

and energetic activity"[9] has developed in particular in Northern Irish writing, which tries to reflect the violent atmosphere of the Troubles, even to the extent of overshadowing other kinds of crime fiction. In fact, critics almost unanimously acknowledge the thriller as the most popular form in Northern Irish literature.[10] Furthermore, the political upheaval of the last four decades has favoured the emergence of a new subcategory, the "Troubles" thriller, which, according to Gerry Smyth, is characterized by the inclusion of stereotyped characters, voyeuristic violence and melodrama.[11]

The list of "Troubles" thrillers published in the last thirty years is certainly wide-ranging. However, as I have mentioned above, not all "Troubles" thrillers fall within the same category. McMinn distinguishes between the documentary type, organized around a predictable pattern that displays the conflict between the IRA and the State,[12] and novels that include some elements of the thriller but in which a love story serves as the point of departure from which the socio-political conflict becomes a threat to the individual.[13] Bowyer-Bell's assessment is more negative since, for him, the main objective of the thriller is to entertain rather than to teach something, and in the same vein, neither Graham-Yooll nor Rolston[14] include the thriller under the

---

[9]   Tony Davies, "The Divided Gaze: Reflections on the Political Thriller", in *Reading Popular Fiction*, 123.

[10]   Keith Jeffery and Eunan O'Halpin, "Ireland in Spy Fiction", *Intelligence and National Security*, V/4 (1990), 115; Neil Corcoran, *After Yeats and Joyce: Reading Modern Irish Literature*, Oxford: OUP, 1997, 162; Patten, "Fiction in Conflict", in *Peripheral Visions*, ed. Ian A. Bell, 128-29; J. Bowyer-Bell, "The Troubles As Trash", *Hibernia*, 20 January (1978), 22; Graham-Yooll, "Belfast, 20-23 October 1993", 290; Bill Rolston, "Mothers, Whores and Villains: Images of Women in Novels of the Northern Ireland Conflict", *Race and Class*, XXXI/1 (1989), 41; Aaron Kelly, "'A Stasis of Hatred, Fear and Mistrust': The Politics of Form in Representations of Northern Ireland produced by the 'Troubles' Thriller", in *New Voices in Irish Criticism*, ed. P. J. Mathews, Dublin: Four Courts, 2000, 109.

[11]   Gerry Smyth, *The Novel and the Nation: Studies in the New Irish Fiction*, London: Pluto Press, 1997, 114.

[12]   He is referring to novels such as *World Without End, Amen* (1954) by Jimmy Breslin; *Harry's Game* (1975) by Gerald Seymour; *Interface Ireland* (1979) by Kevin Dowling; and *Bitter Orange* (1979) by Des Hamill.

[13]   Joseph McMinn, "Contemporary Novels on the Troubles", *Etudes Irlandaises*, 5 (1980), 114.

[14]   J. Bowyer-Bell, "The Troubles as Trash" 22; Graham-Yooll, "Belfast, 20-23 October 1993", 290; Rolston, "Mothers, Whores and Villains", 41.

label of "literature". What these critics are referring to is the sensationalist journalistic thriller, the "Troubles-trash" that has inundated publishing houses since the beginning of the Troubles, offering a vision of a polarized society divided in two monolithic identities.[15]

Having given a brief outline of the wide range of "Troubles" thrillers, I will now focus on the more literary kind and more particularly on a type of thriller that includes the motive of the operation by proxy – this being "the practice of hostage taking and the coercion of civilians into delivering car bombs".[16] This type of operation is found in Benedict Kiely's *Proxopera* (1977), Brian Moore's *Lies of Silence* (1990) and Colin Bateman's *Divorcing Jack* (1995). The three novels chosen exemplify different facets of Northern Irish reality as perceived by both the Catholic and Protestant sides, oscillating between an interest in the individual and a focus on society, covering different social classes and settings, and shifting from a serious to a more comic tone. Stylistically, these novels conform to the popular form of the thriller in its closed patterns, formulaic structure and predictability, and from this viewpoint they would seem to contribute to the consolidation of essentialist positions with regard to nationality, religion, politics or culture – in other words, to identity. In terms of content, they end on a final pessimistic note, resulting from a deterministic atmosphere in which characters are doomed to dissatisfaction. None of the authors chosen for this discussion are professional thriller writers, although, in one way or another, they have all experimented with the form and their names are well known in Northern Irish literary circles. Their "Troubles" thrillers have been concerned with the exploration of

---

[15] According to Deutsch ("'Within Two Shadows'", in *The Irish Novel in Our Time*, eds Rafroidi and Harmon, 149) this is a general characteristic of the first stage of the "Troubles" fiction and not only of the thriller. See Pelaschiar (*Writing the North*, 20) for a commentary of an interview with the criminologist Bill Robton, who manifests his worries about the revitalization of a form that reduces the cultural identity of Northern Ireland to a group of violent "macho-men" terrorists; and see also my own article about Northern Irish literature in the political atmosphere of the Troubles: Marisol Morales Ladrón, "La literatura norirlandesa actual en el panorama político de los 'Troubles'", in *Márgenes y centros en la literatura británica actual*, ed. Fernando Galván Reula, Alcalá: Servicio de Publicaciones de la Universidad, 147-94.

[16] Denis Sampson, *Brian Moore: The Chameleon Novelist*, Dublin: Marino Books, 1998, 276.

moral, psychological and social preoccupations that used to be absent in the most popular and traditional mode.[17]

As we will see in more detail later, the "Troubles" thriller presents the following traits: the inclusion of actual or realistic political facts; the portrayal of characters who feel, in one way or another, responsible for the social, political or historical contradictions of society, the resolution of which would turn them into heroes; the depiction of the conflict in terms of pressure of the community on the individual; and the exploration of questions of identity. Since within these novels the nature of the criminal actions is not analysed, they then seem the inevitable result of a chain of historical events and merely serve to perpetuate violence. Readers do not have the experience of eventually participating in the resolution of a crime nor are they left with a feeling of satisfaction. From this viewpoint, then, it seems valuable to explore the ways in which the "Troubles" thriller both differs from the traditional mode and addresses, through the inclusion of specific symbols and imagery, notions of identity as stable categories. Significantly enough, the evolution of the thriller has paralleled a growing trend within contemporary Irish literature (North and South) that concerns itself with the destabilization of binary notions, problematizing and blurring categories with regard to all kind of boundaries – national, geographical, sexual, racial or cultural – stressing ultimately difference and hybridization.

In the present discussion my main concern is not with the plot, the story of the individual or of the society they present, but rather with the meaning that some representational codes acquire and with the

---

[17] Among the three, Brian Moore has been the most prolific and experienced since he has also published popular thrillers under pseudonym. In an interview, he admitted to having discovered that a narrative form like the thriller, mainly left for second-rate writers, was "tremendously powerful … the gut of fiction" (Colm Tóibín, "Gaelic Gloom", *London Review of Books*, XXII/15 [2000], 8). *Lies of Silence* (London: Vintage, 1992) was short listed for the Booker Prize in 1990. Colin Bateman, who was a journalist before he became a writer, is the most popular of the three authors examined in this discussion. He has published other thrillers and his first novel, *Divorcing Jack*, for which he was awarded the Betty Task Prize in 1994, has been made into a film. Benedict Kiely is probably the most established and best known of the three. His novel *Proxopera* is one of the first attempts to narrate the dynamics of the "Troubles", which would later be followed by Kiely's *Nothing Happens in Carmincross* (1985).

important role they play in a society where signs prevail over facts and where the Troubles seem fated never to find a resolution. It is significant to decode the symbols that construct these discourses because, as Davies suggests, "to study a popular genre is to study lived social relations, not because popular fictions transparently 'reflect' those relations but because the meanings and structures of their narratives are 'actively attributed' by their readers – among whom, of course, must be numbered their writers, and ourselves, who study them".[18] Symbols are created for the transmission of a certain ideology and, especially in Northern Ireland, to set up boundaries that demarcate different sectors. The literature produced in this region echoes this reality through the construction of a discourse in which symbols, colours, murals, banners, graffiti, bonfires, parades and other marks of political or religious identity are used to position characters and attitudes into clear-cut categories.

Kiely's *Proxopera*[19] is a sentimental melodrama about the kidnapping of a family by three IRA men, who force the elderly and sick Mr Binchey, a retired teacher of history and classics, to drive a time bomb to the house of Judge Flynn – according to the narrator, "one of the best men in the north" (78). Since this novel, published in 1977, is a product of the earlier stage of the conflict, the reader encounters within the narrative striking pastoral imagery of peace and a romanticization of the land. This contrasts with a parallel discourse, appearing now and then written in italics, which presents images of violence and destruction. The idyllic and idealized landscape, witness to the events, is eventually made accomplice and victim of the crimes. Being part of Northern Ireland, nature cannot avoid the Troubles:

> ... murderers in the dark had made the sleeping lake their accomplice. The innocent lake had been forced to share the guilt. The lake, out there and fading into another dusk, the lake knew. It could never be the same again. (31)

---

[18]   Davies, "The Divided Gaze", in *Reading Fiction*, 131.
[19]   Benedict Kiely, *Proxopera*, London: Victor Gollancz, 1977. In this novel the protagonist comments ironically on the "operation by proxy" type of crime: "Not even the Mafia thought of the proxy bomb, operation proxy, proxopera for gallant Irish patriots fighting imaginary empires by murdering the neighbours" (58).

Although the novel recounts a terrorist action carried out by the IRA, Protestants are seen in no better light. Violence is thus portrayed as endemic, perpetuated by both groups in a never-ending retaliation for each other's crimes. Against this atmosphere, the protagonist's dreamed-of lake house, symbolically painted in white, is built in an all-too harmonious nature. In opposition to this, references to the "Orange hall" together with ironic allusions to the marching of the Orange order – "July was the best month for perch and the best day was the twelfth" (12-13) – are constant. The entire novel is tinged with references to the green hills, clear water and Orangemen, visibly alluding to the Irish flag.

This certainly points to the violent sectarianism of the village in which Mr Binchey lives, through the use of colour symbolism:

> There were other houses, Orange and Green or Protestant and Cath-
> olic, on the hills around the lakeshore, but they were simple thatched
> cottages and nothing at all in the bay windowed, widefronted style of
> the white house. (15)

At the end, this white house, placed in between the green hills and the orange houses, does not become a symbol of union and peace but of destruction and death. As the protagonist says, then, what has been shattered is more than his family or his town, it is "my dream of a white house" (92) and, with it, the possibility of an end to the conflict. It is perhaps for this reason that the novel, with its romanticizing vision of the land and nostalgia for a better past, blemished now by the atrocities of sectarian violence, is dedicated to the "Memory of the Innocent Dead" (7).

Brian Moore's *Lies of Silence* is also a political and psychological thriller that takes a similar event as its subject matter.[20] The protagon-

---

[20] Brian Moore, *Lies of Silence*, London: Vintage, 1992. Although it might seem that Moore's story grows from Kiely's, he has explained that the plot is based on a real event he himself experienced in 1987, when he was going to receive his doctorate: "I was in the Wellington Park Hotel, near Queen's University, and we had a bomb scare in the middle of the night. We were all put out in the street, and I saw these French tourists there. I was listening to them, and they hadn't the slightest idea what was happening. So I thought about what happened and wondered about what it would have been like if they were killed and they didn't know who killed them" (Sampson, *Brian Moore: The Chameleon Novelist*, 276).

ist's wife has been taken hostage by an IRA group and he is forced to plant a bomb in one of the most important hotels in Belfast if he is to save her life. Although in the two novels neither the protagonists nor the settings have much in common, both have narratives that evolve around the dilemma the main characters have to confront. They are torn between their responsibilities to protect and save their families, which would force them to participate in terrorist activities, and their duty toward society, which sees such actions as simply wrong.

In *Lies of Silence,* published almost two decades after *Proxopera,* we find a marked contrast to the idealized surroundings of the earlier novel. *Lies of Silence* portrays a more realistic Belfast in which sectarianism is seen as a reflection of the existence of two social classes rather than of two violent groups. The novel offers a clear depiction of "those parts of Belfast which had become the image of the city to the outside world: graffiti-fouled barricaded slums where the city's Protestant and Catholic poor confronted each other, year in and year out, in a stasis of hatred, fear and mistrust" (21). However, the protagonist Dillon knows that where he lives, "in the north end of Belfast", away from the ghettos, there is no such distinction since: "Protestants and Catholics lived side by side, joined by class, by economic ties, even by intermarriage, in a way the poor could never be" (22). Moore's thriller focuses on the deeper political aspects that lie beneath the apparently unquestionable bigotry of both groups. Considering his young criminal captors to be dangerous victims of the failure and negligence of politicians, Dillon goes on to blame the lies that sustain this atrocious reality:

> Dillon felt anger rise within him, anger at the lies which had made this, his … birthplace, sick with a terminal illness of bigotry and injustice, lies told over the years to poor Protestant working people about the Catholics, lies told to poor Catholic working people about the Protestants, lies from parliaments and pulpits, lies at rallies and funeral orations, and, above all, the lies of silence from those in Westminster who did not want to face the injustices of Ulster's *status quo.* (69-70)

If *Proxopera* highlighted a violent sectarian society as being the product of history, *Lies of Silence* pictures a reality in which Catholic and Protestant ghettos co-exist side by side with areas where people are completely unaware of the socio-economic injustices that underlie the Troubles. In fact, as Dillon thinks:

> Ignoring the trouble was an Ulster tradition. Another wee bomb, as the local joke had it. By next week the whole incident would be forgotten (110).

At the end of the novel he therefore comes to the conclusion that doing away with the IRA will not bring the conflict to an end. Until Catholics and Protestants share the same opportunities with regard to housing, employment and power the Troubles will go on: "And the only ones who can force them into it are the British Government who haven't got the guts" (196-97).

Divorcing Jack, Colin Bateman's action thriller,[21] offers an alternative vision to the gloom and bleakness of the Northern Irish reality that has habitually been conveyed. It is set in Belfast, its standpoint is the Protestant side, and it approaches the Troubles from a humorous perspective. Playing with tragedy and comedy, the author manages to build a story grounded on absurd situations exaggerated to the point of farce, which makes the novel "the first 'comedy thriller' dealing with the 'Troubles'".[22] Dan Starkey is a Protestant journalist, well known for his wit and his satirical and sarcastic humour, who, involuntarily, finds himself involved in a sequence of events that leads to the murder of his recent lover Margaret – the daughter of a politician – and to the kidnapping of his wife. In this novel, the reality of the Troubles is also exposed to the eyes of an outsider, the American journalist Charles Parker, who is on a special programme to cover elections for a Northern Irish government and gather information about the conflict.[23] Starkey takes him on "the usual terror tour, up the Falls Road to see the Republican wall murals, up the Shankill to see the Protestant equivalent".[24] The frivolous humour with which the protagonist refers to sectarianism is constant throughout the novel.

---

[21]   Colin Bateman, *Divorcing Jack*, London: Harper Collins, 1995.

[22]   Smyth, *The Novel and the Nation*, 123.

[23]   This element of the plot anticipated the establishment of such a body in reality with the election of the Stormont Assembly after the signing of the Good Friday Agreement in 1998.

[24]   Smyth, *The Novel and the Nation*, 46.

From the very first pages, Starkey seems to take the Troubles rather lightly:

> I had this idea about swapping the terrorist wasteland of West Belfast for the Guinness Brewery in Dublin. They could have our troubles and we could drink theirs. (49)

Terrorism seems to be so habitual that it shapes the routines of everyday life. In the city, taxi drivers refuse to enter certain streets that are too risky, people are searched in shops for security reasons, and nobody seems to be bothered about it. In this atmosphere of commonplace violence it comes as a surprise that the Prime Minister to be, Mark Brinn, is the leader of the Alliance Party, whose political programme represents a compromise between Unionists and Nationalists – a promise of hope for Northern Ireland.[25]

However, as the novel will finally reveal, his campaign for peace is as false as his own life. Brinn became a peacemaker politician after having been a member of an IRA unit responsible for the bombing of a restaurant, which caused the death of eight people. In his final attempt to conceal his past he resorts to bribery and plants a bomb to kill a man who is blackmailing him. At the same time, this blackmailer, anticipating such an exploit, also plants a bomb that kills Brinn. Ironically, these acts, which result in the death of both the ex-terrorist and the IRA gangster, take place on the day of the elections. Their outcome is the success of the Alliance party, whose programme has been mockingly presented in the novel as:

> Power sharing, a largely autonomous state, freeport status, British but not British, Irish but not Irish. Independence with a safety harness. A Northern Irish Hong Kong really. Ideas that seem to be generally popular. (83)

In this light, it would seem that *Divorcing Jack* locates the Troubles at the level of a tribal war between Catholics and Protestants although, as I am trying to suggest, these three "Troubles" thrillers offer a much more complex discourse than one merely contrasting binary positions with regard to ideologies, characters or settings.

---

[25] *Ibid.,* 49.

In their representation of conflict the three novels differ significantly from the traditional thriller. This is true also with regard to the
portrayal of characters. Within the conservative ideology of the traditional thriller with its conventional goodies and baddies, the protagonists, according to Palmer, should have an isolated and com-
petitive personality that will eventually prove them

> ... better adapted to the world than everyone else .... What the thriller
> does, essentially, is explore the various ramifications of the prop-
> osition, common enough in our society, that the individual must be
> competitive in order to be an individual.[26]

In most traditional thrillers there is a conspiracy or a threat that the
heroes have to confront and resolve. They need to demonstrate that
they are different and superior to the rest and, above all, to the evil
forces that menace society. In these "Troubles" thrillers, however, the
outcome turns out differently. Heroes do not triumph over evil in any
unequivocal way, and even where – as is the case of Mr Binchey –
they succeed to some extent, they still leave the reader with a sense of
unease. Of the three main characters discussed, both Mr Binchey and
Dillon are apolitical, while Dan Starkey is not. Moreover, all are outsiders: a retired teacher dissatisfied with the reality of his village, a
hotel manager who dreams of the day when he will leave Ireland, and
a Unionist journalist who is only prepared to commit to his ideology
after being pressurized by Republican pretensions of unification. None
of them are willing to have anything to do with Northern Ireland's
strife and it is only circumstances that oblige them to. In all three
cases, they are subject to forces outside their control.

Trying to find the source of the uncontrollable violence that rules
his village, Mr Binchey in *Proxopera* asks himself who "guided or
misguided" (84) these young people. The only answer he can find is:

> Ireland. A long history. England. Empire. King William. The Pope.
> Ian Paisley. Myself. I was a teacher of history.[27]

---

[26]   Palmer, "Thrillers: the Deviant Behind the Consensus", in *The Study of Popular
       Fiction*, ed. Bob Ashley, 194.
[27]   Kiely, *Proxopera*, 84.

Having devoted his entire life to teaching this history, he cannot avoid feeling responsible for the creation and recreation of the national myths that have fuelled the perpetuation of sectarian violence. His age, and his dream of the white house that symbolizes unity, make him refuse to yield to the power of the IRA and, instead of driving the bomb to the indicated target, he reports it to a British checkpoint, becoming then "after all a hero" (86). However, on turning informer he has to pay the price and the IRA retaliates by burning down his white house and kneecapping his son.

Although Pelaschiar argues that *Proxopera* is one of the few "Troubles" novels that does not end tragically since, at the end, order is restored and justice will reign,[28] this does not seem convincing as the reader cannot feel reassurance with the punishment of the criminals. On the contrary, the novel all along has conveyed the message that endemic violence has divided this society into good and evil.

The protagonist of Moore's *Lies of Silence*, like the other protagonists, is an antihero, a frustrated and "failed poet in a business suit",[29] whose position as manager of a hotel does not make up for the empty and monotonous life he shares with his wife Moira. In the novel, he has to face a similar dilemma to Mr Binchey's, though, in this case, Dillon also has to decide whether to tell his wife Moira of his plans to move to England with his young lover Andrea. In addition to this, like Binchey, he is blackmailed into planting a bomb in his hotel, and has to decide whether to save the life of his kidnapped wife or do his duty as the manager of the hotel and save the lives of hundreds of people. In the end, his actions are unheroic, like those of the other protagonists.

In the reality of the Belfast of the Eighties bombs are part of daily life, as the security system of the hotel, bombed only the previous year, reveals. In his attempt to become a hero − but also trying to evade his personal struggle − he tries to save both his wife and the guests in the hotel and succeeds. The bomb has gone off but has only damaged some parts of the hotel and his wife has been released by the IRA, who had assumed he would comply with their demands. When his mission has ended, he exchanges Belfast for London. However,

---

[28] Pelaschiar, *Writing the North*, 77.
[29] Moore, *Lies of Silence*, 12.

having become an informer, like old Mr Binchey, he eventually
encounters his own death at the hands of IRA terrorists, who have
followed him to England to punish his disobedience.

In *Divorcing Jack*, Starkey identifies himself as a "Unionist with a
sense of humour"[30] who does not support terrorism. Although he is the
only protagonist of the three books who has a clear ideology, he is not
willing to fight for any cause, let alone become a hero. Starkey is in
fact an antihero who gets involved in the most absurd situations,
drinks heavily, is seduced by several women, and seems to constantly
find himself in the wrong place, at the wrong time and caught up with
the wrong sort of people. When he finally manages to survive it has
only been a matter of chance. Although the book ends in partial hope
due to the fact that a new government will rule Northern Ireland, it is
clear the civil war will go on, while Starkey witnesses the bombing of
the two cars and watches "the smoke from infernos at either end of the
road rise and mingle high up in the blue" (268).

As Smyth suggests, the significance of Bateman's novel can be
perceived in its attempt to free the Protestant Unionist tradition "of its
image as a narrow reactionary culture and reveal itself instead as a
complex and subtle modern identity".[31] At the same time, *Divorcing
Jack* imparts a similar approach to sectarianism as the previous two
novels, in the sense that the "war" is not primarily presented as the
result of and, indeed, a reaction to violence but rather as a way to
justify its perpetuation. Binchey's son says in *Proxopera* to one of the
IRA men:

> Man, you love the Brits, you couldn't exist without them .... They
> give you the chance to be Irish heroes. They give you targets you can
> easily see.[32]

---

[30] Bateman, *Divorcing Jack*, 9.
[31] Smyth, *The Novel and the Nation*, 125; Pelaschiar shares the same opinion, adding
that "Not only has Bateman's ironic, irreverent and highly entertaining writing
voiced a new perception of Northern Irish reality from a moderate unionist point
of view, but in voicing it in such an unorthodox way it has also contributed to de-
stabilizing the conventional vision of Northern Irish Protestants as reactionary,
bigoted, unimaginative and narrow-minded" (*Writing the North*, 24).
[32] Kiely, *Proxopera*, 27.

Similarly, Moira in *Lies of Silence* tells the IRA men that they cannot make anyone believe they fight for the freedom of anyone, and it is instead hatred that motivates them, since "if the Catholics here stopped hating the Prods, where would the IRA be?".[33]

The North of Ireland, divided by questions of political and cultural identity, has inevitably transposed its own preoccupations onto a literary discourse that plays with archetypal struggles and stereotyped characters and situations to appeal to the reader through the thrill of its own narrative. The reading of these three texts shows that Northern Irish discourse reflects the cultural identity of its own people, an identity which is as different to that of the Irish of the Republic as to that of the British, one that presents division and conflict as the norm. Seamus Deane shares this view that Northern Irish people feel "neither Irish nor British while also being both".[34]

Dermot Bolger, in his Introduction to *The Picador Book of Contemporary Irish Fiction*, has claimed as well that statistical analysis carried out at the beginning of the Nineties has shown that people from the Irish Republic "feel now that they have more in common with the Scottish, Welsh and English than with any section of the population in the North".[35] The term "Northern" serves then not only as a mark to denote a geographical boundary but as an arbitrary space in which binary notions of identity coexist together with a plurality that is increasingly attempting to blur dual categories with regard to nationality, religion and politics. In *Divorcing Jack*, Dan Starkey wittily explains to the American journalist that there are different terms to refer to the tricky identity of the area: "If you're a Loyalist you'll call it Ulster, if you're a Nationalist you call it the North of Ireland or the Six Counties, if you're the British Government you call it the Province." Parker then asks him what he calls it, to which Starkey answers: "Home."[36] Likewise, in *Lies of Silence*, Dillon, who despises Ireland, recognizes at some point that no matter where he moved, he would always know that Northern Ireland was home because it would be the

[33] Moore, *Lies of Silence*, 62.
[34] Seamus Deane, "The Artist and the Troubles", in *Ireland and the Arts*, ed. T. P. Coogan, London: Namara, 1983, 45-46.
[35] Dermot Bolger, "Introduction", in *The Picador Book of Contemporary Irish Fiction*, London: Picador, 1993, ix.
[36] Bateman, *Divorcing Jack*, 46.

only place where he would not feel a stranger.[37] Consequently, it can be argued that Northern Irish fiction, and especially its most popular mode, stands out as a regional category from which writers and artists both articulate and resist notions of stable and fixed identities, a fact that the three novels discussed in this essay clearly illustrate.[38]

[37] Moore, *Lies of Silence*, 199.
[38] The research carried out for the writing of this article has been financed by the Spanish Ministry of Education (DGICYT, research programme BFF2000-0756) and by the University of Alcalá (Vicerrectorado de investigación, research project H015/2001).

DOUBLE DUTCH: IMAGE AND IDENTITY IN DUTCH AND FLEMISH CRIME FICTION

SABINE VANACKER

In 1997 the annual *Detective and Thriller Guide* of the Dutch weekly, *Vrij Nederland,* asked a number of Dutch and Flemish crime authors: "What characterizes a Dutch thriller?"[1] Dirk Aspe, Bob Mendes, Baantjer, Hellinga, Martin Koomen, Jan van Hout, and Tomas Ross emphasized their unwillingness to attach national characteristics to their genre. Others, however, did try to define what would make a thriller specifically Dutch or Flemish.

A number of the authors and critics questioned seriously doubted the actual existence of the phenomenon *Dutch* thriller, designating it as a paradoxical concept or oxymoron. A Dutch thriller, so the reasoning went, is impossible, the conditions for the crime novel are just not present in the Low Countries. Niels Rood, the male half of the crime-writing duo Rood & Rood, commented:

> Een Nederlandse thriller is een min of meer spannend boek, waarin als er al sprake is van een held, deze volstrekt ongeloofwaardig is. Dit vanwege het feit dat Nederland in het echt geen helden kent, alleen bureaucraten en techneuten. In het echt is in dit land de grootste heldendaad het snoeien van de heg, zodat je weer een praatje kunt maken met de buurman.[2]

---

[1]   "De VN-enquête: De misdaadschrijvers over hun vak", *Vrij Nederland's Detective- en Thrillergids,* 14 June 1997, 38-43.

[2]   *Ibid.,* 39: "A Dutch thriller is a more or less exciting book in which, if it indeed can be said to have a hero, this hero is completely unbelievable. This is due to the fact that the Netherlands do not know any real life heroes, only bureaucrats and technocrats. In real life Holland the greatest heroic deed is cutting the hedge, so that you can have a chat with the neighbour" (*Vrij Nederland's Detective- en Thrillergids,* 1997, 39). Since only a few Dutch and Flemish authors have been translated into English, all translations into English are my own.

The feeling seemed to be that the Netherlands could not possibly be a suitable locale for crime. Its structures and organization are too transparent, its communities too small-scale and well known, even the Dutch language itself might present a handicap for the description of action scenes and the snappy dialogue obviously required from a thriller.

While not a representative study of critical opinions of the genre, it is interesting that the questionnaire was conducted in the middle of a literary crime wave. In the Netherlands and Belgium, the last two decades of the twentieth century saw the commercial success and consolidation of the home-grown crime genre. The *Vrij Nederland* questionnaire suggests that this newfound popularity had not yet been translated into a growing self-confidence. Most specifically, the critics and authors, some more tongue-in-cheek than others, here present an auto-image of the Low Countries, in particular the Netherlands: too small, safe, familiar and prosaic to spawn the great adventures of the crime genre.

A second set of answers, however, considered the literary aims of a Dutch thriller, stressing the need for such works to reflect the society in which they are set. The Dutch writer Will Simon phrased the requirements as follows: "In een Nederlandse thriller moet voor mij de Nederlandse maatschappij in al haar facetten zichtbaar zijn."[3]

Indeed, when Dutch and Flemish authors decide to adopt the literary tradition of crime fiction they are clearly issued with a challenge. As with any popular genre, the crime fiction tradition has been constructed as the result of an interaction between conventionality and imitation on the one hand and innovation and emulation on the other. Dutch and Flemish crime writers, open to a dialogue with French, English and American traditions from the very start, must write themselves into this larger tradition.

Consequently, Low Countries writers are not only faced with the challenge of placing the genre in a new, Dutch or Flemish context. By adapting an international genre they are inevitably forced to question how well the genre suits the Low Countries. Dutch and Flemish crime novels adjust conventions and clichés, develop new variations and, in

---

[3]   *Ibid.*: "For me in a Dutch thriller, Dutch society must be visible in all its diversity."

the course of this, formulate theories about national identity, about images of the self and others, about the communities featured in them. It is interesting, therefore, to examine the way in which these imago-typical suggestions of a national, regional or communal identity feature in the crime genre in the Low Countries.

In the Low Countries, Rob van Ginkel notes a vague consciousness of national identity had arisen in response to political and religious events by the end of the sixteenth century. Slowly, over time, a collection of national clichés emerged, which were canonized as national characteristics.[4] These are evident in popular writings of the eighteenth century and were consolidated by the integrationist nationalism of late nineteenth century. As the name implies, image studies do not address empirical, testable reality but study "the discourse of representation qua discourse, in its textual workings and intertextual ramifications". The touchstone for imagotypical statements is "*recognition* value rather than *truth* value".[5]

This leads us to the formulation of the Netherlands and Flanders as imagined communities constructed in response to current challenges, rather than political entities. One initial comment in this connection, however, concerns the peculiar situation of the publishing business in the Low Countries, which also affects the crime novel. Dutch and Flemish-Belgian readers mostly favour novels written by their countrymen and women. They consequently constitute two separate commercial markets. While many publishing houses are represented in both countries, and quite a few literary authors publish across the border, this is far less the case for the commercially more sensitive crime fiction genre,[6] suggesting that in crime fiction terms "het ravijn tussen Essen en Roosendaal" is still present and that any imagotypical

---

[4] Rob van Ginkel, *Op zoek naar eigenheid: Denkbeelden en discussies over cultuur en identiteit in Nederland*, The Hague: Sdu, 1999, 31.

[5] Joep Leerssen, "Image and Reality and Belgium", in *Europa Provincia Mundi: Essays offered to Hugo Dyserinck*, eds Joep Leerssen and Karl Ulrich Syndram, Amsterdam and Atlanta GA: Rodopi, 1992, 282.

[6] Rinus Ferdinandusse, "Misdaad in Vlaanderen: Grensoverschrijdend uitgeven", *VN's Detective- en Thrillergids*, 29 May 1999, 22.

statements identified need to take into account the psychological
border between the Flemish and Dutch towns.[7]

Democratic, small and modest

When Maarten Maartens published his only detective novel, *The
Black Box Murder* in 1889, he became, arguably, the first Dutch
detective writer. The controversial aspect to this statement stems from
the fact that he chose to write in English. In fact, Maartens was only
the start of a sustained tendency among Dutch and Flemish crime
writers towards a dialogue with the international crime fiction genre
and involving the attendant imagotypical comments. In a similar way,
the modern Dutch writer Martin Koomen even muscles in on the
Sherlock Holmes tradition.[8] His somewhat cheesy plot is set in the
Netherlands, and introduces a great number of flattering Dutch in-
jokes. His Watson enthuses about the fairy-tale beauty of the Dutch
Royal palace,[9] while the panorama of Amsterdam looks like a Ruysdael painting. The inhabitants of the Netherlands are described as a
gifted people, a race of solid folk staunchly resisting the dangers from
the sea.[10] Koomen presents a clichéd picture of the Netherlands for
home consumption. At the same time, he also highlights national characteristics of which his Dutch readers feel proud: simplicity, common
sense and especially democracy.

Many novels point to similar characteristics to which the Dutch
and the Flemish gladly subscribe. Tomas Ross displays pride in the
flat country dominated by its low skies, as portrayed in the great paintings of the past, commented on incidentally through the narrator's
rejection of the asthmatic effect of the high Swiss mountains: "Het is
natuurlijk ook geen wonder dat Ruysdael geen Zwitser was."[11] Small-

---

[7]   Ludo Simons, *Antwerpen, Den Haag retour: Over twee volken gescheiden door
       dezelfde taal*, Tielt: Lannoo 1999, 79: "The gorge between Essen and Roosen-
       daal." Simons' often-quoted metaphor refers to the cultural distance between two
       small towns on either side of the Dutch-Flemish border.
[8]   Martin Koomen, "Een delicate affaire uit de praktijk van Sherlock Holmes", *VN's
       Detective- en Thrillergids*, 22 June 1985, 3.
[9]   *Ibid.*, 7.
[10]   *Ibid.*, 9 and 7.
[11]   Tomas Ross, *Van koninklijken bloede*, Bussum: Van Holkema and Warendorf,
       1982, 222: "It comes as no surprise that Ruysdael was not Swiss."

ness is highlighted again and again in connection with the landscape, as in Ross' *Het Poesjkin Plan*. The island of Ameland, seen from a plane, resembles "een vlek eierstruif op het water".[12] A similar opposition is set up in van de Wetering's novel *Het werkbezoek*, contrasting the wild American coastline of Maine with the homely, safe Dutch seaside and its human imprint, "de gele lineaalstreep langs donzige duintjes en daarachter de verse polders .... Daar de netheid, ontstaan door menselijke ijver, hier de oorsprong, de wilde schepping."[13] The geography suggests cuteness, a cosy safe modesty that must reflect the character of its inhabitants, as the quotation stresses human habitation. Indeed, in combination with an ordinariness that rejects the grand gesture or excessive passion, it takes part in what van Ginkel calls "het bescheidenheids-discours" ("the discourse of modesty").[14] Nevertheless, this is also a landscape testifying to the human endeavour that has created it and there is a certain pride in the way the original wildness here has been civilized and organized, a reference to the fight against the sea that looms so large in the national Dutch mythology.

The discourse of modesty can also be noted when the overcrowding of the Netherlands is pointed out with a certain grim pride, as in van de Wetering's *Een dode uit het Oosten* (*The Japanese Corpse*). When a police chase results in the fleeing criminal driving into a female pedestrian, the detective Grijpstra considers the Netherlands as a country too small for this kind of adventure: "Het land

---

[12] Tomas Ross, *Het Poesjkin Plan*, Bussum: Van Holkema and Warendorf, 1984, 23: "a patch of egg spill on the water."

[13] Janwillem van de Wetering, *Het werkbezoek*, Utrecht: A. W. Bruna, 1979, 42. Van de Wetering's novels have been translated into English, most recently by the American Soho Press. Interestingly, but not surprisingly, the translation of *Het werkbezoek*, entitled *The Maine Massacre*, glosses over this section, presumably because an American audience might not recognize this piece of auto-image. I consequently give my own translation, as I do with all van de Wetering quotations: "the yellow line drawn with a ruler alongside small downy dunes and behind this the fresh polders .... Over there the neatness, created by human endeavour, here the origins, the wild creation." The equivalent passage in *The Maine Massacre*, New York: Soho Press, 1996, 39-40.

[14] Rob van Ginkel, *Op zoek naar eigenheid: Denkbeelden en discussies over cultuur en identiteit in Nederland*, 10.

wordt te krap voor al die gein, dacht Grijpstra."[15] Van de Wetering
regularly comes back to this joke: the Netherlands is too overcrowded
to be anything but a well-regulated country; it no longer allows the
space for adventure. In *De ratelrat* (*Rattle Rat*), the plot moves
towards Friesland. This gives van de Wetering plenty of scope for
tongue in cheek references to the wide horizons and space of the
Frisian landscape. However, another police chase across the Wadden
Sea highlights how administratively overcrowded this region is,
involving the Water Defences authority, Fisheries Inspection boats,
the national police force, the Air Force, the Navy and even the For-
estry Commission.[16]

The Weight of the Past

Another characteristic relating to the image creation of the Low Countries in both Dutch and Flemish crime fiction is a contextualization of
the plots by means of reference to a glamorous past. Novels often
suggest that the past weighs on the events of the criminal present. Its
presence can have a debunking effect, contrasting a petty and banal
present to the glorious past. Two older periods feature large in the
collective memory, the glory of the urban Middle Ages (Flanders),
and the Golden Age of the seventeenth century (the Netherlands).

Bob Mendes' detective, embroiled in a plot of corruption and conspiracy typical of modern-day Belgium, ruminates on the venerable,
eternal beauty of the Flemish past and manages in one scene to shore
up the ruins of the present with echoes of the Middle Ages as well as
the glorious eighteenth and nineteenth centuries:

> Het Osterriethhuis aan de overkant van de straat, met zijn 18de-
> eeuwse gevel, was nog even indrukwekkend als twee jaar geleden.
> Toen had hij met Marie op deze zelfde plaats gestaan en had ze zijn
> aandacht gevestigd op de gevelstructuur met de indrukwekkende
> middentravee in rocaille-ornamentiek, zo karakteristiek voor het Ant-
> werpse stadsbeeld van de achttiende eeuw.

[15] Janwillem van de Wetering, *Een dode uit het Oosten*, Utrecht: A. W. Bruna, 1977,
173: "The country is getting too small for all this larking about, Grijpstra
thought."
[16] Janwillem van de Wetering, *De ratelrat*, Utrecht: A. W. Bruna, 1984, 138.

He attends a conference which takes place with a view of "het reus-achtige doek van Robert Mols achter de hoofden van de panelleden, dat de Schelde en de Antwerpse rede in de 19de eeuw voorstelde", while the reception afterwards is held between Brussels gobelin tapestries and showcases with precious manuscripts.[17]

For van de Wetering, the Dutch Golden Age is equally resonant. Indeed, van Sas has referred in general to a Dutch fixation with the Golden Age.[18] Van de Wetering's Amsterdam sees the modern-day intrigue developing amidst canals, quaysides and merchant houses. However, van de Wetering is at pains to point out that the drug pushers and prostitutes of present-day Amsterdam are the modern-day equivalents of the traders and merchant adventurers of a seventeenth century that is never far removed. On a visit to a suspect, the detective superintendent experiences a short, aesthetic illumination, seeing his young colleague Cardozo, wearing borrowed clothes, like the Jewish poet in a Rembrandt painting. A few minutes later the painterly sun-light equally turns the grey hair of a woman into a halo:

> Dat heb je wel eens, dacht de commissaris. Zo'n Rembrandtse bundel zonnestralen die een gaatje vindt in een wolk. Het licht was al weer weg.[19]

Bearing in mind the many Buddhist references in van de Wetering's fiction, one might think that the modern Amsterdam with its gang-sters, pimps and prostitutes ensconced in seventeenth-century mer-chant houses is living out the city's karma, brought about by the greed of the sailors, slave traders and colonizers of the Golden Age.

---

[17] Bob Mendes, *Meedogenloos*, Antwerp: Manteau, 1995, 16-18: "The Osterrieth House across the street, with its eighteenth-century front, was still as impressive as two years ago. Then he had stood on the same spot with Marie and she had drawn his attention to the structure of its façade with the impressive middle bay in rocaille ornamentation, so typical of the Antwerp cityscape of the eighteenth century"; "the giant canvas of Robert Mols behind the heads of the panel members, representing the Scheldt and the Antwerp quay in the nineteenth century."

[18] Van Sas, quoted in van Ginkel, 25.

[19] Van de Wetering, *De ratelrat*, 151: "Once in a while you get this, the *commissaris* thought. Such a Rembrandtian bundle of sunbeams finding a hole in a cloud. The light was gone again."

To a large extent this conceptual past has recently been replaced in modern memory by the Second World War and its consequences. As Rob van Ginkel points out, the Second World War takes over the function of a legitimization of a national sense of identity in the Netherlands. We find many references to the war in Tomas Ross' *Van koninklijken bloede*: the personnel of the Dutch Secret Service is split between those with a war record as resistance fighters and bureaucratic careerists who joined the service later, whereas the wealth of their criminal opponents stems from Nazi connections and a dangerous female adversary is linked with the Teutonic beauties so admired by the fascists. In a recent faction thriller by the Flemish author Bob Mendes, *Vergelding* (*Vengeance*),[20] we see a very conventional representation of the Second World War, one which also appears in many English language novels, with the unfinished business of the war presented as the source of current evil.

It is significant that both Flanders and the Netherlands have strongly developed this particular subgenre, the faction thriller, a genre mixing facts and research with fictional characters and interpretations. In a good faction thriller fact slides into fiction almost imperceptibly, illusion and reality become blurred and the mood is one of paranoia and conspiracy. The auto-images encountered here fracture the mood of cosiness and democracy, suggesting a Jekyll and Hyde split within Low Countries societies.

Tomas Ross, for instance, successfully checks any patriotic instinct during a funny moment in *De vlucht van de 4de oktober*: "Ergens op de gang achter de deur floot iemand het Wilhelmus, dat plotseling afgebroken werd door een diepe rokershoest."[21] The image of the Netherlands presented in this novel shows the psychological end game for the ex-colonizer. The earlier settler's mercantile eye for profit and loss has, in dealing with modern, decolonized Surinam turned into political hypocrisy, selfishness and moral cowardice. The novel opens with the destruction of the Bijlmermeer apartment block in an airplane crash in 1992 and connects this with the murderous drug-running

---

[20]   Bob Mendes, *Vergelding: voorspel tot Saddams oorlog*, Antwerp: Manteau, 1992.
[21]   Tomas Ross, *De vlucht van de 4de oktober*, Amsterdam: Fontein, 1998, 44: "Somewhere in the corridor behind the door someone whistled the *Wilhelmus* [the Dutch national anthem], which was suddenly broken up by a deep smoker's cough."

Bouterse regime in Surinam. The Dutch government, so Ross shows, is prepared to ignore Surinamese corruption, even when the money they have donated for a Surinamese hospital disappears into the accounts of indigenous bureaucrats, officers and building promoters in Cayenne and Miami. As a Surinamese character points out, the chaos and corruption of the former Dutch colony holds up a mirror to the Netherlands itself. Surinam's independence, consequently, is the result of bad conscience and a lack of courage:

> Het was gewoon een kwestie bij jullie van schuldgevoel afkopen, man. Zo'n Joop den Uyl die in zijn broek scheet voor een nieuw Indonesië, maar daar was geen sprake van! Suriname is een Nederlandse uitvinding, dat was het in de zeventiende eeuw, dat was het in '75 en eigenlijk is het dat nog.[22]

Belgian authors operate in a different imagological climate. Recent scandals have only fanned the virulent distrust felt towards the Belgian state and its administrative, judicial and political authorities. Jef Geeraerts' crime novels perform a living autopsy on the diseased body of the state. The image of Belgium he presents is conspiracy driven, characterized by paranoia and loathing: all enveloping conspiracies link a diseased judiciary with small-minded politicians, entrepreneurial *mafiosi*, and ambitious and reactionary church officials.

Geeraerts writes two different types of crime novels, police procedurals and dystopias set in a near future. It is these latter novels that come closest to the paranoia and conspiracy theories of the American hard-boiled genre. Initially, his protagonist, an upstart Attorney General, thinks that he has successfully swum the tides of corruption and nepotism. He plays games with the institutions of the state, and with the power relations between Catholics and freemasons. Typically for the faction thriller, Geeraerts includes issues surfacing in the national press, such as the parliamentary investigation into Opus Dei in the late Nineties. Likewise, Bob Mendes taps into the public unrest of this

---

[22] Ross, *De vlucht van de 4de oktober*, 33: "For you it was simply a question of buying off a guilty conscience, man. Your Joop den Uyl who pissed his pants at the thought of a new Indonesia, but that was out of the question! Surinam is a Dutch invention, it was in the seventeenth century, it was in 1975 and actually it still is now."

period, when large sections of public life came under uncomfortable scrutiny as a result of the Dutroux affair. The faction novels of Mendes and Geeraerts play up to this auto-image of Belgian corruption, while the Dutch author Tomas Ross equally uses the faction novel to warn about societal corruption and governmental conspiracies. He too presents a frightening image of a fearful secret world behind the everyday life of the Netherlands.

Borders and Border Crossings

Societies define the margins of their selves by identifying and marking the Others within their society. Van Ginkel, in his work on the growth of Dutch national feeling, shows how the national project competes with other national cultures and also with local regional ones. For the Flemish sense of identity, the Walloon and French speaking Belgians form one such border to the self, to the own identity. Consequently, both Geeraerts and Mendes feature a lot of French speakers among their corrupt and provincial bureaucrats. The relatively small contact between the language communities in Belgium results in a clear designation of its French speaking inhabitants as Others in a Flemish context.

The mutual images developed in the Netherlands and in Flanders about the other country are also interesting. In Dutch novels throughout the decades, Belgium regularly functions as a kind of moral flipside to the Netherlands. It seems to be a shadow zone, where elements that have been repressed in the North surface. It is the place from which the immoral and the marginal issues. For instance, murderers buy their weapons in Belgium and gangsters go to Belgium to practise their shooting.[23]

Images of the Netherlands in Flemish novels seem far more rare, although in the novels of the Flemish Jef Geeraerts the contrastive function of the two countries is once again strongly used. While Belgium means provincialism, backwardness and small-mindedness, the Netherlands functions as the exemplar of a strong democracy, progressiveness, liberalism and tolerance.

---

[23] See Felix Thijssen, *Wildschut: Dramatische gijzeling in een Nederlands grensdorp; een Charlie Mann thriller*, Utrecht: Veen, 1980, 53-54.

The image of Flanders developed by Dutchman Felix Thijssen in his novel *Cleopatra*, however, is more complex. While searching for the missing wife of a Dutch politician, Max Winter heads for the West Flemish town of Ieper to interview her friend. Thijssen calls up associations of a Flemish land of plenty with pavement cafés, delicious food and strong Belgian beers. Ieper's wartime history is remembered but the cobblestones have been put back, the houses restored and the sun is once again shining. Thijssen stresses the small-town, community atmosphere, where everyone knows each other. But it is also the location of incest connected with a stepfather who reads the Bible every day. The detective reads the guilt in his eyes and relates this to his literary experiences of the Flemish, via Hugo Claus' famous novel of Flemish primitive incestuous farmers:

> Weer die ogen, schichtiger nu, … en ik weet niet waarom ze *De Metsiers* van Hugo Claus uit mijn herinnering te voorschijn riepen. Lust, wroeging en de bijbel?[24]

Flanders is now also loaded with literary connotations of rural primitivism as opposed to the urban, big city North. Also clearly noticeable, in this and other novels, are the repeated references to the soft, melodic accent of the Flemish speakers. It is almost as if the Flemish character of speech needs to be overemphasized, overdetermined. While not so prevalent as to be called a motif, this noting of Otherness towards Belgian or Flemish characters appearing in Dutch novels could be called a recurring trope.[25]

Janwillem van de Wetering

I will conclude this discussion of identity in Dutch and Flemish crime fiction with an examination of the works of one of the most successful detective writers from the Low Countries. As a crime writer Janwillem

---

[24] Felix Thijssen, *Cleopatra: een Max Winter Mysterie*, Amsterdam: Luitingh Sijthoff, 1998, 57: "Those eyes again, now more cagey, … and I don't know why they call up Hugo Claus' novel *De Metsiers* (*The Duck Hunt*). Lust, remorse and the Bible?"

[25] Already in Joop van den Broek's early novel, *Kermis in de regen* (Utrecht: A. W. Bruna and Zoon, 1958) a Flemish murderer shouts "in rollend Vlaams", 18: "In rolling Flemish."

van de Wetering is in a peculiar position. A much-travelled Dutchman now mainly living in the United States, he is more self-conscious about national images than most. He addresses two audiences, currently writing his crime novels in English for a mainly American audience and translating them into Dutch for his readers in the Netherlands. This means that he is producing imagotypical statements that will be interpreted both as hetero-images for the American audience, and auto-images for the Dutch readers and should be recognizable and acceptable to both. Some critics have pointed out that van de Wetering's success in the United States stems from the fact that his chatty, funny, bureaucratic detectives present a counter figure to the cynical, hard-boiled voice of the average American detective novel. Indeed, van de Wetering regularly highlights the everyday, trivial life of the police station: their coffee breaks, where they park their unmarked cars, how they receive their files. All these details underline the ordinary, banal but also cosy lives of the detectives. Their chattiness and their bureaucratic time wasting schemes are exotic to the genre. Thus, van de Wetering's series, recently reissued in the USA, allows an American audience access to a foreign society that is both different and cute. His Dutch readers recognize a pleasant version of the discourse of modesty in his image of Amsterdam.

Van de Wetering's Amsterdam is a town full of prostitutes, pimps, gangsters and drug dealers, but nevertheless it exudes the safety and cosiness of an Agatha Christie. He presents liberal policemen who are very hip and tremendously cool, and who deal with crime benignly. They are still defending a community, admittedly a community of pimps, whores and drinkers, yet a recognizable world where everyone has a name and a place, not the big city anonymity that is the experience of modern-day policemen. However, van de Wetering's games with his country's image in crime fiction are never naïve. A regular feature in his depiction is the resemblance of the Amsterdam police force to the criminals they are pursuing.

Moreover, it becomes obvious quite quickly that there is a wider Netherlands, encompassing immigrants from the ex-colonies. Van de Wetering takes pains to emphasize their Dutchness. However, he also develops a complex argument where images of national identity and ethnic Otherness are turned upside down and inside out.

De ratelrat plays partially in the province of Friesland. Here, van de Wetering introduces a great number of jokes about Amsterdam detectives leaving the metropolis for a marginal, foreign region like Friesland. Suddenly, everybody is considered in terms of his or her ethnic allegiance, not just the Frisian policemen and suspects but also the many Chinese gangsters (immigrants into Friesland), Grijpstra (Frisian emigrant to Amsterdam), de Gier (Hollander), and the young Jewish detective Cardozo. The latter, a very intelligent, ambitious young policeman, is often presented as a clever, sulking child, excessively convinced of his capabilities, although in *De ratelrat* he has an important role in solving the case. Cardozo's Jewishness is flaunted in the text; he is marked again and again as Jewish. Yet van de Wetering uses humour to defuse any intimations of anti-Semitism. When Cardozo's brother asks sardonically if the Jews should be identified by wearing the Star of David, the narrative text points to the Star of David necklace under his shirt.[26] Jewishness, as indicated in van de Wetering's text, is but one of many markers of race and gender that help compose a character's personality. Ultimately, so the cosy world of jokes and quips in the novel implies, they are harmless – labels unburdened by any dark hints of real oppression and racial hatred.

In fact, the central joke in this novel concerns a humorous treatment of race and ethnicity, a *faux naïf* investigation of Frisian nature and its difference from Amsterdam Dutchness. When he arrives in the province of Friesland, de Gier behaves as if he is visiting a foreign country but manages to learn Frisian in record time. Amsterdam is full of immigrant Frisians, who suddenly feel the urge – unsuccessfully – to find their roots up North. In the opening scene a corpse is discovered on a burning ship in the harbour. It is an image that hails from Germanic mythology and calls up associations of the greater Germanic race. Every appearance of a Frisian character brings with it the use of Frisian words such as "blommen" (flowers), or "It Heitelan" (the homeland). There are many jokes about the supposed mystical nature of the Frisians as a motive for the murder, about the attractiveness and toughness of Frisian women and a repressed sexuality said to be typical of the disciplined purity of the province.

Here, van de Wetering is playing a sophisticated game with his readers' hang-ups concerning race and gender. Political correctness seems to be ignored with the sustained use of concepts such as the

---

[26]   Van de Wetering, *De ratelrat*, 46.

Dutch nature now clearly tarnished by associations with fascism. However, they are used not to address racial discrimination but for a bantering debate on Frisian identity. The reader is consequently implicated in an elaborate joke with the narrator.

Van de Wetering's novels display the ethnic variation in the Netherlands and deal to a great extent with Dutch identity, with defining and contrasting a Dutch sense of self, from the perspective of an author living in the United States and faced with fairly extreme hetero-images of rural windmills, clogs and weed-smoking urbanites. At the same time, he must consider the self-images of his Dutch audience. He consequently sets up a confusing double image around the multiculturalism and tolerance so essential for a modern, urban Dutch society, never relinquishing an atmosphere of quirky cuteness and the image of a traditional community. This presents the reader with an ambiguous message. While he advances an image of the Netherlands and Amsterdam as a jolly place of liberalism and tolerance, a society that has moved beyond the need for a petty, humourless political correctness, at the same time the age-old racist jokes and clichés are re-performed and enjoyed, albeit from the superior position of jesters and jokers. While the overall progressive, liberal and tolerant image of these early novels is maintained, racist and sexist clichés remain surprisingly active. As his society's jester and joker, van de Wetering shows more extensively than his literary colleagues how a notoriously conventional and escapist genre is in fact performing a double take on society and its sense of identity.

CULTURAL IDENTITY IN SWISS GERMAN DETECTIVE FICTION

CHRISTOPHER JONES

This essay will take a selection of examples from recent Swiss German detective fiction and analyse the methods that are employed in the construction of identity.[1] I shall demonstrate that on the surface these methods seem to rely on a recycling of stereotypes and clichés to do with an image of the Swiss as rich and insular, coupled with their presentation alongside individuals and groups of foreign (non-Swiss) background who provide a simplistic Other against which Swiss identity is defined. However, I shall then argue that these first impressions are insufficient for a full understanding of the aims of the works discussed. The inclusion of non-Swiss groups is not simply to allow a facile individuation of the Swiss through comparison with the Other. Rather it serves the additional purpose of differentiating Swiss crimes from those perpetrated by outsiders. This is a significant difference because it is not just the individual characters that are worthy of attention but also the crimes they commit. It is those crimes committed by the Swiss themselves that force us as readers to consider the hidden commentary. Are they committed because the perpetrators are turned into criminals by Swiss society, or are these crimes a commentary on or a reaction against this society as it currently exists?

In order to undertake this analysis I will begin by providing a brief theoretical background to the task in hand, starting with a reminder of Homi Bhabha's influential "The Other Question: Stereotype, Discrimination and the Discourse of Colonialism". Bhabha here draws attention to the use of racial and cultural stereotypes as an essential tool in any attempt to confer permanence on the power relationships of

---

[1] I would like to thank Dr William Adamson and Dr Christian Timm at the *Raymond-Chandler-Gesellschaft* for the loan of some of the texts used for this article.

a postcolonial world. Bhabha identifies an anxiety over the success of such an undertaking by pointing out the need for stereotypes to be constantly repeated. For Bhabha this imbues the stereotype with an ambivalence, vacillating "between what is always 'in place', already known, and something that must be anxiously repeated".[2] Bhabha goes on to assert that a stereotype cannot exist in isolation but needs "for its successful signification, a continual and repetitive chain of other stereotypes".[3] I shall argue that it is such a coexistence of a series of stereotypes which forms one of the key structural elements in the texts under consideration here. It should not be forgotten that Bhabha is critical of the limitations inherent in the stereotype as a means of signifying Otherness. Whether these limitations persist or are transformed in an environment such as genre fiction, which provides such fertile ground for them to flourish, is an issue I shall return to in my conclusion.

Of equal significance to the arguments raised in this essay is the work of Tzvetan Todorov in his essay "The Typology of Detective Fiction", in which he illustrates how the detective novel "contains not one but two stories: the story of the crime and the story of the investigation".[4] Drawing on the work of the Russian Formalists, Todorov makes the distinction between the fable (story) and the subject (plot), explaining that "the story is what happened in life, the plot is the way the author presents it to us".[5] This distinction is of particular significance to detective fiction where the reader's enjoyment of the novel is often dependent on the success with which access to the story of the crime is denied. However, I shall be arguing that this distinction is also of relevance to an understanding of the manner in which many recent Swiss detective novels have dealt with the notion of cultural identity through a deliberate marginalization of the Other. This marginalization occurs on the two levels of the detective novel identified by Todorov, relating both to the crime itself and to the manner of its depiction. A few key examples will make this clear.

---

[2] Homi K. Bhabha, "The Other Question: Stereotype, Discrimination and the Discourse of Colonialism", in *The Location of Culture*, London: Routledge, 1994, 66.
[3] *Ibid.*, 77.
[4] Tzvetan Todorov, "The Typology of Detective Fiction", in *The Poetics of Prose*, Ithaca: Cornell University Press, 1977, 44.
[5] *Ibid.*, 45.

Stereotypes as far as the eye can see?

Stereotypes have a close association with popular fiction,[6] but is their prevalence in the works under consideration here a sign of lazy writing or of something else? In order to answer this question it is necessary to look at some concrete examples first, examining the evidence of how Swiss crime writers use stereotypes to describe country and characters. The clichéd images of Switzerland as a rich isolated country surface again and again in Swiss detective fiction, frequently in the company of stereotypically wealthy citizens. Sometimes this wealth is in the hands of individuals, such as Linus in Roger Graf's *Zürich bei Nacht*,[7] Murbach in Peter Zeindler's *Aus Privatbesitz*,[8] or Bucher in Willy Bär's *Tobler*.[9] Of equal, if not greater, significance is the accumulation of wealth in selected families, which are often associated with companies of great financial power, such as the Restelberg family in Ulrich Knellwolf's *Schönes Sechseläuten*[10] or the Belleton family in Verena Wyss' *Die Untersuchungsrichterin*.[11] The *loci* of the novels can also reflect this affluence, through their blatant associative qualities. The art exhibitions in *Aus Privatbesitz* and *Die Untersuchungsrichterin*; the *Sechseläuten* parade in *Schönes Sechseläuten*; and the horse racing track in *Tobler* are just some examples that present an unquestioning portrait of the lives of the rich Swiss citizenry. A strong contrast to this vision is the manner in which outsiders are presented.

The marginalization of those crimes committed by outsiders happens on the two levels of the detective novel identified by Todorov. On the level of subject/plot, which in Todorov refers to the narrative structure of the novel, we see a reduction of the significance of the Other to the level of local colour, as an aid to the creation of a milieu in which there are exotic individuals involved in mysterious or obvious criminal activities. In Rolf Wesbonk's first Dillmann novel *Dillmann: Kein Katzenfall*, for example, the reader is presented with a concatenation of stereotypical observations that serve as a narrative

---

[6] See Scott McCracken, *Pulp*, Manchester: Manchester University Press, 1988.
[7] Roger Graf, *Zürich bei Nacht*, Zurich: Haffmans, 1996.
[8] Peter Zeindler, *Aus Privatbesitz*, Zurich: Arche, 1998.
[9] Willy Bär, *Tobler*, Zurich: Limmat, 1990.
[10] Ulrich Knellwolf, *Schönes Sechseläuten*, Zurich: Arche, 1997.
[11] Verena Wyss, *Die Untersuchungsrichterin*, Berlin: Ullstein, 1996.

shorthand to delineate the criminal underbelly of contemporary city life with little respect for any notion of political correctness:

> Das Bild der Häuserfronten war geprägt von Coiffeurgeschäften, Wettannahmestellen, Kneipen, Spielsalons, Pizzerien und Delikatessen-Läden, an deren Eingangstüren italienische, griechische, türkische und spanische Namen prangten. Und natürlich überall Anzeichen der verheerenden Drogenknechtschaft: zerlumpte, ausgemergelte Gestalten, blutige Spritzen und Fäkalien auf dem Gehsteig, ausländische Dealer mit harten Gesichtern sowie ungewaschene, blutjunge Fixerinnen, die nach Freiern Ausschau hielten.[12]

This image of the foreign dealer permeates many of the detective novels of the Nineties, although its use rarely rises above local colour. In *Tobler*, Bär puts one possible explanation into the mouth of Stefan Winzeler at the *Bezirksanwaltschaft*:

> Nach allem, was wir wissen, ist der Heroinhandel in Zürich auf Kaderebene fast ausschliesslich in der Hand von Ausländern: Türken, Libanesen, Israelis, Pakistanern, gut situierten Geschäftsleuten zumeist. Das soll nicht heissen, dass die Ausländer skrupelloser sind als die Schweizer, überhaupt nicht, sie haben einfach die besseren Beziehungen zu den Anbauländern und den Organisationen, die Produktion und Handel kontrollieren.[13]

Winzeler goes on to define the type of crime the Swiss are more likely to commit, a significant difference to which I shall return in the next

---

[12] Rolf Wesbonk, *Dillmann: Kein Katzenfall*, Berlin: Ullstein, 1997, 34: "The image of the front of the rows of houses was defined by hairdressers, betting shops, pubs, amusement arcades, pizza parlours and delicatessens with Italian, Greek, Turkish, and Spanish names adorning the entrance doors. And of course everywhere indications of the devastating slavery to drugs: ragged emaciated figures, bloodied hypodermic needles and faeces on the pavement, foreign dealers with hard faces, as well as very young and unwashed drug-addicted prostitutes looking out for clients" (all translations my own).

[13] Bär, *Tobler*, 79: "According to everything we know, the heroin trade in Zurich at the top level is almost entirely in the hands of foreigners: Turks, Lebanese, Israelis, Pakistanis – well-placed businessmen for the most part. That's not to say that the foreigners are more ruthless than the Swiss – not at all – it's just that they have better connections to the countries where the drugs are grown and to the organizations that control production and trade."

section. One final point is that since, as we have just seen, the Swiss themselves are also presented with stereotypical qualities, this tends to minimize the racist impact of these passages, by having stereotypes on both sides of the equation.

This marginalization is intensified through the use of the Other in the crime itself, the fable/story level in Todorov's terms, when we see that in most cases the foreign criminals, although present on the perimeter as local colour, have no role to play in the crimes Swiss writers have chosen to focus on. One possible exception to this rule can be found in Zeindler's *Aus Privatbesitz*, one of many Swiss detective novels to exploit the National Socialist period as a backdrop. Unlike Knellwolf's *Schönes Sechseläuten*, discussed below, *Aus Privatbesitz* ignores the commercial and industrial collaboration that occurred, in favour of an examination of the trade in lost works of art. These are paintings, frequently *entartete Kunst*, that were confiscated mainly from Jewish families before finding their way into Switzerland. As in *Schönes Sechseläuten*, but with a less heavy hand, *Aus Privatbesitz* explores the repercussions of past misdeeds in the present day, presenting the reader with a powerful figure, the politician Murbach, who in spite of close connections to this illegal traffic in lost artworks seems invulnerable to prosecution. Here the technique outlined above of presenting foreign crimes and criminals on the periphery is given an interesting twist. Zeindler is able to construct an entire narrative thread in which a foreign investigator tracks down a foreign criminal. Dave, Lucy Brendan's possible love interest, turns out to be a member of the Mossad, the Israeli Secret Service, on the hunt for Kruger, a South African who had been responsible for the death of Samuel (who was Dave's own estranged son). This certainly solves the murder mystery established in the early part of the novel with Samuel's death, but by the time of its solution the reader's attention has been drawn away from this matter to concentrate on the confrontation between Lucy and Murbach.

Having the murder committed by an outsider and solved by an outsider forces them onto the sidelines, and the Swiss issues are brought into sharp focus, with the reader's attention firmly on the moral questions raised by the traffic in stolen artwork, which is seen as a stereotypically Swiss crime. The murder mystery itself, traditionally the key part of a detective novel, is almost the subject of marginalization through this process, allowing Zeindler free reign to explore the moral battle of wills between Lucy and Murbach. Once again the foreign issues are marginalized: here the Otherness of the participants may not merely provide colour and flavour, but clearly they occupy a different layer in the narrative to the main protagonists.

If the crimes and criminals are for the most part Swiss, what are the writers trying to tell us? Are the crimes reactions against a strict society and its laws? Not exactly. Most of these authors take great pains to present contemporary Swiss society as a tolerant environment. The Zurich drug culture depicted in Bär's *Tobler* or Graf's *Zürich bei Nacht* and *Tanz an der Limmat*[14] is seen to be an intrinsic part of a modern urban environment. Indeed Swiss crime writers seem to take great steps to construct a milieu fitting for the late twentieth century in which Switzerland and its cities are susceptible to the same crimes as any other modern metropolis. Wolfgang Bortlik, however, is highly sceptical of this approach, feeling that some writers go too far, and "sich in letzter Zeit Autoren wie Roger Graf so geben, als ob Zürich eine pulsierende Vierundzwanzigstundenstadt wäre, in der an jeder Ecke das Verbrechen lauert".[15] This drug culture may be tolerated with a certain degree of distaste for most of the time but there are then occasions when it becomes the subject of a clean-up campaign, as we read in the drug-using Peter Bigler's hugely ironic diary entry for March 1983 in *Tobler*:

> Die Schmier hat wieder einmal zugeschlagen und die Riviera gesäubert. Seit Jahren wiederholt sich jeden Frühling der gleiche Reigen. Immer wenn die Tage wärmer werden, wenn es die Bürger mit Kind, Köter und Kegel auf die Trampelpfade entlang der Limmat treibt, entdecken sie von neuem die Drogenszene. Mitten in ihrer Stadt müssen sie mitansehen, wie verwahrloste Gestalten Nadeln in die Arme stechen, um sich mit stärksten Schmerzmitteln zu betäuben. So verlangen

---

[14]   Roger Graf, *Tanz an der Limmat*, Zurich: Haffmans, 1997.
[15]   Wolfgang Bortlik, "Löcher in der Schweizer Leiche", in *Das Mordsbuch*, ed. Nina Schindler, Hildesheim: Claassen, 1997, 186: "Authors such as Roger Graf have recently been giving the impression that Zurich is a pulsating city that never sleeps with crime lurking on every corner."

sie empört – im Namen eines Komitees oder anonym – nach ihrem Beruhigungsmittel, der Polizei.[16]

In many detective novels this attitude of *laissez faire* is intensified through the close relationships the central characters have with members of the drug-dealing underground, such as Röfe in *Tobler* or Phil in Graf's two *Marco Biondi* novels. There is also a great deal of tolerance towards individuals who wish to adopt an alternative lifestyle, as seen in *Tobler* through the characters of Marie-Therese and the therapy sessions she organizes, or Frau Meili-Stähelin who attempts to capture voices from beyond the grave on a tape-recorder.

To sum up, then, the narrative approach constructs a portrait of Switzerland as a modern country with an international population troubled by the same problems to do with drugs and drug-related crime as are to be found all over the industrialized world. However, that international population is marginalized as outsiders, and the crimes with which they are typically involved are sidelined in order to achieve a foregrounding of other crimes in which the Swiss investigator and the Swiss criminal stand out in sharp relief. It is now time to examine those crimes and the duality of investigator and criminal.

Two sides of the same Rappen?

As indicated above, the crimes these detective novels choose to explore are not directed against society and the prevailing social norms. They are not a violent reaction to the claustrophobic experience of living in a rigid society. So, what sort of crimes are committed and investigated in these works, and what do they reveal about the aims of the Swiss crime writers? In common with detective fiction the world over the crime is usually murder. Julian Symons in *Bloody Murder* categorizes murder as the staple of detective fiction on the

---

[16] Bär, *Tobler*, 40: "The fuzz have struck once again and cleaned up the Riviera. For years now it's been the same dance every spring. It's always when the days get warmer and the citizens together with their children, dogs, and skittles are drawn to the paths along the Limmat that they uncover the drugs scene once more. In the middle of their city they have to watch how dishevelled individuals jab needles into their arms to numb themselves with the most powerful painkillers. And so in the name of some committee or anonymously they make an outraged plea for their own tranquilliser: the police."

basis of its finality, not so much with regard to the fate of the victim, but with a focus on the killer:

> Murder is in many societies seen as the act which makes its perpetrator finally unacceptable. He may be expelled or destroyed, but never pardoned.[17]

Although at first glance a violent crime in which one individual takes another's life, murder is often endowed with additional significance that takes it far beyond the purely personal sphere. In many of the texts under consideration here this additional significance makes the crime representative of, not a reaction against, serious flaws in Swiss society in its recent history. The crimes and criminals represent the extremes of the stereotypical Swiss desire for money and neutrality at all costs, on an individual level, on a corporate level, and on a national level. It is also surely not without significance that so many people with a criminal past are treated with such tolerance by the rest of society in these texts. In the Preface to his anthology of Swiss detective fiction *Banken, Blut und Berge*, Zeindler observes: "Das Böse lauert hier hinter der biedermännischen Maske."[18]

In my reading of Swiss detective novels, this mask does not hide the evil so much as make it socially acceptable. The investigators therefore become agents of a social conscience and the fact that they are private investigators, for the most part, forcefully suggests complicity between the criminals and the public face of the law.

As already indicated in the discussion of Zeindler's *Aus Privatbesitz*, one of the most fertile periods for Swiss crime writers has been the Nazi era. Knellwolf, for example, draws heavily on the 1933-1945 period for background in two of his detective novels from the Nineties, *Klassentreffen*[19] and *Schönes Sechseläuten*. In the second of these in particular Knellwolf presents a portrait of Swiss society in which the rich and powerful are able to escape justice over many decades, their crimes achieving an almost symbolic quality as representatives of the crimes of Switzerland as a nation, both in the present day and in

---

[17] Julian Symons, *Bloody Murder*, London: Pan, 1994, 21.
[18] Peter Zeindler, "Vorwort" in *Banken, Blut und Berge*, ed. Peter Zeindler, Hamburg: Rowohlt, 1995, 10: "Here evil lurks behind a bourgeois mask."
[19] Ulrich Knellwolf, *Klassentreffen*, Zurich: Arche, 1995.

the Nazi period when powerful Swiss industries exploited opportunities to profit from collaboration with Hitler at the expense of any personal or national honour.

Knellwolf uses the *Sechseläuten* festival, which takes place every year in Zurich on the third Monday in April, as a setting designed to facilitate an association between the major characters, who are mostly connected with one of the historical guilds of the city, and deep-rooted notions of Swiss cultural identity. Knellwolf introduces the reader to the figure of Uta Restelberg very early in the story through the background research into her life undertaken by Frühauf, a journalist. Uta is the matriarch of the RAG aircraft company which did not shy away from selling to Hitler. Although the book only covers a short period of time, there are several murders and mysteries, and at the very end of the story it seems that the instigator of it all, Uta, will not be brought to any form of justice. Uta is concerned about the fate of her family firm and for this reason makes plans to sow suspicion between her son Gerold and his own son.

Although her plans go somewhat awry in a very contrived plot, her original intention is still achieved and Gerold does indeed shoot his son, causing Arnikka, his estranged wife, to stab him. Frauenfelder, the investigating police officer, has nothing to go on even when Frühauf explains how it all must have happened.

Unfortunately the mystery element is built up of a mass of characters with convoluted relationships moving through a sea of contrived coincidence. To the unprepared reader, however, the greatest suspension of disbelief is required for the longest chapter of the novel "Sechseläutenvorbereitung", in which there is another excursion into the days of the Third Reich this time thanks to Uta's memoirs of her meeting with Hitler. The *Führer* had made great plans to seduce her at Berchtesgaden but when the opportunity arrived he was impotent: "Er wütete, er stampfte auf den Boden, kreischte schäumend und blickte erwartungsvoll an sich hinunter. Ohne Ergebnis."[20] Maybe this is some sort of bizarre commentary on German-Swiss relations during the Second World War? Be that as it may, the real problem is that it

---

[20] Ulrich Knellwolf, *Schönes Sechseläuten*, 48: "Raging, stamping his feet, and screeching with foam at his mouth he looked down at himself expectantly, to no avail."

merely adds another barrier to any real understanding of what Knell-wolf is attempting here.

The clarity of purpose seen in *Klassentreffen*, with its remorseless tragic linearity that brought an uncomfortable past tangibly into the present with fatal consequences, has here been replaced by layer upon layer of forgettable characters, weak or contrived motivation, and a predilection for extraneous detail that does not seem even tangentially related to the main thrust of the novel. Using a local festival rooted in centuries of Swiss tradition as a background could have been an opportunity to set current issues against a broader cloth, but the choice to try to fuse so many time periods into a whole (the old Swiss past embodied in the *Sechseläuten* festival; the past of the Second World War; and the present) is clearly beyond Knellwolf on this occasion. Even a charitable view of *Schönes Sechseläuten* which might excuse the artificiality of the plot or the appalling lack of taste would have difficulty in suggesting that Knellwolf has anything to say here that is not in his previous work.

The ruthless opportunism at the heart of the RAG company's dealings during the Nazi era is paralleled in the present-day world of Swiss corporations as portrayed in Wyss' tale of corporate corruption, *Die Untersuchungsrichterin*. The illegal tests of the large chemical company Chemihold form the background to the investigation into a death that at first glance seems to have been an accident, but which is in fact a cleverly staged murder designed to silence the victim. The lack of concern for the individual when there is a financial profit at stake and the moral complicity of most of those responsible for enforcing the law become clear in the confrontation between Cecile Belleton and Wyss' investigator, Simone Wender:

> Ein kleiner Bankangestellter, der in seinem Schrebergartenhaus bei-
> nahe perfekt getötet wird, seine Bohrmaschine war falsch verdrahtet.
> Ein völlig unwichtiger Mensch, um dessentwillen sich der ganze Auf-
> wand einer Untersuchung und Ahndung nicht lohnte, das müßte ihr
> doch klar sein. So klar wie die Tatsache, daß die weltweiten Geschäfte
> der Chemihold ebenfalls in andere Machtzusammenhänge gehören,
> die nicht gestört werden dürfen.[21]

---

[21] Verena Wyss, *Die Untersuchungsrichterin*, Berlin: Ullstein, 1996, 126: "A minor
bank official who had been almost perfectly murdered in his allotment garden

Simone becomes involved with another potential target, the biologist Andres Marchi, whose work has uncovered the illegal testing and made him the target of a professional assassin, Janos Pfeindler. Wyss' green message and the potentially exciting tale of industrial corruption and the murderous steps that some companies are prepared to take to cover up and silence the truth is obscured by a narrative style that relies on a present tense delivery with a point of view very close to Simone's own. The absence of any direct speech, the bizarre dream sequences, and the clichéd romance between Simone and Marchi lend the story an air of unreality that unfortunately does not sit very happily with the subject matter and its claim to contemporary validity and authenticity.

If the investigators are manifestations of a social or individual conscience then Graf's detective Biondi, first seen in *Zürich bei Nacht*, provides the clearest example. In the mould of a flawed hero, he is plagued by demons of depression, thereby lending weight to Bortlik's argument that all Swiss fictional detectives must have some ailment: "Sie [the detectives] stehen der Gesellschaft und der institutionalisierten Gerechtigkeit kritisch gegenüber, lehnen sie unbewußt ab und bekommen dadurch eine schwere psychosomatische Krankheit."[22] Biondi is originally hired by Katharina Boxler to find her missing brother Martin. However Biondi soon finds himself more concerned with past events after finding a photograph of himself, with two old friends Christoph and Linus, amongst Martin's belongings. Todorov's assertion that the detective novel rests on a double narrative of past misdeeds and present day investigations is certainly of great relevance here as Graf links the two time streams to analyse the changes in Biondi and his friends over a period of time.

Zürich bei Nacht is certainly not a formula detective novel in which unchanging characters dance a masquerade of lies and deceptions until a fatal slip of the mask allows the detective to glimpse the

---

shed: his drill had been incorrectly wired. A totally unimportant person, not worth all the bother of an investigation and punishment – surely that much was clear to her. As clear as the fact that the worldwide business of Chemihold also belonged to a different set of power relations which must not be disturbed."

[22] Wolfgang Bortlik, "Löcher in der Schweizer Leiche", 183: "They stand in critical opposition to society and to an institutionalized justice which they unconsciously reject, thereby contracting a psychosomatic illness."

truth. Instead, Graf's novel depends on the notion of change for its impact, charting and chronicling the changes in the trio, imbuing those changes with a symbolic quality that makes them symptomatic of changes in post-war Swiss society. Biondi, Christoph, and Linus are the seeds sown in the past and the novel observes how they have grown, with Graf almost implying that each had the potential to become the other. The central character of Biondi makes this explicit through his vacillation between depression, like Christoph who commits suicide, and satisfaction with his successful role in society, a trait he shares with Linus. Biondi's self-conscious musings highlight a proximity between investigator and criminal, and Graf's detailed portrait of Zurich society endows Linus' successful career path with an emblematic quality, which tempts the reader to consider Linus' ruthless rise to a position of wealth and power as a mirror image of Switzerland's own post-war track record, which has seen it amass great wealth through avenues which are shown, at times, to possess a dubious morality.

There is even evidence to show that with some writers the duality of investigator and criminal is anything but literal. As the gap between investigator and criminal starts to break down, the reader may be tempted into interpreting their battle as a symbolic representation of a moral struggle within Swiss society. Recent mainstream Swiss fiction has been drawing on the detective novel for inspiration, as in Christoph Keller's *Ich hätte das Land gern flach*[23] or in Urs Richle's *Der weiße Chauffeur*[24] which is of particular relevance here. We have already observed how Graf tests the boundary between the investigator and the criminal in the characters of Biondi and Linus, forcing the reader to consider more carefully those few differences that do remain.

Nevertheless the dissolution of the boundary between investigator and criminal which is almost inviolable in the genre itself (with the possible exception of Agatha Christie's *The Murder of Roger Ackroyd*) is more permeable outside the strict boundaries of the genre, and Richle uses this freedom to good effect in *Der weiße Chauffeur*. Here Richle presents us with a detective novel full of twists and turns, that

---

[23]   Christoph Keller, *Ich hätte das Land gern flach*, Frankfurt am Main: Fischer, 1999.

[24]   Urs Richle, *Der weiße Chauffeur*, Munich: Piper, 1998.

takes great delight in toying with the reader primarily through its almost total disregard for the sanctity of individual identity. Imaginary characters become real, as in the case of Dr Walter Herrsberg, and real characters apparently change or die, but not forever. Richle is clearly drawing on the power of the detective novel to present the reader with any number of false statements and identities, using this freedom to monitor in artificial detail how identity is manufactured. Instead of a psychological portrait suggesting how key incidents in an individual's life could account for their psychological make-up, Richle provides a premeditated plan to construct a new identity.

Dr Herrsberg had originally been the brainchild of Karl and Harry, who had set up a bank account for this fictitious individual, and even bought lottery tickets in his name. Harry is eventually fired from the bank, but Karl continues to buy the tickets. When one of the tickets wins a large sum of money, Karl fakes his own death in a swimming accident, with the intention of then slipping into the persona of Dr Herrsberg. However, Karl's plans come to nought and he must go into hiding, but not before he has unwittingly appointed his friend Harry as chauffeur to a non-existent man. Harry is then also obliged to create an identity for Dr Herrsberg, with the help of an actor, to defuse any suspicions on the part of Trix, Karl's old girlfriend with whom Harry is now involved. Richle takes great delight in layering these confusions, but the novel reveals its serious side most clearly through Harry's fictitious accounts to Trix of how he spent his days as Dr Herrsberg's chauffeur and his interpretations of the latter's character.

These explicit acts of construction function as a self-referential allegory of the writer's craft, yet they also attempt to reveal the artificial nature of identity, undermining any notion of psychological predetermination in favour of wilful, often playful choice. By employing a first person narrator, who is at first nameless but who, one assumes, will undertake an investigation of the mysteries of the novel, Richle is able to build on the reader's expectations of fidelity to genre conventions. When that very narrator is himself revealed as Karl, who was not only believed dead but also the instigator of the deception that gave rise to all the convolutions of the novel, this not only shatters those genre conventions, it also disrupts the duality of the investigator and the criminal, suggesting that such a boundary, indeed any boundary between one character type and another, is far more fluid.

From the texts considered here it can be seen that the Swiss detective novel has a strong tendency to present crimes that may be read as symptomatic of moral failures in the recent past of the nation. The interplay between criminals and investigators may therefore also be read on a metaphorical level as the battle between agents of commercial enterprise and manifestations of a social conscience. Recent examples of the detective novel, where the boundary between investigator and criminal threatens to dissolve, prompt a reading in which this struggle is located wholly on the level of the individual who is faced with a moral dilemma. I began by noting that Bhabha's work on the use of stereotypes in postcolonial issues identified them as a tool to reinforce social and political power relationships. Swiss crime writers, as we have seen, have turned to stereotypes not merely to depict the Other, foreigners or outsiders, but have made use of them in the depiction of their fellow citizens. In this endeavour stereotypical qualities such as rich and politically neutral are used in the construction of the criminals and linked to the crimes they commit in order to shine a powerful, revealing light on aspects of contemporary Swiss society and recent Swiss history. In this manner many of the hallmarks of stereotypes such as their aesthetic limitations and their frequent use to reinforce existing power structures or to exclude social or racial minorities have undergone a valuable transformation.

Unresolved Identities in Roth and Rabinovici: Reworking the Crime Genre in Austrian Literature

Marieke Krajenbrink

In recent years, crime fiction in Austria has flourished in an un-precedented way and in a wide variety of forms that increasingly defy classification along boundaries of popular and highbrow literature. It ranges from the *Heimatkrimi*[1] to the political thriller,[2] from adap-tations of the classic whodunnit formula to an Austrian setting, to postmodern experimenting with the conventions of the genre, whether playful[3] or subversive.[4] As Gerhard Fuchs maintains, "kaum ein öster-reichischer Gegenwartsroman kommt ohne Anleihen beim Kriminal-roman aus".[5]

This essay will investigate how elements of the crime genre are used to explore issues of identity within a wider context of debates about Austrianness and about the constructed nature of collective and

---

[1] The term *Heimatkrimi* refers to a crime novel in a traditional rural setting, a close-knit community, a provincial idyll and an ordered world. Alfred Komarek's series featuring commissioner Polt and set in the *Weinviertel* is particularly popular, see *Polt muß weinen* (1998), *Blumen für Polt* (2000), *Himmel, Polt und Hölle* (2001), *Polterabend* (2003), all Innsbruck: Haymon.

[2] See, for example, Josef Haslinger, *Opernball*, Frankfurt am Main: S. Fischer, 1995.

[3] See Wolf Haas, *Auferstehung der Toten* (1996), *Der Knochenmann* (1997), *Komm, süßer Tod* (1998), *Ausgebremst* (1998), *Silentium!* (1999), *Wie die Tiere* (2001), *Das ewige Leben* (2003), all Reinbek bei Hamburg: Rowohlt.

[4] See, for example, Elfriede Jelinek, *Gier*, Reinbek bei Hamburg: Rowohlt, 2000 and Thomas Glavinic, *Der Kameramörder*, Munich: dtv, 2003.

[5] Gerhard Fuchs, "Kolportage und Unterhaltung in Romanen von Lilian Faschinger, Josef Haslinger und Gerhard Roth", in *Banal und erhaben – es ist (nicht) alles eins*, eds Friedbert Aspetsberger and Günther A. Höfler, Innsbruck and Vienna: Studienverlag, 1997, 170: "Scarcely any Austrian contemporary novel gets by without borrowing from the crime novel." I thank Dr Jean E. Conacher for all translations of quotations from secondary sources.

individual identities in two Austrian novels from the Nineties, *Der See* (1995, *The Lake*) by Gerhard Roth, and *Suche nach M.* (1997, *The Search for M*) by Doron Rabinovici. Both of these novels take father-son relations as a framework for a discussion of identity. In particular, I will address to what extent and in what ways these works relate to what has been identified as a "rhetoric of national dissent",[6] typical of post-war Austrian literary production. In order to understand the context in which these books were produced, it is necessary to address the particular significance of the theme of Austria, its images and identities in post-war Austrian literature.

Austrian identity has been a much debated issue, both in literature and in the wider cultural arena.[7] This is intimately related to the history of Austria itself and the formation of the modern state. Due to the different ruptures, realignments and transformations that the country has experienced, Austria provides a particularly striking example of the constructed and multi-facetted character of national identity:

> The Austrian case is a mirror that reflects the various aspects the concept of identity raises: its structures and functions, its cross-cutting elements and its simplifying effects. The Austrian case also underlines the volatility of any given identity.[8]

Among the many factors – linguistic, ethnic, religious etc. – that help shape collective identity, the history of Austria in the twentieth century has been of crucial importance since, within one generation, tremendous changes in what actually constituted Austria occurred. In 1918 the collapse of the multi-national *Vielvölkerstaat* of the Habsburg monarchy led to the First Republic, most of whose inhabitants would have preferred to join Germany. Violent street clashes between

---

[6]   Matthias Konzett, *The Rhetoric of National Dissent in Thomas Bernhard, Peter Handke, and Elfriede Jelinek*, New York: Camden House, 2000.

[7]   See Friedrich Heer, *Der Kampf um die österreichische Identität*, Vienna, Cologne and Weimar: Böhlau, 1996, 9: "Es gibt kein geschichtliches Gebilde in Europa, dessen Existenz so sehr mit den Identitätsproblemen seiner Mitglieder verbunden ist wie Österreich" ("There is no historical creation in Europe whose existence is as bound up with the identity issues of its members as Austria").

[8]   Anton Pelinka, "Austrian Identity and the European Challenge", in *Yearbook of the Centre for Irish-German Studies 2000/01*, eds Marieke Krajenbrink and Joachim Lerchenmueller, Trier: WVT, 2001, 27.

paramilitary forces from left and right marked the Twenties. This First Republic ended when parliament was dissolved in 1933, while the brief civil war of 1934 gave way to the Catholic authoritarian corporate state (*Ständestaat*), modelled on Mussolini's Italy and promoting an ideology that became known as *Austrofascism*. Nineteen-thirty-eight saw the *Anschluss*, the annexation of Austria by Nazi Germany as a mere province, the *Ostmark*. Austria in its present form, the Second Republic, came into being in 1945.

Given these ruptures, it is hardly surprising that in post-war Austria how the past is perceived and categories of continuity and change understood are central in attempts to regain a sense of national identity. Generally speaking, dominant national self-representations involved a radical break with Germany – even to the extent that the language children learnt at school was no longer called *Deutsch* but instead the contrived *Unterrichtssprache*, roughly translated as "teaching language". The attempted disassociation from all things German meant also that little attention was directed towards any Austrian responsibility for atrocities committed during the Nazi era. This was facilitated by the Allies' Moscow Declaration of 1943 describing Austria as the first victim of Hitler's expansionist politics.[9] By stressing this victim discourse and discarding National Socialism as an un-Austrian intermezzo, an accident of history, the myth of Austria as an *Insel der Seligen* ("Island of the Blessed") became vital to the country's self-image for many years. However, in 1986 it became obvious that the past could not be suppressed. This year marked a caesura with its polarized debates on the election of Kurt Waldheim[10] and the emergence of right-wing populist Jörg Haider as the new leader of the FPÖ

---

[9] The Moscow Declaration also explicitly reminded Austria of its shared responsibility for being on the side of Hitler's Germany in the war, but this part was largely ignored in public discourse. See, for instance, Ruth Wodak, Rudolf De Cillia, Martin Reisigl and Karin Liebhart, *The Discursive Construction of National Identity*, Edinburgh: Edinburgh University Press, 1999, 59.

[10] Kurt Waldheim campaigned to become Austria's Federal President in 1986. His wartime record (he served as a junior *Wehrmacht* officer in the Balkans in the Forties), his vagueness about his precise role in the war and his declaration that he had simply done his duty under the Nazis sparked huge controversy and international outrage. Waldheim was elected with 54 per cent of the vote.

(Freedom Party).[11] In 2000, a coalition government including the FPÖ attracted international concern as well as a wave of demonstrations in Austria itself.

In light of this troubled history, it is easy to see why Austrian writers should be so concerned with the whole issue of identity. Gerhard Roth (b. 1942) was a representative of the *Grazer Gruppe*, one of the main groups of writers in Austria which in the Sixties and early Seventies developed a poetological programme that pitted itself against what they saw as false realism and emphasized the constructed character of literary fiction. Influenced by the *Sprachkritik* of Wittgenstein and Hofmannsthal and the language experiments of the *Wiener Gruppe*, as well as by Russian Formalism and the more contemporary French *nouveau roman*, their writing can arguably be regarded as an Austrian variant of early international postmodernism. Many of them embraced the detective genre as a form of defiance, as a gesture of non-conformity with the conservative bourgeois ideas that dominated Austria at the time.[12] What distinguishes Gerhard Roth from other members of this movement is that while many of them abandoned the genre he has carried out a sustained exploration of its creative potential from the beginnings of his *oeuvre* until the present day.

Over the years we can observe shifts in the form and function these detective elements adopt. Roth's writing begins with absurdist experiments (*How to be a detective*, 1972), where semiotic processes of looking for clues and searching for coherence are foregrounded as well as frustrated. Later, he produced more conventionally suspenseful novels. Set in the United States and full of ironic intertextual references to the work of Raymond Chandler, these later works, *Der große Horizont* (1974) and *Ein neuer Morgen* (1976), address such themes as the search for self-identity and a personal way of perceiving reality

---

[11] See Klaus Zeyringer, *Austrian Literature since 1986*, trans. John Nicholson and Sophie Francis Kidd at http://www.liffeyproject.net/content/showthread.php?s=& threadid=311, and Klaus Zeyringer, *Österreichische Literatur seit 1945: Überblicke, Einschnitte, Wegmarken*, Innsbruck: Haymon, 2001.

[12] The most prominent among these writers is Peter Handke. On the transformative use of the detective model in Handke's early novels, see Marieke Krajenbrink, *Intertextualität als Konstruktionsprinzip: Transformationen des Kriminalromans und des romantischen Romans bei Peter Handke und Botho Strauß*, Amsterdam and Atlanta GA: Rodopi, 1996.

or the conflict between convention and authenticity. The fascination with America in these novels, with their emphasis on travelling, the urban jungle and popular culture gives way in the Eighties to a highly critical engagement with Roth's own country.

The analysis of Austrian consciousness becomes the central theme of Roth's seven-part cycle *Die Archive des Schweigens* (1980-1991). As the term "archives of silence" indicates, this monumental work deals with the silence, concealment, forgetting and suppression of the truth, especially silence about the crimes of the Nazi past which for Roth, is the biggest and only genuine taboo in post-war Austria. Although detective elements are employed in a number of books in this cycle, in others no such elements appear. In his collection of essays *Eine Reise in das Innere von Wien* (1991) Roth sets off in search of the skeletons and sewers below Vienna's splendorous edifices and explores what he believes hidden beneath the charming surface: neuroses, violence, cruelty against animals, anti-Semitism. The influence of Freud and Foucault is evident in Roth's portrayal of the way society deals with those on its margins. Roth has recently described his role as a writer as being like a detective investigating the past, and he links this with his experiences as a young man of Austria's historical amnesia:

> Das hat mit meiner Erfahrung als Jugendlicher zu tun, als die ganze österreichische Geschichte tabuisiert war, und ich sehr viele Menschen kennengelernt habe, von denen ich keine Ahnung hatte, wie sie sich im Krieg verhalten haben und welche politischen Ansichten sie vertraten …. Ich bin dann eher in die Rolle eines Rechercheurs gekommen oder eines Detektivs, und damals habe ich auch diesen Zweifel, diese Skepsis in Bezug auf die Unterlagen entwickelt.[13]

---

[13] Daniela Bartens, "Topographien des Imaginären: Zum 'Orkus'-Gesamtzyklus unter Einbeziehung von Materialien aus dem Vorlass", in *Gerhard Roth: Orkus. Im Schattenreich der Zeichen*, eds Daniela Bartens and Gerhard Melzer, Vienna: Springer-Verlag, 2003, 65: "That has to do with my experience as a young man, when the whole of Austrian history was taboo and I got to know lots of people where I hadn't a clue what they had done in the war and what political views they represented …. So I ended up more in the role of a researcher or a detective, and at that time, too, I developed this doubt, this scepticism in relation to the records kept."

Against this background, Roth's use of detective elements takes on a special resonance. The concern with seeking out what lies behind the façade, unveiling what is hidden and remains taboo, and how those untold stories and histories impact on individual and collective identities makes the detective genre the most obvious formal framework for exploring such issues, although the genre is by no means drawn upon in a naïve way.

In Roth's *Der See*, the portrayal of Austria, past and present, and the impact of family and collective history on identity are central, whilst at the same time the very notion of stable categories with regards to identity is destabilized. This fast-paced story of multiple crimes is presented in a hundred very brief and almost cinematographic scenes. It is related by a peculiarly dispassionate narrator, who at the same time stays close to the perspective of the main character, Paul Eck, a heavy user of psychedelic drugs, who spends much of his time hallucinating. Due to the concomitant unreliability about the most basic sensory perceptions, uncertainty and indeterminacy permeate this narrative of increasing violence and disorientation. Through this device of unreliable focalization, the sense of mystification and alienation so typical to the genre, the notion that "things aren't quite what they seem"[14] is heightened. This happens to such an extent that any inclusive reconstruction of the untold[15] is fundamentally frustrated. Instead, the focus shifts to the problem of creating meaningful connections and establishing coherence. As Michael Winkler puts it,

---

[14]   Richard Alewyn, quoting John le Carré, *A Murder of Quality*, and maintaining "Der Detektivroman läßt sich keine Gelegenheit nehmen, die Unverläßlichkeit der Sinne und die Fehlbarkeit der Vernunft zu demonstrieren" (Richard Alewyn, "Anatomie des Detektivromans", in *Der Kriminalroman: Poetik – Theorie – Geschichte*, ed. Jochen Vogt, Munich: Fink, 1998, 70: "The crime novel does not miss any opportunity to demonstrate how unreliable are the senses and how fallible reason.").

[15]   For Ernst Bloch this is the most characteristic feature of the detective novel: "das Aufdeckende geht ... auf Vorgänge, die aus ihrem *Unerzählten, Vor-Geschichte-haften* erst herauszubringen sind. Dies ... ist das charakteristischste der Detektivgeschichte und macht sie, sogar weit vom Detektiv, unverwechselbar." Ernst Bloch, "Philosophische Ansicht des Detektivromans", in *Der Kriminalroman: Poetik – Theorie – Geschichte*, ed. Jochen Vogt, 41: "The process of revelation ... is linked to events which must first be retrieved from their being *untold*, their being *pre-history*. This is the most characteristic aspect of the detective story and makes it unmistakeable, even without the clear presence of a detective figure."

the "question of how webs and strings of sensory and mental data are turned into a story, of how things and people assume an identity, however precarious and contemporary, within a network of other identities is the novel's pre-eminent concern".[16]

The plot at first seems to revolve around a family drama, a conflict between father and son. It soon transpires, however, that the critical concern with Austrian history and society is continued here. Indeed, the motto preceding the narrative already states quite provocatively: "Im Land der Mörder."[17] Yet in this novel, the first in a new cycle Roth is currently working on,[18] we find a much more accessible plot than in previous novels and one which is more clearly linked to the traditional crime narrative. At the same time, the author raises complex issues of identity on both an individual and a collective level; the confrontation with the father is tied to a confrontation with the fatherland and a critique of social attitudes.

Eck, a travelling representative for a pharmaceutical company, accepts an invitation on a sailing trip from his unloved father, whom he has not seen in thirty years and whom he holds responsible for his mother's suicide. Upon his arrival in his native town, he finds that his father, boat and all, has mysteriously disappeared in a storm on Lake Neusiedl on the Hungarian border. The seemingly peaceful shallow lake, a popular holiday resort, takes on a metaphorical quality as appearances again are deceptive and much lies hidden beneath the surface. Storms occur here, sudden and deadly, pollution in the water

---

[16] Michael Winkler, "Afterword", in Gerhard Roth, *The Lake*, Riverside, CA: Ariadne Press, 2000, 169-70. All translations from *Der See* are taken from this translation by Michael Winkler.

[17] Gerhard Roth, *Der See*, Frankfurt am Main: Fischer Taschenbuch Verlag, 1998, 5: "In the Land of the Murderers" (*The Lake*, 1). Gerhard Roth is by no means the only Austrian author to criminalize his country in such an indiscriminate way. Konstanze Fliedl notes how Elfriede Jelinek refers to Austria as a "Nation von Verbrechern" ("a nation of criminals") and Peter Turrini addresses his fellow countrymen as "Liebe Mörder" ("Dear Murderers"). See "Eins nach dem anderen. Ein Nachwort", in *Das andere Österreich: Eine Vorstellung*, ed. Konstanze Fliedl, Munich: dtv, 1998, 205.

[18] The publication of *Der See* was followed by *Der Plan* (1998), *Der Berg* (2000), *Der Strom* (2002) and *Das Labyrinth* (2005), all Frankfurt am Main: S. Fischer. For a discussion of Roth's cyclical writing, see Marieke Krajenbrink, "Van diep in Oostenrijk naar de Orcus: Over het cyclische schrijven van Gerhard Roth", *Armada: Tijdschrift voor wereldliteratuur*, 24 (2001), 86-98.

breeds parasitic worms, and gruesome evidence of crimes is found in the lake: discoveries of body parts point to multiple murders. Also in other respects the locale is anything but idyllic; the recurrent imagery of bird hunting generates an atmosphere of wanton violence and cruelty.

Eck becomes the main suspect in the disappearance of his father, as he appears to have both motive (avenging his mother) and no sound alibi (the drugs leave even him unsure about his own memories). Moreover, what makes him all the more suspicious is that he is operating under a false identity and attempts, whilst revisiting the scenes of his childhood, not to be recognized as the son of his father. Under a false name, he buys a revolver and reluctantly starts investigating. Soon he hears rumours of a multitude of shady affairs in which his father, a prominent local politician and businessman, is apparently implicated, ranging from political corruption and environmental scandals to human trafficking and the illegal arms trade. As in the hard-boiled tradition of social criticism the crime here serves as a focal point for social issues of much wider relevance. Unsurprisingly, there are links to international crimes far surpassing the Austrian context, while other aspects can be seen as specifically Austrian flavoured variants of global problems.

Much more striking is the way in which the novel time and again brings up reminders of both recent Austrian and more distant Austro-Hungarian history. In themselves, these are often inconspicuous and seem mostly unrelated to the plot, yet together they form a network of historical reference, including the lost grandeur of the Empire and, more particularly, the repressed period of National Socialism. Significantly, the novel opens in Trieste – the main port of the Austro-Hungarian Empire – where Eck visits the *Miramare Schloss* of Archduke Maximilian, the short-lived Habsburg Emperor of Mexico, and the *Risiera di San Sabba*, a rice factory dating from 1913, which during the Second World War served as a transit camp to Auschwitz. Later, in the Neusiedl region, we find descriptions of a forgotten Jewish cemetery, where Eck encounters an old Jew, who tells him that he is considered insane because he could not help returning after the war, whilst the heirs of the disinheritors now live in his grandfather's house. Also mentioned are a *Schloss* used as summer residence by the Austrian empress Maria Theresia and a channel dug by order of the Princes Esterhazy, which now marks the border with Hungary.

The existence of this border reminds us of the changes to the former Austro-Hungarian Empire, and the more recent shifting boundaries reflecting geo-political changes within Europe are clearly alluded to in this novel. Whilst the end of communism in Eastern Europe and its implications for this border region are mentioned repeatedly, we find that in the present moment of the novel, Austrian soldiers are engaged in what they call "die Grenze zumachen",[19] in policing this border against illegal refugees from the war-torn Balkans. Part of the border runs through the lake itself, and Roth highlights how difficult it can be on the water to know which side one is on. At one point, Eck views the region from an airplane and notices the differences in the agricultural landscape in Austria and Hungary. However, on the lake itself, there are no fixed markers. Along with the references to history, this reminds us that borders, like water, can be fluid and changeable. In Eck himself we have a product of both nations, as he is descended from a Hungarian grandfather, who was a fervent supporter of the Monarchy. Eck's investigation leads him across the border on several occasions where he visits his Hungarian relations.

In the foregrounding of the past, a scene where Eck meets the quaint Dr Goriupp, an old friend of his father is particularly interesting. Here, the scattered discourse on Austria's history is connected to and alternates with the story of the investigation into the vanished father. Past and present intersect as Goriupp, with an army of tin soldiers, re-enacts the 1866 Battle of Königgrätz, whilst simultaneously disclosing the clandestine arms business he and Eck's father so lucratively pursued. It is as if for Goriupp the trauma of Königgrätz, a pivotal moment that marked an end to aspirations for a unification of Austria and Germany and allowed Prussia, with its superior modern weaponry, to take prominence in the creation of modern Germany, somehow serves as a justification for these dealings:

> "... Sehen Sie" – er hörte auf, die Figuren zu verschieben, aus der Krallenhand ragte eine Zinnkanone, wie die Beute eines Adlers – "es ist wichtig, mit den neuesten Waffen ausgerüstet zu sein – ... Das wissen auch die Kroaten und ... unter uns gesagt – sie zahlen jeden

---

[19] Roth, *Der See*, 55: "closing the border" (*The Lake*, 36-37).

Preis dafür. Ihr Vater machte mit ihnen Deckgeschäfte, mehr will ich
darüber nicht verraten."[20]

Goriupp expresses his hope that Eck will follow in his father's foot-
steps. Eck indeed tries to find out more about his father's past and
especially about his war record, but discovers only that: "Die vergan-
gene Zeit verschwor sich gegen alle Nachforschungen."[21] He quite
deliberately remains an outsider, assuming a position of dissent both
with regards to his family and the nation.

We see this in a scene where Eck finds himself at a political
gathering where a young ambitious politician is ironically referred to
as "der 'Hoffnungsmann' ... der auf alle Probleme eine Antwort
wußte".[22] In front of a cheering crowd, this "man of hope" with
increasing rhetoric fervour warns against foreigners inundating the
country and thus casts his "Netz aus Vorurteilen, Ängsten, allgemei-
nem Unbehagen und offenen Mißständen, mit dem er die Wähler
einfing".[23] Eck, again under the influence of pills, observes how the
old men of the Veteran's League (*Kameradschaftsbund*) in subdued
voices compare the speaker with the *Führer*. Eck, feeling hatred rise
within him, releases the safety catch of his revolver and pulls the
trigger – but nothing happens, the revolver simply does not work.[24]

This is not the only instance in which Eck comes close to resorting
to violence. In a hallucinatory state, Eck also believes, and makes the
reader believe, that he shoots Dr Goriupp, but then later, the doctor
reappears again, alive and well. This is typical of the way in which the

---

[20] *Ibid.*, 177-78: "'... You see' – he stopped moving the figures, from his claw-hand
      protruded a tin canon like the prey of an eagle – 'it's important to be equipped
      with the latest weapons – ... The Croatians know that also and ... between you
      and me – they pay any price for them. Your father was engaged in clandestine
      business with them, that's all I am prepared to reveal about this'" (*The Lake*, 123).
[21] *Ibid.*, 183: "The time that had passed conspired against every sort of enquiry"
      (*The Lake*, 127).
[22] *Ibid.*, 185-86: "'the man of hope' ... who had an answer for every problem" (*The
      Lake*, 129).
[23] *Ibid.*, 186: "net of prejudices, anxieties, general discontent, and open grievances in
      which he caught the voters" (*The Lake*, 129).
[24] This scene has caused political commotion as the FPÖ accused Roth of incitement
      to assault on Jörg Haider and demanded in Parliament that all state prizes Roth
      had received be reclaimed (see documentation in *Gerhard Roth: Orkus*, eds
      Bartens and Melzer, 90-91).

novel fundamentally undermines the idea of reliability of perception and thus deconstructs the faith in the possibility of uncovering a true version of events which characterizes conventional detective fiction.[25] Yet, it seems possible to establish a kind of motive for Eck's two wished-for murders, in as far as both the "man of hope" and Dr Goriupp attempt to make Eck part of a larger venture, on the one hand based solely on him being his father's son and on the other on the assumption that he will subscribe to a certain notion of Austrianness. In both cases, Eck seems to resist false historical continuities, the populist anti-foreigner rhetoric with its Nazi overtones as well as the proposal to keep the family business going, which itself is again linked to a bizarre justification of the clandestine arms-deals through reference to the trauma of Königgrätz. Indeed, Eck resists any attempt by anyone to involve him at any level in collective identities in his hometown.

Towards the end of the novel, we find a series of denouements and a spectacular shoot-out, resulting in a conflagration of apocalyptic proportions. Yet, many questions remain unanswered and there is no reassuring sense of closure. The dominant version of events with regard to the death of Eck's father is that it was an accident. However, sabotage and murder cannot be entirely ruled out, and with these the possible, if unlikely, scenario of a connection between the multiple murders, involving worldwide networks of terrorist gangs trafficking arms to the warring parties in the former Yugoslavia. Eck leaves the lake resort in a state of LSD-induced bliss before the investigations have come to an end, flying off in a small airplane, while the starlings, that have figured so prominently throughout the novel, begin to paint their mysterious signs into the air.

While many of Roth's concerns are also taken up by author Doron Rabinovici, his novel *Suche nach M.* addresses issues of identity in contemporary Austria from a different perspective, that of the Jewish

---

[25] See also Renate Giacomuzzi-Putz, "Verdrängte Geschichte in seichten Gewässern. Zu Gerhard Roths Roman 'Der See'", in *Gerhard Roth: Orkus*, eds Bartens and Melzer, 78-79.

minority in post-Holocaust Vienna.[26] The presence of the past, relationships between generations and questions of both individual and collective identity are central, as in Roth's *Der See*. The exploration of such themes is, again, intricately connected to a highly creative and innovative use of elements of the detective genre. Yet, the novels differ markedly in many ways. To concentrate on a Jewish perspective implies a concern with alterity and with ambivalent, hyphenated identities, typical of minority writing. More specifically, what is at stake here is the relationship between children of Holocaust survivors and children of the perpetrators. [27] In this context, issues of crime and guilt, the search for justice and truth, for a possibility of resolution and a reconstruction of the untold have a different resonance. In Rabinovici's novel, detective elements take on a poignantly new dimension, which is in stark contrast to any notions of simple resolutions and reassuring restorations of narrative and ethical order.[28]

Rabinovici, who was born in 1961 in Tel Aviv and has lived in Vienna since 1963, is a writer of fiction, a historian and a political

---

[26] As with Roth, Rabinovici's biography impacts significantly on his work: "Ich bin ein nationaler Doppler, ein hochprozentiges Gemisch, ein Kind der Migration. Meine Identität ist eine Melange, und das bringt mich dazu, in mir immer auch einen anderen zu erkennen .... Alle mir nächsten Menschen leben zwischen den Sprachen, Kulturen und Kontinenten" (Alexandra Eberhard, "Wer Essays schreibt, kommt von Aussen, von anderswo: Ein Gespräch mit Doron Rabinovici", in *Clemens Brentano Preis der Stadt Heidelberg 2002*, ed. Alexandra Eberhard, Heidelberg, Amt für Öffentlichkeitsarbeit, 2002, 6-7: "I am a national double, a high-proof blend, a child of migration. My identity is a melange, and that leads me to always recognize another person in myself .... Everyone nearest me lives between languages, cultures and continents.").

[27] *Suche nach M.* is often discussed in the context of an increasing interest in Jewish identity in Austrian literature. See Andrea Kunne, "Jüdische Identität in der österreichischen Nachkriegsliteratur: Peter Henisch, Robert Schindel, Robert Menasse und Doron Rabinovici", in *Jüdische Identitäten: Einblicke in die Bewußtseinslandschaft des österreichischen Judentums*, ed. Klaus Hödl, Innsbruck, Vienna and Munich: Studienverlag, 2000, 271-306; Eva Reichmann, "Identität als Problem: Leben als Jude in Österreich im Werk von Doron Rabinovici, Robert Menasse und Robert Schindel", *Ide: Informationen zur Deutschdidaktik*, XXV/2 (2/2001), 40-48.

[28] See Dagmar Lorenz, "Holocaust Literature and Film as Crime Fiction", *Modern Austrian Literature*, XXXI/3/4 (1998), 35-48.

essayist.[29] One collection of short stories, *Papirnik*,[30] includes crime stories with bizarre twists and narratives about miscommunication between Jews and non-Jews, and he has also published a historical study on the Jewish Council, *Instanzen der Ohnmacht. Wien 1938-1945: Der Weg zum Judenrat*.[31] He is perhaps best known as a vocal campaigner in the movement against Jörg Haider's FPÖ.

His novel *Suche nach M.* in twelve episodes tells of the lives of first and second generation Holocaust survivors in Vienna since the Sixties. A complex network of family and community relations gradually unfolds whilst the episodic structure allows for a multiplicity of different perspectives, narrative voices and configurations, thus creating a multifaceted panorama of contemporary Vienna in its diversity. Bizarre and surreal elements feature strongly, and particularly striking are the use of mirror structures, mirror images and doubles, and the recurring pattern of mistaken identity, devices that are combined with a whole array of variations on the detective model. As the title, *Suche nach M. (The Search for M)*, – with its reference to Fritz Lang's famous film *M. Eine Stadt sucht einen Mörder* (1931, *M. A City Searches for a Murderer*)[32] – suggests, the search is the central driving force of this novel. Here, the search for the murderer, the attempt at resolving crimes from the past, coincides with a search for identity.

---

[29] See Doron Rabinovici, *Credo und Credit: Einmischungen*, Frankfurt am Main: Suhrkamp, 2001; *Ohnehin. Roman*, Frankfurt am Main: Suhrkamp, 2004. See also his edited collections of political essays, including *Republik der Courage: Wider die Verhaiderung. Essays*, eds Doron Rabinovici and Robert Misik, Berlin: Aufbau, 2000; *Österreich: Berichte aus Quarantanien. Essays*, eds Doron Rabinovici and Isolde Charim, Frankfurt am Main: Suhrkamp, 2000 and *Neuer Antisemitismus? Eine globale Debatte*, eds Doron Rabinovici, Ulrich Speck and Natan Sznaider, Frankfurt am Main: Suhrkamp, 2004.

[30] Doron Rabinovici, *Papirnik: Stories*, Frankfurt am Main: Suhrkamp, 1994.

[31] Doron Rabinovici, *Instanzen der Ohnmacht: Wien 1938-1945: Der Weg zum Judenrat*, Frankfurt am Main: Jüdischer Verlag bei Suhrkamp, 2000.

[32] The most overt allusion to Lang's film in the novel occurs where Mullemann is confronted with old police files from the archives: "Er bekannte alles, auch einen Kindesmord, jammerte dabei: 'Ich kann doch nichts dafür!' Das Verbrechen hatte im Berlin der dreißiger Jahre stattgefunden – lange bevor Mullemann geboren worden war" (Doron Rabinovici, *Suche nach M.*, Frankfurt am Main: Suhrkamp Taschenbuch 1999, 233): "He confessed to everything, even a child murder and wailed: 'I can't help it!' The crime had taken place in the thirties in Berlin – long before Mullemann had been born" (*The Search for M*, trans. Francis M. Sharp, Riverside, CA: Ariadne Press, 2000, 162).

The mission to reconstruct what had remained untold thus becomes a search for the self.

As in Roth's *Der See*, family relations and the lack of knowledge of sons about their fathers' past are central to the structure and development of the narrative. However, in *Suche nach M.* this takes shape in very different ways. The plot revolves around two Jewish families and their sons, Arieh Scheinowiz and Dani Morgenthau. Of central importance are the identity problems arising from the specific difficulties in relationships between Holocaust survivors and their children. As in *Der See*, the lack of communication between parents and children is very much a silence about the past. However, inter-generational tensions differ for perpetrators and victims, as the narrator in *Suche nach M.* emphasizes: whilst the non-Jewish population for the most part chooses to remain silent about the Holocaust, the survivors are incapable of speaking about their experiences with their children. These in turn learn to intuit what remains untold and secret, for, as the narrator puts it with regard to Dani, "Schweigen war Teil der mündlichen Überlieferung seiner Familie".[33] In an attempt to name the unnameable they develop a predisposition for investigative thinking.[34] This takes on bizarre forms, as the obsession with crime and guilt enables, or indeed, forces both protagonists to identify almost entirely with perpetrators of crimes.

The burden of the past weighs heavy on Dani Morgenthau, who under the pressure of parental expectations develops peculiar forms of behaviour. From early childhood on he feels compelled to confess to the misdeeds of others and to take the blame upon himself. Moreover, he is able to sense and describe criminal schemes embarked upon in his environment in full detail even before the deed is done, which only further contributes to his guilt complex. He feels that for his parents he is supposed to make up for the loss of entire families, to represent in his very existence the ultimate victory over genocide, and thus to legitimize their survival where so many others perished. Not only does

---

[33] *Ibid.*, 35: "silence was part of his family's oral tradition" *(The Search for M*, 20).

[34] *Ibid.*, "Fähigkeiten, das Verborgene zu benennen", 35: "abilities to summon up things hidden and out of sight" *(The Search for M*, 20). This refers to Dani, but is echoed in the words describing Arieh's excitement about a "Formel ..., mit der das Unbekannte benannt werden konnte", *ibid.*, 58: a "formula, with which the unknown could be named" *(The Search for M*, 37).

he absorb their feelings of guilt, he also feels increasingly responsible for their present and past suffering. Indeed, Dani's implausible self-accusations, his compulsive confessions turn clearly pathological when he grows older. This is aggravated by the emergence of itching pustules, boils and carbuncles, which can only be alleviated by his false confessions of: "Ich war's. Ich bin schuld. Ich hab's getan."[35] This completely overturns the traditional whodunnit structure. Dani's unusual faculties obviously equip him well for the unmasking of criminals, and large parts of the novel are concerned with the bewildering effects his confessions have on actual perpetrators. At the same time his identity increasingly dissolves and he becomes the mysterious Mullemann, who, completely covered in layers of gauze, haunts Vienna with his proclamations of guilt. He occupies, as Dagmar Lorenz has observed, "a position of almost mythical proportion: he is an avenger, a victim, and, by assuming the crimes and suffering of everybody, a Jesus figure".[36]

In much the same way as Dani/Mullemann expresses his father's guilt complex and the anxiety of having to legitimize his existence, his counterpart Arieh unconsciously mirrors his father by developing a remarkable gift for mimicry and frequently changing his name and identity. As Arthur Bein aka Arieh Arthur Fandler aka Arieh Scheinoviz, he is very much the son of Jakov Scheinoviz aka Adam Kruzki aka Jakob Fandler, whose very survival was based on a case of mistaken identity.[37] Like Dani, Arieh displays an unusual investigative talent, which is connected to an identity disorder that complements Dani's compulsive contrition.[38] He is capable of surmising who is guilty of a crime by unconsciously assuming the perpetrator's demeanour. By becoming increasingly similar to his criminal counterpart in appearance, bearing and fashion preferences, he eventually finds the culprit, even before the crime is committed. As a young man this enables him to track down a neo-Nazi responsible for a racist attack, whom he inadvertently kills. This is one of the instances in which the roles of detective and murderer intersect, a device that also plays an

---

[35] *Ibid.*, 37: "It was me. I'm guilty. I did it" (*The Search for M*, 22).
[36] Dagmar Lorenz, "Holocaust Literature and Films as Crime Fiction", 44.
[37] Rabinovici, *Suche nach M.*, "Mein ganzes Überleben war eine Verwechslung", 101: "My survival depended on a mix-up" (*The Search for M*, 67).
[38] See also Eva Reichmann, "Identität als Problem", 42.

important part later on in the novel. Arieh flees to Israel, is recruited by the Israeli secret service, and ends up ferreting out enemies of the state and setting them up for elimination by Mossad. This activity is portrayed as anything but heroic, and the problematic moral and political dimension is underscored in an episode where Arieh/Arthur's Palestinian target turns out to be his eerily similar counterpart and mirror image. Thus Arieh's ability to find the culprit by becoming like him is turned against itself. By implication, boundaries of the self again appear permeable. The investigative device of slipping into the adversary's mind, a typical feature of crime and spy writing, is exploited in a highly unusual way that questions notions of stable identity and radically undermines simplistic ideologies of good and evil.

Unlike Paul Eck, who insists on remaining an outsider, in *Suche nach M.* both Dani and Arieh are very susceptible to succumbing to outside pressure. This problem of the self being defined by others is highlighted by the older generation:

> "Wenn du du bist, weil du du bist, und ich ich bin, weil ich ich bin, dann bist du du, und ich bin ich; wenn aber du du bist, weil ich ich bin, und ich ich bin, weil du du bist, dann bist du nicht du, und ich bin nicht ich."[39]

This implies the possibility of a self-contained identity, integral to the individual, an idea that seems unattainable now for either the protagonists of *Suche nach M.* or of *Der See*.

The critical concern with Austria we encountered in Roth's novel is also strongly present in *Suche nach M.*, where the accent lies more on the country's Nazi past. The protagonists' fragile sense of belonging is emphasized, as is their ambivalent position between cultures in an Austria that one of the characters refers to as the "Heimat Luegers und Schönerers, Hitlers und Eichmanns".[40] Arieh relates xenophobia

---

[39]   Rabinovici, *Suche nach M.*, 59 and 189: "If you are you because you are you and I am I because I am I, then you are you and I am I. If, however, you are you because I am I and I am I because you are you, then you are not you and I am not I" (*The Search for M*, 37 and 130).

[40]   *Ibid.*, 203: "the native land of Lueger and Schönerer, Hitler and Eichmann" (*The Search for M*, 140).

and anti-Semitism in present day Austria to the Nazi past, and ponders:

> Kriegsverbrecher wurden nicht vor Gericht gestellt, und alles, was sich auf die Untaten, die hier einst begangen worden waren, berief, zu Hatz und Massenmord aufrief, wurde nicht verfolgt, sondern geflissentlich übersehen. Schuldige durften nicht zu finden sein in einem Land, das allgemeine Unbeflecktheit vorgab.[41]

It is suggested in the novel that Dani would not have developed his pathological condition had he lived in another country. This makes the Mullemann figure all the more interesting. At one level, he goes from being a suspected monstrous serial killer to an internationally acclaimed master detective, who by his confessions helps bring real criminals to justice. In raising issues of collective identity and collective guilt Mullemann provides a focus for national self-reflection. In Austrians' reactions to him we find a clear generational gulf between the older people, who would prefer the past, and particularly the Nazi past, to remain buried, and the younger citizens, who find a positive catharsis in such declarations as:

> "Genug mit dem Lügen und Leugnen dieses Landes. Schluß mit dem Schweigen. Wir müssen Zeugnis ablegen, müssen künden: Ich war's. Ich bin's gewesen. Ich hab's getan."[42]

Both novels clearly make recourse to elements of the crime genre, while moving far beyond traditional crime novels. Their anti-detective mode with its undermining of fixed categories and structures proves the medium par excellence for exploring the more complex issues of unstable and multiple identities.

However, there are considerable differences between these two novels which, among other things, may be connected to the gener-

---

[41] *Ibid.*, 47: "War criminals were not brought to court and everything recalling the crimes once committed as well as actions provoking persecution and mass murder was deliberately ignored rather than persecuted. Guilty parties were just not to be found in a country that claimed to be without blemish" (*The Search for M*, 29).

[42] *Ibid.*, 252: "'Enough of this country's lies and denials. This silence must cease. We must testify and bear witness: I was the one. It was me. I did it'" (*The Search for M*, 175).

ational difference between the authors. Whereas in Roth we have an unremittingly pessimistic view of Austria, and of its past and present, Rabinovici potentially foresees a more positive vista. In *Suche nach M.* we find at least some sense of resolution, both with regards to many of the crimes in the novel and the protagonists' search for themselves. Dani finally unravels the entanglements of his Mullemann persona and escapes the prison of his role as scapegoat and confessor to begin a new life. Similarly for Arieh a more liberated identity and a new beginning come into view as he leaves the Israeli secret service and resolves to visit his ancestral Cracow and the camps, thus following the advice of his father's friend:

> ... mag sein, daß ihr mit den Hypotheken unseres Erbes leben müßt, aber wenn ihr euch davon befreien wollt, müßt ihr in das Grundbuch der Geschichte schauen. Der einzige Weg aus der Vergangenheit in die eigene Zukunft führt über die Erinnerung."[43]

In relation to the collective level and a resolution with the past Rabinovici appears to find a way forward in the exploration of the past in order to create a future. Although Roth shares the belief in the importance of recovering memory, his greater concern with the problems of perception and of representation of the past makes traditional closure even less possible and instead leads to a deferral of any potential resolution.

---

[43] *Ibid.*, 188: "It may be that you've been forced to live with the legacy of our burden of guilt, but if you want to set yourselves free from it, you have to look into history's register. The only way out of the past into your own future goes through memory" (*The Search for M*, 129-30).

CRIME NOVELS IN ITALY

COSTANTINO C. M. MAEDER

Is there such a thing as typically Italian crime fiction, and, if so, what are the features that characterize this variant of the genre? Of course, we can assume that a *giallo*, as detective novels are called in Italy,[1] is set in Italy, in Milan, in Rome or in Tuscany. Many thematic elements are recurrent: Italian novels often deal with the Mafia, with corrupt politicians and with religion. Of course, Italian investigators do not really believe in law and order, because institutions are compromised by dishonest and incompetent politicians, policemen and judges. Italian investigators are often highly sophisticated and cultured. They like food, literature and art and they love their cars and women. Needless to say, they love to talk. Also, as with any typical sleuth, they display strange, idiosyncratic behaviour. But are all these commonplaces, these typical, but superficial ingredients really an expression of italianità, or are there other dimensions that oblige us to review these commonplaces?

I believe that certain culturally determined main axes pervade most national productions, at thematic level and in deep structures. There are probably a few common elements typical of Italian detective stories. Of course, we are speaking of tendencies and cultural patterns which do not have to appear in every specific *giallo*. Evidently, it is possible to find all of these elements in English or American detective novels, but in Italy they can be perceived as a kind of cultural isotopies. Those isotopies are not necessarily related, and may even be opposed or indeed mutually exclusive.

---

[1] *Giallo*, yellow, is the Italian term for crime and mystery novels. It was the colour of the cover of many crime novels in Italy, notably the collection published by Mondadori from September 1929 – only interrupted by Fascist policy during the Second World War.

An unprecedented surge

Recently, crime novels have enjoyed incredible success in Italy. For a number of years now, Andrea Camilleri has been topping the best-seller lists with his acclaimed detective stories, sometimes with two, three or more titles in the top ten. However, it is mostly the young generation of writers who show a strong affinity to this kind of literature. In the early Nineties, a group sometimes referred to as "young cannibals"[2] started to publish short stories and novels presenting daily violence with an incredibly (and sometimes even disgustingly) ironic, playful lightness and comic tone, which revealed the influence of American minimalists like Bret Easton Ellis and director Quentin Tarantino's *Pulp Fiction* or *Reservoir Dogs*. Language fulfils an important function and juvenile slang, a gusto for intellectual puns and play on words, a playful predilection for iconic experiments and references to many cryptic technolects and idiolects characterize these texts. This gives them an astonishing new dimension which is quite distinct from the usual literary idiom in Italy, and very open to new influences, such as game shows, television serials, pop, trance, hip hop and underground. The works of Camilleri – an established and successful scriptwriter and playwright who authored many famous Italian television serials but remained unknown to the general public until recently – and of most other new crime novelists are characterized by velocity and cross fertilization and, therefore, by a new poetic background which many critics today would describe as horizontal, and no longer vertical.[3]

In addition to the newcomers, many important and established writers like the old guard represented by Umberto Eco or Leonardo Sciascia and even Antonio Tabucchi, have discovered and developed this genre. This vigorous growth of crime novels has been accompanied by an explosion of new, unpredictable formal solutions. A detective story cannot be understood, despite what many Italian scholars still believe, either as an application of a minimal set of

---

[2] Daniele Brolli, *Gioventù cannibale: La prima antologia italiana dell'orrore estremo*, Turin: Einaudi, 1996.

[3] See Clive Bloom, *Cult Fiction: Popular Reading and Pulp Theory*, London: Macmillan, 1996.

ingredients (for instance Van Dine's famous rules)[4] or, alternatively, as a ludic parody of mass literature.

Lack of theory and abuse of it

The protean variety of forms of the recent *giallo* and its appeal to certain major contemporary writers do not interest Italian critics who dismiss mystery stories as being a kind of simple, dull, trite form of telling, governed by a reduced set of rules, and therefore without any literary or aesthetic merit. The renowned Eugenio Scalfari, founder of the newspaper *La Repubblica*, recently attacked the new vogue for detective stories that apparently is killing serious literature. Even his reply to his critics[5] reveals his preconceived image of detective stories as only a kind of crossword puzzle, rebus or enigma.

This polemic is outdated but revealing because it shows the strong resistance this genre still has to face in Italy. Forty years ago, Oreste del Buono complained about the vogue for detective stories. Previously, in 1931, Antonio Bruers identified in the growth of interest in detective stories the wish to return to classic plots and story telling.[6] Primo Levi, like many others before and after, thought the whole discussion obsolete, describing the division between literature and *gialli* as fictitious.

Discussing detective stories in Italy is not a simple task. While there are detective stories that are characterized by commonplaces and foreseeable plots, there are also very inventive, peculiar and innovative novels that critics do not classify as genre fiction. Many Italian authors mimic Agatha Christie and her peers, and adapt this model to particular Italian cultural and sociological circumstances. Others prefer to develop the questioning initiated by Poe, and understand

---

[4]   S. S. Van Dine (W. H. Wright), *Twenty Rules for Writing Detective Stories*, preface to *The Great Detective Stories*, New York: Scribner's, 1927. The first partial Italian translation was included in the appendix to J. S. Fletcher, *Il motto rivelatore*, Milano: Mondadori, 1938. Many critics assume that the rules mentioned in this text form a sort of classic standard that every authentic crime story has to follow.

[5]   Eugenio Scalfari, "Il vetro soffiato. Ringraziamo gli autori di gialli, ultimi supplenti della parola scritta", *L'Espresso*, 45 (11 November 1999), 254.

[6]   Antonio Bruers, "L'insegnamento dei romanzi polizieschi", *L'Italia che scrive*, October, 1931.

detective novels as a kind of epistemic machine that permits pondering about the limits of knowledge and the existence of any kind of
values. Still others continue Chandler's line of sociological investigation.

Different types of crime novels should provoke a range of critical
responses and more subtle and differentiated theoretical reflection.
Yet, there is still insufficient theoretical investigation of Italian detective stories. Only a few scholars have been interested in this genre and
in its literary value. There are many reasons for this official disdain for
crime stories, not only in Italy.[7] Structuralist and semiotical approaches have contributed to the negative image of detective stories
associated with a minimal set of forms and rules. Propp's research in
the field of fairy tales has led scholars to look for other genres with a
similar foreseeable structure, suitable for analysis in order to discover
the mechanism of narrativity.[8] The questioning of literary genres,
guided by the philosopher and critic Benedetto Croce, had a far-
reaching negative impact on the reception of novels that tend to
choose clearly defined structures for their plots. Most foreign crime
novels of literary value were not properly translated since many
editors exploited the success of *gialli* and reduced them to pulp literature by inundating the market with cheap translations and editions.

During the Fascist era, crime novels were considered a kind of
foreign, non-Italian genre that appealed to the most primitive human
instincts. The Fascist veto even obliterated the flourishing Italian tradition in crime novel writing from memory. It is commonly believed

---

[7] Giuseppe Petronio, in his *Sulle tracce del giallo* (Rome: Gamberetti Editore,
2000), has pointed out the particular academic and cultural background that even
today is conditioning the reception of crime stories.

[8] Obviously, this perspective has led scholars to ground their research on arbitrary
corpora, responding to the criteria of uniformity and similarity – thus excluding
crime novels not suiting those criteria. This approach is scientifically speaking
valid, but does not allow other forms of crime stories to be regarded as parodies,
as anti-detective stories (Stefano Tani, *The Doomed Detective: the Contribution of
the Detective Novel to Postmodern American and Italian Fiction*, Carbondale
Illinois: Southern Illinois University Press, 1984), as "esogialli" (Antonio
Pietropaolo, *Ai confini del giallo: Teoria e analisi della narrativa gialla ed
esogialla*, Napoli: Edizioni Scientifiche Italiane, 1986). Many of the critics quoted
above repeat that a strong codification is a typical feature of the *giallo*. Melchiori
("L'arbitrio della ragione. Le regole del gioco", *Rinascita*, IV/2 [23 January
1976]) even claims that detective stories have been codified since 1920.

that there is no Italian tradition of detective novels. Only a few writers are still known: Carlo Emilio Gadda (1893-1973) and his highly acclaimed *Quer pasticciaccio in via Merulana* (1957); Giorgio Scerbanenco (1911-1969); Augusto De Angelis (1888-1944) or Alessandro Varaldo (1876-1953), the first Italian author to be included in the series *I Gialli Mondadori* in 1931. However, this assumption does not reflect reality. Many Italian novelists wrote crime novels under English pseudonyms.[9] Astonishingly enough, there were even writers who anticipated the great Anglo-Saxon and American crime novelists. In the nineteenth century, novelists such as Francesco Mastriani (1819-1891) and later Matilde Serao (1865-1927) wrote crime novels at a time when this genre was not yet configured and coded.[10] This short-sightedness on the part of certain critics can be seen in Sormano's study of the crime novel and its mechanisms which refers to Simenon, Spillane, Christie and Stout, but does not mention any Italian writer – this at a time when Leonardo Sciascia had, for decades, been writing very peculiar and acclaimed crime novels that were certainly not imitations of foreign examples.[11]

Returning to the present we find that many critics cannot abandon their traditional frameworks and tend desperately to uphold the distinction between detective stories and literature, while most writers do not bother with such distinctions at all. They choose a genre they clearly consider one of the most appropriate for talking about our times and our problems, without being bothered by any structural, narrative constraint.

---

[9] Pino Belli, for example, between 1956-67, wrote about 145 crime novels, under at least twenty names such as Ray Kendall or Iris White (see Roberto Pirani, Monica Mare and Maria Grazia De Antoni, *Dizionario bibliografico del giallo*, Florence: Pontassieve, PBE, 1996).

[10] Matilde Serao's *Il delitto di via Chiatamone* was published in 1892 by Perrella in Naples. In 1853, Francesco Mastriani, also from Naples, published a trilogy of crime novels that anticipated Conan Doyle and Gaboriau. Other renowned nineteenth- and early twentieth-century authors wrote detective novels: for example, Cletto Arrighi, one of the *Scapigliatura*, the Italian Bohème, Carlo Collodi (author of *Pinocchio*), Carolina Invernizio, Salvatore Farina, Luigi Natoli, and Emilio De Marchi. Even De Roberto wrote a detective novel: *Spasimo*, republished recently. For an exhaustive discussion, see Renato Crovi, *Le maschere del mistero: Storie e tecniche dei thriller italiani e stranieri*, Florence-Antella: Passigli Editori, 2000.

[11] Elena Sormano, *Il romanzo giallo e i suoi meccanismi*, Turin: Paravia, 1979.

Leopardian and Pirandellian legacy

Despite the incredible structural variety of novels and short stories, there are certain main axes that are culturally determined. Some of them refer to themes, others to certain discourses, others, finally, to deep structures, closely tied to Italian culture.

The nineteenth century has strongly influenced the twentieth century: the fight for freedom forced Italian intellectuals to deal with patriotism and with strong values and precise ethical and moral expectations. Very early on, the gap between reality and patriotic and religious rhetoric caused many intellectuals to deconstruct official readings and to reflect on the contradictions in ethics. Those doubts can be referred to as the *Leopardian Legacy* and the *Pirandellian Legacy*. Leopardi (1798-1837) and Pirandello (1867-1936) have considerably influenced the Italian way of thinking and writing, and continue to do so today, although in obvious contrast to Catholic doctrine. Their texts are still widely studied at school and form a sort of intertextual discourse that re-emerges in many other writers and eras. Leonardo Sciascia, one of the most important Italian crime writers is explicit: "Si potrebbe dire di me che ho introdotto il dramma pirandelliano nel romanzo poliziesco."[12]

Leopardi combined a pessimistic philosophy with poetry. In his poems and other, often philosophical writings, he emphasizes the futility of the human being, lost in an unlimited, unknown and unknowable universe, where there is no god, and providence and determination do not exist since they are a simple human projection. Leopardi deals with this dilemma of the individual who longs for values. Faced with the indifference of the universe, with its own rules and unpredictable events that can destroy Pompeii with a simple eruption or Lisbon with an earthquake, the idea of human beings as the centre of creation is untenable. Scientific progress and growing knowledge about existence and nature continually underline this and thus destroy the divine image human beings made of themselves. Luigi Pirandello continues this thinking, but instead of scepticism, he prefers a kind of mocking, Homeric laughter. Pirandello is no longer shocked by the relativity of life and values, but fascinated by the variety of micro-systems that

---

[12]   Leonardo Sciascia, *La Sicilia come metafora*, Milan: Mondadori, 1989, 88: "You could say of me, that I have introduced Pirandello's drama into the crime novel."

determine modern and postmodern society. Therefore, in his work he does not propose a choice of one system or one grand narrative.

Most recent Italian detective stories are profoundly influenced by these attitudes, and disbelief in values, comic and humoristic relief and apparently playful quotations are thus very important components. This attitude informs the different textual levels, syntax, semantics, and the poetic and aesthetic dimension of many recent works.

Sciascia

Leonardo Sciascia (1921-1989), a Sicilian modernist writer, is known for his commitment to social issues, for his battle against totalitarianism and governmental abuse of power, and the unholy conspiracy of Mafia, church and politics. He is often described as a kind of Voltairian, whose main aim was to educate society and to denounce social iniquities. Therefore, next to his essays and historical reconstruction of past events, Sciascia chose detective stories as a medium for this project. The simple, linear, straightforward form of his novels was chosen to reach a broader public, and to enhance the magic of narrative tension. However, several antinomies show that Sciascia does not believe in a better society and that his writings are intrinsically pessimistic.

In many of his novels the crimes are not solved. The investigator, who wants to reveal the truth to society (and therefore to the reader), dies or is removed from his task by the authorities. The reader comes to understand that the real criminals are social behaviour and the political parties with their criminal allies in the Mafia. Sometimes, the investigator succeeds in solving a crime but the reader is not informed about the truth. This omission of the most characteristic aspect of a crime novel, and that most longed for by the reader, is essential. Sciascia, or rather the implicit author in his texts, does not believe in detection. To know anything, for instance the identity of the criminal and the real motive of a crime, is not a public, but a private aim. To know the truth does not change society. More controversial still, evil is just a part of our existence and cannot be defeated. Thus, every reaction to evil can only be an individual act, and only secrecy permits both personal fulfillment and perhaps revenge.

The short story *Western di cose nostre*[13] is revealing. It is a kind of classic fairy tale, situated in a little town in Sicily during the Second World War. Here the Mafia reigns, untroubled by the police. Of course, sometimes there are feuds between different factions, but everything follows clear rules. For every murdered member of one faction, a member of the other will lose his life. Sometimes freshmen want to take power and the older men try to retain power. At a certain moment, the killing rate increases substantially. The Mafia bosses do not know what to do and call in *mafiosi* from outside as arbiters. They find out that an unknown hand has perpetrated most of the murders. At the end they discover that a simple citizen has taken the law into his own hands. He is avenging a rather petty injustice he suffered years ago when the mob convinced his sweetheart not to marry him. The whole town, and the murderer himself know that the Mafia has discovered the culprit. Yet, the murderer does not flee. At the end, knowing he will be killed, he accepts his execution because he shares the same values as the Mafia.

This short story overturns the expectations of a reader who is not familiar with Italy. When we apply Propp to this story, or theories based on his studies (for example, Greimas), the hero of the tale is the Mafia. In the beginning the text outlines the *status quo*, then the foe causes disorder and obliges the hero to act (manipulation), the hero has to acquire a certain competence before passing to the performance and the positive sanction: order has been re-established.[14] The lonesome avenger, the foe, does not act driven by civil courage. His motives are purely individualistic and self-centred. This explains his initial success and even why he does not flee at the end – with his vengeance fulfilled, his reason for living has gone, and he knows it.

Sciascia's last crime novel, *Una storia semplice* (1989),[15] a not at all simple story, concisely presents all of his thoughts. It looks as if the reader is confronted with a classic mystery. A professor, returning to Sicily from abroad, finds something strange in his cottage. He alerts the police. The following day a warrant officer pays him a visit, but

---

[13] Leonardo Sciascia, *Western di cose nostre*, in *Opere*, ed. Claude Ambroise, Milan: Bompiani, 1991, I, 1361-65.
[14] See the single entries in Algirdas Julien Greimas and Joseph Courtés, *Sémiotique: Dictionnaire raisonné de la théorie du langage*, Paris: Hachette, 1979.
[15] Leonardo Sciascia, *Una storia semplice*, in *Opere*, III, 729-62.

finds just the corpse of the professor. The investigator is able to un-ravel the straightforward, linear mystery and find the culprit, his su-perior, who is involved in the traffic of stolen art works. In order to spare the police from a scandal, the whole affair is hushed-up and the hero gets a promotion. However, in one of the last sections of the novel, a witness recognizes a priest as a criminal who was certainly in-volved in the crime. The solution was only partial or even wrong and the mystery remains. The witness, maltreated by the police when he voluntarily offered to testify, now simply prefers to continue on his way, whistling a melody.

Even this last novel implies that action is individual and self-centred, and that solutions cannot be foreseen or trusted. Grand Narratives do not exist. An individual cannot find a general truth, except, perhaps, that there is none, and that is not satisfying. Some-times Sciascia's sleuths do find an explanation, but in these cases, they do not reveal it to the reader who has to guess at a solution. We find this in *Todo modo* (1974)[16] where the narrator himself could be the avenger of a series of murders, but no clue definitely permits this con-clusion. Apparently, he knows something (the truth?), but he with-holds the final revelation.

Italian modernist crime novels often do not explain and reveal, but rather deconstruct the idea that it is possible to find the truth. There are only human beings who believe in values and narratives and who act without any possibility of succeeding. Even when they believe that they have reached some kind of conclusion, the reader is confronted with textual elements that contradict this, without, however, offering alternative solutions. The thirst for knowledge is only a kind of indi-vidual instinct, without any real effect on humanity.

Sciascia's crime novels prepare the ground for the recent crime novel. And his last novel, with its comic ending, is an important *trait d'union* with the main tendency of current Italian crime stories and the earlier stories, mostly founded on clear patterns, where good and bad are clearly defined (such as in the novels of Scerbanenco). Therefore, we have to distinguish between two levels: the narrative one and the utterance that is the relation between the implicit author, the text and the implicit reader. Heroes in Sciascia's works are often either inte-

---

[16] Leonardo Sciascia, *Todo modo*, in *Opere*, II, 97-204.

grated or apocalyptical.[17] They believe or do not believe in society and its values. Only the sleuths who do not want to reveal the truth (*Todo modo*) or do not find a solution (*Una storia semplice*) survive. Thus, readers, confronted with results without any final interpretation can only imagine solutions, often guided by their own preferences and expectations. The integrated characters, who believe in the constitution and classical moral values, are killed or removed from their tasks (*Il giorno della civetta*,[18] *A ciascuno il suo*[19]). Therefore the reader will only imagine a solution, without being certain that his conclusions are really sound.

Do Sciascia's novels denounce the realities of Italian politics and society? Certainly, he writes about Sicily and Italian politics, but his main focus is on the human condition. Sciascia is apocalyptical, in other words the implicit author creates a world where morals and ethics are deconstructed, something that the implicit reader shares. The dénouement of the plot of most Sciascian crime novels is not at all important. The negative view of the human condition prevails. In this sense, Sciascia's texts are modernist. They deconstruct the simplistic view that cognition can decipher truth, that truth exists. Comic elements in his texts underline this fact and are sarcastic rather than truly humoristic or comical. His intertextual component in telling is classic and vertical (references to Gide, Pirandello or Voltaire) and is not ludic and horizontal.

The fall of the Iron Curtain, the Unification of (Western) Europe, along with the awareness that we are living in a postmodern condition completely changed the horizon of Italian literature and contributed to the rise of new kinds of *gialli*. Many problems now had to be faced: corruption or the obsolete nature of the essentially corporate system that determined social and political issues, and the intrinsic vacuity of obsolete post-war values (that is, the Marxist, Capitalist and Catholic meta-narratives with their Manichaean systems of global values which determined most of the twentieth century). Most writers previously exhibited a didactic approach to literature: a novel had to teach, to reveal, or to denounce, and this was no longer possible. Whereas in the Sixties and Seventies, literature was mostly bound by a number of

---

[17]   See Umberto Eco, *Apocalittici e integrati*, Milan: Bompiani, 1964.
[18]   Leonardo Sciascia, *Il giorno della civetta*, in *Opere*, I, 387-483.
[19]   Leonardo Sciascia, *A ciascuno il suo*, in *Opere*, I, 775-886.

straitjackets, now it was free, and this freedom did not entail chaos, but an incredible choice.

The new giallo: between apparent concision and logorrheic explosion

Carlo Lucarelli[20] began his literary career with several historical crime novels, based on his studies at the University of Bologna. These first novels feature a classic structure. Just as in Agatha Christie, the plot in itself is not interesting, but the main appeal resides in the particular ambience Lucarelli tries to create, by reconstructing an almost forgotten and removed past: the Fascist era and the post-Second World War period. The stories are linear and straightforward. In these plots the investigator, a policeman, has to, or rather wants to solve a crime where a high-ranking Fascist might be implicated. Alternatively, the investigator, an agent in Fascist times, tries to solve a crime after the war or during the chaotic days of liberation and encounters difficulties with the new order which is suspicious about his past.

Without really changing the core structures of the plots, his novels set in the present, are completely different. There is still a policeman (or a pair of incompatible investigators) who has to investigate a crime against all odds. But the tone and style are incompatible with his former novels. There is no simple transposition to today's Bologna of techniques Lucarelli experimented with in his historical novels. We notice many typical postmodern features such as cross-fertilization, fragmentation and irony. The writing techniques are heavily influenced by pop music and by narrative strategies borrowed from television serials and commercials. One of Lucarelli's sleuths, Coliandro, is a totally incompetent, naïve, illiterate and not very intelligent investigator. A sentimental macho, longing for love, but incapable of communicating seriously with women, he lives in an illusionary world

---

[20]   The works of this prolific novelist can be divided into three different fields: historical crime novels, crime novels set in the present, and faction based on famous crimes. Historical crime novels are *Carta bianca* (Palermo: Sellerio, 1990; *L'estate torbida*, Palermo: Sellerio, 1991) and *Indagine non autorizzata* (Milan: Mondadori, 1993). Postmodern novels set in the present are the astonishing *Almost blue* (Turin: Einaudi, 1997), *Falange armata* (Bologna: Granata Press, 1993) and *Il giorno del lupo* (Turin: Einaudi, 1998). *Mistero in blu* (Turin: Einaudi, 1999) discusses famous present-day cases.

of television serials, porn stars, cinema, cars, formula one and a vague desire to solve cases. His social background is simple and his vision of life is outdated, but this does not prevent him from being tempted by *viados*, transvestite prostitutes. His fellow sleuth is a young student, a kind of post-punk, a multicultural intellectual who is against any out-dated order and is unwilling to collaborate with the police. Everything happens by coincidence, but at the end the incompetent investigator shows incredible willpower and solves cases without really under-standing all of the implications, and falls miserably in love with his colleague.

This twofold way of writing is really interesting. In Italy, after Eco's *Il nome della rosa*,[21] many authors have chosen to write histor-ical crime novels. Almost every age is represented: ancient Rome,[22] the Middle Ages,[23] the Renaissance, the Baroque era, the eighteenth and nineteenth centuries, and the Fascist era. However these texts are very far from Eco's marvellous and ambiguous novel. They feature mostly traditional, stereotypical crime plots that are no longer found in Italian crime novels set in the present day. In this sense, Carlo Lucarelli's paradoxical experience is revealing. It seems that today it is not possible to tell a simple, mainly linear crime story (or any other classic story, with an exposition, real intrigue and a final solution, all linked by temporal, logical and causal chains). In modern times, with myriads of incompatible value systems, where everything can be ques-tioned, a crime novel has to reflect the precarious situation of the in-vestigator and investigation. Choosing to place traditional crime novels in the past reveals a melancholic nostalgia for a time where precise logical deduction within closed systems was considered pos-sible.

Andrea Camilleri uses a technique similar to Lucarelli's in his con-temporary crime novels: his texts seem very traditional, despite his

---

[21] Umberto Eco, *Il nome della rosa*, Milan: Bompiani, 1991.

[22] We find Roman investigators like Danila Comastri Montanari's Publio Aurelio Stazio or Rosario Magri's Ponzio Epafrodito.

[23] There are Medieval monks like Rino Camilleri's Corrado da Tours, and Medieval historians like Comastri Montanari's Agnello Ravennate.

highly innovative language.[24] He mixes standard Italian with a sort of idiolectal Sicilian in an unusual manner.[25] However, the texture, the plot in itself, is perhaps even too classic: there is a crime; a police officer, named Montalbano (probably a homage to the Catalan writer Vázquez Montalbán), searches for clues and at the end, there is a solution. The plots are straightforward, but nevertheless we can observe interesting features that question the causal chain of a classic narration. The key to these features is the sleuth himself and his relation to his actions. He seems to be an investigator in the typical Italian tradition. He is cultivated, he loves literature and, of course, gastronomy. He has a stable but complex love affair with a woman living in the North. He does not really believe in law and order, or that the existing laws are really equitable or that it is possible to implement them. The Leopardian and the Pirandellian legacy shine through everywhere. Most actions have many angles to them, there is no exclusive truth, and a certain humoristic approach pervades the stories. These features seem to imply that Montalbano's actions can be foretold which, in fact, is never the case. This is one of the characteristic features of many crime novels of recent years in Italian literature.

In modernist stories, investigators are often opaque. By this I mean that, as in Dashiell Hammett's *The Thin Man* or *The Glass Key*, the reader never exactly knows what the sleuth is doing or thinking, unlike the protagonists in an Agatha Christie novel. The reader knows everything about how Poirot and Miss Marple investigate, even when the two are withholding vital clues. Their moral and ethical positions are not questionable. In modernist stories investigators try to establish order without really believing in society and its law, but this does not imply that the sleuth does not believe in a system of values or that he is not consistent in his choices and actions. Chandler and Sciascia's heroes ultimately do know, for themselves, what is right and what is wrong. It is simply the world they live in that no longer believes in

---

[24] Andrea Camilleri novels featuring the investigator Montalbano include: *La forma dell'acqua*; *Il cane di terracotta*; *Il ladro di merendine*; *La voce del violino* (all Palermo: Sellerio, 2000).

[25] Dialects are usually quoted in direct speech or single words as a kind of exotic ingredient in authors like Verga, one of the fathers of Italian Verismo, or in Sciascia. Camilleri, however, integrates his Sicilian dynamically into his texts, mixing it organically with standard Italian.

right and wrong or that can no longer enforce ethical rules. Of course, sometimes they question their values, perhaps they do not even know why they want to be different, but in the end they are committed to their values. Another fundamental aspect of this kind of novel that creates differences and opacity, concerns the relation between the reader and how a crime novel is presented. As we have seen, Sciascia plays with the expectations of a common reader. But Camilleri's sleuth is not opaque in this sense. Camilleri's investigator is unpredictable not because we do not know what he is thinking, but on the contrary because we know all of his actions and reflections, and thus we regularly observe Montalbano's completely erratic and unreliable behaviour. The police officer is a kind of fool, a crazy person, as is frequently stated in the texts themselves. Montalbano's actions depend on his mood and on the situation, but are not driven by a single narratological or ethical concern.

We will finish this discussion by considering two very recent crime writers, Andrea G. Pinketts[26] and Santo Piazzese.[27] Pinketts' investigator Lazzaro Santandrea, a strange kind of poet who is unable to write books, is not very different to Montalbano. In what is a typical feature of crime novels, Lazzaro has many strange habits, just like Poirot or Pepe Carvalho. Piazzese's sleuth is as unpredictable as Camilleri's Montalbano or Lucarelli's Coliandro. His actions defy any logic. While many storytellers, like Lucarelli or Camilleri, prefer a concise style of writing, Pinketts' and Piazzese's novels are completely different. They suffocate their plots with many digressions, unnecessary descriptions and a lot of sidelines that are not continued. Sometimes the investigators find their way back to the main storyline and we may even learn the solution of the crime. Inserts are overwhelmingly present and constantly divert the reader from what would usually be considered the main plot and centre of interest of a crime novel. Pirandello's humoristic approach is always present, deconstructing the seriousness of classic detection and, of course, the tragic dimensions of life. Apparently, even death and murder have lost their importance today. Life could be a joke.

---

[26] Andrea G. Pinketts, *Il senso della frase*, Milan: Feltrinelli, 1995, and *Il conto dell'ultima cena*, Milan: Feltrinelli, 1999.

[27] Santo Piazzese, *I delitti di via Medina-Sidonia*, Palermo: Sellerio, 1996 and *La doppia vita di M. Laurent*, Palermo: Sellerio, 1999.

There are many points of contact between Lucarelli, Camilleri, Pinketts and Piazzese. Their detectives have much in common and, in their novels, morality, re-establishing order, solving a crime are absolutely secondary. The protagonists of these four writers are investigators who are interested in knowledge and knowing/solving, but not in solving as metaphor for re-establishing order. Not even for themselves.

The main reason for choosing crime novels as a genre is certainly the quest for knowledge and the pondering about the limits of our intellect, but another aspect is as important. Today, most taboos are obsolete. Society is fragmented, homosexuality is accepted, fathers and sons listen to classical music, Hip Hop and U2, women work and have children without being married, and mixed marriages are reality, at least in literature. Even when in the real Western world it is still not simple to deal with these facts, literature has successfully and extensively discussed everything for more than two centuries. To investigate social injustice or describe how we fail to live in this complex world is simply outdated. Murder is probably the last aspect of morality and ethics we can still question, where right and wrong probably could still exist without only being an opinion we can deconstruct.

For most Italian authors, law and order are insignificant. Most investigators are neither apocalyptical nor integrated, they are just sleuths, and their main stimulus is not finding the truth or re-establishing order, but simply knowledge itself. Often the solution is only a kind of casual outcome, with a limited effect on the social context. Sometimes a dangerous killer gets arrested, and Montalbano, Camilleri's investigator, thinks he has achieved justice, but in the next case his behaviour cannot be foreseen and is completely incompatible with his previous actions.

Stereotypical crime novels are often situated in the past, as if the authors want to show that positivistic approaches to investigation and knowledge are no longer possible. Novels set in the present are characterized by cross-fertilization and horizontality. There are mostly two different approaches. Some authors prefer concise writing focused on a linear plot, others prefer a dispersive and distracting logorrheic writing where investigation and detection have lost their importance. Yet, both approaches share the same basis. While in modernistic crime novels the investigator still seems to believe in values or the implicit author seems to regret the absence of values and of grand narratives, now there is a playful acceptance of the freedom permitted by this lack of common ground. Investigators are fools, crazy people, whose actions cannot be calculated, who make decisions following strategies they conceive *ad hoc* and that nobody can predict. Investigation and detection are often a sort of hobby, without any real impact on society. Most texts are humoristic: death has lost its impact. Discourses on art, pop music or jazz, gastronomy or philosophy are often more important than the solving of a puzzle which is reduced to a kind of aesthetic pleasure. Learning the identity of a murderer is often just a minor, casual output. Therefore, it is not accidental that in Antonio Tabucchi's *Il filo dell'orizzonte*,[28] the investigator will be told the truth upon entering a building, but the reader will never know what happens inside. Whether the investigator will survive or not does not matter anymore. The investigator enters the building. The door shuts. The text just stops there.

---

[28]   Antonio Tabucchi, *Il filo dell'orizzonte*, Milan: Feltrinelli, 1986.

THE DETECTIVE AND THE DISAPPEARED: MEMORY, FORGETTING AND OTHER CONFUSIONS IN JUAN JOSÉ SAER'S *LA PESQUISA*

PHILIP SWANSON

Even a casual glance at the consumption and production of detective fiction in Latin America will render obvious what Amelia Simpson has called "the gap between readership and authorship".[1] There has been relatively little autochthonous mystery fiction written in Latin America, while translations of foreign whodunnits or thrillers have been avidly devoured. The temptation of a straightforward post-colonial understanding of this phenomenon is apparent. Detective fiction – be it the classic, hard-boiled or contemporary police procedural model – is still associated with English social order, US urban modernity, a functioning justice system and, more generally, in social, economic, political and literary terms, the sort of supposedly superior cultures against which Latin America is perceived to define itself. Moreover, if Howard Haycraft's famous 1941 essay emphasizes the link between detective fiction and Northern/Western democratic institutions,[2] the Mexican critic Carlos Monsiváis asserts "we don't have any detective literature because we don't have any faith in justice".[3]

Hence, in Latin America, the emergence of detective fiction is often seen as a project of creating a specifically non-Anglocentric and non-formulaic version of the genre, which takes account of and stems from national and subcontinental realities. Latin American mystery fiction questions the conventions of the genre and in so doing ques-

---

[1] Amelia Simpson, *Detective Fiction from Latin America*, London: Associated University Presses, 1990, 16.
[2] Howard Haycraft, *Murder for Pleasure: The Life and Times of the Detective Story*, New York: Biblo and Tannen, 1968.
[3] Vicente Francisco Torres, *El cuento policial mexicano*, Mexico: Diógenes, 1982, 13 (cited in Simpson, 21).

Philip Swanson

tions neocolonial assumptions about the continent's status. In particular, there is a strong trend in serious Latin American fiction after the Sixties to blur the boundary between High Art and Popular Culture (often in a political context), so that a playful or subversive style of detective fiction develops which appears to offer a postmodern challenge to traditional notions of hierarchy and order, while erecting a model that recreates either a dysfunctional or, more happily, plural and multicultural society. The idea is that what has developed in Latin America is a kind of geographically and politically aware detective fiction based on a meaningful transgression of the original and fundamentally alien or foreign model.

However, the very inevitability of a process of interaction between model and revision should alert us to the potential limitations of an easy reductive reading. There is certainly a strong and effective strain of political and interrogative mystery fiction in Latin America, but the overall reality is more complex. The foreign model remains popular and, as Simpson's survey clearly shows, there is plenty of evidence of mimicry of that model. Internal production is largely centred in big countries with long-standing metropolises such as Argentina and Mexico, as well as Brazil. Much of it does very much go against the conventional model, although in Cuba (the other main centre of production), until recently, it did so for highly conservative purposes. Though the situation with regard to detective fiction there has moved on dramatically in the last decade, after the early Seventies, police or crime writing was officially encouraged as it was seen to represent an ideal model of solution-orientated social instruction in the Revolutionary context. Moreover, the embracing of popular genres after the Sixties and the emergence of what has been called a Post-Boom bring their own problems.

This has been discussed in detail elsewhere,[4] but essentially, many of the key Latin American writers of the literary boom of the Sixties began in the following decades to move away from the profoundly ambiguous tortuously-structured or fantastic works typical of the *nueva narrativa* or "New Narrative" to write novels that were, along with other Post-Boom works, relatively speaking, more traditional,

---

[4]   See Philip Swanson, *The New Novel in Latin America: Politics and Popular Culture after the Boom*, Manchester: Manchester University Press, 1995.

more accessible, more socially-focussed and often keen to embrace forms from popular culture such as film, soap opera or the detective genre. But these writers – the first generation of genuinely international novelists – owed as much to Europe as they did to Latin America and in many ways came to prominence on the back of high Modernism. The attempts to accommodate a Modernist instinct with a growing postmodernist ethos, to combine politics with ludic play, or social commentary with the problematization of literature's link to reality, to situate popular models in an elitist "New Narrative" framework, led to some uncomfortable results. For instance, Mario Vargas Llosa's Post-Boom detective novel *¿Quién mató a Palomino Molero?* appears to criticize authority while simultaneously asserting a strong need for order and structure;[5] Gabriel García Márquez's sortee into detection, *Crónica de una muerte anunciada,*[6] might seem to demand a socio-political reading given its author's public posture, yet clearly – with its emphasis on myth, ambiguity and literariness – undermines the application of fiction to the external world; and the media-friendly cosmopolitan Carlos Fuentes' 1978 spy thriller *La cabeza de la hidra* seeks to create "un héroe del Tercer Mundo ..., el James Bond del mundo sub-desarrollado",[7] yet creates a highly unstable intertextual narrative in which one of his own characters says that "en una novela, ... las palabras acaban siempre por construir lo contrario de sí mismas".[8] The function of the postmodern detective is fundamentally foggy and the facile explanation of literary play or pluralism as subversive of bourgeois forms and practices is simply inadequate.

---

[5]   Mario Vargas Llosa, *¿Quién mató a Palomino Molero?* (*Who Killed Palomino Molero*), Barcelona: Seix Barral, 1986. For more on this novel, see my article in the special edition of the *Bulletin of Hispanic Studies, Studies in Latin American Literature and Culture in Honour of James Higgins*, Liverpool: Liverpool University Press, 2004, 216-27; some of the opening remarks are drawn from this piece.

[6]   Gabriel García Márquez, *Crónica de una muerte anunciada* (*Chronicle of a Death Foretold*), Diana: Mexico, 1981.

[7]   *Simposio Carlos Fuentes: Actas*, eds Isaac Jack Lévy and Juan Loveluck, Columbia: University of South Carolina Press, 1980, 217: "... a Third-World hero ..., a James Bond of the underdeveloped world." Translations throughout are my own. In the case of a title, the name of an available translation has been used.

[8]   Carlos Fuentes, *La cabeza de la hidra* (*The Hydra Head*), Barcelona: Argos Vergara, 1979, 240: "... in a novel, ... words always end up constructing the opposite of themselves."

The attractiveness of the detective model in the Latin American context is readily comprehensible. Traditionally, the detective investigates a rupture in the social order (a crime) and, in solving the mystery and bringing the culprit to justice, restores epistemological and societal cohesion. Yet the detective is often a maverick figure or outsider. Even in the reputedly conservative classic model, Agatha Christie's main detectives are a little old lady and an eccentric Belgian. The most cited examples are the hard-boiled heroes of North American detective fiction from Raymond Chandler's Philip Marlowe onwards, with – amongst other variations – female detectives like Sara Paretsky's V. I. Warshawski or black ones like Walter Mosley's Easy Rawlins reviving the topic of detective-as-outsider in recent years. Nonetheless, these mavericks do not in any sense seriously destabilize the values of civilization and order. As Peter Messent points out: "The private eye … may appear to see and act from an individualistic and autonomous perspective, but the detective's agency is in fact subordinated to larger forms of social monitoring and control, and her or his vision is limited by the 'private' basis on which he or she operates."[9]

What is more, the trend away from the P.I. or "P.I., private eye" to the police procedural novel reduces individual agency even further and stresses the detective's function as an arm of an overarching system of order and control, to the extent that "the relationship between the detective's role and the agency of the state is necessarily foregrounded".[10] The emphasis is firmly back to order and authority again. But even here the pattern is not so transparent: there are still plenty of mavericks within the system, such as Colin Dexter's Inspector Morse or Ian Rankin's Rebus, while many modern investigators have jobs which are in some ways tangential to the system, like Patricia Cornwell's pathologist Kay Scarpetta or Janet Evanovich's bounty hunter Stephanie Plum, or figures such as the lawyer, journalist, criminal psychologist or profiler. Again, while such characters in many ways test the system, they often operate a kind of modern pseudo-chivalric honour code (for instance, Rebus) or a strict, even absolutist, moral code in which transgression is repeatedly linked to the anxious category of "evil" (for example, Scarpetta). Despite the

---

[9]   *Criminal Proceedings: The Contemporary American Crime Novel*, ed. Peter Messent, London and Chicago: Pluto Press, 1997, 10.
[10]   *Ibid.*, 12.

degree of formula, the detective novel revolves around what is really a rather complex interaction of authority and rebellion, control and excess, the fixed and the random. In this sense, it – and especially the "High" take on it – is a potentially ideal yet simultaneously hugely problematic vehicle for an exploration of Latin American identities.

Juan José Saer and *La pesquisa*

The Eighties and Nineties vogue for Juan José Saer outside his native Argentina and his publication of a playful detective novel, *La pesquisa*, in 1994[11] may encourage the casual academic reader to make an identification between his work and the Latin American Post-Boom, particularly the politically-inflected reading of the phenomenon favoured by cultural critics who link it to the trauma of dictatorship and disappearance in the Southern Cone of the Seventies and Eighties. However, the characterization by Antonio Skármeta of his generation's writing (associated by its leading literary historian Donald Shaw with the Post-Boom) as "anti-pretentious by vocation, pragmatically anti-cultural, sensitive to the banal, and seeking, rather than to re-order the world, ... simply to present it"[12] could hardly be less applicable to Saer, whose work is essentially heavy, a stylistically and philosophically complex meditation on the nature of life and language.

Moreover, Saer moved to France in 1968 and, as Daniel Balderstone has already observed, "his literature is only obliquely related to the literature of political commitment and the denunciation of the military dictatorships".[13] Indeed, Saer's fiction has more in common with the scepticism of Jorge Luis Borges or, even more so, the gloominess of Juan Carlos Onetti than it does with many of the writers usually

---

[11]   Juan José Saer, *La pesquisa*, Buenos Aires: Seix Barral (*The Investigation*, trans. by Helen Lane, London: Serpent's Tail, 1999). A version of the comments on Saer that follow is included in a special edition of the *South Atlantic Review* LXVII/4 (2002), 46-62, on Spanish American fiction in the Nineties.

[12]   Original comments by Antonio Skármeta, "Al fin y al cabo es su propia vida la cosa más cercana que cada escritor tiene para echar mano", in *Del cuerpo a las palabras: la narrativa de Antonio Skármeta*, ed. Raúl Silva Cácares, Madrid: LAR, 1983, 139 and quoted in translation in Donald L. Shaw, *The Post-Boom in Spanish American Fiction*, Albany: State University of New York Press, 1998, 9.

[13]   *Encyclopedia of Latin American Literature*, ed. Verity Smith, London and Chicago: Fitzroy Dearborn, 1997, 743.

associated with the Post-Boom, even in its more pluralist conception.[14] Saer has been writing fiction since around 1960 and has long been respected in Argentina as a major literary figure. Moreover, the French connection has repeatedly led to his work being linked to the French *nouveau roman*, more so than with the Latin American *nueva novela*. The Nineties superficial brush with popular culture (in the shape of a detective novel) cannot disguise the connection with the experimental intellectualizing Sixties tradition. At the end of the twentieth century, Saer, despite attempts to absorb his work into the new Anglo-American academy, continued to be a reminder of the relativity of formulations such as the Post-Boom and of the institutionalized political values of the new orthodoxies of cultural studies. What is more, he showed that the dilemmas and uncertainties raised by the Boom fiction of the Sixties are by no means resolved, while, behind the contemporary rhetoric of pluralism or strategic reading, a good deal of confusion and even inconsistency remains.

Ostensibly then, and as the title implies, *La pesquisa* is a detective story. In a snowy Paris, shortly before Christmas, police captain or *comisario* Morvan is investigating the brutal murder of a string of old ladies by a serial killer. However, there is very little investigation. Morvan spends much of his time looking out of the window, hanging around or walking about the city. The resolution, such as it is, seems to come about by chance. Morvan spots a piece of paper on the floor of the twenty-eighth victim's apartment, which happens to be a fragment of a letter torn up in his office by his assistant and number two, Captain Lautret. This leads him to deduce that Lautret is the killer and he sets a trap by waiting for him at the residence of the intended twenty-ninth victim. However, when Lautret arrives, the old lady is already mutilated and dead while Morvan is emerging from the bathroom covered in blood. Morvan has a split personality and is himself the killer.

This is an obvious transgressive twist: the detective, the supposed repository of rational deductive intelligence, is, in fact, the very source of disorder, chaos and irrationality. In a sense, though, the transgression is merely part of an Argentine tradition: the twist is an obvious

---

[14]   See Shaw, *The Post-Boom in Spanish American Fiction*, 12.

echo of Borges' "La muerte y la brújula"[15] or Hunter's proposed detective novel in Ernesto Sábato's *El túnel*.[16] But there is more to it than this.

If the detective narrative is conventionally suggestive of order and resolution, the novel's repeated pattern of digression disrupts the security of any anticipated inexorable movement towards disclosure. By Chapter 3, almost halfway through the novel, the action has not moved on at all from the opening page: Morvan is still, as he was, at the window looking out. A pattern of systematic digression continues throughout the novel and is complemented by interruption, as it emerges that the story of the Parisian murders is being related in Argentina to a group of friends by the expatriate Pichón Garay who has returned to the litoral Santa Fe area from France for a vacation.

Not only do interlocutory interventions disrupt the progress of any plot, much of the narrative is actually given over to the relationships and activities of the Argentine friends. In particular, there is a focus on a manuscript (referred to as a dactylogram) of a novel found amongst a dead friend's belongings and the question of whether or not the deceased, Washington Noriega, is its author. This sets up a parallel literary mystery, suggesting a more complexly subversive detective narrative and echoing much postmodern fiction's use of the detective.

This literary mystery is never resolved. On top of this, the manuscript's contents, dealing with the Trojan War, link to another aspect of the Paris story – the repeated and unexplained incursions into classical mythology, that serve, at least on the narrative surface, to deflect attention from the solving of the crime and to increase the novel's sense of enigmatic inconclusiveness. Furthermore, one of Pichón's friends, Carlos Tomatis, offers an entirely different version of the solution to the Parisian mystery, in which Morvan is innocent and has been framed by an elaborate plan (echoes again of Borges) laid out by a fiendish Lautret, the real serial killer. Whatever the implications, the detective narrative's traditional guarantee of knowledge and reassurance has been comprehensively destabilized.

If this last point can be agreed upon, the operation of this process of destabilization occurs on multiple levels: social, psychoanalytical,

---

[15] Jorge Luis Borges, "La muerte y la brújula" ("Death and the Compass"), in *Ficciones*, Madrid : Alianza, 1987.
[16] Ernesto Sábato, *El túnel* (*The Tunnel*), Madrid: Cátedra, 1987.

existential, literary. Contemporary criticism of Hispanic detective fiction tends to emphasize the social, almost obsessively dwelling on the links between the detective and hegemonic order. Indeed, as has been noted, the movement away from the independent private eye to the police procedural underlines the individual's dependency on systems and the maintenance of the *status quo*.[17] Morvan is part of such a system and is eventually (and possibly) trapped and undone by it, yet the narrative itself seems to dwell on his individual psychology, presents him, to some degree, as a loner and privileges personal reflection over active investigation. His police colleagues are described as almost a single conformist entity, constructed by the now unnoticed forces of their civilization, yet who believe their natures are as much a given as "las formaciones geológicas o la circulación de la sangre". For Morvan too, these are "las leyes naturales de la existencia", yet "se apartaba de esas normas".[18]

Similarly, the frequent digressions on materialism and consumerism present the individual as an "autómata" or robot whose actions are "idénticos y previsibles", even when they are supposed expressions of "individualismo orgulloso".[19] This idea of social construction is taken to a Jamesonian extreme of postmodern saturation when it is implied that one can no longer think in terms of "vida real" or real life and it is said that "la inmensa mayoría de los habitantes de ese continente ... confunde el mundo con un archipiélago de representaciones electrónicas y verbales".[20]

This is extended further into Baudrillard's idea of the simulacrum. The reference in the mysterious manuscript to the tale that the Trojan Paris kidnapped merely an identical copy of Helen suggests that the cause of the Trojan War is a simulacrum (124). The repeated references to "ese lugar llamado París" – that place called Paris – may suggest the idea of a totally constructed humanity living in essentially a virtual reality.

---

[17]　See *Criminal Proceedings*, ed. Messent, 12.
[18]　Saer, *La pesquisa*, 81-82: "geological formations or the circulation of the blood", "the natural laws of existence" and "he strayed from these norms".
[19]　*Ibid.*, 137: "identical and predictable", "proud individualism".
[20]　*Ibid.*, 32: "the immense majority of the inhabitants of that continent ... confuses the world with an archipelago of electronic and verbal representations."

Yet Morvan as observer seems conscious of the processes of construction and seems to challenge them. Moreover, the theoretically aware notion of identity construction often seems to fuse with a less theorized notion of the universal. For example, in the opening digression on old ladies, the meticulously documented characteristics of a specific social group become so generalized as to deny specificity, to the extent that the old ladies are "vueltas ya casi, de materia que eran, símbolo, idea, metáfora o principio".[21] The position on memory meantime is completely ambivalent: Morvan's memory of the rather peculiar circumstances of his own upbringing "parecía haber sido entresacada de un fondo de experiencia perteneciente a otros hombres, a la especie entera quizás, excepción hecha de sí mismo".[22] Yet, later, construction seems to be abandoned in favour of something close to universal experience:

> no es en la tierra natal donde se ha nacido, sino en un lugar más grande, más neutro ... al que nadie podría llamar suyo ..., un hogar que no es ni espacial ni geográfico, ni siquiera verbal, sino más bien ... físico, químico, biológico, cósmico, y del que lo invisible y lo visible, desde las yemas de los dedos hasta el universo estrellado, ... forman parte.[23]

In fact, the human dilemma as presented in this novel often comes very close to the supposedly old-fashioned idea of the human condition. Most people "se han dejado corroer por la desesperanza" and "la obstinación por durar" is "más misteriosa todavía que el concurso de circunstancias que puso al mundo en funcionamiento y más tarde ... a nosotros en el mundo".[24] Such views may, in part, be behind a further series of digressions on the natural world and the forces of the

---

[21] *Ibid.*, 12: "almost transformed now, from matter that they once were, into symbol, idea, metaphor or principle."

[22] *Ibid.*, 21: "appeared ... to have been selected from a depth of experience belonging to other men, perhaps to the entire species, with the exception of himself."

[23] *Ibid.*, 78: "it is not in one's native land that one has been born, but in a larger, more neutral place ... which no one could call his own ..., a home that is not spatial or geographical, cosmic, and of which the invisible and the visible, from one's fingertips to the starry universe, ... form a part."

[24] *Ibid.*, 11-12: "have allowed themselves to be gnawed away by despair" and "the stubborn will to live" is "even more mysterious than the concatenation of circumstances that set the world to functioning, and later on ... us ... within this world".

universe in general, in which the city of Paris is seen as clinging to the earth in the same way that a mollusc might cling to a rock (136) or men are seen as essentially at the mercy of "las fuerzas que tiran hacia lo oscuro".[25] The very pointlessness and repetition of the serial killings underscore the sense of aimless futility. This is the world of existential and metaphysical anguish that Shaw used to see as typifying the (now traditional) New Narrative.[26]

The perspective, then, in *La pesquisa* is, to say the least, unstable. But, in between the realms of the social and the metaphysical, there is some concentration, as one might expect in a novel about a serial killer, on the psychological. Detective fiction criticism tends to emphasize the social roots of psychological malaise. Linking to the theme of consumerism, Brian Jarvis locates anxiety in "consumer society", where "the body is defined as a private space, but in practice it is increasingly subject to a variety of forms of regulation".[27] Talking of Patricia Cornwell's Kay Scarpetta, Peter Messent claims that the prevalence of stranger killings "signals the loss of affect which is so noted a feature of the recent social landscape: the collapse of that web of domestic and community relationships that have conventionally located the subject and which have, in past times, aided the detective in her or his reconstruction of narrative legibility".[28] In the sense that the detective's brief is the restoration of a coherent narrative explanation for madness and chaos, that is to promote "[community] health",[29] the social role of the detective is close to that of the doctor or psychoanalyst. Sally R. Munt links this to repetition as the detective retraces the criminal's tracks, but wonders, with Daniel Gunn, "does repetition point towards some original movement of unity or always towards division and loss?".[30]

---

[25] *Ibid.*, 172: "the forces exerting their pull towards darkness."
[26] See Donald L. Shaw, *Nueva narrativa hispanoamericana*. Madrid: Cátedra, 1992.
[27] Brian Jarvis, "Watching the Detectives: Body Images, Sexual Politics and Ideology in Contemporary Crime Film", in *Criminal Proceedings*, ed. Messent, 225.
[28] *Criminal Proceedings*, ed. Messent, 15.
[29] See *Criminal Proceedings*, ed. Messent, 10 and Marty Roth, *Foul and Fair Play: Reading Genre in Classic Detective Fiction*, Athens: University of Georgia Press, 1995, 170.
[30] Sally R. Munt, *Murder by the Book?: Feminism and the Crime Novel*, London and New York: Routledge, 1994, 147 and Daniel Gunn, *Psychoanalysis and Fiction*, Cambridge: Cambridge UP, 1988, 5.

Given our earlier comments, the answer here is probably the latter and this answer tends to weaken the connection with a socially-theorized psychoanalysis and implies a looser model easily linked with the idea of the existential. Given that he is, it seems, the serial killer, Morvan's investigation is a psychoanalytical process in an obvious sense in that it is ultimately an investigation of himself. It is regularly said that the bizarre ritualistic murders have their own internal logic for the perpetrator if the detective could only divine it. Also, when Morvan is accused, the psychiatrists reduce his alleged actions to a pattern of psychological logic. His father, a wartime member of the resistance, committed suicide after revealing to Morvan – prompted by the break-up of his son's marriage – that the policeman's mother did not die while giving birth as he thought, but abandoned him, leaving his father for a member of the Gestapo. The crimes began at the time of this revelation, nine months earlier, and end with the discovery of a naked, bloody and helpless Morvan – a species of exorcism in the form of a monstrous second birth.

The sexual crimes are thus a form of raging against the mother, who would be approximately the same age as the victims. Added to this is a further complex layer of revenge connected to Lautret's usurping of his boss' place through his relationship with Morvan's ex-wife Caroline. Yet the convincing psychological explanation is not without its difficulties. It is not clear who Morvan's father is: the good hero or the evil villain? This may be an indication of the split nature of Morvan's personality, but – as a literary metaphor – may also allude to the possibility of Morvan's innocence and the culpability of the evil Lautret, who in Tomatis' version kills not unknowingly, as Morvan is alleged to have done, but for pure pleasure. In the version that has Morvan as the killer, Julio Premat points out that this shows up the instability of the self (the opposite of explanatory logic) and that such horrific or exceptional behaviour comes from someone who represents the social norm and social order, thereby indicating "una culpabilidad universal".[31] And, of course, we do not even know if Morvan really did it. Worse, if Tomatis' version is correct, then "la impunidad y la lucidez del criminal dan una visión de los comportamientos humanos mucho más escalofriante que la paciente construcción justificadora de

---

[31]   Saer, *La pesquisa*, 22: "a universal guilt."

la culpabilidad eventual de Morvan".[32] Once more social theory and recuperative psychoanalysis seem to collapse into the world of universal existential anxiety and the realm of the inexplicable.

All that is left are words. The truth cannot be seen, so only discourse remains, and the various versions of the truth simply exist side-by-side in writing. Indeed the obsession with language and writing is probably the most commented upon feature of Saer's prose. Mirta E. Stern, for instance, has already asserted in relation to Saer that "cada texto narra una historia, que a su vez trata, obsesivamente, la historia de su propia producción textual".[33] Hence the narrative produced by investigation and psychoanalysis is really the narrative of the text itself. But the serial killer, who is presumably a detective as well, is also linked to narrative.

It is well known that Saer's novels are mostly written in a kind of serial form, featuring the same characters (such as most of the Argentine characters of *La pesquisa*) and set in the same area, the Zona of Santa Fe and particularly the city suburb of Colastiné. This obsessive pattern of return and repetition is reinforced further by one of the narrative's many stylistic tics, what Víctor Gustavo Zonana calls "una voluntad exasperante de rectificación",[34] the constant and extended returning to words or objects to modify or qualify their possible meaning. Moreover, the elusive internal logic of the killer's acts is similar to the internal logic of an infuriatingly slippery and obscure text. The killings are like the novel itself: fascinating, repulsive and meticulous, inexplicable but with possible hidden meaning – "cada acto, cada objeto y cada detalle, ocupaba el lugar exacto que le acordaba en el conjunto la lógica del delirio".[35] Indeed the pattern of mutilation is

---

[32] Julio Premat, "El crimen de la escritura: la novela policial según Juan José Saer" in *Latin American Literary Review*, 24 (1996), 26: "the impunity and lucidity of the criminal offer a vision of human behaviour that is much more horrifying than the patient justificatory construction of the guilt of Morvan."

[33] Mirta E. Stern, "Juan José Saer: Construcción y teoría de la ficción narrativa", *Hispámerica*, 4 (1984), 22: "each text narrates a story that at the same time deals obsessively with the story of its own textual production."

[34] Víctor Gustavo Zonana, "Estrategias de des-simbolización literaria en la narrativa de Juan José Saer" in *Revista de literaturas modernas*, 28 (1995-96), 144: "an exasperating urge or desire to rectify or correct."

[35] Saer, *La Pesquisa*, 38: "each act, each object and each detail occupied the precise place accorded to it within the whole by the logic of delirium."

such that the killer is referred to as an "artista" (101), whose canvas is human flesh.

At the same time, there is a parallel mystery and a parallel investigation, which establishes an even clearer link with writing. Who wrote *En las tiendas griegas* (*In the Greek Tents*), the manuscript found amongst Washington Noriega's possessions? As Premat has observed, the examination of the manuscript is similar to the examination of a body, Soldi's investigation into the provenance of the text matches Morvan's, and the opening line of the text could easily be the opening line of *La pesquisa*. This mystery, of course, also begs another related question: who is writing here, who is the narrator of *La pesquisa*? Again as Premat has suggested, one might be forgiven at first for thinking the narrator is to be associated with Saer (the narrator even lives in the same *arrondissement* as Saer used to).[36] Then in the second chapter and a good way into the novel, the narrator is clarified as Pichón. But what does this mean? Pichón is supposedly narrating the story to a group of friends, but it is highly unlikely that anyone would tell a story at such length and in such a complexly literary fashion. Moreover, the intervention of Tomatis, with his alternative version of events, destabilizes narrative perspective even further. And, in any case, who is narrating the story of Pichón in Argentina and the story of Pichón telling a story? The answer has to be similar to the question asked about the authorship of *En las tiendas griegas*: we just do not know.

So, once more the explanatory project implied in detection (or psychoanalysis) is undone. The suggestion is even that the quest for any originary meaning outside of language is impossible. "En las tiendas griegas" is the title of a poem by the Peruvian poet César Vallejo, from the "Truenos" or "Thunderclaps" section of *Los heraldos negros* (The Black Heralds). The idea is that external meaning is a fiction or artifice and that literature is only really about itself. Indeed one of the most commented on features of Saer's work is the scepticism towards meaning and the concentration on language. Moreover, his work has been repeatedly associated with the objectivism of the French *nouveau roman* which creates "un efecto de antirrealidad o antinaturalidad",

---

[36]   Premat, "El crimen de la escritura", 30 and 27.

thus bringing out "la ininteligibilidad del mundo".[37] Any reading of *La pesquisa*, with its constant digressions, reflections, descriptions of external details, rectifications, qualifications, linguistic self-consciousness, dual narrative, dual conclusions, multiple levels and ultimate indeterminacy, leaves a sense that this narrative investigation has been a self-referential exercise, leading nowhere except back to the process of its own creation.

Saer's own attitude to the relationship between fiction and reality is ambiguous. Though he says, in *El concepto de ficción*, that "la ficción no solicita ser creída en tanto que verdad, sino en tanto que ficción", he also claims that "la ficción ... no vuelve la espalda a una supuesta realidad objetiva". Instead he sees "lo falso" (that which is false) and "lo verdadero" (that which is true) not "como opuestos que se excluyen, sino como conceptos problemáticos que encarnan la principal razón de ser de la ficción". [38] This leads to his definition of fiction as an "*antropología especulativa*" (speculative anthropology), a sort of investigative quest for a more complex kind of truth somewhere in between the objective and the subjective.

This is a rather indeterminate concept and extremely literary in nature. It sits somewhat ill at ease with the political transparency sometimes associated with Southern Cone fiction of the Post-Boom period. However, there is a political dimension to *La pesquisa*, in a way that may or may not be seen as inimicable to the anti-novelistic trends noted above. The unspoken subtext of this novel is the horror of dictatorship and disappearance. Pichón Garay is living in exile in France and has, in some ways, turned his back on his country. His brother, Gato Garay, and his lover Elisa disappeared during the military dictatorship. Pichón barely acknowledges this here and the references to Gato and Elisa are oblique in the extreme. This is obviously the third key mystery in the novel, arguably the only real mystery. But

---

[37]   Myrna Solotorevsky, *La relación mundo-escritura en libros de Reinaldo Arenas, Juan José Saer, Juan Carlos Martini*, 1993, 159-60: "an effect of anti-reality or anti-naturalness" and "the unintelligibility of the world".

[38]   See Juan José Saer, *El concepto de ficción (The Concept of Fiction)*, www.literatura.org/Saer: "fiction does not seek to be understood as truth but as fiction", "fiction ... does not turn its back on any presumed objective reality" and "as mutually exclusive opposites, but as problematical concepts that embody the principal *raison d'être* of fiction".

this is the only one that is not investigated. Indeed it is almost studiously avoided.

During a river trip to Washington's former residence, the friends pass the house from which the lovers disappeared. Little commentary is made on this, the friends do not talk about the matter, and no truth about what happened has been identified. At the end of the novel, Soldi notices what could be a mixture of recognition, repression and guilt in the old friends Pichón and Tomatis: "A Soldi le parece notar que sus miradas se encuentran, fugaces, y casi en seguida, por alguna razón que se le escapa, se rehúyen."[39] Having returned from a trip to investigate the source of Washington's manuscript and having exchanged alternative versions of the outcome of the Parisian murder mystery, this is perhaps a tacit acknowledgement that the one mystery which has not been investigated or resolved, by implication a real mystery rather than one existing only within the pages of a text, is the disappearance of Gato and Elisa and perhaps of countless others.

The now familiar themes of collective guilt at the suppression of memory and the failure to come to terms with a traumatic past are central, despite, like the memory itself, being buried deep in a contemporary narrative. The crime drama could be seen to underline these themes. Morvan's suppressed past psychological scars and his repressed penchant for violence and torture beneath a respectable exterior parallels the Argentine nation's dilemma with respect to its national unconscious. Tomatis' version of the crimes makes more or less the same point: Lautret is the nation's dark side, an enemy in the midst whose abuses have not been properly acknowledged or exorcized; and Tomatis' version even suggests the idea of an establishment cover up of the truth.

Florinda F. Goldberg has exhaustively documented a number of links between the novel's narrative levels and the military repression. She also notes the metaphorical implications of Washington's daughter Julia's refusal to allow a proper investigation to establish the authorship of her father's manuscript, a text that deals with violence and civil war. And she sets Gato's disappearance in the context of Saer's earlier novels, noting how in *Glosa* (*Gloss*) (1986) Gato's dis-

---

[39]   Saer, *La pesquisa*, 174: "Soldi seems to notice that their eyes meet, fleetingly, and almost immediately, for some reason that escapes him, they avoid each other."

appearance is mentioned only in passing and with no detail, while much of the novel concentrates on the imaginary narrative reconstruction of a party in Washington's house by those who were not present.[40] This echoes the apparent technique of *La pesquisa*, where the Parisian detective mystery could be seen as a self-indulgent distraction from the repressed truth of what should be the main concern, the disappearance of Gato and others. In a sense, Saer's elaboration of a complex fiction, infuriatingly peppered by digression and apparent nitpicking, may be taken as a dramatization of the collective national will to forget the past and avoid the truth, to the extent that political reality has itself become a species of fiction and history an act of digression.

The problem is that Goldberg's convincingly articulated political reading depends, to some extent, on a removal or neutralization of the ambiguity and indeterminacy that seems so crucial to Saer's literary universe. As tends to happen elsewhere, particularly since the rise of cultural studies in the wake of the theoretical revolution, narrative plurality and uncertainty can actually be turned to a very specific and even reductive (if valid) end. Thus the whole novel, here, for instance, comes to be seen to be about that which it seems not to be about. This may be a persuasive argument for a reading based on cultural memory, but is itself dependent on a strategic forgetting, ignoring or presumptuous dismissal of much of what does appear to be central in the narrative. In any case, given that the investigative, psychoanalytical and literary recuperative processes are so thoroughly undermined in *La pesquisa*, how can any literary critic reasonably claim to have uncovered a core meaning?

Stern has already suggested that Saer's narrative technique "consiste en borrar, suprimir o eludir una determinada realidad (histórica, social, política, afectiva, etc.)".[41] And, while Jorgelina Corbatta has noted that "la memoria ocupa un lugar importantísimo en los textos y en la concepción literaria de Saer", she equally says that "sin embargo, la negatividad ... tiñe también la confianza en la capacidad de recor-

---

[40]   Florinda F. Goldberg, "*La pesquisa* de Juan José Saer: alambradas de la ficción", *Hispamérica*, 26 (1997), 96-97.

[41]   Stern, "Juan José Saer: Construcción y teoría de la ficción narrativa", 20: "consists of erasing, suppressing or avoiding any given reality (historical, social, political, emotional, etc.)."

dar".[42] Indeed Saer himself hints at the potential limitations of "national" readings when he complains of the tendency to interpret the great Argentine gaucho epic *Martín Fierro* in terms of "la supuesta identidad nacional que habría allí".[43] Although in another interview he says, "I've got nothing against politics in art", he still talks of "the universal human condition" and asserts that "I'm not interested in the particular".[44]

The centrality of France alongside Argentina in *La pesquisa* problematizes further the idea of an exclusively national focus, as does the centrality of European mythological reference. Morvan's obsession, for example, with what appears to be Zeus' rape of Europa while disguised as a bull and his anxious delirious visions of Scylla, Charybdis and the Gorgon may echo the ideas of deception, abuse of power and monstrosity beneath an apparently normal surface.

But despite the possibly Argentine national overtones of these allusions, they are equally suggestive of dilemmas in human psychology, friendship and relationships, literary interpretation, reality and the hazardous journey through life in general. The key idea seems to be that things are not what they seem: that is, that we are back to the idea of the problematic nature of reality and literature's attempts to portray it. In fact, the mythological references are really profoundly enigmatic and pretty unfathomable. The story of Morvan ends with him in detention asking for his case notes and a book on mythology, but he ignores the file and loses himself in the book's illustration of a white bull violating a terrified nymph beneath a Cretan plane tree. This appears to be an indicator of metaphorical significance, but in reality provides an obscure and impenetrable conclusion to the narrative's central story. Meaning is not to be found in this tale. At the same time, the framing of the story in terms of classical Greek mythology does seem

---

[42]   Jorgelina Corbatta, "Algunas notas sobre 'la praxis poética' de Juan José Saer", *Cuadernos hispanoamericanos*, 561 (1997), 104: "memory occupies an extremely important position in Saer's texts and in his conception of literature" and "nonetheless, negativity ... also taints any confidence in the capacity to remember".

[43]   Saer quoted in *La caja de la escritura: diálogos con escritores y críticos argentinos*, ed. Marily Martínez-Richter, Frankfurt am Main: Vervuert, 1997, 17: "the supposed national identity that might be there."

[44]   Saer quoted in Caleb Bach, "Writer on the Rivers of Time", *Américas*, 51 (1999), 50-51.

to universalize the human drama, suggesting that the failed quest for meaning is at the heart of the human condition.

This puts *La pesquisa* back in the territory of the Latin American new novel of the Boom and before. The end of the twentieth century, then, with the embracing of popular genres such as the detective format now firmly embedded in Latin American cultural practice, does not necessarily mark that much change or development in the subcontinent's narrative. The sharpened political awareness of the Seventies onwards does not erase radical scepticism. Perhaps the real problem of much Latin American fiction of the later twentieth century is an unresolved urge to have it all ways, as the popular/elite or political/existential tensions appear to signify. Whether the commentator praises multiplicity or criticizes inconsistency, the same old difficulty remains: how to reconcile any examination of reality with extreme doubt about its nature and the ability of writing to grasp it. The postmodern detective novel does not necessarily represent that much of a step forward and indeed the Latin American novel at the turn of the century was probably, in some ways, not all that far away from where it had been for some time.

CASES OF IDENTITY CONCEALED AND REVEALED IN CHILEAN DETECTIVE FICTION

KATE M. QUINN

Throughout most of the twentieth century detective fiction remained a marginal form in the field of Chilean literature. Few authors cultivated the genre and, for the most part, literary critics paid scant attention to their efforts. It was only in the Nineties that the genre achieved mainstream acceptance with the success of a new generation of authors of what came to be known as *neopolicial latinoamericano* or *nueva novela negra latinoamericana* (new Latin American hard-boiled). In this variant, the cynicism of the hard-boiled takes on an edge of socio-political criticism and is applied to Latin American realities such as social and economic inequality, repressive political regimes, widespread political corruption, drugs trafficking and violent crime. In the specific context of Chile, authors like Ramón Díaz Eterovic[1] and Roberto Ampuero, the most prolific of the new crime writers, recognized the potential within this form for examining the legacy of political radicalism and military dictatorship and for chronicling the years of transition to democracy. The *neopolicial* model dominated detective and crime fiction production throughout the Nineties and into the new century,[2] but the success of this particular form also created a

---

[1]   Díaz Eterovic actually published his first book in the Heredia series, *La ciudad está triste*, Santiago: Sinfronteras, 1987, prior to the restoration of democracy and in this, and subsequent novels such as *Solo en la oscuridad*, Buenos Aires: Torres Agüeros Editor, 1992, and *Nadie sabe más que los muertos*, Santiago: Planeta Meridion, 1993, he examines the legacy of human rights violations committed under the dictatorship.

[2]   For more on *neopolicial* and Ramón Díaz and Roberto Ampuero, see Kate Quinn, "Chilean Writers and *neopolicial latinoamericano*", in *Latin American Detective Fiction: New Readings*, eds Shelley Godsland and Jacky Collins, Manchester: MMU Press, 2004, 52-67.

wider interest in detective fiction that attracted authors from outside
the genre and encouraged a broader range of approaches.

This essay will look at two novels from the Nineties by Roberto
Ampuero and Marcela Serrano that foreground issues of identity, linking these to an examination of contemporary society. Both authors
were supporters of Salvador Allende's political project[3] and, from the
perspective of the Nineties and with different focuses, re-examine the
utopian impulses that informed their generation. In both Ampuero's
¿Quién mató a Cristián Kustermann?[4] and Serrano's *Nuestra Señora
de la Soledad*[5] we find plots that centre around investigations into the
identity of absent individuals, and the reconstruction of the details of
these individual lives sheds light on contemporary issues. Ampuero's
novel looks critically at the legacy of left-wing political militancy and
its place in the Chile of the early years of transition to democracy,
while Serrano's looks at the position of women in contemporary society from a feminist perspective.

Roberto Ampuero's *¿Quién mató a Cristián Kustermann?*

Roberto Ampuero is best known in Chile for his Cayetano Brulé
detective series, and *¿Quién mató a Cristián Kustermann?* is the first
of five novels to date.[6] The title of the novel makes the issue of
identity central to the narrative, even implying a whodunnit quality.

---

3   Allende came to power in 1970 at the head of the Popular Unity government.
    Although the main party in this group was Allende's own socialist party, there
    were other coalition members and a number of these pursued policies more radical
    than those favoured by Allende. This government was overthrown on 11
    September 1973 in a military coup. General Pinochet emerged as the leader of the
    subsequent military *junta*, ruling by decree until 1980. Then he consolidated his
    position in a controversial plebiscite which allowed him to draft a new consti-
    tution and assume the title of President. This constitution confirmed him as Presi-
    dent until 1989, at which point elections were to be held to see whether he would
    be confirmed in power for a further term. The constitution also outlined the frame-
    work for an eventual transition to democracy.
4   Roberto Ampuero *¿Quién mató a Cristián Kustermann?*, Santiago: Planeta, 1993.
    The title of this novel clearly echoes that of Mario Vargas Llosa's *¿Quién mató a
    Palomino Molero?*.
5   Marcela Serrano, *Nuestra Señora de la Soledad*, Santiago: Alfaguara, 1999.
6   The others are *Boleros en la Habana*, *El alemán de Atacama*, *Cita en el azul pro-
    fundo*, and *Halcones de la noche*. All Santiago: Planeta, 1995, 1996, 2001, and
    2004 respectively.

However, the reader soon discovers that the real centre of interest in the investigation is not so much who killed Cristián Kustermann, but rather who Kustermann really was. In order to uncover the identity of the killer, the detective must retrace the victim's steps, examine his past and engage in a reconstruction of his life. This in turn provides a pretext for a wider exploration of the turbulent recent history of not only Chile, but the whole of Latin America and, indeed, also of Europe.

The novel clearly fits within the category of *neopolicial* and begins conventionally enough when businessman Carlos Kustermann retains private detective Cayetano Brulé to investigate the murder of his son, restaurateur Cristián. There are many theories about the killing; that it may be a drugs-related crime, a crime of passion, a robbery gone wrong, or the act of a vengeful employee. Brulé explores all of these possibilities, discarding them one by one. He gradually uncovers a political dimension to the crime when he learns that Cristián, who had moved to Germany in 1980, ostensibly to study, had instead joined an underground opposition group and it is this involvement in opposition to the Pinochet regime that holds the key to solving the case. Yet, Ampuero frustrates any expectation on the reader's part that supporters of the dictatorship are behind the killing and presents us with a motive based on a falling-out among members of an armed revolutionary group. Young Kustermann has not been eliminated by his former enemies, but by a former friend and colleague.

The trajectory of Kustermann's life uncovered by Brulé is fascinating. Using a cover story of wishing to study in West Germany, he used this as a stepping stone to reach East Germany and, from there, eventually travelled on to Cuba. In Cuba he received training in guerrilla warfare and he later participated in various armed conflicts in Central America. Finally he was assigned to a Cuban-trained group charged with attempting to overthrow the Pinochet regime through armed insurgency. When the transition to democracy came about peacefully in 1990, Kustermann was already questioning his previous allegiances and beliefs. Brulé discovers that he was murdered by a colleague who opposed the young man's attempts to re-orientate this insurgency group, the *Frente*, and persuade them to abandon their arms and participate in the new democracy. The *Frente* alluded to mirrors the real *Frente Patriótico Manuel Rodríguez* which was established in 1983 as the armed wing of the Communist party and whose members were indeed trained in Cuba and remained active during the early years of the Transition.[7] Ampuero does not evade the issue of the problems of the Chilean transition to democracy and the difficult compromises that were reached to facilitate this – among which was an adherence to the formula outlined in the 1980 constitution drafted by the military government – but he insists that it is necessary to acknowledge that the political radicalism that preceded the coup of September 1973 was two-sided. For the author, a mature reassessment of the history of the Left is as critical as the ongoing examination of the legacy of the dictatorship in providing a complete overview of the recent history of Chile. He also expresses a keen desire to see the phenomenon of exile and the impact of those returning with new ideas and new experiences reflected in Chilean literature.

Commentators on the novel were swift to draw parallels between the career of the fictional Kustermann and that of Ampuero and when we look at the author's biography it is easy to see why this temptation is so strong. Roberto Ampuero left Chile in 1973 because, as a young Communist, he did not wish to live under the military dictatorship. He travelled to East Germany where he rapidly became disillusioned with the kind of socialism he found in operation there. He did not, however, immediately give up faith in the Socialist cause, but instead decided to move to Cuba. He reasoned that, unlike in East Germany where socialism had been imposed by force and was maintained by a strong Soviet military presence, in Cuba the idealism of the Revolution must have produced a better system. In addition to this, as a South American he thought he would feel more at home in Cuba. Nonetheless, there too he was disillusioned with the Socialist system, finding that power was held by a minority and no attack on the orthodoxy of the Revolution was tolerated. It was in Cuba that Ampuero renounced his allegiance to the Communist Youth. He returned to East Germany where he studied for some years prior to moving to West Germany. While there, he witnessed the collapse of communism and the Reunification of the two Germanys. He finally returned to Chile in 1992, after

---

[7]   The FPMR made an assassination attempt against General Pinochet in 1986, attacking his motorcade and killing members of his security team, although he himself escaped unhurt. The FPMR has renounced violence in recent years and maintains an official party website at http://www.fpmr.org.

the restoration of democracy, having spent half his life in exile.[8]

In addition to the similarity between the careers of both author and character, there is further scope for comparison of the two in Ampuero's subsequent publication of a fictionalized memoir based on his experiences in exile, *Nuestros años verde olivo*.[9] This book displays the same desire to explore the shifting nature of political commitment in the turbulent Seventies and Eighties. Further criticism of the political regime in Cuba can be found in Ampuero's second Cayetano Brulé novel *Boleros en la Habana*, and in the more recent novel *Halcones de la noche*, and in interviews the author has been consistently impatient with those who criticize the Pinochet regime in Chile while refusing to censure Fidel Castro's regime in Cuba.

Criticism of the unreformed Left is a strong element in *¿Quién mató a Cristián Kustermann?*, with the author presenting many satirical portraits of paranoid hard-line Communists. In the course of his investigation, as Brulé attempts to establish the precise nature of Kustermann's beliefs, he interviews various supporters of the Communist cause who knew him, and these reveal widely divergent views about the transition to democracy. One of the first consulted is Luis Berrios of the *Oficina de Retorno*, a bureau set up by the new democratic government to facilitate the return of political exiles and those who left the country for economic reasons. Such a bureau existed in reality and was set up by the Aylwin government with just such a remit. Berrios is optimistic about the transition to democracy, despite having been imprisoned and tortured under the dictatorship because of his Socialist beliefs. However, this is not the case with Ernesto Cardona, another former prisoner and torture victim, who now owns a bar which provides a meeting place for nostalgic Communists. Ernesto's cynicism is clear in his words to the detective: "¿crees que esto es democracia? Aquí sigue mandando Pinochet, y los partidos de izquierda trabajan a dos niveles, por lo que pudiera ocurrir."[10] Cardona points

---

[8]   Information on the author based on personal interview conducted in June 1994.

[9]   For Ampuero's response to the polemical debate this book provoked in Chile, see http://docs.tercera.cl/especiales/2001/verdeolivo/capitulo01/columna.htm.

[10]   Roberto Ampuero, *¿Quién mató a Cristián Kustermann?*, 82-83: "do you think this is democracy? Pinochet is still in charge here, and the left-wing parties operate on two fronts, because of what might happen" (all translations are my own).

Brulé in the direction of Martín Chacón who reveals that Cristián had recently broken with the *Frente* but he does not believe that they are responsible for the murder and is convinced that Cristián was a victim of state repression. Chacón's views on the crisis in the Left are interesting:

> "nosotros creemos que es un proceso ... de purificación del movimiento revolucionario .... Hoy muchos de los revolucionarios de los setenta son socialdemócratas de derecha y se avergüenzan de su pasado, y reniegan del socialismo y de Cuba .... Estamos en una época de resaca revolucionaria, pero la rueda de la historia sigue rodando"[11]

Similar views are expressed by Cristián's old acquaintances from Germany who all assume that the Chilean security forces must be behind the killing, an attitude that seems paranoid and outdated to Brulé since he knows that many of the political leaders who criticized the military regime during their years of exile are now members of the new democratic government.

When the action moves to Cuba, Cristián's ex-wife Magali, the daughter of an exiled Allende minister, confirms that Cristián had participated in armed conflicts in Guatemala, El Salvador and Nicaragua, but reveals that he had later distanced himself from the revolution and returned to Germany where he obtained a job as translator for a firm exporting to Latin America. Magali provides information on a Chilean of German descent who worked for the same company, information that will eventually help the detective unmask the killer. She too blames the dictatorship for Cristián's death and when Brulé replies that in Chile "ya no hay dictadura ... hay un gobierno democrático desde hace más de tres años"[12] she remains sceptical. Brulé understands the reasons for this attitude, reflecting "no creía en el retorno pacífico a la democracia y por ello despreciaba a los políticos que

---

[11] *Ibid.*, 98: "We believe this is a process ... of purification of the revolutionary movement .... Today many of the revolutionaries of the Seventies are right-wing Social Democrats and are ashamed of their past and reject socialism and Cuba .... We are in an age of revolutionary hangover but the wheel of history keeps turning."
[12] *Ibid.*, 184: "there is no longer a dictatorship there has been a democratic government for over three years."

aceptaban las reglas de Pinochet".[13] Despite his political change of direction, no one in Cuba believes that Cristián was killed by the *Frente*. Nonetheless, it is in Cuba that Brulé finds the key to solving the case. Another former comrade, Alejandro Barra describes how four members of their guerrilla group had identical rings made as a symbol of their solidarity: "Era una especie de símbolo de nuestra identificación, y quedamos en que los usaríamos siempre, hasta la victoria final o la muerte."[14] These rings are symbolic of the collective aspect of their shared political aspirations and the utopian ideals for which they fought. Their vow now takes on a sinister tone since two of them are dead, Cristián and his friend Samuel Léniz who died in a supposed car accident. Of the remaining two, Barro has chosen to remain in Cuba and the last member, the man of German descent, is finally revealed to be the killer.

Although there is no real attempt to provide a psychological explanation for the murders of Kustermann and Léniz, it is clear that the motive is personal as well as political. Both victims were rejecting the armed path and the killer was unwilling to accept this political defection, unwilling to accept this challenge to the collective identity even though this identity had already become fragmented and discredited. Speaking of the crisis in the Left after the fall of the Berlin Wall, Jorge Amado summed up the general feeling of disorientation that struck a whole generation:

> I know of men and women, magnificent people, who suddenly find themselves unprotected, empty, submerged by doubts, lonely, lost and crazed. What inspired them and led them through life, the ideals of justice and beauty for which they fought, for which they suffered persecution and violence, exile, jail and torture, and for which so many others were murdered, turned into smoke, into nothing, into something worthless, into a lie and an illusion, a miserable and ignominious trick.[15]

---

[13] *Ibid.*, 185: "she did not believe in the peaceful transition to democracy and therefore despised the politicians who accepted Pinochet's rules."

[14] *Ibid.*, 195: "It was a kind of symbol of our identification and we swore to wear them always, until final victory or death."

[15] Jorge Amado, "Sólo el futuro es nuestro", in *La Jornada Semanal*, Mexico City, 29 December 1991 and quoted in Jorge G. Castañeda, *Utopia Unarmed: The Latin American Left after the Cold War*, New York: Alfred A. Knopf, 1993, 39.

In *¿Quién mató a Cristián Kustermann?* we find an attempt to shed light on an area of Chilean history that Ampuero believed had been neglected or deliberately ignored, that of the involvement of Chileans in armed revolutionary struggle at home and elsewhere in Latin America. As Brulé collects individual statements about Cristián they form part of a jigsaw that the detective must reassemble and this jigsaw says as much about the history of communism during the lifetime of the victim as it does about Kustermann himself. The novel gives the reader an insight into the individual experiences behind the transformations that communism has undergone in the last thirty years and the impact this political system has had on Latin America and particularly on Chile. Just as individual lives cannot be divorced from their sociopolitical context, the history of individual nations cannot be properly understood in isolation.

Yet, in all of this Cristián Kustermann remains a compelling absence. Since he is already dead when the investigation begins, neither the detective nor the readers have the opportunity to encounter him directly. Instead they must rely on others' impressions of him. Brulé conscientiously interviews Kustermann's friends and acquaintances and follows up the leads they provide, but everything we learn of the victim is second-hand and mediated through the subjective perceptions of these people. Although some witnesses are hostile to Kustermann, the majority are sympathetic and as readers learn more of his personal history and his struggle with his own beliefs, they form a sympathetic image of this idealistic young man and his involvement in what was for many of his generation a genuine quest to create a utopia based on Socialist and Communist ideals. The lasting impression formed is one of genuine loss, of a missed opportunity with all that Kustermann might yet have accomplished.

Marcela Serrano's *Nuestra Señora de la Soledad*

Throughout the twentieth century Chilean detective fiction remained a resolutely male-dominated affair, both in terms of authors and protagonists. However, at the end of the Nineties Marcela Serrano made a surprise contribution to the genre with her novel *Nuestra Señora de la Soledad*. Serrano came to the genre as an already established author, whose works were well known outside of Chile. In all her novels she looks at various aspects of contemporary women's lives, from the domestic to the professional, and from the romantic to the political.[16] *Nuestra Señora de la Soledad* is her fifth novel and, although new in terms of genre affiliation, it has much in common with the rest of Serrano's production in terms of its major themes and preoccupations. With its publication Serrano became the first female author in Chile to write a detective novel. In addition to this, the novel presents the first professional woman detective in Chilean literature.[17] This novel brings a new focus on women's lives to the genre and explores the possibility of women creating a utopian space for themselves in the modern world.

Where Brulé is a readily recognizable P.I., the detective in this novel does not belong to the hard-boiled tradition. Rosa Alvallay is a fifty-four-year-old, separated mother of two who works for a detective agency. The novel is a first-person narration and opens with Alvallay being allocated the choice assignment of investigating the disappearance of detective writer C. L. Avila. Although Serrano's detective is an agency worker, the missing author is a writer of hard-boiled detective novels. It is an honour for Alvallay to be assigned this case, given the author's international fame and the notoriety surrounding her

---

[16] Serrano is a feminist but is impatient with those who try to categorize her novels as feminist works. She is particularly impatient with the designation "women's literature", viewing this as an attempt to devalue and ghettoize books by female authors that deal with female characters. For more on the author's political views and her literary works, see Marisa Pereyra, "Sobre orfandad y utopías: Entrevista a Marcela Serrano", *Hispanic Journal*, XXIV/1 (2003), 223-33.

[17] Ramón Díaz introduced a female journalist as adjunct detective in *Nadie sabe más que los muertos*, only to kill her off in the next book, *Angeles y solitarios*, Santiago: Planeta, 1995. Mauro Yberra (the pen-name of José Leal and Eugenio Díaz) created a team of adolescent sleuths, including one girl, in *La que murió en Papudo*, Santiago: Ediciones Linterna Mágica, 1993. Bartolomé Díaz (another, solo, pen-name of Eugenio Díaz has written *Linchamiento de negro*, Santiago: Ediciones Linterna Mágica, 1994, an agency detective novel with women employees, but this is set in Kenya. Alejandra Rojas has written a number of novels such as *Legítima defensa* and *Noches de estreno*, Santiago: Planeta, 1993 and 1994, that could be classified as crime fiction, but not as detective novels in the strictest sense, since they do not have professional detectives. For more on Alejandra Rojas and for a discussion of Marcela Serrano, see Clemens A. Franken Kurzen, *Crimen y verdad en la novela policial chilena actual*, Santiago: Universidad de Santiago de Chile, 2003, 179-202 and 217-29.

disappearance but she downplays the significance of this, saying "pues sí, supongo que me eligieron por ser una mujer. Y porque México ha permanecido acuartelado en mi conciencia."[18] This familiarity with Mexico that she shares with the missing author is due to her having lived there for a number of years with her husband who was exiled for his political beliefs after the military coup. After their separation he remained in Mexico while she returned to Chile with their children.

We are given the background to the author's disappearance; she had attended an international book fair in Miami and was due to fly back to Chile. She took a taxi to the airport but never boarded her flight. Some months have gone by and the police have been unable to turn up any leads. Now her husband, university rector Tomás Rojas, has engaged the services of the private agency in the hope that they may succeed where the police have failed.

Alvallay believes that in order to solve the case she must have some understanding of the missing author and so questions friends and family members in order to gain a picture of her personality and her life. Carmen Lewis Avila is the daughter of a Chilean mother and US father. She led a nomadic existence since being abandoned by her hippy parents who went to seek enlightenment in India in their own quest for a personal utopia. Left in the care of her mother's family in Chile, she suffered the trauma of witnessing her grandmother's murder at the hands of a family member. She then went to live with her paternal aunt in San Francisco. As an adult she herself became a traveller and, as her friend Jill tells Alvallay Carmen "solía decir que primero siguió a sus padres sin rumbo alguno, luego a sus hombres".[19] She did settle for a time in Mexico City where she had a son Vicente, and a second mystery in the text is that of the identity of the boy's father. Carmen has invented a story of a US citizen who died in a car accident, but most believe that Vicente was the product of an affair with guerrilla fighter, Luis Benítez. However, this too turns out to be a deliberately planted false lead, designed to protect the true father, married Mexican author Santiago Blanco. Following a long period of

---

18   Marcela Serrano, *Nuestra Señora de la Soledad*, 13: "well yes, I suppose they chose me because I am a woman. And because Mexico has remained in my consciousness."

19   *Ibid.*, 59: "She used to say that first she followed her parents with no particular direction and then her men."

emotional turmoil Carmen married Tomás Rojas and settled in Santiago with him. Her marriage provided a refuge and stability for a time, but eventually it came to feel like a prison.

Those interviewed by Alvallay – family, friends and employees – propose a number of theories with regard to the author's disappearance, the most outlandish of which is that she may have been kidnapped by Luis Benítez, the guerrilla fighter with whom she once had an affair, and that she may be held by the *zapatistas* in Chiapas. The existence of this theory for a time might lead the reader to believe that this is another political crime novel, albeit one with a romantic twist. However, this theory is soon discarded, and indeed derided by Alvallay who believes that it reveals a complete lack of understanding of the aims of the *zapatista* movement.[20] Soon more prosaic possibilities are raised.

Her best friend believes she has committed suicide, while her stepdaughter is convinced that she has simply run away. This turns out to be closest to the truth as Rosa Alvallay discovers that Avila has carefully planned and staged her own disappearance in order to cut all ties with her previous existence. Although it seems that her husband does love her, there is a strong indication that he treats her as a sort of trophy wife and revels in the attention that her fame attracts, while she herself shies away from the spotlight. When Alvallay examines the author's wardrobe she discovers the informal clothes favoured by Carmen and the more formal outfits that are described as the "*disfraz*" (disguise) that she wears to transform herself into the Rector's wife. This notion of deliberately playing a role and consciously engaging in self-invention is reiterated throughout the novel. An author friend says that Carmen claimed her great-grandmother was a gypsy but that this is "¡Mitos! ¿Qué escritor no los necesita para posicionarse a sí mismo como un personaje?".[21] Her stepdaughter warns "No ... se deje llevar por los mitos. Creo que Carmen ... se había cansado de inventarse a sí

---

[20] A concern with Mexico is also to found in Serrano's *Lo que está en el corazón*, Barcelona: Planeta, 2001, a novel set against the backdrop of the Chiapas uprising.

[21] *Nuestra Señora*, 47: "Myths! What writer does not need them in order to set themselves up as a character?"

misma cada día" going on to say that "pienso que Carmen trató de doblegar su verdadera naturaleza, pero a la larga ésta venció".[22]

Alvallay turns literary sleuth seeking clues in Avila's novels and in interviews she gave to the press. She tries to get under the skin of the missing woman and in her reliance on empathy and intuition she resembles Avila's own fictional detective Pamela Hawthorne, who has argued that "las mujeres eran más agudas en el campo de la investigación criminal que los hombres" because they have "una cierta *percepción no objetiva*".[23] This privileging of the subjective runs counter to genre tradition but it is interesting to note that it is just such skills that permit Serrano's detective to solve this case.

Carmen Avila's book collection reveals a broad-ranging familiarity with the detective genre, with a marked preference for the hard-boiled. Her collection includes books by Patricia Highsmith, P. D. James, Sue Grafton, Ross Macdonald, Chester Himes, Vázquez Montalbán, Luis Sepúlveda, as well as the complete works of Chandler and Hammett. Both Avila and Alvallay have an academic interest in the genre and the detective, herself a keen reader of crime fiction, has heard Carmen lecture on this subject. We are told that Avila wrote one novel set in Chile which is described as "una novela política, aunque se disfrace de historia policial".[24] Thus the writing of the fictional C. L. Avila resembles that of real writers like Díaz Eterovic and Ampuero. Serrano has created a very self-aware detective novel and a very literate detective. She also counts on the reader being familiar with the detective genre as she leaves intertextual clues that point to the true fate of Carmen Avila. Avila's last Pamela Hawthorne novel mentions the story of a secret agent named Jim Thompson who one day vanished without a trace, never to be found. Alvallay thinks this story may have given Carmen the idea to stage her own disappearance. Carmen's fictional Jim Thompson shares his name with the real life author of *The Getaway* which includes a flight to Mexico, although one with an ultimately unhappy outcome. Escape to Mexico may also bring to

---

[22] *Ibid.*, 79: "Don't get carried away with the myths. I believe that Carmen had grown tired of inventing herself every day"; and 84: "I think that Carmen tried to suppress her true nature but in the long run it defeated her."

[23] *Ibid.*, 71: "women were sharper in the field of criminal investigation than men" and "a certain non-objective perception".

[24] *Ibid.*, 106: "a political novel, although it disguises itself as a detective story."

mind Terry Lennox from Chandler's *The Long Goodbye*, who changes his appearance and assumes a new identity after fleeing the USA, and like Lennox, Carmen Avila has had cosmetic surgery to alter her appearance. We finally learn that the main catalyst for Avila's radical break with her old life lies in a near miss with death when she agreed to give up her seat on a flight that subsequently crashed, killing those who had taken her place. This incident is reminiscent of the Flitcraft episode from Hammett's *The Maltese Falcon*.

Alvallay learns that there are plenty of conventional reasons to explain the author's flight from the marital home since Tomás Rojas has been having affairs with younger women, including Carmen's assistant. Satisfied that Vicente has an excellent relationship with his stepfather and that he has the security of having recently married, Carmen has abandoned her husband and son to begin a new life under an assumed name in Oaxaca, Mexico. The real problem is accounting for the radical nature of her flight. In order to understand her motivation, Alvallay must try to identify with the author. Avila is motivated as much by a desire to escape from her own fame and the popularity of her fictional detective as from the circumstances of her domestic life. Alvallay suggests that she could simply have killed off the detective but a friend of Avila's reminds her of Conan Doyle's frustrated attempt to kill Holmes. Avila leaves everything behind because she has come to feel trapped and because she longs for complete freedom.

In addition to referencing classics of the detective genre, Serrano's novel also alludes indirectly but quite clearly to Virginia Woolf's *A Room of One's Own* and the problems faced by women in the creative sphere. Carmen Avila has a study in her husband's house but she is constantly interrupted. She dreams of an ideal space, a refuge that she hopes to find in a blue house in Mexico. Alvallay empathizes with this desire because her own domestic situation is characterized by compromise and is far from conducive to work. As she herself puts it: "Lamenté una vez más que el departamento tuviera únicamente tres habitaciones: o un escritorio para mí o los dos niños en la misma pieza; la decisión se tomó por sí sola. El resultado es que llevo muchos años trabajando sobre mi cama."[25] In addition to this, Alvallay too makes unfavourable comparisons between Chile and Mexico. She dislikes the way in which neoliberal economic policies and global-ization have affected Chile and, like Carmen Avila, sees Mexico as a country that has managed to resist the dehumanizing pressures of modernization.

These comparisons are not limited to the author, Alvallay also compares herself ironically and self-deprecatingly with Pamela Haw-thorne:

> Pamela Hawthorne, la investigadora heroína de sus novelas, era abo-gada como yo y nuestros trabajos no diferían mucho uno del otro. Claro, el mío no llevaba anclado a su escencia ningún glamour y tam-poco yo llegué a esto por vocación … sino por una cadena de fracasos consecutivos …. Y si sigo con las comparaciones, ella no es madre de dos hijos, no dejó a un marido en el otro hemisferio ni atiende sola una casa, amén de financiarla. Y por supuesto, dato crucial, yo no cuento con los esplendorosos treinta años de Miss Hawthorne.[26]

Alvallay may envy Avila's bid for freedom but she cannot choose such a radical option since she does not enjoy Avila's financial in-dependence, nor can she count on someone else to look after her chil-dren.

Nonetheless, her sense of female solidarity is sufficiently strong to outweigh the demands of her profession and so, when her intuition and investigative skills lead her to Avila's refuge in Oaxaca, she chooses to keep the author's secret safe. Solidarity is more important than the prestige and rewards she could have earned upon revealing

---

[25] *Ibid.*, 12: "Once again I regretted the fact that the apartment had only three rooms and if I were to have a study the two children would have to share the same room. The decision was easily made. As a result, I have spent many years working on my bed."

[26] *Ibid.*, 38: "Pamela Hawthorne, the detective heroine of her novels was a lawyer like me and our jobs were not that different. Of course, mine did not have any glamour attached to it, nor had I taken this up through a sense of vocation … but rather after a series of consecutive failures …. And if I continue with comparisons, she is not the mother of two children and she didn't leave a husband in a different hemisphere, she doesn't have to take care of a house by herself, nor pay for one. And of course, another crucial piece of information, I am not a splendid thirty-year-old like Miss Hawthorne."

the truth. Alvallay succeeds in solving this case, although she leaves us with an unconventional resolution, where the truth is concealed from the client. The detective is satisfied that she understands Avila's motivation, that her attempts to identify and empathize with the author have given her a privileged insight. Indeed, imagination, intuition and empathy are privileged over reason. Yet, the reader has reason to question Alvallay's conclusions. Her reading of the motives behind the author's actions may simply amount to projections of her own frustrations. It is telling that all of those who know Carmen Avila formulate their own theories about her disappearance based on their own understanding of her character and many of them are mistaken. The fact that Alvallay reads her well enough to discover her whereabouts does not mean that she truly knows her any more than anyone else. Despite her late, very brief appearance in the novel she remains a mystery.

Ampuero's *¿Quién mató a Cristián Kustermann?* and Serrano's *Nuestra Señora de la Soledad* are novels that put the issue of identity centre stage. Both are concerned with absent characters with a history of leaving false trails and of re-inventing themselves. In Ampuero's novel the motive for these transformations is political and the victim ultimately dies because of his wish to break free from a specific political identity. Serrano's missing author is also motivated by a desire for freedom but one that is based on a personal longing to break away from the expectations of others, to be answerable only to herself as she pursues her solitary vocation. In both novels we also find a concern with place and identity. Ampuero's novel has been described as a novel of Valparaiso, the city in which Cayetano Brulé has his office, but it also links the local to the international. Kustermann's familiarity with Chile, Germany and Cuba finds a parallel in the detective who was born in Cuba, grew up in the USA, spent time in Germany as a soldier in the US army, and moved to Chile when he fell in love with a Chilean woman. This helps him follow the victim's trail but does not lead him to any greater identification with Kustermann. In Serrano's novel Carmen Avila has also led a nomadic existence and the action again moves beyond the local when the detective pursues the author to Mexico. In this case it is precisely through a process of identification that Alvallay manages to find the whereabouts of the missing writer.

Just as their detectives have different investigative styles, Ampuero and Serrano have different apprashes to the genre. What Ampuero brings to the field of Chilean detective fiction is a concern with examining the legacy of left-wing politics, and an insistence on equal criticism of all authoritarian regimes. In terms of influence, Ampuero has expressed admiration for authors like Greene and Le Carré, and for a number of Cuban crime writers and has stated that he regards the detective genre as a suitable vehicle for looking at the recent history of Latin America. He has also made it clear that he rejects the idea of writing committed literature. His primary aim is to produce an entertaining story which also deals with important issues but in a way that integrates these smoothly into the narrative and *¿Quién mató a Cristián Kustermann?* does just this. Despite the spy story elements, Ampuero works within the established conventions of the genre in terms of detective, procedure and resolution. There is a murder and an investigation that leads to the arrest of the guilty party. The detective follows conventional procedure to achieve this outcome. This is not the case in Serrano's novel where there is no real crime and where the detective chooses to conceal the truth. There is a resultion of sorts, in that the author is found, but no real closure since there are still many unanswered questions about Carmen Avila. Serrano foregrounds an awareness of genre tradition, of important authors and schools and critical approaches within the novel itself. Building upon this, she brings a new sensibility to the genre in Chile and examines new concerns from a new perspective.

FROM A GOOD FIRM KNOT TO A MESS OF LOOSE ENDS: IDENTITY AND SOLUTION IN MARTIN AMIS' *NIGHT TRAIN*

BRIAN DUFFY

Detective fiction survived for quite a while on the simple formula of a crime and its detection, and in the process reassuringly brought order to disorder, understanding to enigma, answers to questions. But from Dashiell Hammett through to our own sceptical, unstable times it has all gone wrong. Realism and anti-detective fiction have disturbed the rational, teleological narrative, the inexorable causal movement towards a solution. Detective narratives have gone the way of other grand narratives: they have lost their way, they have lost the plot, they have lost the answer. In keeping with, and articulating, the spirit of the age, they have lost faith. We might say they have gone postmodern.

Martin Amis' exploitation of the detective fiction genre in his novel, *Night Train*, is indeed a text of impeccable postmodern sensibility, but one which, in its appropriation of the styles, conventions, and intentions of different schools of detective fiction, reveals itself ultimately to be a thoroughly hybrid and restless creation, mixing detective and anti-detective fiction modes, drawing upon the hard-boiled American *noir* idiom and the decentred postmodern sensibility, blending ugly realism and metaphysical speculation, and challenging throughout facile solutions to the question of identity, be it of genre, character, or reality.

The novel's postmodern credentials are displayed in its treatment of two of the quintessential concerns of detective fiction, namely identity and solution. The conventional and essentially comforting who-dunnit understanding of identity at the heart of detective fiction is subverted in *Night Train*, transformed into a whydunnit, into a question that can only be answered by what is at once a more fundamental and more metaphysical interrogation of the concept of identity, one initiating a shadowy existential dance between the identities of the female detective and the female victim.

This essay will seek to trace the development of these interweaving modalities and concerns of the text, and proposes to do so in accompanying the unfolding of the narrative itself, a reading and interpretive strategy that receives a kind of justification in the novel by way of the narrator/detective's own metaphor for the narrative dynamic of her account and the troubled condition of her investigation: "I have taken a good firm knot and reduced it to a mess of loose ends."[1]

What is it in *Night Train* that allows it to turn so fiercely on its traditions, to actually reverse detective fiction's habitual movement from disorder to order? It is surely the nature of the crime, the change from homicide to suicide, but it is also the identity of the perpetrator of the particular crime in *Night Train*. For what does it mean that a woman who has everything kills herself? This is the task of the detection in *Night Train*, the imposing question that cannot be avoided, the source of the great unravelling. "Suicide is the night train, speeding your way to darkness" (67).[2]

The narrative takes the form of a first-person account by Detective Mike Hoolihan of what she calls "the worst case I have ever handled". The main part of the narrative is retrospective, but, at the moment of its narration, the investigation has not yet reached its conclusion. What we read brings us up to date, before the events at the end of the book take place, when Mike herself will discover where the investigation finally leads. The narrative, then, is something of an attempt to achieve what it is given to narrative to achieve: to find links, to establish cause and effect, to produce coherence, to supply an answer. This matters to Mike because it is the worst case she has ever handled, "for me, that is" (1). And because "I am part of the story I am going to tell" (4). Life and literature are full of self-narrations, of the narrative construction of selves and identities. But if this is such a bad case for Mike, it is because her police investigation has drawn her into an unwelcome personal examination, and the identity she finds herself

---

[1]   Martin Amis, *Night Train*, London: Cape, 1997, 4 (all further references will be given in the text).

[2]   The darkness, the particular brand of *noir*, on display in *Night Train* has not everywhere found a receptive audience. John Updike read *Night Train* as exemplifying what he sees as Amis' "writ[ing] out of a sensibility on the edge of the post-human" (John Updike, *More Matter: Essays and Criticism*, New York: Knopf, 1999, 364-65).

articulating and constructing in her narrative contains no comfort at all. It is this bifurcating investigation, initially of an act of suicide that is grotesquely the wrong conclusion to the valuable and valid life it terminates, which pitilessly confronts Mike with the value and validity of her own life.

That everything has become mixed up for Mike in the experience of the investigation is clear from the outset of her narration of the investigation. What is supposed to be the delineation of the facts of the case is deflected by and tinged with an existential anxiety about her identity and a metaphysical apprehension about where her story and investigation is leading her. Mike is a woman with a man's name, a man's physique, and a deep voice, "further deepened by three decades of nicotine abuse" (2). What should go without saying (her fundamental, self-evident identity as a woman) has to be said, because it is not self-evident, not to others, and, somewhere – if for different though not unrelated reasons – not quite to herself either. The name, the build, and the voice have Mike frequently taken for a man, and not just on the phone – "This is happening to me more and more often: The sir thing" (31). Mike's body is not as she would like it to be. She describes herself at one point as "a forty-four-year-old police[3] with coarse blond hair, bruiser's tits and broad shoulders" (43). This is the outside, the body that she and others see. What she alone sees, and feels, is inside her body, "[my] body, so ordinary and asymmetrical, the source of so little pleasure or pride, so neglected, so parched" (25). And this is not the only wound, the only obstacle to an enabling, stable sense of self. She was "raised by the state" (3) from the age of ten, from the moment everything blew apart at home. And there was the alcohol, which nearly killed her. And then there is the business, the trauma, of being a murder police, of having seen too much human ugliness and horror:

> I have seen the bodies of bludgeoned one-year-olds. I have seen the bodies of gang-raped nonagenarians. I have seen bodies left dead so long that your only shot at a t.o.d. is to weigh the maggots.

---

[3] "Among ourselves, we would never say I am a policeman or I am a policewoman or I am a police officer. We would just say I am a police" (*Night Train*, 1).

The hard-boiled tough talk here is as much a measure of the corrosive wear and tear on Mike's sensibility as it is an appropriation of an idiom. She apologizes for "the bad language, the diseased sarcasm, and the bigotry" (4) in her account, and will shudder later on at "how hardbarked" (141) she has become. But there are limits, and after eight years in Homicide Mike reached hers: "I entered my own end-zone and couldn't do it anymore." Now she works in Asset Forfeiture. But one more dead body had to be looked at, the last, the worst: "of all the bodies I have ever seen, none has stayed with me, in my gut, like the body of Jennifer Rockwell" (4).

All of this – what Mike is, why she has become so, what she thinks of herself – matters because of what this investigation does to her. The body of Jennifer Rockwell carries the force of an accusation against the body of Mike Hoolihan. The life of Jennifer Rockwell, as it emerges through the investigation, incriminates the life of Mike Hoolihan. This is why Mike becomes part of the story she is going to tell.

But what is it about Jennifer Rockwell that will not leave Mike alone?

This will not leave her alone: when you are young, beautiful, intelligent, loved, admired, healthy, well balanced, financially secure, professionally successful to the point of having a reasonable opportunity of making a lasting contribution as an astrophysicist – when you are happy, this happy, when everything about you and your life is so scandalously right, you are not supposed to kill yourself. Mike had known Jennifer – the daughter of Mike's former Squad Supervisor in Homicide, Colonel Tom, the man who had guided Mike and saved her from alcohol – for twenty years, since Jennifer was eight years old:

> She was a favorite of mine. But she was also a favorite of everybody else's. And I watched her grow into a kind of embarrassment of per-fection. Brilliant, beautiful. Yeah, I'm thinking: To-die-for brilliant. Drop-dead beautiful. And not intimidating – or only as intimidating as the brilliant-beautiful can't help being, no matter how accessible they seem. She had it all and she had it all, and then she had some more. (7)

And one Sunday evening she made love with her adored and adoring partner, put a gun in her mouth and shot herself three times, still naked in the aftermath of love-making, and just moments after her partner, Trader Faulkner, had left their apartment. Everything at the scene says it was a suicide, but Colonel Tom wants a homicide, which is at least bearable, settling on Trader as the perpetrator: "Bring me something I can live with. Because I can't live with this" (19), he says to Mike, asking her to investigate. Colonel Tom wants a homicide, because in the domain of violent, unnatural death, homicide is the intelligible option. It is brutal and shocking, but is, within its own macabre imperatives and primitive logic, wholly understandable, allowing simple answers to simple questions, as Mike reflects:

> Police really are like footsoldiers in this respect at least. Ours not to reason why. Give us the how, then give us the who, we say. But fuck the why. (31)

Colonel Tom wants a who, but there is none – Trader did not do it. It was suicide, and it is Trader, in beating off Mike's Colonel Tom-inspired attempts to pin the murder on him, who makes the metaphysical leap across the gulf separating the simple questions about homicide from the powerful and inscrutable questions about suicide:

> Mike, you've tied yourself up into all kinds of knots trying to make a mystery of this thing .... Some little mystery, all neat and cute. But there's a real mystery here. An enormous mystery .... A woman fell out of a clear blue sky. And you know something? I wish I *had* killed her .... Because that's better than what I'm looking at. (57)

From homicide to suicide: from the intelligible to the unintelligible, from the investigation of the circumstances of a death to a confrontation with the enigmas of a life. In changing the nature of the crime, and in exploring the existential resonances of suicide, Martin Amis has hugely extended the scope of the inquiry of his novel, has opened it up to the vast philosophical interrogation that accompanies suicide. Amis reflects on his preoccupation with suicide in his recent memoir,[4] and quotes G. K. Chesterton who observed that "suicide was a heavier undertaking than murder. The murderer kills just one person. The suicide kills everybody."[5] From homicide to suicide: from an

---

[4] Amis speaks in the memoir of the "fundamental trinity of significant suicides" that has marked his life, including that of the mother of his eldest child (Martin Amis, *Experience*, London: Cape, 2000, 226).

[5] *Ibid.*, 281.

isolated human act to the general human condition, from a judgement on one to a judgement on every-one.

And, of course, from the who to the why. "If it's a suicide, I'm going to feel an awful big why" (31), muses Mike before the autopsy confirms that Jennifer has indeed killed herself. The move from a whodunnit to a whydunnit seems at first sight to shift the inquiry away from identity, as the goal of the investigation is no longer to determine the identity of an individual. But this latter, traditional preoccupation of detective fiction has more to do with identification than identity, with simple naming rather than with a radical inquiry into the philosophical and existential dimensions of the notions of personal identity and selfhood. Paradoxically, then, it is precisely in moving from a whodunnit to a whydunnit, with the subsequent shifting of focus from a death to a life, that the more profound implications of the concept of identity may be explored.

The why question, in fact, is simply another formulation of the who question, but this time with all the complexities and obscurities, enigmas and uncertainties, associated with personal identity. That this is the new question to be answered by Mike becomes clear on the day of Jennifer's funeral, when she speaks to Miriam, Jennifer's mother. Jennifer is dead, but her dead body has given up a secret about her life:

> You didn't see the toxicology report. Tom made it disappear. Mike, Jennifer was on *lithium*. (63)

In other words, the shiny, happy life was contaminated by something that had no business there – a mood stabilizer. It is Miriam who draws the inevitable conclusion, who formulates the necessary question, the big identity question:

> See, Mike, we were looking for a why. And I guess we found one. But suddenly we don't have a who. Who was she, Mike? (64).

We have arrived at the end of the first part of *Night Train*, by which time in the novel Amis has disconcerted and diverted the genre within which he is working, has both exploited and played with its idioms and conventions, has subverted the expectations it generates, and has substantially expanded the horizons – the thematic and philosophical possibilities – of its traditional inquiry. We have gone from who to why, then back to who again. But the difference between the initial and the revised who is profound: it is the distance between the who of doing and the who of being, the disparity in metaphysical density between a single act and an entire existence. The former is the preoccupation of traditional detective fiction, while the latter represents the larger ambition of *Night Train*, its stab at the universal. Mike intuits as much when she agrees to seek an answer to Miriam's question – she senses that "the death of Jennifer Rockwell was offering the planet a piece of new news: Something never seen before" and she knew that it would lead to "something absolutely sombre" (64).

Mike investigates the events preceding Jennifer's death and finds out this: along with the lithium there was Arn Debs, a graceless, tasteless hulk from Texas, whom Jennifer had met in a bar and whom she had promised to meet the next time he was in town; there was Jennifer's momentous professional error in her calculations about the age of the universe, made the week before her death, but which only came to light the day after she killed herself; there was the uncharacteristic buying of things, such as the paintings which began to arrive at her apartment after her death; there was the book on suicide she had been reading, *Making Sense of Suicide*; and there was the suicide note, explaining everything, telling Trader that "Almost exactly a year ago I started getting the sense that I was losing control of my thoughts", that she had been on stabilizers for months, and comforting him with the assurance that he "couldn't have done *anything any different*" (117). What Mike found was an emerging, typical suicide pattern, a concatenation turned up by basic detective work, culminating in the suicide note that confirmed that here was a life that appeared to be lived in a clear blue sky but which was in fact blighted by an illness that became unbearable and uncontrollable. So Jennifer Rockwell killed herself.

As Mike sifts through the evidence, considers the pattern that is beginning to emerge, and reflects on the past, the subsequent evolution and the possibilities of a woman's life, she becomes deeply uneasy, almost inconsolable: so much has gone wrong, has been so wrong for so long – in her own life. Miriam asked Mike to investigate because she felt that a woman would see and understand things about a woman's life that a man would not. But the investigation into Jennifer's identity, into her life, into the love and tenderness and happiness and beauty assumed with the natural and easy grace of a birthright, sucks Mike into a confrontation with her own woman's life, which, when set beside the radiance of Jennifer's existence, seems sordid and vicious and mean. Slowly, but inexorably, the attempt to construct a narrative of a self has Mike as much as Jennifer as its existential subject.

Mike's presentation of herself at the outset revealed a sensitivity, a nervous vulnerability, a deep anxiety, about herself and her self-image, disclosed in the almost self-reproachful details about herself and her life – the male features, her overall appearance, the frequent mistaking of her for a man, her under-loved body, the booze, the vileness. The narration of the investigation articulates the stages of this evolving self-narrative, consisting essentially of a disinterment of Mike's past, going back to what began to happen when she was a little girl:

> My father messed with me when I was a child …. Yeah he used to fuck me, okay? It started when I was seven and it stopped when I was ten. I made up my mind that after I hit double figures it just wasn't going to happen …. On the morning after my birthday he came at me in my bedroom. And I almost ripped his fucking face off …. Then my mother woke up. We were never a model unit, the Hoolihans. By noon that same day we ceased to exist. (86-87)

Mike does not construct a rigidly causal narrative, where what happens before explains, uniquely and inevitably, what happens after, but the detective in her sees a pattern, that of finding herself "hanging on the arms of woman-haters and woman-hitters".

She ends up with a succession of violent men: "These guys didn't just slap me around: We had fistfights that lasted half an hour" (146). Here was a pattern that had hardened into a destiny: "Long ago I learnt that I cannot get the good guys" (111). Now she is with Tobe, and Tobe is a big improvement – Tobe does not beat her. But here he is "watching a *taped* quiz show" (36), and here he is off "attending a video-game tournament" (143). Tobe does not beat Mike, but Mike has taken too many beatings already, and, more than anything, her sense of being a woman has taken a beating – the harsh judgement of herself as being "just another big blonde old broad" (7) is one articulation of how her body is a reminder, is the experience, of her un-fulfilled womanhood. Forty-four-year-old Mike intimates that she is menopausal, producing particular physical sensations but also a time-of-life – her expression – reflection about her "unused womb" (40), which culminates in another bitter self-assessment, a response to Trader's explanation that Jennifer wanted to have children because "She was a woman" and "Women want children":

> He looks at me, my town flesh, my eyes. And he's thinking: Yeah. All women except this woman. (49)

Mike will insist later that she "never wanted a kid" (87), but her reaction to Trader's remark nonetheless displays a preoccupation about her sense of being a woman and an anxiety about her inability to fully assume a woman's identity.

Mike's father abused her, violent men abused her, and Mike abused herself, with alcohol, and was saved only by Colonel Tom before one last, fatal binge. But she remains on this threshold, functioning, almost expectantly, under the shadow of her self-induced, and willed, Sword of Damocles: "We keep booze in the apartment and somehow I like to know it's there even though it will kill me if I touch it" (21). It is as if the accumulated effects of violence and disappointment, abuse and neglect, have pushed Mike to this delicate hovering between stoic acceptance and self-destruction, and as if she has willingly assumed this condition, understood by her as at once a limit and a possibility, a place to make a last stand in the quiet determination that there can be no more excesses, and that there is no more tolerance for the abuse that life so casually metes out.

Mike's investigation, then, becomes an interrogation of two lives – of a life upon which the ultimate judgement has already been passed, and of one that is, increasingly, and increasingly harshly, being judged. If the narrative that Mike is constructing of her life, and if the identity she is assuming as her story advances, are haunted by disappointment and caustic self-condemnation, it is because it is impossible for Mike not to compare the life still being lived by one woman with the life that had to be ended by another. From the moment Mike takes on the investigation, Jennifer becomes an ominous presence in her consciousness, insisting that her suicide will be relevant to whatever is to be discovered, that it has greater meanings that go beyond the ending of a single life, and that these meanings will have to be faced: "Now I feel that someone is inside of me, like an intruder, her flashlight playing. Jennifer Rockwell is inside of me, trying to reveal what I don't want to see" (67). About what? About whom? It may be that Mike herself, with this ambiguous formulation, does not yet know what category of knowledge Jennifer's life and death have to offer, but it soon takes the form of a verdict, by way of a comparison of the two lives, upon the quality and value of Mike's own experience and existence. Trader's gushing love letters to Jennifer – "the words a woman wants to hear" (79) – are contrasted with the *billets-doux* – "GET SOME TOILET PAPER FOR CHRIST SAKE" (80) – left in the kitchen for Mike. The effortless harmony represented by Trader and Jennifer, exemplified by the arrangement of their study – "The peer lover, ten feet away: Silence, endeavour, common cause. Isn't that what we're all supposed to want?" (78) – precedes, and surely generates, the withering conclusion by Mike on the couple formed by herself and Tobe: "half a ton of slob and slut" (144). Jennifer's body – "a thrilling embarrassment" (109) – is the measure for Mike in dealing with the pleasureless experience of her own.

Mike becomes less and less capable of thinking about her life and of constructing her identity within the limitations and possibilities set by her own existence; the life of this other woman, like a distorting mirror image, stands as an accusation and a verdict:

> It's not too late. I'm going to change my name. To something feminine. Like Detective Jennifer Hoolihan. (105)

As the investigation slides towards "something absolutely sombre", Mike's darkening mood crystallizes into a self-flagellating direct comparison (131-32):

Astrophysics	Asset Forfeiture
Trader	Tobe
Colonel Tom	Pop
Beautiful	

How are we to read the meaning of this ominous, almost desolate blank space? At the symbolic level, as an absence revealing an emptiness in Mike's existence, or as signifying an unspeakable truth about it? Or at a more literal level, as a confusion in Mike about her identity, or as an importunate question that cannot yet be, but that ultimately will have to be, answered? Mike's investigation of Jennifer's life has led her to the threshold of a conclusion about her own life and her own identity, a conclusion that is stalled as it awaits the word that cannot, or will not, be uttered.

Who is Mike Hoolihan, and what is the meaning of her life?

Early on in her investigation, this thought comes to Mike:

> But she's a cop's daughter. This means something. This has to matter. (83)

After Jennifer's funeral, Mike draws up a list of Stressors and Precipitants, the division of Jennifer's life and experience into sources of potential significant stress, from which may have come the irresistible propellant towards suicide: Money? Job? Physical Health? Trauma? Childhood? The list goes on. There are, of course, the accumulating clues – the lithium, Arn Debs, and the rest – and there is the clinching proof of the suicide note, but none of these answers quite match up to the questions: the clues and the note conform to suicide patterns, but they do not conform to Jennifer's suicide. As her investigation ends, Mike strikes off the last, lingering, inadequate questions on her Stressors and Precipitants list: "Now there's nothing" (132). Mike has asked the right questions, but Jennifer's life has given up the wrong answers.

Then Mike reads the following sentence highlighted by Jennifer among the banalities and platitudes of *Making Sense of Suicide*: "virtually all known studies reveal that the suicidal person will give warnings and clues as to his, or her, suicidal intentions." Jennifer had certainly done that:

> Clues. Jennifer left *clues*. She was the daughter of a police. That did matter. (134)

Now Mike understands the wrong answers:

> She was the daughter of a police .... She knew that [her father] would follow her trail. And I believe she knew also that I would play a part in the search .... As she headed toward death she imprinted a pattern that she thought would solace the living. A pattern: Something often seen before. Jennifer left clues. But the clues were all blinds. (145)

Mike's investigation had uncovered a solution to the unbearable mystery of Jennifer's suicide. But her revisiting these clues now reveals it to be an elaborate and calculated *faux* solution, carefully concocted by Jennifer to leave the living with something they could live with: Jennifer knew her suicide would trigger the great anguished existential questioning, so she set about supplying an answer. But if this answer is not an answer, if the detection has led only to a false solution, then who was Jennifer Rockwell, and what is the meaning of her suicide?

Far from answering the questions about Jennifer's identity and existence, Mike's narrative has only deepened the enigma. And her account has even formulated another question about identity, this time concerning her own, but here too her narrative has stalled on a question, faltering in the face of the unnamable, or the ineffable. *Night Train*'s short last section deals with this unfinished business, but it deals with it in a manner that is true to the epistemological condition of its telling. As far as Mike's self-interrogation is concerned, it will not provide the missing, or unutterable, word; it will allow her to narrate herself to her own conclusion, and to act accordingly. But if this, in the unforeseen existential quest in the novel, does not assuage our anxieties or return us to order, neither does it withhold from us the evidence for well-founded apprehension.

But who was Jennifer Rockwell, and what is the meaning of her suicide? We might say that the detective set out to answer the first question, and the novel to investigate the second. Both fall silent at the moment of closure. The identity question, the detective's quest, was, on reflection, an impossible one, because the *a priori* assumptions informing the quest – about temporal and self coherence, and about the unity, intention, and stability that ground and delimit the concept of personal identity – are so comprehensively sundered, so irrevocably negated, and are rendered so thoroughly irrelevant, by the finality, conviction, and sheer otherness of suicide. Intelligibility and coherence are precisely what Jennifer's suicide mocks and destroys. Identity seems a puny, fragile impostor in the wake of suicide's verdict.

The two questions are, in fact, one, a way of saying that the detective's quest to construct the victim's identity and the novel's teleological drive towards a solution are inseparable. The latter subsumes the former. If we know why Jennifer Rockwell killed herself we have a solution, in so far as we can re-interpret and re-inscribe her life, and construct for her an identity, within the context of the reason for her suicide. We will have an explanation, we will understand, and the novel will have both returned us to a form of order and assumed the responsibilities of its own teleology. But *Night Train* does not do this – it does not offer us a solution, it does not tell us why Jennifer killed herself. The detective and reader alike are left staring into the same metaphysical void, futilely sifting through the same inklings and intimations for something as concrete as a reason for the suicide. Jennifer's decision to kill herself seems close to being a gratuitous act, although it is a decision whose metaphysical context is her work as an astrophysicist. We learn that her staring into the vastness of the universe was never reduced for her to velocities, algorithms and pixels, but that she retained, rather, a romantic, entirely human wonder at the grandeur of the cosmos and the puniness of human striving. We are allowed to consider that the world – the human condition, with the "rat-race, turf-war, dog-eat-dog stuff we do all day" (93), as Jennifer's boss describes it – suddenly appeared impossibly vain and hollow to Jennifer, although this whispered speculation is not endorsed by the narrator. Suicide kills everybody, but does it also, in Jennifer's final gesture, deliver a verdict on the planet, on the entire human endeavour?

Night Train leaves the reader with these sombre metaphysical musings, an outcome that has not been appreciated by all its readers. The novelist Anita Brookner considers the narrative's quest for the truth as "an assault on the reader's good faith",[6] a serious, and wholly unfair, charge that smacks of a depressing conservatism and a failure, or an unwillingness, to appreciate the genre conventions within and against which Amis is writing. Amis has taken a genre whose tradition and, for a long time, practice epitomized and enacted rational inquiry, the discovery of truth, a return to order, and a faith in the value of solution and closure, and he has confronted it with the enigma and incoherence of suicide. He has, in other words, deliberately and disinterestedly challenged the archetypal discourse of order by means of the ultimate human act of disorder and chaos. If *Night Train*, then, comes dressed

---

[6]   Brookner's comments appeared originally in her review of *Night Train* for *The Spectator* (27 September 1997), which is reproduced in *The Fiction of Martin Amis*, ed. Nicolas Tredell, Cambridge: Icon, 2000, 175-76.

up in these postmodern clothes and either refuses or fails to permit the detection to posit a solution in what appears to be a resolutely anti-detective mode, it is less that it consciously and ideologically wishes to do so, than that it is obliged to remain true to the existential uncertainties and metaphysical anxieties that inhabit the act, and contemplation, of suicide.

Content and form in *Night Train*, in their resistance to solutions to questions about identity, are, indeed, in harmony. The novel's impressive weave of styles and idioms, tradition and innovation, homages and subversions, thwart simple categorization, and, in its breezy borrowings and multiple poses, *Night Train* confronts the reflective reader with the elusive, mutating, and unstable nature of identity. Who was Jennifer Rockwell? Who is Mike Hoolihan? As always in literature, we learn more from troubling questions than from facile answers.

Notes on Contributors

Beate Burtscher-Bechter is Assistant Professor of Comparative Literature in the Department of Languages and Literatures at Innsbruck University, Austria. Her research focuses on francophone Mediterranean literatures, postcolonial studies and transcultural writing. She is the author of *Algerien – ein Land sucht seine Mörder* (IKO, 1999) and has recently co-edited *Grenzen und Entgrenzungen* (Königshausen and Neumann, 2006, with P. W. Haider, B. Mertz-Baumgartner and R. Rollinger).

Theo D'haen is Professor of American Literature at Leuven University, Belgium. He has published widely on modern literature in European languages, (post)modernism and (post)colonialism. His most recent book publication is *Contemporary American Crime Fiction* (Palgrave, 2001, co-authored with Hans Bertens).

Brian Duffy is Lecturer in French and English in the School of Applied Language and Intercultural Studies at Dublin City University, Ireland. He wrote his thesis and has published on the topic of narrative and identity in Samuel Beckett, and his most recent publications are on the work of Beckett, John Banville, and Richard Ford, including the book *Morality, Identity and Narrative in the Fiction of Richard Ford* (Rodopi, 2008).

Eva Erdmann lectures in the Department of Romance Literature at the University of Erfurt, Germany. She has published widely on the areas of poststructuralism and comparative literature. She is editor of *Der komische Körper* (transcript, 2003). With Immacolata Amodeo, she is currently working on an online World Atlas of Crime Fiction (see www.crime-and-nation.de).

Hans Ester lectures in comparative arts at the University of Nijmegen, the Netherlands. He wrote his dissertation on Theodor Fontane. His most recent book publications include: *Künstler-Bilder* (Rodopi, 2003, along with G. van Gemert), *Im Schatten der Literaturgeschichte* (Rodopi, 2005, with J. Enklaar), *Geborgenheit und Gefährdung in der epischen und malerischen Welt Adalbert Stifters* (Königshausen and Neumann, 2005, with J. Enklaar).

Shelley Godsland is Senior Lecturer in Spanish at Manchester Metropolitan University, UK, and was formerly the Jubilee Research Fellow in Hispanic Studies at Royal Holloway, University of London. She has published two monographs, thirty scholarly papers, and a number of collections of essays, and has been guest editor for a range of special issues of internationally leading journals.

Sjef Houppermans lectures in modern French literature in the Department of French Language and Culture at Leiden University, the Netherlands. He has published widely on twentieth-century authors such as Proust, Robbe-Grillet, Simon, and his most recent books are *Samuel Beckett et Compagnie* (Rodopi, 2003) and *Renaud Camus, érographe* (Rodopi, 2004).

Christopher Jones is Senior Lecturer in German in the Department of Languages at Manchester Metropolitan University, UK. His main research interests are in the field of German popular culture, with a particular emphasis on crime fiction. Recent work has included a comparison between Agatha Christie and Sabine Deitmer; an analysis of Pieke Biermann's short fiction; and a case study of the TV series *Kommissar Rex*.

Stewart King is Senior Lecturer in Spanish and Latin American Studies at Monash University, Australia. He has published extensively on twentieth-century Spanish and Catalan authors. His most recent publications include *Escribir la catalanidad* (Tamesis, 2005), and the edited book *La cultura catalana de expresión castellana* (Editions Reichenberger, 2005).

Marieke Krajenbrink lectures in German at the University of Limerick, Ireland. She has published widely on contemporary German and Austrian literature, particularly on national myths, intertextuality and crime fiction. She is author of *Intertextualität als Konstruktionsprinzip* (Rodopi 1996) and has recently co-edited *Connections and Identities: Austria, Ireland and Switzerland* (Peter Lang, 2004, with G. Holfter and E. Moxon-Browne).

Costantino C. M. Maeder is Professor of Italian at Leuven Universityn, Belgium. His main research interests include modern Italian literature, intercomprehension in Romance Languages, and the relationship between text and music in Italian opera. He is co-editor of *Outside-In – Inside-Out* (John Benjamins, 2005, along with O. Fischer and W. J. Herlofsky).

Agnès Maillot is Lecturer in French and Intercultural Studies at Dublin City University, Ireland. She has published a number of articles on Northern Ireland politics and her most recent book is *New Sinn Fein: Irish Republicanism in the 21st Century* (Routledge, 2004).

Marisol Morales Ladrón lectures in Modern Languages at the University of Alcalá, Spain. She has published extensively on contemporary Irish authors and has co-edited two volumes on feminist criticism. Her publications include the books: *Breve introducción a la literatura comparada* (Universidad de Alcalá de Henares Press, 1999), and *Las poéticas de James Joyce y Luis Martín-Santos* (Peter Lang, 2005).

Kate M. Quinn is Lecturer in Spanish at the National University of Ireland, Galway. Her main research interests are in Hispanic crime narrative and historical narrative in Chile. She has published on contemporary Chilean crime writers such as Roberto Ampuero, Ramón Díaz and Marcela Serrano.

John Scaggs lectures in the English Department at Mary Immaculate College, Limerick, Ireland. His main research interests are in literary theory and the modern novel. He has published articles on Raymond Chandler, James Crumley, and Cormac McCarthy, and he is the author of *Crime Fiction* (Routledge, 2005).

Philip Swanson is Professor of Hispanic Studies at the University of Sheffield, UK. He has published extensively on Latin American literature, including books on the New Novel, José Donoso and Gabriel García Márquez. His most recent books are *Latin American Fiction: A Short Introduction* (Blackwell, 2004) and the edited volume *The Com-*

panion to Latin American Studies (Arnold, 2003). Professor Swanson has taught in a number of universities in Europe and the USA.

Arlene A. Teraoka is Professor of German and Associate Dean for Undergraduate Programmes in the College of Liberal Arts at the University of Minnesota, USA. She is the author of books on Heiner Müller and on Third World discourse in postwar German literature. Her essays on multiculturalism and German cultural studies focus on representations of Turks in German politics and literature.

Sabine Vanacker lectures in English literature at the University of Hull, UK. Her research interests include literature and gender – especially with regard to Modernist women writers, and crime fiction in Dutch and English. She has published on Sayers, Paretsky, Grafton and Cornwell, and has co-authored *Reflecting on Miss Marple* (Routledge, 1991, with Marion Shaw).

Anne L. Walsh is Lecturer in the Department of Hispanic Studies at University College, Cork, Ireland. She has published on Gonzalo Torrente Ballester. Her particular area of interest is the narrative development of the Spanish novel since the 1940s, especially the areas of post-war fiction, fiction by women writers, postmodernism and detective fiction. She is currently finishing a book on Arturo Pérez-Reverte.

Willem G. Weststeijn is Professor of Slavic literature at the University of Amsterdam, the Netherlands. His main areas of interest are the Russian avant-garde and contemporary Russian literature. His most recent books are the collection of essays *Russische literatuur* (Meulenhoff, 2004) and, together with Arthur Langeveld, *Moderne Russische literatuur: Van Poesjkin tot heden* (Pegasus, 2006).

Anne M. White is Senior Lecturer in Spanish at the University of Bradford, UK. She has published on a broad range of topics relating to European popular cultural forms including crime fiction, advertising, film and television. She is co-editor (with Shelley Godsland) of *Cultura popular: Studies in Spanish and Latin American Popular Culture* (Peter Lang, 2002).

Index

Abahri, Larbi, *Banderilles et muleta*, 190

Aïssa, Salim, *Adel s'emmêle* and *Mimouna*, 191

Akkouche, Moloud, *Avis déchéance* and *Causse Toujours*, 183

Akunin, B., 161

Albrecht, Hans-Jörg, "Ethnic Minorities, Crime, and Criminal Justice in Germany", 119

Albrecht, Peter-Alexis, "Die strafrechtliche Auffälligkeit des 'Ausländers': Kriminologische Verarbeitung und kriminalpolitische Verwendung", 120

Albrecht, Richard, "Krimi – made in Germany: Literatursoziologischer Nekrolog auf den progressiven bundesdeutschen Serienkrimi", 114

Alewyn, Richard, "Anatomie des Detektivromans", 248

Allen, Dick (with David Chacko, eds), *Detective Fiction: Crime and Compromise*, 115

Ali Benali, Zineb (with Bouba Tabti), "Le Roman d'espionnage algérien: Mourad Saber ould James Bond", 186

Allende, Salvador, 296

Álvarez, Blanca, *La soledad del monstruo*, 50

Amado, Jorge, "Sólo el futuro es nuestro", 301

Amari, Chawki, *De bonnes nouvelles d'Algérie*, 183-84

Amis, Martin, *Experience*, 315; *Night Train*, 8, 311-24

Ampuero, Roberto, 8, 295-302, 306, 309-10; *Boleros en la Habana*, 296, 299; *Cita el el azul profundo*, 296; *El alemán de Atacama*, 296; *Halcones de la noche*, 296, 299; *Nuestros años verde olivo*, 299; *¿Quién mató a Cristián Kustermann?*, 296-302, 309-10.

Anderson, Benedict, *Imagined Communities: Reflections on the Origin and Spread of Nationalism*, 28, 30, 38, 44

Arjouni, Jakob, 4, 6, 14, 113, 117-28; *Ein Mann, ein Mord*, 113, 124-26; *Happy birthday, Türke!*, 113, 124-25; *Kismit*, 113; *Mehr Bier*, 113, 124-25, 127-28; Interview with Georg Hoffmann-Ostenhof and Ernst Schmiederer, "Besatzer sollen bleiben", 122; Interview with Christian Seiler, "We Have Great Jobs and Earn Heaps of Money", 122

Arrighi, Cletto, 265

Asensi, Matilde, *El salón de ámbar*, 50

Ashcroft, Bill (with Gareth Griffiths and Helen Tiffin), *The Empire Writes Back: Theory and Practice in Post-Colonial Literature*, 36

Ashley, Bob, ed., *The Study of Popular Fiction: A Source Book*, 201, 210

Aspe, Dirk, 215

Aspetsberger, Friedbert (with Günther A. Höfler, eds), *Banal und erhaben – es ist (nicht) alles eins*, 243

Assman, Aleida (with Heidrun